Holocaust Testimonies

זכור ימות עולם
בינו שנות דור ודור
דברים ל״ב

Remember the days of yore,
Understand the years of generation after generation
DEUTERONOMY 32:7

Holocaust Testimonies

European Survivors and
American Liberators in New Jersey

EDITED BY

JOSEPH J. PREIL

FOREWORD BY ELIE WIESEL

Rutgers University Press
NEW BRUNSWICK, NEW JERSEY, AND LONDON

Frontispiece photograph by Roman Vishniac. *Students of the Talmud,* Czechoslovakia, 1937. © Mara Vishniac Kohn, courtesy The International Center of Photography.

The maps were created by the United States Holocaust Memorial Museum and published in *Historical Atlas of the Holocaust* (New York: Macmillan Publisher, 1996). Used with permission of the United States Holocaust Memorial Museum.

Library of Congress Cataloging-in-Publication Data

Holocaust testimonies : European survivors and American liberators in New Jersey / edited by Joseph J. Preil.
       p. cm.
  Includes bibliographical references (p.) and index.
  ISBN 0-8135-2947-6 (alk. paper)
   1. Holocaust, Jewish (1939–1945)—Personal narratives. 2. Holocaust survivors—New Jersey—Biography.   I. Preil, Joseph J.

  D804.195 .H74 2001
  940.53′18—dc21

                       00-045746

British Cataloging-in-Publication data for this book is available from the British Library

Manufactured in the United States of America

Design by John Romer

Contents

Maps

Foreword

Nowadays, when we are witnessing, on more than one level, a widespread assault on Jewish memory of the Holocaust and the survivors who embody it, I think that this work is more important than ever before. It is comprised of testimony that we must read and reread, if we wish to better understand something about the most troubling and the most tormented period in history.

These accounts are narrated by survivors of the ghettos and the camps. What they tell, no one can articulate in their place. Each one evokes, in his or her own way, his or her personal suffering and agony. Certain passages reopen ancient wounds; others heal them. All bear witness so that future generations will remember.

In the beginning, survivors attempted to recount their misery. After all, it was the obsession of both the victims and the fighters to respond to the appeal of the great historian Shimon Dubnov, who was assassinated in 1941 in the Riga ghetto: "Jews, take notes and write, write about everything!" They were anxious to teach the world about the horrible scope of the crimes that the Germans and their collaborators had committed against the Jewish people in occupied Europe.

Unfortunately, in the free world people refused to listen and to believe them. The truth was frightening. So the survivors kept silent. They asked themselves, "Why bother? After all, those who had not known Auschwitz and Treblinka would never understand."

With time, attitudes have changed. Thanks to certain events (the Eichmann trial, the Six Day War, the creation of the President's Commission on the Holocaust by President Jimmy Carter, the construction of the Holocaust Museum in Washington), Americans have begun to show genuine interest in the words of the witnesses, so tragically qualified to speak, like those who have created this book. In reading their narrations we can only admire the strength of their courage and their faithfulness to memory.

What have they done with their ordeal? What kind of scar has it left on the remaining years of their lives? Ruth Stern Friedman does not hesitate to confess that while visiting Germany after the war she was overwhelmed by anger and hatred for the Germans: "I am full of vengeance. I am full of hatred. I hear the German language and I start to freeze up inside." Many among us strongly oppose hatred everywhere, but who would pass judgment on Ruth who wished, doubtless, to hate the Germans out of love for the Jews? Halina Goldberg Kleiner says, "The Germans tried to strip us of our humanity, of this ability to think about other people. . . . They weren't able to do that. We looked out for each other, and we would have risked our lives for each other." And Sylvia Blau Wirtzbaum says: " We didn't feel anything in Auschwitz. We weren't human." Is this true for all the inmates? Weren't they themselves more human than their torturers? Rose Gluckstein Kramer relates a distressing memory of her arrival in Birkenau: her sister was so attached to her little niece that, to help her overcome her fear and to reassure her, she took her in her arms and went with her when she could have joined those whom the SS had selected for work.

Let's stop.

Read this collection. The cruelty of the killers, the cowardice of the bystanders, the brutality of the collaborators, the desperate faith of the believers, the solitude of the condemned, the magnificent bravery of the liberators: all of these themes appear here.

These survivors and their liberators are speaking to you.
Listen to them, and you will be grateful to them.

ELIE WIESEL

Preface

The purpose of publishing *Holocaust Testimonies* is threefold: first, to teach the Holocaust to all citizens by using the firsthand experiences of witnesses, both survivors and liberators, most of whom are or were New Jersey residents; second, to provide teachers with testimonies of witnesses who were in Europe during the Holocaust (the teachers may assign these narratives for reading or they may invite some of these survivors to their schools); and third, to enable scholars to locate survivors or liberators with specific backgrounds of interest to their studies.

Holocaust Testimonies is presented country by country and its arrangement is based on the march of German troops through Europe. We begin in chapter 1 with the testimonies of thirteen German and three Austrian witnesses. Forced return to Poland, *Kristallnacht,* and the *Kindertransport* program are highlights of this period. With hindsight, we begin to detect features of the evolving Holocaust.

Chapters 2 and 3 are devoted to the testimonies of ninety-nine Polish witnesses. Nazi policy in Poland develops into bureaucratically efficient mass murder. We hear about the organization, for the destruction of all Jews, of ghettos and the brutal camp system—four camps used exclusively for murder; another three large concentration camps for murder and some slave labor prior to death; 1,798 slave labor camps; and 136 refugee camps. Cattle cars for transporting Jews were used throughout. Finally, as Germany is faced with defeat, death marches from Polish camps defy human understanding.

Testimonies from witnesses in Western Europe (chapter 4), Lithuania and Russia (chapter 5), and Central Europe (chapter 6) provide some insight on the Holocaust in these places. The differing reactions of the citizens of various countries merit further study.

Questions regarding human conduct arise throughout these incredible stories. In the concluding year of the war, with German defeat imminent, what motivated the Germans to continue the murder program at its highest degree of efficiency? And with the American and British armies marching victoriously through France and Germany, what was done, if anything, to thwart the Holocaust in the murder camps? These questions are raised as we hear the testimonies of our twenty-eight Central European survivors.

The interviews with twenty liberators (chapter 7) reveal a different perspective on this most tragic event in human history. Thus this volume takes us from the interviews of German and Austrian survivors (revealing the incredible, yet enthusiastic, acceptance of brutal antisemitism by the apparently enlightened populations) to the end of the Holocaust decade, with American liberators describing the sights, sounds, and smells that confronted soldiers entering the concentration camps as World War II was ending.

Table 1. Holocaust Testimonies, by Country of Origin

Country	Testimonies
Germany/Austria	16
Western Poland	68
Eastern Poland	31
Western Europe	6
Lithuania/Russia	3
Central Europe*	28
United States (Liberators)	20
Total	172

*Consists of Czechoslovakia, Hungary, Romania, and Yugoslavia.

It is appropriate to record how Kean University's oral history program developed into this book. At the very beginning of our activities in 1983, Holocaust Resource Foundation (HRF) president Murray Pantirer foresaw the advisability of producing such a publication. This was discussed at an early foundation meeting. I believe the book is faithful to the guidelines formulated at that meeting: a brief introductory description of each survivor's background, followed by the survivor's Holocaust experiences, and concluding with a short statement of each individual's status at the time of testimony.

As indicated in the appendix, the Kean University oral history program was guided by the highly regarded program at Yale University. We had also been fortunate in appointing an outstanding committee of oral history scholars to advise and monitor our work. This helped us to organize (a) the pre-interview preparations; (b) the interview itself; (c) the post-interview recording procedure, a most important and demanding aspect of the entire program; and (d) the criteria for determining which interviews would be published. During the course of our fifteen year history (1983–1998), a questionnaire was developed to prepare the survivor and the interviewer for the experience. A copy of the questionnaire appears in the Appendix.

Table 2. Estimated Jewish Losses in the Holocaust, by Country

Country	Initial Jewish Population	Minimum Loss	Maximum Loss
Austria	182,000	50,000	50,000
Belgium	65,700	28,900	28,900
Bohemia & Moravia	118,310	78,150	78,150
Bulgaria	50,000	0	0
Denmark	7,800	60	60
Estonia	4,500	1,500	2,000
Finland	2,000	7	7
France	350,000	77,320	77,320
Germany	566,000	134,500	141,500
Greece	77,380	60,000	67,000
Hungary	825,000	550,000	569,000
Italy	44,500	7,680	7,680
Latvia	91,500	70,000	71,500
Lithuania	168,000	140,000	143,000
Luxembourg	3,500	1,950	1,950
Netherlands	140,000	100,000	100,000
Norway	1,700	762	762
Poland	3,300,000	2,900,000	3,000,000
Romania	609,000	271,000	287,000
Slovakia	88,950	68,000	71,000
Soviet Union	3,020,000	1,000,000	1,100,000
Yugoslavia	78,000	56,200	63,300
Total (rounded)	9,800,000	5,600,000	5,860,000

SOURCE: *Encyclopedia of the Holocaust,* Israel Gutman, ed. New York: Macmillan, 1990, p. 1799.

Acknowledgments

Many people have made significant contributions to the successful completion of this book. The members of the Holocaust Resource Foundation have inspired and encouraged all our activities from the time that Kean College's Holocaust Resource Center[1] was merely a dream until today (see appendix). It has been my privilege to work closely with and appreciate the friendship of all these people and, particularly, the foundation's two presidents, Murray Pantirer and Clara Kramer. All three presidents of Kean University—Nathan Weiss, Elsa Gomez, and Ronald Applbaum—have encouraged and supported the HRC in our first two decades.

Henry Ross and Michael Lampert, administration liaisons to the HRC, served with great commitment and effectiveness at all times. Jeffrey Glanz assumed this vital position in 2000 and his involvement in preparing the book for publication is deeply appreciated. Our professional partnerships in these endeavors have helped to forge very precious personal friendships.

A number of people in the Office of the Vice President for Academic Affairs have displayed much interest and cooperation in our endeavors. Among others, we recognize the concern and efforts of Livingston Alexander, Vera Farris-King, Louanne Kennedy, Bonnie Kind, Catherine Dorsey-Gaines, and Eleanor Laudicina for HRC achievements.

School of Education Dean Ana Maria Schuhmann displayed remarkable perception and involvement in the continuing expansion of HRC activities. This is especially true of her leadership role in the impressive development of the Diversity 2000 Council of Kean University, an incredibly effective group of sixty-two school districts. Myra Weiger, chair of the department of instruction, curriculum, and administration, supported my continuing involvement in HRC programs even though it impinged greatly on my other departmental endeavors.

In many respects, this book owes its publication to Vincent Merlo and Claude Everhart of the Instructional Resource Center. Their talent and commitment provided the foundation for the success of our oral history program.

Mark Lender has been involved in the oral history testimonies from the very beginning. He always understood the possibilities of the program, and his expertise and creative ideas have been essential to our progress throughout our history.

Benton Arnovitz, director of Publications at the United States Holocaust Memorial Museum in Washington, D.C., was always most gracious and cooperative in offering effective suggestions. He was especially helpful in guiding us to obtain the museum's permission to use their maps. Dewey Hicks, former museum cartographer, assisted in the transmittal of the maps to Rutgers University Press.

Mere words are insufficient to thank Elie Wiesel for inspiring all of us to ponder our responsibility to remember and teach the Holocaust. The latest example of his many writings can be appreciated in his challenging foreword. Irene Gnarra of the foreign language department responded most graciously to our request that she translate Elie Wiesel's foreword from French to English.

It is difficult to express how much this publication owes to Edith Jaskoll, Helen Walzer, and Lois Saidel. Their HRC involvement has been a labor of love. Kean University is fortunate, indeed, to have such friends.

As the book was nearing completion, knowledgeable people suggested that Rutgers University Press would be the appropriate publisher. The thought became reality when Arthur Kurzweil of Jason Aronson became familiar with the manuscript and made his recommendation to David Myers, social science and religion editor of Rutgers University Press. Consequently, the path to publication has been a smooth process. This has also been assured by the outstanding professional staff at Rutgers and the much appreciated efforts of Brigitte M. Goldstein, production editor.

Finally, a word about my family. I am truly blessed with my partner in life, Dvorah Leah. She has always encouraged my career with love, with devotion, with keen intelligence and, most significantly, with amazing patience. It is our hope and prayer that all our children and grandchildren will understand fully the significance of the events described in these testimonies and will conduct their lives in a manner appropriate to the tradition of our people and of benefit to all humankind.

Holocaust Testimonies

Chapter One
Germany and Austria

THREE events should be noted in the evolution of the Holocaust in Nazi Germany. First is the series of national elections held during the economic crisis of the 1930s. Just before the crisis, in 1928, the Nazis garnered only 3 percent of the vote. During the crisis of 1930, the National Socialist Party took 18 percent of the vote, and in 1932, they captured 37 percent and had 230 members in the Reichstag, Germany's national legislature.[1] Thus, Hitler and the Nazis gained political control of Germany legally.

Second is the expulsion from Germany of some 15,000–17,000 Jews of Polish origin in October 1938. The Polish government refused to accept these Jews, and they were suspended in a no-man's-land between the two countries.[2]

Third is *Kristallnacht,* the "Night of Broken Glass," 9–10 November 1938, when "hundreds of synagogues and thousands of Jewish businesses were burned down, destroyed, or damaged. Some thirty thousand Jews were put into concentration camps, and almost one hundred Jews were murdered."[3] All of this persecution, organized by the government, led to a determined effort by the Jews to emigrate from Germany. Of the approximately 500,000 Jews in Germany when Hitler took office, about 200,000 perished in the Holocaust and about 300,000 were saved, mostly by emigration.[4]

The prewar population of Austria was less than 7 million; the Jewish population was 185,000 (170,000 in Vienna). The German army marched into Austria in March 1938 and annexed Austria to Germany, an agreement documented as the *Anschluss.* The Austrian population generally accepted this development enthusiastically, and Austrian Nazis outdid German Nazis in persecuting the Jews.[5]

As the reader moves from the historical background of the Holocaust in Germany and Austria to the testimonies of our sixteen survivors, the tragedy becomes real in each individual family. Although these witnesses were youngsters at the time, we live through the shock of Kristallnacht with each retelling of this early event in the story. Lisbeth Brodie-Judelowitsch returned to Poland and worked in the Pawiak Prison, the main prison used by the Germans in Warsaw during this period, and provides us with her memory of Janusz Korczak and his young orphans marching toward the deportation train. Jola Schulsinger Hoffman's masterful descriptions of being expelled from Germany followed by her experiences in the Warsaw ghetto are most effective. Hans Fisher's family sailed to America in May 1939 on the ill-fated *St. Louis,* only to return to Europe. Thus, efficient bureaucrats protected the free

■ 1

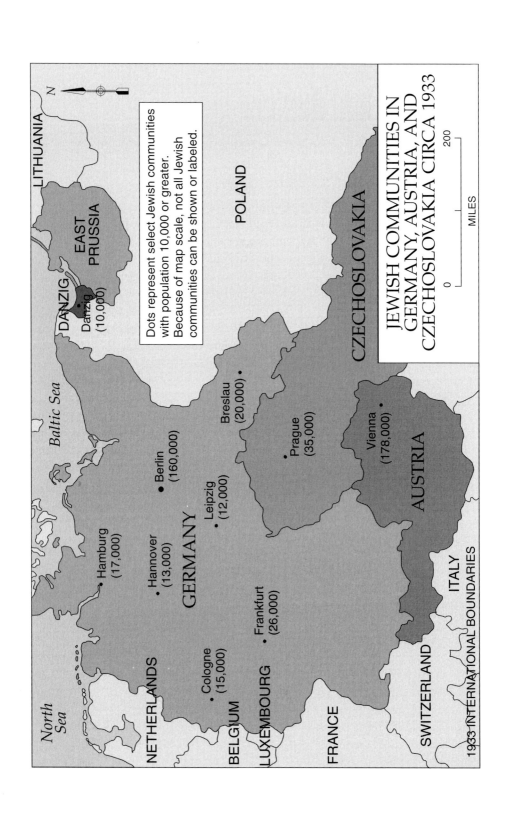

JEWISH COMMUNITIES IN
GERMANY, AUSTRIA, AND
CZECHOSLOVAKIA CIRCA 1933

Dots represent select Jewish communities
with population 10,000 or greater.
Because of map scale, not all Jewish
communities can be shown or labeled.

North
Sea

Baltic Sea

LITHUANIA

EAST
PRUSSIA

DANZIG
Danzig
(10,000)

POLAND

NETHERLANDS

Hamburg
(17,000)

Hannover
(13,000)

Berlin
(160,000)

Leipzig
(12,000)

Breslau
(20,000)

GERMANY

Cologne
(15,000)

BELGIUM

Frankfurt
(26,000)

Prague
(35,000)

CZECHOSLOVAKIA

LUXEMBOURG

FRANCE

Vienna
(178,000)

AUSTRIA

SWITZERLAND

ITALY

1933 INTERNATIONAL BOUNDARIES

N

0   200

MILES

world from these people who were suspected of being (though never proven to be) dangerous aliens. The Fishers managed to return to America, to the benefit of Rutgers University where Hans Fisher eventually pursued his career as a professor of nutritional biochemistry.

A number of survivors were saved by the *Kindertransport* program to England. Herta Laster Erreich and Walter Nachtigall reveal to us the importance of the people who cared for them, both those who knew and those who did not know how to deal with children in such emotionally difficult periods. And all of the survivors provide insight on the lifelong impact of this tragic period.

Thus, it is quite appropriate that we begin this history with the German-Austrian experience, even though the total and inescapable organization of the Holocaust took place following the German conquest of Poland.

Sixteen Survivors from Germany and Austria

GERMANY

Hella Lowenstein Bailin	Hans Fisher	Rosalie Weiser Klein
Lotte Baum-Zwaab	Ruth Stern Friedman	Liesel Hess Mayerfeld
Lisbeth Brodie-Judelowitsch	Jola Schulsinger Hoffman	Susanne Heymann Prager
Herta Laster Erreich	Marguerite Gunther Jeremias	Martin Radley
		Amalia Petranker Salsitz

AUSTRIA

Lilly Kanfer Gottlieb	Lucie Pressburg Jacobson	Walter Nachtigall

Germany

HELLA LOWENSTEIN BAILIN, 1915–

[Holocaust testimony (HRC-941, videotape: 1 hour, 23 minutes), 21 May 1987; interviewed by Bernard Weinstein and Robin McHugh, indexed by Bernard Weinstein. D804.3/.B155 1987]

Hella Bailin as a young married woman in New York, ca. 1939–1940.

Hella Lowenstein Bailin [HB] was born in Düsseldorf, Germany, in 1915. She lived in Berlin, in Seville, Spain, and then in Nuremberg and Cologne in Germany. The family's location depended on the father's employer, Siemens, for whom he worked as an engineer. HB learned to read and write by the time she was four years old. She attended about twelve schools in Germany and Spain. Her older brother died of an ear infection when he was about eleven years old. HB was then the only child in the family.

HB remembers a few instances of antisemitism in the 1920s and 1930s. While attending a Catholic boarding school for girls in the Rhineland, one sixteen-year-old girl tried to drown HB, who was one of two Jewish girls in the school. The situation in Nuremberg was especially serious. One day a Nazi entered the school and threatened her with a gun. She dropped out of the school immediately. In general, HB felt there was more antisemitism in Nuremberg and the rest of Bavaria, in the smaller towns, than in the larger cities and Berlin. Her family then moved to Cologne, where HB did not feel singled out for being Jewish.

The situation deteriorated after Hitler assumed power in 1933. Book burnings were particularly upsetting for HB. Inasmuch as conditions were now quite difficult and frightening, arrangements were made for HB to travel to New York to her maternal uncle, but this did not work out well. Her uncle had developed lung cancer, and his wife was a "miserable person." HB had to move in with distant relatives and, in essence, this young person had to make her own way in a new country. She found employment and was married in 1937.

HB tried to bring her parents to the safety of America. As the months and years rolled by, Germany was deeply involved in World War II. Finally, after much difficulty and heartache, HB arranged for her parents to enter Cuba as a first important step toward the United States. Tragically, a new German decree went into effect on the projected day of departure, banning her parents from leaving Germany because her mother was under sixty years of age. HB holds and reads the postcard she received from her father explaining this tragic turn of events. She says, "They knew what was in store for them."

HB reviews the fate of many of her family members. Her parents were sent to

Theresienstadt and perished in Auschwitz. Most of her relatives in Germany were sent to Auschwitz. She concludes by relating, "I have four cousins left, all in all, out of a family of about sixteen aunts and uncles. . . . There were about thirty people killed in different concentration camps."

HB reports that at times she feels guilty for not having done enough to save her parents. She cannot rationalize her feelings of guilt, but she feels a certain self-reproach for being here in the United States while others perished in her native land. In addition to her husband, HB has one son and one daughter. She has made a life for herself and has become a recognized artist.

LOTTE BAUM-ZWAAB, 1915–

[Holocaust testimony (HRC-935, videotape: 23 minutes), 5 March 1987; interviewed by Phyllis Ziman Tobin and Bonnie Kind, indexed by Bernard Weinstein. D804.3/.B347 1987]

Lotte Baum-Zwaab [LB] was born on 9 August 1915 in Essen, Germany. Her mother was also born in Germany, her father in Holland. She had one brother, one year older than she was. Of the four persons in her immediate family, LB is the lone survivor. LB describes her home as comfortable and not very religious, although her father did attend religious services every Saturday. All of her friends were Jewish.

LB graduated from public school and then from secretarial school in 1931. Antisemitism was becoming more ugly and more dangerous. She took a position as secretary to a Jewish lawyer. The lawyer was persecuted and died shortly after Hitler assumed power in 1933. LB's father died in 1931; her mother in 1936. Her brother fled to Holland in 1933, and she never saw him again.

LB describes *Kristallnacht* in November 1938, the suffering of Jews, and the massive destruction, including the destruction of the most beautiful synagogue in Essen.

LB fled to Holland in 1941. She married a man who owned a factory, which the Germans expropriated in 1942. LB and her husband were imprisoned in the Westerbork concentration camp in Holland in 1943. She worked in the laundry, and the couple paid "in gold" to avoid deportation to Poland. Nevertheless, they were shipped on the last transport to Auschwitz-Birkenau in September 1944.

LB and her husband had no idea of what awaited them in Auschwitz. They were separated immediately upon arrival. She was stripped from head to toe, all her clothing and belongings were confiscated, and she had a number tattooed on her arm. She was assigned to carry sand from one place to another, without any purpose. In January 1945, she was transferred to work for four months in a Sudetenland munitions factory. LB was liberated by the Russians. She went to Leipzig in the American zone and then returned to Holland. Her husband did not return—he had perished in Auschwitz.

LB remarried in 1947. Her second husband was also a German. She reports that he had been with the Resistance during the war. The couple emigrated to the United States in 1947. Their daughter was born in 1948, their son in 1952. They moved to New Jersey in 1974 to be near a cousin of LB. Her second husband died in 1982.

Lisbeth Brodie in Warsaw 1943. The Pawiak prison is in the background.

LISBETH BRODIE-JUDELOWITSCH, 1911–

[Holocaust testimony (HRC-1006, videotape: 58 minutes), 28 January 1988; interviewed by Bernard Weinstein and Phyllis Ziman Tobin, indexed by Anne Kaplan. D804.3/.B763 1988]

Lisbeth Brodie-Judelowitsch [LB] was born on 15 May 1911 in Poznań, Poland. She was an only child. Her family moved to Germany after World War I in order to escape living under Russian domination. Her father left his profession of synagogue cantor and became an unsuccessful businessman in Germany. After completing her education, LB worked for German newspapers. She lost her job in 1937 as anti-semitism became state policy. Her father died in 1928.

LB and her mother returned to Poznań before the outbreak of World War II in 1939. She describes the difficulties for Jews, which began immediately after the German invasion. She fled to Warsaw and earned a meager livelihood by teaching German. She then invited her mother to join her in Warsaw. Eventually, LB worked for a Gestapo member in Warsaw's infamous Pawiak Prison. She was responsible for translations into Polish and German. She quotes her employer as saying that he had nothing against Jews and that he was responsible for saving hundreds of Jews, including LB and her mother. Nevertheless, her mother died of insufficient food in the prison. LB testifies on her Pawiak experience:

> I didn't know what was going on outside the prison. I mean, I have seen the outside of the prison. I was one of the people who, at that time, worked for the Germans, and I was not in the Pawiak yet, and saw the transport of Korczak. I was upstairs and I saw him go downstairs and that's something I will never forget in my life. Not knowing about Korczak. I saw an elderly man and little, you know, rows of two children, two children, and two children, maybe some twenty rows, with shaven heads, terribly emaciated, and he was carrying one of the tiniest ones. Going to the *Umschlagplatz* ["transfer point"], where they sent the transports.

She continues her sensitive, vivid account of the emotional impact of her time in Pawiak:

> I am speaking about the prison itself. There were horrible things that you learned not to see. Like before that, when I passed, there were dead people in the street covered with newspaper, completely stripped bare because people needed the clothes they had died in. You didn't see them anymore. You got so numbed that, up until now, I know that I am missing one quality. I cannot mourn. I cannot, I cannot feel the sadness that other people feel. There is something inside me, that's the one thing I'm left from the war that's left me. There's a certain impossibility of feeling. I see and I don't see. I feel and I don't feel. As if a glass partition were between me and what was happening.
>
> *INTERVIEWER:* Can you recall how you felt then?
>
> *LB:* It was starting that way because I could not have survived otherwise. Things were happening around me that are very hard for *me* to describe. There are people who can roll in these things. I cannot. There was only one thing I could do: Detach myself, from *myself* even. That's all I could do.

After her mother died, LB was alone in Pawiak with the Gestapo until she went to the Theresienstadt concentration camp as the Russians were liberating Poland. She left Pawiak with the Germans on 8 August 1944 because they knew she could still be useful to them. As the months passed, the retreat from Poland evolved into a horrible death march toward Germany. Eventually, LB arrived in Theresienstadt for the chaotic concluding six weeks of the war. She was liberated by the Russians.

LB managed to leave for England after the war. She worked there as a domestic for three years until she was able to emigrate to the United States. She settled in New Jersey, attended Rutgers University, graduated from Kean College, and became a kindergarten teacher.

HERTA LASTER ERREICH, 1931–

[Holocaust testimony (HRC-1085, videotape: 58 minutes), 16 March 1993; interviewed and indexed by Joseph J. Preil. D804.3/.E71 1993]

Herta Laster Erreich [HE] was born in Schwäbisch-Gmünd, Germany, in March 1931. Her father died of a heart attack in 1933. Her mother then moved with HE and the two older children to Munich where she opened a laundry to support the family. HE's mother had two brothers in Munich who were married, and each had two children.

HE's father and her maternal grandparents were born in Poland. Thus they were all viewed as Polish Jews. They were sent to Poland in 1939 by the SS, but Poland refused to accept this Jewish family, which remained at the border for twelve hours. Finally they returned to their home in Munich on the Sabbath. HE's mother then began her effort to send all three children to England.

HE describes her memory of Kristallnacht as a seven-year-old in 1938. Her mother succeeded in sending HE and her older sister to England in 1939 as part of the *Kindertransport* program. HE was placed in an Orthodox home for girls in Sunderland, located near Gateshead and Newcastle. She describes some of the difficulties of living in the home as a young girl. Looking back on these years as a mature person, HE realizes that she received a fine education and she remains very appreciative of the care provided in the home.

HE's sister was assigned to a young family as a maid. This family sent an affidavit for HE's brother on condition that he attend the Manchester Yeshiva. HE's mother remained with her own elderly mother in Munich in 1939, planning to join her children in England after the Jewish High Holidays. In the meantime, the war started. HE's mother perished in Auschwitz, her grandmother in Theresienstadt. Her two Munich uncles fled to China with their families.

After the war, the two uncles emigrated to the United States with their families, one to New York City and the other to Newark. HE joined her uncles in the United States in 1953 and married a survivor from Poland one and a half years later. HE became a travel agent; her husband went into business. They have a son, who is a lawyer, and a daughter, who is a teacher. They have ten grandchildren. The family remains deeply committed to their religion.

Hans Fisher, Rutgers professor, 1993.

HANS FISHER, 1928–

[Holocaust testimony (HRC-948, videotape: 1 hour, 20 minutes), 27 April 1987; interviewed by Bernard Weinstein and Margaret Dunn, indexed by Bernard Weinstein. D804.3/.F533 1987]

Hans Fisher [HF] was born in Breslau, Germany, on 4 March 1928. His mother was also born in Breslau, and her family lived there. His father came to Breslau to study law.

HF describes the antisemitism he experienced as a child in the 1930s. He had to attend a Jewish school because he was not allowed to enter public school. He remembers the bullying and beatings he suffered from German boys. He felt danger in 1938 when Polish Jews were rounded up and sent back to Poland.

Kristallnacht in November 1938 was the climactic event for HF's family. His father was incarcerated in Buchenwald for six weeks. His mother obtained his father's release when she showed the Gestapo the father's merit award for World War I service and also his visa for travel to Panama. His father left Germany quickly and switched his destination to Cuba.

HF's mother then arranged to leave Germany for Cuba with her two children. The children had stopped attending school, and HF remembers this tense period in his life as a "surrealistic existence." The departure date for Cuba was 13 May 1939, on the ill-fated *St. Louis.* Practically all of the ship's passengers were forced to return to Europe because the required documents had not been obtained. Finally, the Fishers obtained the visas for Cuba and arrived in Havana from France in February 1940. They were thus reunited with their father and husband.

HF's father never spoke about his Buchenwald experience. HF describes his family's religious leanings as observant Conservative. They identified themselves as strongly Zionistic. The two sisters of HF's mother were permanent settlers in Palestine in the 1930s. In early 1938, his parents tried to emigrate to Palestine, and if it had not been for the British White Paper, they would be Israelis today.

HF's grandparents were murdered in the Theresienstadt concentration camp. When HF's mother learned the fate of her parents, she suffered a nervous breakdown that he attributes to the accumulation of events and concerns.

HF's family arrived in New York in February 1941. His father struggled to adjust to his new country, finally settling in Vineland, New Jersey, as a poultry farmer. HF earned his undergraduate degree at Rutgers University, his master's degree at the University of Connecticut, and his Ph.D. degree at the University of Illinois. HF is a professor of nutritional biochemistry at Rutgers University. He is married, has three children, and lives in New Jersey.

RUTH STERN FRIEDMAN, 1926–

[Holocaust testimony (HRC-1064, videotape: 1 hour, 44 minutes), 28 June 1988; interviewed by Bernard Weinstein and Jodi Frank, indexed by Bernard Weinstein. D804.3/.F769 1988]

Ruth Stern Friedman [RF] was born on 20 June 1926 in Hamburg, Germany. She was the youngest of three sisters. Her father was from Budapest, her mother from Galicia in Poland. The family was very assimilated religiously and culturally. RF refers to her father as a "holier than thou" German who could never believe the extent of evil apparent in the Germany of the 1930s. RF's two sisters were much older than Ruth and left Germany to live in Palestine before the outbreak of war in 1939.

RF attended a Jewish school rather than a German school. She says that, "it was the thing to do." It was a good school and "everybody went there." The first time she felt danger was when German children her age began to throw stones at her on the way to school and called her names. This was followed by *Kristallnacht* in November 1938. By 1939, neighbors who had been good family friends stopped talking to them, their most accommodating grocer rushed her mother out of the store, and children stopped playing with RF. Her father, who had already been arrested twice, was warned one day to leave Germany within twenty-four hours. He escaped to his native Budapest in June 1939, followed by RF and her mother in January 1940.

Life was difficult for the Stern family in Hungary. RF was refused entrance to a Hungarian school because she had attended a Jewish, not German, school. These mounting difficulties caused her to become ill, and she was hospitalized for two months. By the time she was released from the hospital, she had learned to speak Hungarian. Nevertheless, "Budapest was a nightmare."

The Germans occupied Hungary in 1944. RF and her parents now experienced the culminating fury of the Holocaust. The Stern family was sequestered in the Budapest ghetto. They moved into an apartment where thirty-two people lived together in two rooms. Her father, a man in his sixties, became very bitter, and he hated the Hungarians. Her mother had worked as a domestic before moving into the ghetto and now made skirts from drapes and sold them.

One day, all people between the ages of sixteen and forty were ordered to report to a stadium. RF sensed the danger in following the instructions and maneuvered, miraculously, to return to her parents in the ghetto. The others were marched to the railroad station, packed into cattle cars, and taken to Auschwitz.

RF's parents arranged to hide her with a local couple. The husband was a German-Jewish building "super," the wife a gentile. One night in December 1944, RF dreamed the ghetto was burning. By sheer determination, she returned to her parents' quarters in the ghetto and remained with them through the climactic weeks of the war. As the Russians advanced, the conflict moved to Budapest, and Ruth's father was killed in the ghetto crossfire.

After liberation, RF and her mother went to Austria, Belgium, and then France for departure to Palestine. In 1947, they set sail for Haifa on a crowded ship. She could not get off at Haifa, but her mother did. RF was taken to Cyprus, where she married her first husband. They had a daughter. She returned to Israel, divorced her husband, and married a second time. Her new husband had a daughter about the same age as RF's daughter. He also had a large American family. RF wanted "to see the world," especially America. In order to come to the United States, her husband had to give up his career in the Israeli army. They arrived in the United States in 1961 and settled in New Jersey. Their daughters live in Israel.

Toward the end of the interview, RF describes a return trip to Germany that she made with her mother at her mother's request. They visited their former apartment house and neighbors. This is the background for RF's assertions:

> I am full of vengeance. I am full of hatred. I hear the German language and I start to freeze up inside. You know why? They took away my best years. . . . I hate them with a passion. . . . Look what they did to me. They killed my young years and for that I will never forgive them. . . . I have seen too many dead bodies. . . . I was ready to kill for food. . . . That's why I won't forgive them.

JOLA SCHULSINGER HOFFMAN, 1931–1994

[Holocaust testimony (HRC-973, videotape: 1 hour, 45 minutes), 3 November 1987; interviewed by Bernard Weinstein and Jodi Frank, indexed by Anne Kaplan. D804.3/.H755 1987]

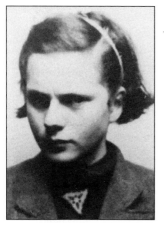

Jola Schulsinger, age twelve, in Warsaw, 1944. She survived with false ID as Maria Oracz.

Jola Schulsinger Hoffman [JH], an only child, was born in Leipzig, Germany, on 13 June 1931. Her mother was a concert pianist and her father a wholesale fur dealer. Her family was upper middle class, highly educated and cultured for generations. They were originally from Poland. Practically the entire extended family remained in Poland and perished in the Holocaust. JH reports, "We were assimilated, but we never denied the fact that we were Jewish." She remembers visiting her maternal grandparents in Łódź, Poland, for Jewish holidays.

JH sensed danger and the end of her happy, serene childhood in this remarkable recounting of events in Germany.

It changed in 1938. My father was away; my mother and I were alone in the apartment [with] the housekeeper. In the middle of the night, there was banging on the door and Mother opened the door. There were SS people, German soldiers, standing in front and they told us to leave the apartment right away, and the housekeeper, too.

They wouldn't let us take anything. I wanted to take something with me, even a toy. . . . We had no time. *Schnell! Schnell!* We had to be very quick. My mother grabbed a hat box, which I never forget why she grabbed the hat box. And this is how we were literally chased outside. And my grandmother lived on another floor . . . my father's mother . . . and she also had to leave. The four of us were chased.

We met a whole group of people. And we were moved on, very quickly, into trains. . . . It was in the middle of the night. As a matter of fact, while we were being moved, a woman was carrying a baby in front of us, and the baby fell. And the German would not let her pick up the baby. And I don't know whether the baby ever was picked up later. But the woman who dropped the baby could not pick up the baby.

And then we were chased to the trains. The trains were closing. We didn't know where we were going. The rumor was we were being sent back to Poland because that night they deported all the Polish Jews who lived in Germany, without any warning. Thousands of us, I don't know how many, but thousands of us. And we traveled at least . . . for a night and a day, and we got there the following night, to the Polish border.

And the Polish government did not know that we were coming. They did not expect it. So they were not prepared to take us in. And we had to spend a whole night, I think it may have been more than a night, at the border. And I remember it was cold, and it was raining, and it was frightening, very frightening. The Polish peasants who were there did help out. They gave us some soup, they gave us some tea, they gave us some hot stuffing. It was cold [outside] and it was horrible.

Then what happened was we were distributed and sent to different cities where we had relatives. And my mother, of course, had relatives in Łódź and in Warsaw. So we went to Łódź to her parents. We arrived there, and that's where I stayed.

All of this happened before Kristallnacht in November 1938. JH's father had been in England on a business trip. He decided to return to Germany before joining his family in Poland. He returned for Kristallnacht. German gentile friends hid him and then they helped break the seal on his apartment. He took some family clothing and left for Poland.

JH does not recall how she and her parents came to Warsaw, but they were in Warsaw when war broke out in September 1939. She paints this memorable picture of the Warsaw ghetto.

The most horrendous experience of the war that I had was the Warsaw ghetto. . . . And that's when one became aware that it could be the end. . . . You saw so much death around you. . . . For myself, I was scared. You know, seeing people starving, seeing dead bodies. We saw every day new bodies. . . .

My mother would suddenly point out the beggar, and say he was a student with her in the Leipzig Conservatory. And people, who were not ordinary people, who led normal lives, to be in such a condition!

I think the scary part of the Warsaw ghetto for me was when they started liquidating the ghetto and they chased us out. . . . In other words . . . they would close up a street, a block, and they would empty out the houses, everyone who was in the house, and take us downstairs. And then they would take some of us, some of us would go. They'd say they would resettle us, take us to another place. And some of us would stay. And the relief of staying told us something. . . .

In other words, we were told these people would be resettled. We did not want to be resettled, basically. So there was an indication, more than an indication. . . . And the first people they took were the old people. They started with the old people and then the children.

She describes the crowded, unsanitary conditions in the ghetto, although the Jews did organize schools and education for the children.

They were trying—this is a marvelous thing—they were trying to make life normal in this very abnormal environment. But I would see children, my own peers, running across the wall or across barbed wire, onto the Aryan side to get some food. And the Germans would see that, and they would shoot the children. I saw [she then describes children's theater in apartment house courtyard—*ed.*]. There was a lot of love given to me and through my family. . . .

The most unbelievable months of my war years . . . I actually had to pinch myself when I was in the ghetto to think that . . . maybe it was all a bad dream, and it wasn't happening for real. Because it couldn't be. For instance . . . it must have been a rabbi, but it was an Orthodox Jew, on a Friday night, kneeling by a dead horse on the street . . . and taking a piece of meat for food . . . and take it home for food. I mean this is something you just can't imagine.

JH's parents had gentile friends on the Aryan side of the wall. False papers were obtained for JH so that she could join these friends. She spent a total of eight months in the ghetto. JH's mother was also able to leave the ghetto and pass as an Aryan. Her father was deported to Auschwitz, and after the war JH heard that her father had died there of typhoid.

In 1944 the Warsaw Jewish population was deported to Germany for slave labor. JH was taken to a labor camp in Breslau. She describes the brutal conditions. Russians liberated her camp. This was after she had recovered from typhoid.

JH and her mother returned to Poland for one year after the war. She was brought to England in 1946 by Rabbi Solomon Schonfeld to participate in a special program sponsored by British Chief Rabbi Joseph Hertz. Her mother was able to join her in England in 1948. JH arrived in the United States in 1949 and lived with an uncle and aunt in Newark. Her uncle was an ophthalmologist who had left Poland before the war for professional and career reasons.

JH's husband was born and raised in Newark. They have four sons, all highly educated professionals. JH earned her college degree and teacher's license from Kean College and taught in the Newark public schools for many years.

At the conclusion of her testimony, JH pondered the meaning of the Holocaust for herself.

The meaning is that you make your life worthwhile. You do what you can. I said at one point that I'm glad I was part of everything that has happened. . . . It doesn't sound right, but on the other hand, it has a meaning to me. There was a Holocaust. . . . It was all right that I was there because I experienced it and I know what it is. Maybe that's why I wanted to work in the city, because I wanted to see what it's like to be in there, to be an activist. Not to just sit back and say, "It's there, but there's nothing I can do about it." I think once you put yourself into it . . . you are responsible for your actions. I think that's the lesson.

MARGUERITE GUNTHER JEREMIAS, 1926–

[Holocaust testimony (HRC-1015, videotape: 1 hour, 29 minutes), 2 November 1988; interviewed by Bernard Weinstein and Anne Kaplan, indexed by Bernard Weinstein. D804.3/.J474 1988]

Marguerite Gunther at a French children's home, 1945.

Marguerite Gunther Jeremias [MJ] was born on 10 February 1926 in Heidelberg, Germany. Her family moved to Hoffenheim when she was a little girl. MJ had one older sister. Her father was successful in his dry goods store, and the family enjoyed conveniences, including a domestic servant. Her family was Orthodox. They went to shul [synagogue] every Friday night and Saturday and did not travel on the Sabbath.

Before 1933, MJ's family and all of their gentile neighbors had enjoyed excellent relations. As she begins her very effective testimony of the Holocaust in Germany, MJ reports the significant changes in her life, beginning in 1933. Her father's store and other Jewish businesses were closed. In school, her assigned seat was changed to one in the back of the classroom. Two or three hours each week were devoted to racial, antisemitic education. Children were taught to hate Jews. Finally, in 1937, MJ was transferred by her parents to an all-Jewish school in Heidelberg, which required traveling by train for one hour to school and another to return. MJ states, "I guess I felt it more because I had only non-Jewish friends. I was completely isolated at the time . . . for me, it was even worse than if you lived in a city and you still have other friends."

MJ's sister was able to leave Germany for the United States in 1938, where she accepted employment as a maid. MJ reports that she and her parents were the only members of their extended family who could not escape from Germany at this time.

MJ recalls Kristallnacht in November 1938, the burning of the synagogue and the holy Torahs, and the deportation of her father to Dachau. Her father remained in Dachau for five weeks until her mother obtained his release because he had been awarded the Iron Cross during his military service in World War I. MJ reports the impact of Kristallnacht on her mother.

My mother took Kristallnacht, November 10, as a fast day. She felt this was like the destruction of the Temple [in Jerusalem—*ed.*], being that all the synagogues in all of Germany were burnt the same night or destroyed. She felt this warranted a fast day. So she fasted, even in the . . . concentration camp, on that day; from '38 until, I presume, she got killed.

In October 1940 the SA (storm troopers) confiscated the family property and shipped them to the concentration camp in Gurs, France. They were transferred to Rivesaltes in April 1941. One year later, MJ was separated from her parents and taken to a children's home. Shortly thereafter, her parents were deported to Auschwitz where they perished.

MJ and other girls moved several times in France in a continuing effort to hide from the Germans. They were in a convent school in Brieve and then in another Christian school in Ussel. The Germans searched for Jewish youngsters but were unable to find MJ and her group. MJ then moved in with a family and served as a nurse for their baby.

MJ provides details of the Holocaust years in France. She was liberated in August 1944 by the Maquis, the French Resistance group, and rehabilitated by the Children's Aid Society (OSE), a worldwide Jewish organization for health care and children's welfare. She trained to become a baby nurse.

MJ emigrated to the United States in 1946 to join her sister's family in New York. She married in America and settled in New Jersey. Her husband is a German Jew who escaped to Italy in 1936 then to the United States in 1939. They have two daughters and seven grandchildren.

Weiser family in a Berlin park, 1936.
Front row, from left: *Rosalie and younger sister Fanny;* back row: *father, mother, and older sister Sophie.*

ROSALIE WEISER KLEIN, 1927–

[Holocaust testimony (HRC-2016, videotape: 1 hour, 27 minutes), 23 May 1995; interviewed and indexed by Joseph J. Preil. D804.3/.K429 1995]

Rosalie Weiser Klein [RK] was born on 12 September 1927 in Berlin. She was the second of three sisters. Her parents were born in Poland and married there. She and her mother survived the Holocaust; her father and two sisters perished. They were also the only survivors of their extended family of at least nineteen persons, through first cousins.

RK remembers a normal early life—school, friends, afternoon Hebrew school twice a week. This was until "Hitler started up." One day in school all of her friends, including her best friends, suddenly stopped talking to her and completely avoided her. Jewish businesses were closed, and Kristallnacht took place. RK's father, a successful tailor, was sent back to Poland by the Germans in 1938. "The neighbors wouldn't bother with us."

In 1939, RK's mother decided the family should be together. Her mother and the three daughters left Berlin for Kraków to rejoin the father. RK did not speak Polish.

Her father decided she should learn a trade, hairdressing, rather than enroll in school. This helped RK in the concentration camp where she received extra bread for doing the hair of the German women.

RK describes the Holocaust in Poland, beginning with the plunder of valuables. Then the Jews were ordered to wear armbands bearing the Star of David. In 1940, the Germans organized the Kraków ghetto in order to gather all of the city's Jews in one section. This meant one room to a family. There was no gas or electricity. RK's parents were assigned to factory work while RK had to clean toilets in Nazi offices. One day at the end of a long work session, a Nazi soldier entered the room and said to RK, "Dirty Jew, I'll give you more work." He urinated in front of her, pushed her head and nose into the urine, and stamped on her head with his foot.

RK's two sisters remained at home with the older sister's baby while RK and her parents went to work. One day, the older sister disappeared and was never seen again.

RK describes the selection process for assignment to Płaszów, the new concentration camp constructed on a Jewish cemetery outside Kraków. The Gestapo officer placed her father and mother on the "good side," for transfer to Płaszów. He pulled the baby out of RK's arms and placed RK with her parents. RK asked, "What will be with the children?"

> He answered, "*Die Kinder kommen nach.*" This meant, We will send them after you. He pulled the children away, he pushed the younger sister on the truck with other children, and threw the baby against the wall of the house, killing the baby.
>
> As we walked away from the ghetto, we heard gun shots. They murdered all the children in the truck.

RK and her parents were among the first prisoners in Płaszów, the camp under the control of the infamous Commandant Amon Goeth. She reports that "the food was not fit for a pig." She provides insights regarding the camp's organization and cruel procedures. A young boy's whistling of a Jewish song was sufficient reason for a public hanging. Her father became ill. Mother and daughter arranged for him to enter the "hospital." One day, a young boy attempted to escape from Płaszów. For punishment, the Germans emptied the "hospital," pushed RK's father with all the patients into a pit nearby, and murdered them. "We discovered what happened when we returned at night from work. . . . You could smell the flesh burning from bodies when you had to pass by the pit."

In 1943, RK and her mother were selected for transfer to Skarżysko-Kamienna. They worked in a munitions factory near the camp.

> INTERVIEWER: Were conditions better, without Goeth there?
>
> RK: No, it was the same thing. What do you think—one Nazi is better than another?

RK and her mother were transferred to Leipzig, Germany, in an eight-hour cattle car train trip, "squeezed in like herrings." Conditions were similar to their previous camps. In April 1945, they were sent on an eleven-day death march with about eleven hundred women. Only three hundred survived the march. Her mother begged her, "Please leave me. You walk on." RK and another girl managed to carry her mother. Finally the Germans fled, and the remaining prisoners were liberated by Americans and Russians.

RK worked in a beauty parlor in Liegnitz (Legnica) after the war. She met her future husband there, and they were married two months later. The couple and her mother arrived in the United States in September 1949. They lived in Brooklyn for several years, moving to New Jersey in 1956 in order "to improve their surroundings." RK worked as a beautician, her husband as a tailor. RK's mother lived with them until she died in 1986. RK's husband died in 1993.

RK has three children, a son born in Germany and two daughters born in Brooklyn. The son is a dentist in New Jersey, the older daughter a special education teacher in California, and the younger daughter an occupational therapist in Massachusetts. RK has four grandchildren.

LIESEL HESS MAYERFELD, 1933–

[Holocaust testimony (HRC-1090, videotape: 33 minutes), 14 October 1993; interviewed and indexed by Joseph J. Preil. D804.3/.M387 1993]

Born in Frankfurt, Germany, in 1933, Liesel Hess Mayerfeld [LM] was the middle child in a family with an older sister and a younger brother. Although not quite five years old in November 1938, the time of *Kristallnacht,* LM remembers this traumatic period quite vividly. Within one week of *Kristallnacht,* her pregnant mother shipped LM and her older sister to an unmarried uncle in Holland. Her mother then worked tirelessly for the release of LM's father from Buchenwald, where he was imprisoned even though he had earned a medal for service in the German army during World War I.

The effort to leave Germany began in 1937 and assumed urgency with *Kristallnacht.* The two girls fled first. The father went to England in July 1939, and on 17 August 1939, just two weeks before the outbreak of World War II, the mother and infant brother were able to join him. The mother then arranged for the two little girls to come to England from Holland in January 1940.

The sudden uprooting of the family from Germany, one or two persons at a time, had a profound psychological impact on little LM.

LM: As children, we felt abandoned. At least, I did.

INTERVIEWER: Because you were shipped to Holland?

LM: We were shipped to Holland. I felt thoroughly abandoned.

INTERVIEWER: Do you remember that your father was taken to Buchenwald?

LM: No, I just remember confusion. I don't remember a happy childhood any more. . . .
I was happy, and then I wasn't. That's what I remember.

The five persons in LM's family left England for the United States on the last ship
to make the journey before America entered World War II. They became impover-
ished refugees. Finally, they moved to Michigan where the father became a janitor
in a Hebrew day school. Adjusting to a new country and language was very difficult.
Nevertheless, the children were educated, married, and have begotten sixteen American and Israeli children. LM and her family moved to New Jersey when her husband became a Hebrew day school principal in this state.

SUSANNE HEYMANN PRAGER, 1923–

*[Holocaust testimony (HRC-997, videotape: 1 hour, 16 minutes), 24 February 1988; inter-
viewed by Selma Dubnick and Henry Kaplowitz, indexed by Bernard Weinstein. D804.3/.P895
1988]*

A librarian assistant at Jersey City State College at the time of the interview, Su-
sanne Heymann Prager [SP] was born in Oppeln (now Opole, Poland), Upper Silesia, Germany, in 1923. In 1938, her immediate family consisted of her parents, SP,
and her younger sister. The parents perished in Auschwitz. The sisters were sent to
Stockholm during the winter of 1938–1939 and lived in Sweden throughout World
War II.

SP describes the antisemitism she experienced as a schoolgirl in Germany during the 1930s. She was the last Jewish student remaining in her school after the few
other Jews in the school had left. She was shunned by the other pupils and her teachers. SP recalls an incident involving her and a Jewish girlfriend one day when they
were chased by a mob of girls in Nazi uniforms. The two friends hid in a pharmacy.
The Nazi girls threw rocks into the store because SP "had laughed at them." SP's
parents then sent her to a boarding school.

SP recalls the *Anschluss* with Austria and Kristallnacht in 1938. She describes
the vandalism and plundering of Jewish property, the burning of synagogues, the destruction of businesses, and the deportation of men to concentration camps. With
the help of an uncle, SP and her sister were sent to Stockholm when SP was fifteen
years old. Her perception of the German danger was quite different from that of her
parents.

I have to say, I really had been begging my parents, over the years, to leave. I could
see what was happening. But, you see, I was more exposed, because I was in school

and I could see what was going on. While my parents lived in their little world, and they didn't see it as much, you know.

They knew Germany the way it used to be. They said, "Oh, the German people are good. Everything is going to calm down."

I felt, look, I have the opportunity. Yes, I want to go. I said, "Yes, I do want to go. I want to leave." Because I couldn't see any future for myself and my sister anymore. My mother said, "Yes, you can leave. The only thing is you have to be responsible for your sister." I said, "That's fine with me."

In Stockholm, SP worked as a governess in order to be independent. The two sisters lived in Sweden for nine years, until 1947, when they were able to emigrate to New York. An uncle met the two girls when their ship arrived. They moved into the German-Jewish neighborhood that had developed in Washington Heights.

The sisters studied, worked and, finally, married. SP has two daughters who live in California. One daughter is married and has given birth to SP's first grandchild.

MARTIN RADLEY, 1924–

[Holocaust testimony (HRC-1079, videotape: 58 minutes), 17 December 1992; interviewed and indexed by Joseph J. Preil. D804.3/.R107 1992]

Martin Radley [MR] was born on 27 July 1924 in Beuthen, Upper Silesia, Germany. He was the middle of three brothers. The oldest emigrated to Palestine shortly after Kristallnacht in November 1938. MR and his younger brother left for England in 1939 in the Kindertransport program. His parents perished in a murder camp.

MR, who was fourteen years old at the time, remembers Kristallnacht. He was sent by his parents to check on the condition of his grandparents. He saw smashed stores and heard someone say, "There goes a Jew." He ran away and hid in a public toilet for two hours.

The fifteen members of his Beuthen extended family are recorded on the official municipal list of Jews deported to murder camps. MR interprets this to mean that, of eighteen family members, only he and his two brothers survived the Holocaust.

In England, MR was assigned to a family in the glass business. His brother lived with distant relatives who were in the grocery business. In 1943, when he was nineteen years old, MR was inducted into the British army. When the war ended, he was assigned to the Bergen-Belsen area as an interpreter. He spoke to survivors who participated in the death march from Auschwitz to Bergen-Belsen, a distance "of five hundred miles." He helped the Jewish chaplain officiate at the funerals of many survivors who died after liberation. MR recalls this incident during his testimony.

A guy comes, I never met him before. He told me his name. His name was Friedrich. That was his second name. I said, "Did your parents have a store, with good feathers? That was near the synagogue?"

"Yeah, how did you know?"

I remember that store. Friedrich, he was originally a Polish Jew. His parents and family were deported after Kristallnacht. And somehow, he lived in Poland and lived through the camps. And he's talking and he tells me that he has a sister that married a guy by the name of Rudy Weiner and they emigrated to Brazil. I said, "That's my mother's cousin, Rudy Weiner."

We didn't know the address. He couldn't write a letter because the civilian mail didn't go through yet. I wrote a letter, addressed to Mr. Rudy Weiner, São Paolo, Brazil. I got a reply. The letter got to him. . . . It was the cousin, and it was his sister. He was out within three months. They got him out.

After MR related how a Jewish Kapo was beaten by survivors, the following section of the interview occurred:

INTERVIEWER: But it was a no-win situation. Whatever you did was not good. . . .

MR: A Jewish policeman had the job to go and arrest them and bring them down there.

INTERVIEWER: Which remains a source of controversy until the present day.

MR: Right. I think to myself, what would I have done if I was in that situation? I don't know.

INTERVIEWER: Did you ask the survivors that question? "What would you have done?" Probably not.

MR: I don't think so. . . .

INTERVIEWER: So that was the story, really, of the existence of the people at that time. Whatever they did was impossible.

MR: It wasn't wrong, it wasn't right, you know. I think to myself in the position: If I was in the camps, and I was in the age where they make me a policeman, and I got the order, "Go and arrest this and this people," I don't know what I would have done.

INTERVIEWER: It was better to be in the British army.

MR: Definitely.

After the war, MR married a Czech survivor in Germany and adopted her son from a previous marriage. They lived in England, had twin sons, and the entire family emigrated to the United States in 1951. They settled in New Jersey when MR bought a glass store in Newark. His first wife died in 1961. MR's second wife is a librarian in a suburban New Jersey school district. All three of MR's sons are in business, two in New Jersey and one in Alabama. His two brothers live in Israel. At the time of this interview, MR had two grandchildren.

AMALIA PETRANKER SALSITZ, 1922–

[Holocaust testimony (HRC-974, videotape: 3 hours, 25 minutes), 24 April and 27 October 1987; interviewed by Bernard Weinstein and Ruth Harris, indexed by Bernard Weinstein. D804.3/.S174 1987]

Amalia Petranker Salsitz [AS] was born in Munich, Germany, on 21 October 1922, the middle of three sisters. Her father was in the lumber business. AS remembers living in a loving, comfortable family.

The family moved to Stanisławów, in the Galician region of Poland, after Hitler assumed power in 1933. This region was under Russian control between September 1939 and June 1941. After Germany extended the war to Russia, life became much more difficult and dangerous for the Jews in eastern Poland. From November 1941 until October 1942, AS and her family were in the town ghetto organized by the Germans. She was in Kraków from the end of 1942 until 1945. She was saved because she had obtained certification in Kraków that she was a Christian with the name of Felicia Milaszewska. Despite this successful effort to pass as a non-Jew, AS describes a number of occasions when her life was in danger each time she was suspected of being a Jew.

As the war was ending, AS joined the Armia Krajowa, the Polish underground military organization popularly referred to as the "AK." She married a fellow survivor. Both husband and wife worked for the AK and both protected themselves with false identification papers. AS and one sister were the only family members to survive the Holocaust. The parents and one other sister were murdered by the Germans.

After the war, AS and her husband lived in Kraków, Breslau (Wrokcław), and Liegnitz (Legnica) before they arrived in the United States on 17 January 1947. They have one daughter and three grandchildren and live in New Jersey.

Austria

LILY KANFER GOTTLIEB, 1925–

[Holocaust testimony (HRC-1022, videotape: 57 minutes), 7 February 1988; interviewed by Bernard Weinstein and Devorah Lichstein, indexed by Bernard Weinstein. D804.3/.G693 1989]

Lily Kanfer Gottlieb [LG] was born on 20 May 1925 in Vienna. She transferred from public school to a Jewish day school at the age of ten. This was her choice because she "was oriented toward Zionism and the Hebrew language." Her family came to Austria from Poland. Her grandfather was a Hasid with a beard who wore traditional Hasidic clothing. She describes her family as "very Jewish, not assimi-lated." LG's father was in the import-export business. Her mother sold wool and yarn. LG was an only child. The family appeared to live comfortably. Her mother lost her business during Kristallnacht in November 1938.

LG experienced fear the first day the Germans marched into Austria during March 1938 and the soldiers sang, "When Jewish blood flows from our knives." LG knew a number of people who were sent to the Dachau concentration camp at the time of Kristallnacht. Many returned, some never did. LG's family was friendly with the family of Raul Hilberg, who has become a distinguished Holocaust historian. She recalls that Hilberg's father was incarcerated in Dachau.

LG's parents and other family members in Austria made preparations to leave. Her parents and LG left in 1939 and managed to settle in Antwerp, Belgium. Many Jews would not leave Austria. "They could not believe" these destructive actions would not abate. When the Germans invaded Western Europe on 10 May 1940, LG's father was interred by the Belgians because he was considered to be a German. When Germany won speedily, LG's father remained interred by the Germans. He was transferred to two holding camps in France by the Germans, to Saint-Cyprien and Les Milles. This brought LG and her mother to France. Because they had finan-cial means, they had visas and were able to buy food. They "were never hungry in France."

The family sailed from France on 9 January 1942 in a ship built for 350 passen-gers but carrying 800 people anxious to escape the European turmoil. They stopped in Casablanca, Morocco, then continued the journey to the American continent and finally arrived in Cuba. LG's family lived in Cuba for twelve years, leaving finally and permanently for the United States in 1961, at the time of Castro's assumption of power. They had alternated living in Cuba and the United States between 1948 and 1961.

LG married a Holocaust survivor from Poland in Cuba. Their two sons were born in Cuba. When the family moved permanently to the United States, they settled in New Jersey. Mr. G. went into real estate construction. One son is a physician, the other a lawyer. LG has two grandchildren.

LG reports that her family assumes that all relatives left in Vienna and in Poland were killed. The same applies to the Jews they knew in southern France, all of whom have also vanished. LG and her husband have always talked with their sons about their experiences during the Holocaust. She summarized her Austrian experience very effectively near the conclusion of the interview.

> For me, these things were not traumatic. I mean, it was traumatic as a child to walk down the street where I was born and to have kids tell me, "Get off the sidewalk, you dirty Jew." Or to go by the apartment where I played all the years when I was a child and to see a big sign saying, "Entrance for Jews Forbidden." . . . It had an impact. . . .

I think it was easier for us who were very Jewish oriented. There were some people in Vienna who were very Austrian . . . who hardly were aware of the fact that they were Jews. It was terrible for them. I mean being in the Jewish school and the Jewish youth organization helped . . . our self-esteem. . . . I don't think any of us ever felt inferior.

LUCIE PRESSBURG JACOBSON, 1924–

[Holocaust testimony (HRC-1012, videotape: 59 minutes), 15 November 1988; interviewed by Bernard Weinstein and Anne Kaplan, indexed by Bernard Weinstein. D804.3/.J336 1988]

Lucie Pressburg in Vienna, 1938.

Lucie Pressburg Jacobson [LJ] was born in Vienna on 9 March 1924. She was an only child. Her father managed an architectural firm; her mother worked in an office and was also a dressmaker.

LJ provides several examples of antisemitism experienced by the family in Austria in the 1930s. In school, she says, "I just didn't feel at home." In May 1938, two months after the Anschluss with Germany, LJ's father and his brother were shipped to Dachau. LJ and her mother were expelled from their apartment in September 1938. Their extended family tried to flee from Austria. Her mother began to carry poison to commit suicide should her husband die in the camp.

In January 1939, her mother managed to send LJ to England on the Kindertransport created to save refugee children. The family's possessions were sent to Haifa in the hope that the family would succeed in emigrating to Palestine. Mother courageously traveled to Gestapo headquarters in Berlin in her endeavor to obtain the release of her husband from Dachau. Her husband and his brother were released. LJ's parents fled to Palestine and managed to have LJ join them before the outbreak of World War II.

In 1946, LJ married a British soldier who had been stationed in Palestine during the war. The young couple lived in England, where their daughter was born. LJ's parents emigrated to the United States in 1953. When her first husband died in 1962, LJ left England with her daughter to join her parents in New Jersey.

She married again in the United States and had a son. Both her children are married, and she has two grandchildren. Her daughter is a lawyer, a graduate of Douglass College and Rutgers Law School. Her son is a doctoral candidate in Temple University's mental health program and a summa cum laude graduate of Princeton University.

As she concludes her testimony, LJ articulates her post-Holocaust philosophy:

As a survivor—although I really don't count as a survivor because I didn't survive such terrible things as people who stayed beyond 1939—you are left with the question: Why me? Why not Martha, with whom I had such a wonderful time? Why not . . . all the others, who never made it? And you ask yourself, why? What can I do? It's got to be a reason. It cannot be for no reason at all. And being Jewish has always been the motivating force in my life.

And when my son was born and started Hebrew school, I became very active in the synagogue. And I've gone from knowing instinctively to knowing by learning. And the whole thrust of my existence now is to let people know not only what took place but also how important it is not to be a bystander. Whether you live in America, or you live in France, or in England, or anywhere else in the world, the world should remember that it wasn't Hitler alone who destroyed so much of the Jewish people. That it was America who did not let people in, who did not expand their quota. . . .

At the time when we were fighting for a place to live under the sun, in Evian-les-Bains, in 1938 in July, the nations had no room. Not for children, not for adults, not for Jews. Except the very small countries. I think Holland and Denmark . . . offered places to Jewish children. And, consequently, the Danes were wonderful. And so were some of the Swedes who took in a friend of mine and saved her life.

But we've got to remember that by doing nothing, we are helping, just as much as if we actually took a gun and shot a Jew, or pushed them into an open ditch.

WALTER NACHTIGALL, 1931–

[Holocaust testimony (HRC-1042, videotape: 1 hour, 4 minutes), 8 February 1989; interviewed by Bernard Weinstein and Peppy Margolis, indexed by Bernard Weinstein. D804.3/.N329 1989]

Walter Nachtigall [WN] was born in Vienna, Austria, on 2 February 1931. He was the youngest of three children. His father was in the leather business. He remembers a happy early childhood. The world of WN and his family was altered radically in 1938. The Anschluss between Germany and Austria took place in March, followed by Kristallnacht in November. WN's description of Kristallnacht is truly remarkable, especially so because he was younger than eight years old at the time.

Only my parents and my sister were still at home when the door was forced open. [His older brother had been forewarned and understood that his best choice was to hide that night—*ed.*] And in marched about a half-dozen SA troopers . . . they were the Brown Shirts. At the time they were considered the thugs of the Nazi party, versus the Black Shirts, or the SS, who were the so-called elite.

And again, the ages of these Nazis were rather young—late teens, early twenties. And much to our surprise, our father recognized at least three of them, because of his business being in the building. And again, the same type of humiliation ensued—

jostling, pushing, cursing. And my father would ask, Fritz, or Hans, "What did we do to you?" And the response: "You're a Jew! You're a Jew!" That was it.

They proceeded to ransack our apartment, throwing furnishings, pillowcases, blankets, right out of the window to people waiting down in the street. It was a free-for-all. Grab what you can. I was simply terrified at what was happening, to see my father pushed and punched, and to see that being done to my mother—a frightening and painful experience—and there was no hitting back, weathering the storm. And I asked even then, "Why? Why? What's going on?" And my mother was trying to keep me quiet, simply out of fear that I wouldn't arouse the Nazis from doing any greater harm.

My father was arrested, taken away . . . to Dachau, one of the notorious concentration camps. We had no idea who, what would be happening. This was happening all over the city, so most Jews, all Jews, were in the same sad state of affairs.

WN then describes the burning of the synagogue across the street from his family's apartment. The fire department rushed to the fire. Hoses were connected to fire hydrants, but the SA did not allow the fire to be doused and the synagogue was completely destroyed.

Several months later, while his father remained incarcerated in Dachau, young WN and his siblings were sent on the Kindertransport to England. He and his sister were assigned to Jewish families in Edinburgh. His brother was sent to southern England.

WN was unhappy in the doctor's home where he had been assigned. He found it cold and unpleasant. When the doctor and his wife left for a golfing vacation shortly after his arrival, WN went to stay with a Christian family in Dysart, a nearby fishing community. Young WN was treated with love and warmth in his new home, and the arrangement became permanent.

In the meantime, WN's father was released from Dachau and his parents managed to come to Edinburgh. They obtained employment as domestics.

The family was able to emigrate to the United States in 1940. WN completed his education through college and is now a sales executive. He is married, has three American children and two grandchildren. The family lives in New Jersey. He reports that he has returned to Scotland to visit with his Scottish "family" and is in constant contact with these wonderful people who made a home for him during a traumatic period of his childhood. His "love for this family knows no bounds."

In 1994, WN was invited by his community to make a presentation based on his Holocaust experience. He telephoned his Scottish "sister" and asked her to record her memories of those critical times. The "sister's" letter, as typed by her, follows:

Re: Walter Nachtigall
From: Mae (Salmond) Elder, Kircoldy, Scotland
You asked Walter "how did it happen"? Through our church, dad and mum took children from the Church of Scotland Home and gave them a holiday. There was no

payment involved. One day the Matron of the Home went to our Minister Mr. Menzies and said she had a little boy. A Jewish refugee, in the Home, and they would like to find a good home for him for 1 week only.

Apparently in the synagogue in Edinburgh the congregation was asked if they would take in a little refugee. It was a Doctor and his wife whom you were with, but they were going on vacation, so I guess he was the Doctor to the Home, and he was able to take you there.

Our Minister said to the Matron, he would take her down to the Salmond's. While they were in the house Dad came home from work. When the Matron explained you were only 8 years old, taken away from your family and had no one apart from your sister, but they didn't know where she was, both dad and mum said bring the little boy to us, we will look after him. The following day you came to the Salmond home. You were a frightened, sad little boy. We didn't have a lot of money but we had a good comfortable happy home with good food and were well clothed, but above all we were brought up with love, lots of love. Dad and mum explained to Bill (my brother) and I how you were far from your mum and dad and we were to look after you while you were here for a holiday. At the end of your week when you were due to go back to Edinburgh you asked if you could stay another week. Mum phoned the Doctor and his wife and asked, they said yes it would be alright. At the end of your second week, when again it was time to go, you asked, please can I just stay one more week when I will go. Mum phoned Edinburgh, yes it was alright.

We were all going to Perth for one weeks holiday and you were coming too. While we were at Perth, war was declared and dad got a telegram saying send Walter back immediately to be evacuated. I remember dad, mum, Auntie Peg and Uncle John speak about this. Then dad and mum went in to the Police Station in Perth with the telegram and asked if they could keep you. They explained, here was a little 8 year old boy taken away from his parents, brought to a strange country, put with strangers then into a home. When brought to Dysart to be with more strangers and now being asked to be sent back to Edinburgh to be evacuated. The Police were very understanding and said Dysart was not an evacuated area and asked dad what his plans were. He said to keep you safe until your parents came for you. They then asked what if his parents don't come dad said we will adopt the lad. We came home to Dysart, mum phoned Edinburgh to say we were going to keep you and to send on your clothes.

Bill and I thought this was great, we had a little brother. He was special because he had come from a long way to stay with us. Dad and mum had such a lot of love to give and more for three of us. They told us how lucky we were, we had so much and we were to love Walter. Mum took you to school, Miss Duncan your teacher was very good with you and so kind to you. The kids all thought you were great. You kept following dad around saying he was "marvelous." Mum said, why is Jimmy so "marvelous" and you said "cause he is so big. He could fight Hitler—my papa was small and couldn't fight him." You asked if it was your new mama and papa, mum said no—

you have a mama and papa and you said what shall I say, Isa and Jimmy, Bill said that's right.

At nights we would all sit around the fire talking and playing games, sometimes you would say Isa I'm just going to have a cry I'm thinking about my mama and papa but don't you cry, you can't help it. So there we were all sitting together crying, sometimes Lord Haw Haw would speak on the radio with German propaganda, you would translate in English and say Jimmy, he said the Germans are coming over here. You would sit on dad's knee and he told you no they will never get here. Dysart being such a small close-knit village, everybody knew each other. They all took you to their hearts, you sure were a celebrity. At christmas most kids hang up a stocking for Santa to fill but, Bill and I being spoilt, we hung up a pillow case and of course showed you what to do. I can still see the look on your face on christmas morning you not knowing anything about christmas. I think all Dysart gave you a present. Remember the time you were out playing at the play park with your pals when dad asked how you had been that day. You were a bit unhappy all your friends had been able to slide down the shoot, but because your trousers were suede you were sticking, so dad said, right, we must get some more trousers. Only once do I remember saying to mum do you love Walter more than Bill and me? She said no, your dad and I love you, Bill and Walter all the same, but just listen to me. If you or Bill wants anything or needs to talk to your mum and dad you only have to come to us, but if Walter wants to talk to his mum and dad or if he would like something who does he come too, he is far from his mum and dad so we all have to take care of him and look after him for his mum and dad. So Bill and I thought no more about it and whatever we got or wanted you always were there with us. Often we were told how lucky we were always being together with our mum and dad. One Sunday you were out playing and came in crying. Dad and mum wondered what was wrong. You said Jimmy who told Hitler I was here, he has come for me, dad held you and told you then Hitler wasn't here and would never come and take you away from him. You took him outside to show him the little red van like the one which took your dad away but it was our mail van collecting the mail at the Post Office. We had read in the papers and heard on the radio about Hitler and what he had done to the Jewish people, but I guess because Germany was so far away and we didn't know any of the people it didn't get home to us, but after you came to stay with us. Here was an 8 year old so involved with all that horrific brutality, we paid more attention to the happenings. Dad and mum thought you had suffered more than enough in your young life, so they were going to do their best to give you love and security till you met up your parents. I remember mum saying, those poor Jewish families they are all god's people, she never could understand how it should happen. Dysart people then realised the sufferings and the tragedy which was put upon the Jewish people and I would say yes emotions were high because you were Jewish and the feelings were very strong for your parents. The torture they went through plus having their children taken from them not knowing where they were going, what kind of people they would be staying with and would they ever see you all again. It must have been traumatic, the end of the world. I remember your mum and dad coming to visit you, the first time they saw you since that awful day when you left on the train, you were in the park with your friends. We all came looking for you. The look on your parents face.

In many ways it was a sad time but we all had happy times too. Dad and mum loved you as their own. Bill and I loved you as a brother. The love you had for the Salmonds was the richest payment.

When that sad day for us came for you to leave and be united with your parents, brother and sister, we cried and cried. You crying saying Jimmy you promised you wouldn't let me go. Dad trying to tell you he promised to keep you till your mum and dad came for you. At the railway station you said Isa when I grow up I'll be back. Which you did.

The first time you came back home again you were on a return journey from a business trip to Europe. We picked you up at Edinburgh Airport, the bond of love was still there. We took you down to Dysart, you recalled everything as it was many years before, our home, the bake house, van shed where Jimmy kept his milk fleet, the crossing where you went to visit Fairfull's Chemist. Then down to the sea shore—in your eyes nothing had changed. As we walked along the High Street, one lady came forward saying "is that you Walter?" As she spoke with you she said "My Mr. & Mrs. Salmond loved you" your reply was "yes and I loved them, that's why I'm back." We then went down to the harbour, this time a man called out, "Mrs. Salmond that's Wee Walter?" He was the road sweeper, who had a trash can on wheels and you used to run and push it.

Not only are you a part of the Salmond family but part of Dysart. People still ask for you and your family. You came as a small Jewish boy to a small village of Dysart and made us all aware of the sad plight of the Jewish people.

Chapter Two
Western Poland

THE statistics on Jews murdered in Poland during the Holocaust are staggering in terms of both the number and the percentage of Jews who perished. Poland's prewar Jewish population was 3.3 million, of whom 3 million, or 90 percent, perished during World War II.

The Germans created an enormous camp system in Poland for the Holocaust. This included four extermination camps—Chełmno, Treblinka, Sobibór, and Bełżec—which were used for the immediate murder of Jews transported there; three large concentration camps—Auschwitz, Majdanek, and Płaszów—which were used for murder of most Jews immediately upon arrival, while some young Jews were used for slave labor before they were also burned and cremated; and 1,798 slave labor camps and 136 refugee camps. In addition Jews were murdered in transit camps, prisons, and ghettos.[1]

The totality of Jewish losses in Poland has been summarized by Israel Gutman: "In Poland, a country where Jews had been dwelling for a thousand years, only two Jews are left out of every thousand who lived there before the war broke out in 1939."[2]

Christopher Browning provides us with a seemingly clear perspective of the terrible speed of Holocaust murders in 1942 in the introductory paragraph of his chapter, "One Day in Józefów."

> In mid-March of 1942, some 75 to 80 percent of all victims of the Holocaust were still alive, while some 20 to 25 percent had already perished. A mere eleven months later, in mid-February 1943, the situation was exactly the reverse. Some 75 to 80 percent of all Holocaust victims were already dead, and a mere 20 to 25 percent still clung to a precarious existence. At the core of the Holocaust was an intense eleven month wave of mass murder. The center of gravity of this mass murder was Poland. . . . The German attack on the Polish ghetto was not a gradual or incremental program stretched over a long period of time, but a veritable blitzkreig, a massive offensive requiring the mobilization of large numbers of shock troops at the very period when the German war effort hung in the balance.[3]

The testimonies in the two chapters on Poland make it possible to understand the Holocaust as the experiences of different and distinct individual persons. We should make every effort to understand the Holocaust in this manner, because the numbing

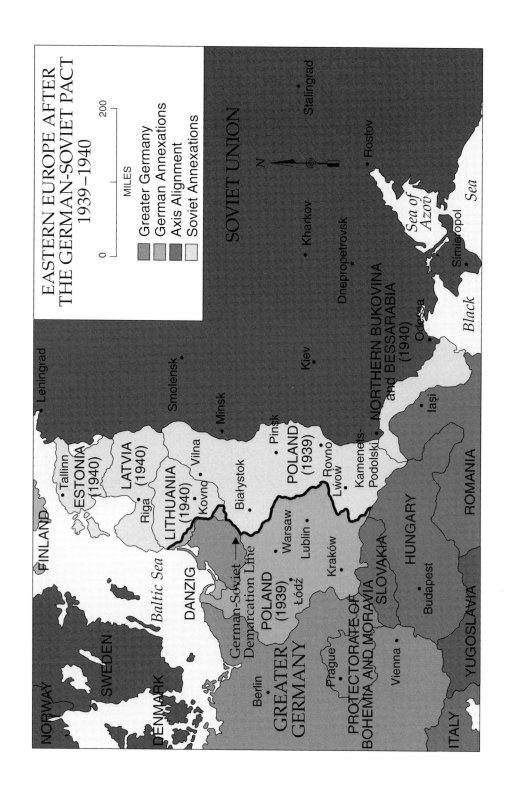

EASTERN EUROPE AFTER
THE GERMAN-SOVIET PACT
1939–1940

MILES

0   200

Greater Germany
German Annexations
Axis Alignment
Soviet Annexations

NORWAY

SWEDEN

DENMARK

FINLAND

Leningrad

Tallinn
ESTONIA
(1940)

Baltic Sea

Riga
LATVIA
(1940)

LITHUANIA
(1940)

Kovno

Vilna

Smolensk

Minsk

DANZIG

Berlin

GREATER
GERMANY

POLAND
(1939)

Łódź

German-Soviet
Demarcation Line

Warsaw

Lublin

Białystok

Pinsk

POLAND
(1939)

Rovno

Lwów

Kamenets-
Podolski

Kiev

SOVIET UNION

N

Kharkov

Dnepropetrovsk

Stalingrad

Rostov

Prague

PROTECTORATE OF
BOHEMIA AND MORAVIA

Kraków

SLOVAKIA

Vienna

HUNGARY

Budapest

NORTHERN BUKOVINA
and BESSARABIA
(1940)

Iaşi

Odessa

Sea of
Azov

Simferopol

ITALY

YUGOSLAVIA

ROMANIA

Black
Sea

statistics are beyond our ability to comprehend. This explains the universal appeal of *The Diary of Anne Frank*[4] and is the major theme of Judith Miller's *One, by One, by One.*[5]

What do we learn as we analyze the testimonies of the survivors from Poland? We see a clear picture of the German murder program. In general, you will note that older Jews and children were murdered upon arriving at the concentration camps. These two age groups rarely survived. Young people and adolescents were allowed to work for the Germans for the short period of time they had strength to live. The "food" provided by the Germans was far from sufficient to ensure survival for the Jewish work force. As Shlomo Weinglas reports: "A lot of people gave up and they died, yes. A lot of people lay down. . . . They could not go farther, and that's it. We got the food rations, what's just barely enough to survive, not to live and not to die. But you couldn't die from it and you couldn't live with it."

The ninety-nine testimonies are divided into two chapters: sixty-eight witnesses who were in German-occupied western Poland from the beginning of the war and thirty-one who were in the eastern sections of Poland occupied by the Russians between the outbreak of war in September 1939 and the beginning of the German invasion of eastern Poland and Russia in June 1941.

In these testimonies, the reader will note insignificant differences between the German-occupied territory (Jewish population, 2.1 million) and the Russian-occupied territory (Jewish population, 1.2 million). For example, of the sixty-eight witnesses from German-occupied Poland, twenty-six (38 percent) are lone survivors of their families; in Russian-occupied Poland, nine (32 percent) of the thirty-one witnesses are lone survivors of their families. Holocaust events become more real to the reader in these narratives than in general histories. The philosophical challenges addressed in a number of interviews include such issues as the motivations of the Germans and other perpetrators; resistance by the victims; the effect of inhuman hunger; and the meaning of the Holocaust for post-Holocaust generations.

It should be noted that Ada Abrahamer based her testimony on a diary she wrote as a young girl during the Holocaust.

Sixty-eight Survivors from German-Occupied Western Poland, 1941–1944

Ada Breitkopf Abrahamer	Sally Silberstein Chase	Leon Faigenbaum
David Altholz	Jeanette Rottenberg Ehrlich	Regina Debowska Faigenbaum
Mila Zagorski Bachner		
Morris Bergen	Sol Einhorn	Max Findling
Shlomo Biezunski	Henry Erlich	Joel Frish

Paul Gast

Eliasz David Glanz

Nat Glass

Gladys Bresler Helfgott

David Katz

Luna Fuss Kaufman

David Kempinski

Eva Chawa Horowitz Kempinski

Halina Goldberg Kleiner

Henry Kolber

Edith Frohlich Kornbluth

William Kornbluth

Rose Gluckstein Kramer

Rose Korcarz Laiter

Eva Apozdawa Laks

Naftali Laks

Henry Landsberg

Philip Lederman

Isak Levenstein

Sally Banach Levenstein

Henry Lowenbraun

Manya Reich Mandelbaum

Jerry Miron

Paul Monka

Murray Pantirer

Helen Faigenbaum Raff

Maurice Rauchweld

Rabbi Jack Ring

Aron Rosenblum

Celina Spira Rosenblum

Idek Rosenblum

Lillian Kronenberg Ross

Dora Lampell Roth

Morris Rubell

Rosalyn Leisten Rueff

Norman Salsitz

Rose Pariser Schwartz

Aaron Schwarz

Ida Furst Schwarz

Bennett Silberstein

Mala Hoffnung Sperling

Jack Spiegel

Miriam Shapiro Spiegel

Leo Stahl

Samuel Stimler

Rabbi Isaac Suna

Enoch Trencher

Sol Urbach

Lee Laufer Weinberg-Erlich

Shlomo Avraham Weinglas

David Werdiger

Henry Yungst

Abraham Zuckerman

Millie Mark Zuckerman

Teddy Zweig

ADA BREITKOPF ABRAHAMER (DATES UNAVAILABLE)

[Holocaust testimony (HRC-1052, videotape: 1 hour, 52 minutes), 10 October 1989; interviewed by Bernard Weinstein and Patricia Widenhorn, indexed by Bernard Weinstein. D804.3/.A245 1989]

Ada Breitkopf in Kraków, 1940.

Much of Ada Breitkopf Abrahamer's [AA] testimony is based on her diary written in Kraków and in three concentration camps. An only child, AA was born and raised in Kraków. She has fond memories of the prewar era when she belonged to Akiba, a Zionist youth organization. Her family in 1939 consisted of four persons: her parents, a grandmother, and AA. Her father perished at the very beginning of the war. It was reported to AA that he was murdered as he was trying to flee to Russia. Her grandmother died during the last days of the Kraków ghetto, in early 1943.

AA recalls acts of persecution by the Germans when the war started in September 1939. These included the curfew, the decree for all Jews to wear identifying armbands, the closing of schools for Jewish students, the plundering of valuables, the ripping off of beards, and the general humiliation of pious Jews. AA describes how the Jews of Kraków were compelled to move into a ghetto in March 1941. Her family was assigned one room and a young woman added as a "tenant." AA and her mother were involved in forced labor both before and after the ghetto was opened. She reports a life of cruelty, beatings, and constant hunger during the ghetto's two years. The lives of AA and her mother were in danger when the ghetto was being liquidated in March 1943. Would they be assigned to an extermination camp or would they continue to work in a Kraków munitions factory and be transferred to the nearby Płaszów concentration camp? At last, the German army captain who was in charge of their factory arrived at the ghetto assembly place and took his employees for continued work in his plant and for transfer to Płaszów.

AA's inherent optimism about life is revealed in the following:

> I only heard that . . . this particular captain, who was a very stern man, and he never showed any . . . softness or emotions, he expressed himself, and I will never forget his words, he said in German, ". . . I damn it what is occurring now in the ghetto." Because he saw what was happening, you know, and that came from a German. This was always my hope, when they talk now about antisemitic incidents. This is always my hope that there are enough people, there will be enough people with good sense, to know that these kinds of happenings, like the Holocaust, like persecution of people because they are anything else that they are, is not good. And it will never, *ever* . . . win. I believe that deeply.

AA recounts her Holocaust experience by reading extensively from her diary. She is a talented writer both in the original Polish and in her own English translation. She describes the horrible life in Płaszów under Commandant Amon Goeth; her move from Płaszów to Oskar Schindler's factory; the trip by cattle car to Auschwitz-Birkenau and her three weeks in those infamous camps; her transfer to Lichtewerden-Freudenthal in Sudetenland, Czechoslovakia, where she suffered the chaotic conditions of the concluding six months of the war (her mother was transferred to the Skarżysko-Kamienna camp in the Radom, Poland, district and AA never saw her again); liberation by the Russians; her wedding in a DP camp kitchen in a ceremony performed by an American chaplain in front of twenty guests.

The descriptions of her liberation and wedding come through as beautiful literature that will surely be appreciated by students and others. AA and her husband arrived in the United States in 1948. They have two children, a daughter and a son.

DAVID ALTHOLZ, 1928–

[Holocaust testimony (HRC-912, videotape: 1 hour, 27 minutes), 20 June 1984; interviewed by Sidney Langer, indexed by Joseph J. Preil. D804.3/.A467 1984]

David Altholz [DA] was born in Krosno in 1928. His family moved to Tuchów, Upper Silesia, in 1932. His father was a watchmaker who provided comfortably for the family. His immediate family in 1939 consisted of four persons: his parents, DA, and a younger sister. When the war started in September 1939, DA and his mother and sister were on a vacation visit to the maternal grandparents in Tuchów. His father was able to join them in October. The family moved somewhat later to Krosno to live with the paternal grandparents.

DA recalls how the Germans, at the very outset of the war, removed the intelligentsia from their homes and murdered them. They had information containing names and addresses, provided by the local Poles. DA recalls the roundups of Jews and the executions of those who tried to avoid the roundups. Young DA was included in one roundup. After three months, his group was informed they would be in a work detail. After one year of war, in late 1940, DA was twelve years old. What does he remember of the situation at that time? "What I remember clearly . . . would be hunger, lice, and fear in that order."

After about six months in the work detail, DA and his group were moved by trucks to Szebnie, a small concentration camp, and then to Płaszów, a large camp on the outskirts of Kraków. "There, by coincidence, I met my father," who told him that his mother and sister had been sent to Auschwitz. They were never seen again. DA points out that Płaszów has one of the few memorials in Poland that identifies Jewish victims as Jews, not merely as Polish citizens. (The memorial was erected by the Jewish community.)

DA and his father remained in Płaszów about eighteen months. He describes the horrible living conditions in the camps, fit for animals and not for people. He remembers *Appell*s (roll calls) where every tenth person was executed for no reason whatsoever. How did he and his father manage to remain alive? "What saved my father was the fact that he was a watchmaker. What saved me was that I claimed to be a watchmaker."

About religious observance, DA states, "There were people who prayed, especially Hungarians." A minyan [prayer group]? "There must have been."

After Płaszów, DA and his father were transferred to Sachsenhausen concentration camp in Brandenburg, Germany. Toward the end of the war, DA was in a group of about two hundred youngsters sent to Ludwigslust to work in a munitions factory. It was bombed often, and they could hardly do any work. They remained in Ludwigslust about nine months, and DA continues: "Conditions were miserable. The worst part was just before liberation. Many died from diarrhea and malnutrition. I suspect some of the corpses were used for [unclear; probably "food"—*ed.*]."

DA estimates that only approximately twenty of the original two hundred young prisoners survived until liberation by the Americans. He and the other survivors were taken to a hospital by the liberators, where for three weeks they were fed carefully. DA went to Berlin with a survivor friend. He heard conflicting reports about his father's survival. Finally, after much effort, father and son were reunited in Lübeck, in the British zone. This was "some reunion." An aunt of DA was also there.

Father and son were able to emigrate to the United States in 1949. They came to distant cousins in New York. Father was employed by Omega, and DA was drafted for the Korean War. "That's when I learned English." DA wanted to avoid returning to Europe, but the army sent him to Germany because he spoke German fluently.

DA married a fellow survivor. They have a son who is a lawyer and a daughter who is an arts editor. DA and family settled in New Jersey because of his work, and they selected a community with a reputation for an excellent school system. At the very end of his testimony, DA spoke with great feeling.

The first thing I teach my children is that the word, hate, even though kids very loosely use that term—Oh, I hate this one, I hate that one—I have simply forbidden that word. I've stricken it, in my household, from the dictionary. That word should not be used at all. I don't hate the Germans and I don't hate the Poles. I perhaps feel hatred for those who have been doing these cruel things. But not all people have done it. And a lot of them have simply taken the easy road. Well, if you won't bother me, I won't bother you. Many people here are the same way. People are the same all over the world, certainly the civilized world. . . .

I fault people when I hear them speak with passion against the Poles or Germans. People who were born here have never experienced anything remotely comparable to what we have experienced. They simply, as if to justify—or rather cleansing their soul of guilt—they hate that much more, those they have not even met.

I took my kids to Poland, both of them, with my wife. . . . I showed them where Copernicus studied, and I took them to Auschwitz, and I took them to Płaszów, and I showed what these same people, only a very few years ago, did. . . . If you want to hate somebody, you'd have to hate the entire world's population, because we are all subject to the same weaknesses and the same shortcomings and imperfections. And the right circumstances can bring out the worst in us. There are, I am sure, exceptions to this rule. But as a rule, that's what we are.

MILA ZAGORSKI BACHNER, 1927–

[Holocaust testimony (HRC-962, videotape: 1 hour, 15 minutes), 9 July 1987; interviewed by Bernard Weinstein and Phyllis Ziman Tobin, indexed by Bernard Weinstein. 804.3/.B124 1987]

Mila Zagorski Bachner [MB] was born on 15 March 1927 in Chrzanów in the Galicia region of Poland. She was one of six children in a strict Orthodox Jewish family. All the girls attended the Bais Yaakov school. She describes instances of anti-semitism experienced by members of her family in Poland in the 1930s. She heard the blood libel and the accusation that Jews killed Jesus although, in both instances, these lies had been disavowed by the established Church leadership.

When the war started, MB's family tried to flee to Russia, but they were forced back to the ghetto in Chrzanów and experienced the beginning of the persecution and suffering that developed into the Holocaust. Most of MB's family perished in Auschwitz. MB herself remained in the town's ghetto until 1942. She was then taken to Neusalz in Germany, near Breslau, where she was assigned to making coats for the Germans. MB describes her effort to maintain a semblance of human and Jewish existence in this camp.

As the war situation became desperate for the Germans in 1945, MB and the approximately nine hundred girls imprisoned in Neusalz were ordered on a death march. "We marched to nowhere." Hitler Youth threw rocks at them. Finally, they arrived at the Flossenbürg concentration camp. During eight or nine days at Flossenbürg, they viewed "many hangings." They were given "no food, no water, nothing." They were then ordered to the train station and into a cattle car. "We were totally without any food, any water, any air. No toilet facilities. Like cattle. But the only exception, for the cattle, they would have opened a little window for air. For us, they did not do that."

The girls were taken to Hanover, near Bergen-Belsen. "When the British came, I was a living dead." When liberated by the British in April, MB weighed only fifty pounds. She was nursed back to health by a German couple who lived near the Hanover camp. After a doctor confirmed that MB's lungs were clear (which meant she did not have tuberculosis) she reports: "From that moment, I was part of the family. I had my own little room and I sat with them at the table. They were very good to me. . . . Their sons-in-law were Nazis. They were SS men."

MB's only surviving relative, her brother Moniek, learned of her whereabouts. Brother and sister had a highly emotional reunion and then crossed the border to Moniek's DP camp in Austria. MB was hospitalized for several weeks. Sister and brother emigrated to the United States to join their paternal uncle in New Jersey. MB married a fellow survivor in 1952. They have three children, two sons and a daughter, and three grandchildren. The sons are lawyers, and the daughter has a master's degree in social work.

MORRIS BERGEN, 1918–

[Holocaust testimony (HRC-1005, videotape: 1 hour, 53 minutes), 3 February 1988; interviewed by Bernard Weinstein and Freda Remmers, indexed by Bernard Weinstein. D804.3/.B457 1988]

Morris Bergen [MB] was born in 1918 in Tarnów, an important city east of Kraków. Its twenty-five thousand Jews comprised 55 percent of the community's population. Of the seven persons in his immediate family, only MB and one brother survived the Holocaust. He experienced much antisemitism in school and in his community. He remembers life in Tarnów as difficult for Jews. He states the relationship in these words: "We loved the country. We loved Poland. Most Jewish people loved Poland. But we were considered second-class citizens."

MB's family and the Jews in town were very poor and lacked such essentials as adequate food. Immediately after his bar mitzvah, at the age of thirteen, he began to learn the tailoring trade to help support the family.

The war started in September 1939 and the first murders of Jews in Tarnów occurred in December. The Germans rounded up forty World War I veterans and killed them. MB was by this time doing forced labor in a tar factory.

MB experienced all the Holocaust conditions, first in the Tarnów ghetto and then in six concentration camps: Pustkow, Płaszów, Zakopane, Mauthausen, Melk, and Ebensee. He was in Tarnów's Ghetto A, the working ghetto. Older people were assigned to Ghetto B. As elsewhere, the town suffered a series of murderous German *Aktionen,* which resulted in the deaths of twenty-five thousand Jews by the end of 1943. This included nearly all of Tarnów Jews and many from surrounding communities.

MB was in Pustkow about six months before returning for a short time to the ghetto where he worked in a garment factory. After the total destruction of the ghetto, MB was among those transferred to Płaszów. Although this camp was not far away, the cattle car journey lasted three days. The infamous Amon Goeth was the Płaszów commandant. MB describes the cruelty of Płaszów in this incident.

> It was on Yom Kippur, this I remember. They came in, a group of Nazis—one, his name was Jan—and he was like a cripple, he was an officer. He came in, and we were just sitting and shaking in there. And we didn't face him, the machines were facing each other. And he was from the back going like this [pointing], and within five minutes, he took out fifty people. . . . They shot fifty people, just took them out, on Yom Kippur. And then they came back and took out another bunch. I was among them, too. We had to make fire, wood, and put the people on the wood. . . . The burning, the smell, was horrible. And we kept working. . . . And Goeth was living down, and we worked on top of the hill. He used to come up with his Great Dane, his pleasure [required] the Dane eat people and bite them and then he would shoot them, you know, "for mercy."

A very intriguing exchange then occurs; MB's response requires thought and study.

INTERVIEWER: Did you think you would survive?

MB: No, of course not. I guess, I had hope, only because I was curious to know what's going to happen. This . . . partially kept me alive, I am sure. Just, the curiosity. And I think a lot of people . . . if you ask them, you will find they felt the same way. Curiosity made you stay.

From Płaszów, MB was shipped to Zakopane and then to Mauthausen, Austria. Léon Blum, the prewar French premier, was also imprisoned in Mauthausen. MB testifies: "He was locked up, he did not come out. . . . The sergeant was the biggest sadist I ever saw. We were only there for ten days. But horrible days. Working in the quarry was the worst thing. . . . Not many survived in this place."

MB's travels took him to Melk and Ebensee. The Germans were now experiencing the chaos of their defeat in the closing days of the war. Nevertheless, and incredibly, they held on to their remaining Jews, providing them with no food but continuing the murderous death marches. MB states, "People died like flies on those marches." With death all around him, MB was liberated by the Americans on 8 May. How did he feel at liberation? "I had nobody, nowhere to go."

At the time of liberation, MB weighed only seventy-five pounds and was quite ill. He lived several years in Austria and, mainly, in Italy. He married an Italian woman. They arrived in the United States in 1951. He and his first wife were divorced. MB married a second time, and they settled in New Jersey and have two children. MB is employed as a bank messenger; his son is a lawyer and his daughter a restaurant manager in San Francisco. He has two grandchildren. MB's second marriage also ended in divorce.

SHLOMO BIEZUNSKI, 1926–

[Holocaust testimony (HRC-1004, videotape: 1 hour, 44 minutes), 12 May 1988; interviewed by Bernard Weinstein and Jeanne Miller, indexed by Bernard Weinstein. D804.3/.B549 1988]

Shlomo Biezunski [SB] was born in 1926 in Łódź, "the Manchester of Poland." Łódź was the second largest city in Poland, with a population of more than six hundred thousand of whom one-third were Jews. SB's father was a pharmacist; the family was middle class and "lived in the best part of Łódź." The immediate family consisted of four persons: his parents, an older sister, and SB. The father was murdered by Germans shortly after the war started in September 1939. Mother and sister perished in Auschwitz. Thus SB is the lone family survivor.

SB reports that he never personally experienced antisemitism in Poland in the prewar years. Coming from a well-to-do background, he attended a private school. His family had been in Poland for many generations, some "five hundred to six hundred years."

In May 1940, the remaining three family members were moved into the Łódź ghetto. SB comments this was his "first contact with the Jewish proletariat." A hundred thousand Łódź Jews were squeezed into the ghetto. When it was liquidated in 1944, only twenty thousand Łódź Jews had survived the four difficult years. The other Jews in the ghetto in 1944 were not from Łódź but from other communities.

SB describes the food shortages in the ghetto and his family's efforts to cope. His widowed mother broke down mentally and physically. She was arrested because she could serve no useful purpose for the Germans. A former customer of their pharmacy arranged for the mother to be released. The family was then transported by cattle car from Łódź. They were informed that their destination was Germany where they would have "food and a good life." They arrived instead in Auschwitz-Birkenau. Men and women were separated immediately upon arrival. SB never saw his mother or sister again.

SB recalls that during their first three days at Birkenau, the new arrivals received no food. They did stand, however, for numerous *Appell*s (roll calls) "day and night, counting . . . never ending." When asked how he managed to survive, SB struggles and recounts this incident.

> I was always determined to survive. I was like a ghetto kid. . . . I was street smart, you know. If you have four years [in the Łódź ghetto] . . . I had a friend over there, a kid . . . was sitting over there. . . . I don't know, I look back, how I survived. . . . Only will. You had to have will to survive. I want to tell you about the kid sitting next to me.
>
> "Salig," my name in Polish was Salig, "we're not going to survive." [SB] replied, "Stop talking like that. You're a young kid, only seventeen years old. . . . You have a long life. The war is going to end. You're going to survive. You have to be strong." The next day, I look at him. He was dead. Because the will was gone. He said, "I want to be dead. I want to die." And he died, even without somebody touching him.

SB was quite firm in analyzing the lack of physical resistance by the prisoners. He discusses the situation in the Łódź ghetto.

> There was no resistance . . . because there was no way to resist. We were surrounded by a hostile Polish population. They just laughed at us. When I walked to work, I walked along a street, and along the street there was a fence, you know, with steel wires along the fence. And each few hundred meters, you had a German guard. But the trolley used to go over there, you know, and the Poles used to travel . . . through the ghetto. They used to laugh at us, you know, and make a sign and show like that and . . . cut your throat.
>
> The Jew in Poland had no protection at all. There was in the concentration camp, it

was known, if you escape, you had no way to survive. Only if you had somebody, if you knew somebody, who'd really want to help you out. If you don't have the means to pay him for it, in gold or diamonds, he's not going to do it; because the Germans offer him for it, for each Jewish head, a kilo of sugar and a bottle of vodka. That was the price, the worth of a Jewish life.

That was after hundreds and hundreds of years, what the Jews gave to Poland, and did for Poland, and fought for Poland. That was how the Polish population paid them back in time of need. They just deserted the Jews. Not only they deserted the Jews, they were happy to get rid of them because they took their houses, they took their businesses, they took everything.

After two weeks in Birkenau, SB was transferred to the vicinity of Fürstengrube to work in a coal mine. He then volunteered to become a metalworker. This was a most fortunate change for him because metal workers were the elite and were treated much better by the Germans than the other prisoners.

In January 1945, the prisoners were taken on a death march to Gleiwitz, then a horrible seven-day train journey to Prague, and finally to the Nordhausen concentration camp in Germany. Very few of the prisoners who started the death march survived these experiences in the deadly chaos of the war's closing days. SB's moment of liberation was far from a celebratory occasion. He had been marched onto a boat in Neustadt with eight thousand others. SB describes how he was one of only thirty-seven to survive the bombing of the ship by the British.

After the war, SB remained in Neustadt for two and a half years. He was then able to emigrate to Israel where he remained for nineteen years. He fought in Israel's wars in 1948, 1956, and 1967. He moved to the United States with his Israeli wife and their two children in November 1967 and settled in New Jersey where he has worked as a toolmaker.

SALLY SILBERSTEIN CHASE, 1931–

[Holocaust testimony (HRC-932, videotape: 1 hour, 15 minutes), 9 February 1987; interviewed by Bernard Weinstein and Carole Shaffer-Koros, indexed by Carole Shaffer-Koros. D804.3/.C487 1987]

Sally Silberstein in Berlin, 1946.

Sally Silberstein Chase [SC] was born on 20 November 1931 in Radom, whose Jewish population in 1939 was thirty thousand, about one-third of the city's total. SC remembers a joyous childhood wherein religious traditions were important. Her family consisted of her parents, five brothers, and three sisters. One brother and the three sisters survived the Holocaust; six family members perished.

SC describes the development of the Holocaust in Radom, an important Polish city. Eight days after the German invasion in 1939, the Jews were sent into the ghetto being established at that time. The Germans began their *Aktionen* against Jews by murdering intellectuals. In an effort to save her life, the eleven-year-old SC worked twelve-hour shifts daily for the Wehrmacht.

SC relates a remarkable story that encapsulates the unremitting fear hounding the Jews constantly during the Holocaust. Three German storm troopers entered the family's living quarters "in the ghetto, in their black uniforms with red swastikas." They asked for Mr. Finkelstein, the head of another family squeezed into the same apartment with SC's family, but Mr. Finkelstein was not home. Mrs. Finkelstein was there with her two children—a three-year-old boy and a nine-month-old baby—and Mrs. Finkelstein's mother. Mrs. Finkelstein said her husband had not yet returned home. The SS men responded, "If you don't tell us [where he is], we will take you and the baby and shoot you." Mrs. Finkelstein's mother volunteered to go in her daughter's place. SC, whose family had been observing the entire scene, comments, "If somebody had a weak heart, I think he could have a heart attack." The SS men pushed the mother away, took Mrs. Finkelstein and her baby outside, and murdered them on the steps. SC concludes, "I'll never forget this because I used to dream about this particular incident." She was eleven years old at the time.

SC then describes the murderous *Aktionen* in Radom on 28 August 1942, "the last time I saw my parents." The Germans rounded up twenty-eight thousand Jews, practically the entire Jewish population of Radom, and shipped them by cattle cars to Treblinka where they were gassed and cremated. The children were thrown into the pits while still alive. SC, in her barrack outside Radom where she worked, heard the cries and screams on the cattle cars from a great distance.

The remaining two thousand Jews of Radom were liquidated gradually until

June 1944, when only three hundred of the original thirty thousand Jews remained. SC reports: "We were always in fear . . . never knew what the next step was." SC and her sisters were assigned work in Ostrowiec, a small town nearby. In June 1944, the last three hundred of Radom's Jews were shipped to Auschwitz. This contingent included SC and her two sisters. SC describes conditions in Auschwitz during the second half of 1944.

In December 1944, as the Russians were advancing, the three sisters were in a group shipped from Auschwitz to Gabersdorf, Germany, to work as welders in an airplane factory. As the war was winding down, they participated in a three-day death march, in the bitter cold of winter, to the Sudetenland in Czechoslovakia, where they were liberated by the Russians.

SC and her surviving siblings have all emigrated to the United States. She arrived in June 1946. While working full time, she completed high school at night in eighteen months. She then enrolled in Brooklyn College as a nonmatriculated student and graduated after nine and a half years. She married a young lawyer, settled in New Jersey, and raised her two daughters here.

JEANETTE ROTTENBERG EHRLICH, 1923–

[Holocaust testimony (HRC-975, videotape: 1 hour, 31 minutes), 17 November 1987; interviewed by Bernard Weinstein and Joan Bang, indexed by Bernard Weinstein. D804.3/.E279 1987]

Jeanette Rottenberg Ehrlich [JE] was born in Kraków in 1923. She and her family were living in Myszków when the war started. Her father owned a chemical factory and was a partner in a coal mine. Apparently he was a man of wealth and influence. Of JE's immediate family of six persons—her parents, three girls, and one boy—only JE and one of her sisters survived the Holocaust.

JE's father was determined to keep his family out of the most dangerous situations, especially the murder camps. His wealth and his connections with non-Jewish associates were helpful indeed. Nevertheless, JE describes a number of horribly dangerous experiences. One was the removal by the Gestapo of her uncle and cousins from a home where they were staying for safety. She then tells how she and her sisters were saved from deportation to Auschwitz and sent to a labor camp as a result of her father's intervention; the cruelties experienced by the sisters in their first labor camp; their removal to the Będzin ghetto; and their father's successful intervention once again to save the girls a second time from being deported to Auschwitz. JE never saw her parents again after this episode.

She describes other instances of seemingly futile efforts to find safety. Finally, Hanoar Hazioni, a Zionist underground organization, helped JE and a group of some twenty young people to escape from the Kamionka slave labor camp and Będzin. In the dark of night, the young people stealthily crossed the border into Czechoslovakia and Hungary. This feat was accomplished with the assistance of a number of kind Polish citizens.

JE married one of the young men in her group when they reached Hungary. She was separated from the group in 1944, when Hungary came under German domination. She managed to convince the Germans that she was not Jewish although her husband was. Once again, Hanoar Hazioni helped JE, this time to board a ship for Tel Aviv. She was pregnant at the time and the ship had to land in Istanbul, Turkey, for her to give birth. The young mother and her month-old son finally arrived in Haifa, Israel, in December 1944, via Syria.

At the beginning of 1946, JE heard that her husband was still alive. She managed to come to Munich with her little son. They were reunited at the end of 1946. The young family lived in Israel several years before emigrating to the United States in August 1951 in order to be near some of JE's relatives. She and her husband had friends in New Jersey. They bought a farm here before going into business.

JE has three children. Her two sons are lawyers. One lives in Florida, the other in California. Each son is married and has one daughter each. JE's daughter, a schoolteacher in New Jersey, is married and mother of three.

JE concludes the interview by commenting that she has not spoken about her Holocaust experiences for many years. She has decided to testify today, however, in order to bear witness against those who deny the Holocaust and to serve as an antidote to the antisemitism she perceives as still existing in many places.

SOL EINHORN, 1922–

[Holocaust testimony (HRC-967, videotape: 2 hours, 53 minutes), 28 May and 16 July 1987; interviewed by Marcia Weissberg, Phyllis Ziman Tobin, and Bernard Weinstein, indexed by Anne Kaplan. D804.3/.E369 1987]

Sol and Rose Einhorn in Germany, 1946, the year of their marriage.

In 1922, Sol Einhorn [SE] was born into a pious family in the small town of Gorlice, fifty yards from the Czech border. His father rented a sawmill to provide lumber for farmers. SE was the only member of his family (parents, sister, brother, and maternal grandparents) to survive the Holocaust.

In a lengthy and articulate interview, SE provides many details of the Holocaust years as experienced by a boy who was seventeen when the war started in Poland. He describes his grandfather's face wrapped in a kerchief after the old man's beard was torn out. Evidently, the tradition of family piety remained firmly implanted in SE throughout the war as he describes the two occasions in the closing days of the war when he ate nonkosher food. In addition, he reports that he risked his life in the forced labor camp by donning tefillin [phylacteries] for morning prayers.

SE's story provides the listener with a revealing view of the Holocaust. This includes the ghetto in their town until it was liquidated in July 1942, the difficulties and dangers experienced in forced labor camps in Poland (especially Płaszów and Skarżysko-Kamienna), and the chaotic conditions in the German concentration camps (Buchenwald and Dachau) during the closing weeks of the war. SE reports that Skarżysko-Kamienna was "the pits," that after six or seven weeks of slave labor there, only 10 of 180 men in his unit were able to survive the sixteen to eighteen hours of work daily.

SE explains his philosophical and psychological frame of mind as he confronts four issues of living during the Holocaust. First is the extreme emphasis on food as a consequence of starvation.

> If you don't know where your next meal comes from . . . if you fill up your stomach full, a minute later, you're hungry. I'll give you an example, we went through a gasoline crisis. . . . People were lining up. You could have a half-tank of gas, yes, but if you had a gas station that was giving five gallons of gas, people were running. . . . A person who has a full stomach will never believe a person who is hungry. If you weren't there, you cannot get the feeling.

The second issue: How could the Germans treat fellow human beings as they treated the Jews?

> And the same thing . . . I always used to tell people, as far as the Germans in treating the Jews. The first thing you got to keep in your mind, if you can't pass that stage you can't go further: If you can imagine that the Jew to the German was like a cockroach. In the United States, if you step on a cockroach . . . it doesn't mean anything to you. The same thing, exactly the same thing, the Jew was to the German—a cockroach. . . . One particular Shabbos, they shot twelve or thirteen people in my area. In other words, the German had the right, if he saw me, any Jew that he saw in the street, he could go over to you, calmly take out his revolver, and put it to your head, and shoot you down like a . . . roach. He didn't have to fill out a form, he didn't have to go to the police. . . . Nothing, absolutely nothing. It was a free-for-all.
>
> INTERVIEWER: Did you personally witness any of these events?
>
> SE: Yes, yes, yes. . . . As a matter of fact . . . it was just exactly like a cockroach. As I said, if you can pass it through your head, then you can imagine it. Otherwise, it doesn't mean anything.

The third is: How did Jewish prisoners perform inhuman tasks?

While being over there in camp [Płaszów] . . . me and another guy, we had to take away . . . behind the barracks they used to make the executions. Me and another guy had to take them away. . . . What I want to bring out is, under the circumstances . . . given, I mean . . . the "right circumstances," a human being can turn in worse than an animal. Because with all the things going on . . . I mean it was a question. Today it's him, tomorrow it's you. . . . I mean you lived it from minute to minute. And it didn't mean anything. I mean right after that, after the execution taken away, if I had some food to eat, I just sat down calmly. . . . Even today, when I talk about it, if I watch a movie . . . sometimes, you know, you well up inside, I will well up. But when it comes to talk about the Holocaust and all the things . . . I turn into a stone. I mean it has no effect on me whatsoever. I can talk about it. . . . It was part of, you know, my built-in safety valve. . . . Otherwise, I would have gone bananas. . . . You know, I cannot shed a tear over it. It isn't in me. I cannot bring it up.

The fourth is religious faith and interpersonal relationships.

My motto was, I kept saying to myself, . . . God, whatever you want to dish out, I'll take everything, except, please let me live. At least, I should be able to survive. . . . I'll accept any punishment. Just let me live. Over there, the work was unbelievable. . . . It stands out more than anything else. We had to load the cartridges [unclear; probably "ammunition wagons for the Russian front"—ed.]. . . . I remember one winter night, it was a Friday night. We were saying: "How could God punish us that much?" . . . It was coming down snow. Cold, it was coming down. You know, Poland . . . and it kept covering the track [making it practically impossible to move the just-loaded wagons—ed.]. . . . Now you asked me about helping out each other. I'll give you an example. . . . We had every ten people on a car load. So we had some people inside and some people outside. . . . What happened was, these things were going to the Russian front [describes loading procedure]. . . . What happened was, one particular Passover, with all that going through, we still had some very Orthodox people. They stuck to principle. They wouldn't eat bread on Pesach. So we used to steal potatoes, something like that. They were weak. So what we did, we pushed in the car load, they should stay in the car load. And we would do the work. Because outside, you couldn't do anything. Because right away, he would have gotten whipped. Inside, at least, we tried to keep them in there. And we did the work . . . because they wouldn't eat the bread. I mean we all were weak. But still in all . . . in order to show, in order to let them be able to do it.

SE was liberated by the U.S. Seventh Army on 30 April 1945. His group was already in the cattle cars as the Germans tried to transfer them to Mauthausen. The day after liberation, SE volunteered to work for UNRRA. He was deemed qualified for this work being knowledgeable in English because of his Berlitz self-study prior to the war. He met his future wife, and they were married in February 1946. Through an army chaplain and the *New York Daily Forward,* SE located his aunt who lived in the Bronx, New York.

SE and his wife arrived in the United States on 7 May 1947. The young couple struggled to earn a living as recently arrived immigrants. They moved to New Jersey in 1958 for a better job and to live with friends. SE worked at repair and sales of commercial laundry machines.

SE and his wife have two sons. One, a lawyer, is married and lives in California with his wife and three children. At the time of this interview, the younger son was studying in the internationally famous Yeshiva of Lakewood, New Jersey.

HENRY ERLICH, 1919–

[Holocaust testimony (HRC-1019, videotape: 1 hour, 46 minutes), 19 October 1988; interviewed by Bernard Weinstein and Anne Kaplan, indexed by Anne Kaplan. D804.3/.E67 1988]

Henry Erlich [HE] was born in Kraków in March 1919, the youngest of three children. His father died in 1929, when he was not yet ten years old. HE recalls his happy school years and a pious Orthodox family life.

In a very effective, detailed, and authoritative testimony, HE describes the Holocaust as experienced by a young man of Kraków. He remembers dispossessed Jews being forcibly returned from Germany to Poland in 1938; *Kristallnacht* in Germany with forebodings that Poland would be next; the German invasion in September 1939, followed by orders to surrender fur coats and valuables on pain of death; forced labor, food shortages, construction of the Płaszów concentration camp on a Kraków cemetery; and establishment of the Kraków ghetto for the city's entire Jewish population.

The next development was the selection process, beginning with the systematic murder of the old and young, the expendable and useless population. Community intellectuals and leaders were among the first to be selected for murder. When the ghetto was liquidated in August 1943, HE was imprisoned in Płaszów, and he recalls the daily murders, the tortuous *Appell* routines that took place out-of-doors in all kinds of weather, and the torture of starvation combined with slave labor.

> Anybody who couldn't work was destroyed. After a while, there was actually no room where to bring the people because it was all saturated. They were putting one layer, after another layer, after another layer, and that was full. So they started to burn the bodies. There was no crematorium over there. They were just piling the bodies and throwing the gasoline and burning. . . . You became numb. You couldn't feel anymore. If you see a person on a street being hit by a car, you are in shock. But when you see ten thousand people being hit by the car, it numbs you. . . . So everyone was watching, trying to stay alive. The rations that we were getting were not enough to live, and too much to die. So we were starving.

HE's testimony continues to the "worst part," the seven-day trip by cattle car from Płaszów to Dresden, Germany, where he was imprisoned in the Tschechowitz forced labor camp from December 1944 until March 1945. He suffered from lice and a typhoid epidemic. He weighed seventy-five pounds. In this weakened condition, he was ordered to join the death march to Theresienstadt, Czechoslovakia, during the war's closing weeks. He was finally liberated by the Russians in Theresienstadt when the camp was suffering from a dysentery epidemic and people were "dying like flies."

In a state of complete exhaustion, HE then walked most of the twenty-five miles to Prague, where he was reunited miraculously with his fiancée. The young couple felt alone—only three cousins and HE survived in his extended family of almost forty persons; his fiancée lost her entire family except for one uncle. The couple moved to Germany and managed to emigrate to the United States in 1947, where they struggled to make ends meet as new immigrants.

HE and his wife had two children, a son who is a physician and a daughter who is "also educated." He moved to New Jersey in 1985 when he married his second wife, a resident of this state. During his testimony, HE made this statement regarding the question of Jewish resistance during the Holocaust.

I said before I would like to make a statement on my own about the way the Germans prepared the annihilation of people. It was done scientifically by doctors, professors, engineers, psychologists, psychiatrists. It was all planned. It was done in a way, in such stages, that people were drawn into it step by step. It wasn't done rapidly that they came in and killed everybody. . . .

Before they destroyed us physically, they destroyed us mentally. We were so confused that we didn't know what to do. Because people who live outside, as free people, cannot understand why we didn't fight back. Why . . . three and a half million people in Poland let themselves be slaughtered, like sheep. I have to explain, how did this happen? We never could believe that a man could destroy a man in the way they did it. A normal person cannot visualize that it is possible to destroy millions of people. We knew about war. When a soldier goes to war, and he might lose his life. We knew that a plane can come over and bomb a city . . . a hundred people, a thousand people. But we didn't believe that someone would come and destroy three million people.

That's number one. Number two. It happened several times that Jewish people, and Polish people, committed some act of violence against German people. Resistance. If they didn't catch the person who did it, they always had several hundred hostages on hand all the time. And they liquidated the hostages. If I as a Jew would throw a bomb . . . at a place in Kraków, immediately they would take the hundred hostages and execute [them].

How could you defend yourself . . . with bare hands? We didn't get any help from outside, from Polish people. . . . We didn't have any weapons. How could you defend yourself with bare hands against the German army? So, the question I am getting from

American people and from [non-]American people: How come you let yourself be slaughtered without any resistance? How can you resist? With what? Of course, after we knew what was going on, there were several organizations who resisted. So they gave their life too . . . So, we had help from nobody. We were on our own. And we were being destroyed, day after day after day, until the complete destruction.

LEON FAIGENBAUM, 1924–

[Holocaust testimony (HRC-2003, videotape: 1 hour, 47 minutes), 17 March 1994; interviewed and indexed by Joseph J. Preil. D804.3/.F156 1994]

Born in Jędrzejów on 11 March 1924, Leon Faigenbaum [LF] and his family suffered the full weight of the Holocaust. His immediate family consisted of eight persons: his parents, five sisters, and LF. Only LF and one older sister survived; the six others perished in Treblinka. His extended family consisted of about a hundred people in Poland. Only LF, his sister, and one cousin survived.

When the war started, LF's family tried to escape to Russia. This was a futile effort because Germans confronted the family everywhere. In early 1940, young LF was sent to a labor camp in Ciechanów, near the Russian border. This was his "worst experience." LF's group was then transferred to Makow Podhalanski in Galicia, near the Austrian border. LF's family moved in with his maternal grandmother in nearby Wodzisław. LF and about three hundred other men were then marched to nearby Sedziszów, near the Russian border, where the Germans were preparing to invade the Soviet Union. He remained in Sedziszów from January 1941 until October 1942 and was then transferred to Skarżysko where he stayed until October 1943.

LF describes the miserable conditions in the labor camps where he was assigned to factory work producing materials for the German war effort. Toward the end of 1943, LF was moved to Buchenwald in Germany for several weeks, then to Schlieben for ten months, until September 1944. He was returned to Buchenwald for several weeks when the Schlieben factory was destroyed in an explosion. LF was then transferred to Bergen-Belsen for five months, from October 1944 until March 1945. The production program there was very secret. Finally, LF participated in a death march to Theresienstadt, Czechoslovakia, in March 1945. He was liberated there by the Russians in May 1945. He "saw children for the first time" in Theresienstadt.

After the war, LF returned to his hometown in Poland, where he received postcards from his sister in Russia, the only other immediate family member to survive. He and his friends felt unsafe in Poland. They moved on to Prague, then to Germany, where he got married in Landsberg at the age of twenty-one. He and his wife arrived in the United States in 1949, settled in Newark, and opened a tailor shop. He had retired at the time of this testimony, though he has remained a New Jersey resident. He and his wife have two children, a daughter who is a teacher in California, and a son who is an accountant in New Jersey. They also have five grandchildren.

LF refers to Polish antisemitism twice in the interview. In an early statement, he mentions its existence in his community and says: "The town was a gentile town. We did the best we could." In a later section of the interview, he refers again to the role of many Poles in the Holocaust.

> We knew with whom we're dealing. They really don't want us. They never did. . . . I've got to mention one thing. Why did the Germans build . . . crematoriums in Poland? Why not in Norway? Why not in Denmark? . . . Or in Germany? . . . Just because they had the people to help them. Simple as that. As much as I hate to say it, but the truth is, this is exactly what happened. They helped them, and that's what it was.

REGINA DEBOWSKA FAIGENBAUM, 1926–

[Holocaust testimony (HRC-921, videotape: 1 hour, 43 minutes), 1984; interviewed by Sidney Langer, indexed by Joseph J. Preil. D804.3/.F159 1985]

Regina Debowska Faigenbaum [RF] was born on 22 January 1926 in Jędrzezów, a small town between Kraków and Kielce. In 1933, her family moved to Sosnowiec, as recommended by the Pinchever Rebbe to her father. RF's immediate family consisted of nine persons: her parents, three boys, and four girls. Only one sister and RF, the youngest child in the family, survived the Holocaust.

RF reports that she experienced much antisemitism in Poland before, during, and after the war. When the Germans arrived in Sosnowiec, they took the most prominent Jews and murdered them. Her father's beard was forcibly shaved off. In April 1940, a Polish family reported RF's whereabouts to the SS after she had avoided being taken by the Germans in a roundup of Jews. She was then shipped to a labor camp in Parschnitz, Czechoslovakia. One of her sisters was in the same camp. They remained there until they were liberated by the Russians in 1945.

RF describes the camp routines, living conditions, and work assignments under cruel female SS guards. She tells the story of how she was nearly sent to Auschwitz. What was her crime to earn such a punishment? A German guard had accidentally left her wallet on RF's worktable at the end of the workday. RF found the wallet and returned it to the guard when she saw her the following day. This was interpreted to mean that she was involved in business with the guard, which merited deportation to Auschwitz.

RF returned to Sosnowiec after the war. She was greeted by her neighbors with: "What a shame he didn't finish you. He left the job for us." She could find no family survivors but she did meet her future husband in Poland. The couple returned to Landsberg in the American zone in Germany, and married in 1946. They emigrated to the United States in 1949 and settled in Newark.

RF relates how her husband obtained employment as a tailor at twenty-five dollars a week immediately after arriving in New Jersey. They were "proud" and did not wish to depend on material assistance from the United Jewish Appeal. "We came here to work." She concludes her testimony by referring to the severe emotional toll of the Holocaust on survivors.

> It doesn't get any easier to live with it. Plenty of nights, we have dreams and we scream. One wakes the other one up. And we know what happened. Because screaming like this. . . . You have dreams that the Germans are chasing you. Are they killing you? Are they killing your relatives that you watch?

RF and her husband have two children, a daughter, who is a teacher in California, and a son who is an accountant in New Jersey. They also have five grandchildren.

MAX FINDLING, 1923–

[Holocaust testimony (HRC-1076, videotape: 3 hours, 36 minutes), 3 and 22 December, 1992; interviewed and indexed by Joseph J. Preil. D804.3/.F515 1992]

Max Findling in 1949, the year of his marriage.

Max Findling [MF] was born in Zmigród on 28 July 1923. His paternal family had lived in Zmigród for "about two hundred years." Zmigród is near the Czech border, about a hundred miles from Kraków. MF's mother was born in Hungary. Her siblings emigrated to the United States before the war. The extended paternal family in Poland consisted of "a couple of hundred people." MF's immediate family consisted of five persons: his parents, their two sons, and one daughter. MF is the only known survivor of his immediate family of five and of his extended family of a couple of hundred.

MF provides an excellent and incredibly detailed description of the Holocaust experience in Poland, from the first day of war in 1939 until liberation and, finally, his return to Germany in 1972 when he was invited to testify at a war crimes trial of a number of people involved in the murder of Jews in Zmigród. During this interview, MF told of his plan to return to Zmigród in 1993 to set up a memorial for the murdered Jews of Zmigród, including thirty-five to forty of his own relatives.

MF describes the antisemitism in his community before the outbreak of war. Polish boys his age would bully him, trying to remove his yarmulke from his head or by force-feeding him nonkosher food. Good Friday and Easter Sunday were particularly unpleasant times for the Jews of Zmigród.

The year 1942 was an especially dangerous time for the Jews in the town. MF recalls 7 July, when 1,250 Jews were taken from the town and murdered in a German

Aktion. The remaining were primarily young people who were assigned to forced labor. Later that day, MF saw a truck return with clothing. This meant that the victims had been stripped naked before being murdered.

One week later, MF was in a group of 150 taken to Jasło near Zmigród. Later, they were shipped in cattle cars to the Płaszów concentration camp outside Kraków. He describes the prison in Jasło where he was incarcerated, for no reason, together with his sister and a neighboring rabbi, among others. One day, while MF was out on forced labor, his sister and all the others disappeared, murdered by the Germans. MF's reaction: "What could I tell you? Crying, screaming, you couldn't cry any more because you didn't have any more tears."

MF describes his escape from Płaszów and his return to Zmigród via Jasło. His "freedom" was short-lived, however, and he was back in Płaszów later in 1942. MF and his brother were both shipped to labor camps in 1943. His brother was sent to the Skarżysko-Kamienna concentration camp where he contracted pneumonia and died in 1944. MF was taken to Częstochowa–HASAG Warta, where he worked on munitions until liberation in 1945.

On the day of liberation, MF walked to Radom. Eventually, he made his way back to his hometown. A Polish family had taken over his family home and did not allow him to enter. Later that day, MF was told that the head of the Polish family in his home was planning to murder him. This convinced MF that he must leave Poland.

> I was alone. In the beginning, it was terrible. All the time I said, What have I got in life? It would be better if I could be dead. I had nobody. I saw the antisemitism again in Poland. It was terrible. I came to my town, I went in for a piece of paper. I didn't even have a piece of paper who I am. They asked me, Who are you? I said, I was born here in Zmigród. I want a piece of paper. Then they told me, Why are you here? Why don't you go to the army? I said, I just came from the concentration camp. I am sick. . . . And then there was the pogrom in Kielce. I better leave here. There's no place for me here. . . . I went to Italy. . . . Finally, I came to Israel.

MF met his future wife in Israel. She was also a Polish survivor, the only member of her family to survive. They married in 1949. MF felt he must have a family. He and his wife emigrated to the United States in 1955 with their oldest son to join MF's maternal aunts and their families. Eventually he had three sons.

MF relates: "Everything was fine. . . . Good children, good wife. . . . But I couldn't sleep [unclear; probably "some nights"—*ed.*]. I would wake up in the middle of the night. I have to go back to Zmigród and see the grave of my parents." He did go back with his oldest son and others. This group has succeeded in collecting funds to place a tombstone in the Zmigród cemetery to memorialize the martyrs who lost their lives during the Holocaust.

MF has lived in Brooklyn for many years. He supported his growing family as a taxi driver. His sons are an accountant, a physician, and a self-employed business-man. He has five grandchildren. MF was brought to this interview by a son who lives in New Jersey.

JOEL FRISH, 1924–

[Holocaust testimony (HRC-1082, videotape: 1 hour, 35 minutes), 25 February 1993; inter-viewed and indexed by Joseph J. Preil. D804.3/.F788 1993]

Joel Frish [JF] was born on 11 November 1924 in Tuczyn, near Łódź. His immedi-ate family in Poland in 1939 consisted of seven persons: his parents and their three sons and two daughters. Of these seven, only JF and one brother survived the Holo-caust. His extended family, through first cousins, consisted of thirty-five to forty people. JF and his brother are the sole survivors.

The Frish family and the Jews of Tuczyn were moved to Moszczenica, a nearby town, in November 1939. After about six months, they were moved to Srock. JF and his brother David were assigned to forced labor by the Germans. The other five fam-ily members perished in Treblinka.

In 1942, the two brothers were transferred to Piotrków. JF tells of the labor as-signments and the cruel treatment of all Jews in Piotrków, including the workers. JF and his brother were working elsewhere when the 560 remaining Jews were as-sembled in Piotrków's main synagogue. All were taken outside the city and shot. Twenty-two Jews were assigned to dig mass graves and bury the victims, dead or alive. JF reports that all twenty-two gravediggers, with the possible exception of one person, eventually committed suicide.

In 1945, as the Russians and the Allies were advancing, the two brothers were transferred to Buchenwald, near Weimar, then to Rehmsdorf-Troglitz; and, finally, to Theresienstadt, Czechoslovakia. They were liberated in Theresienstadt, but both brothers were seriously ill. The conditions in these camps, and on the roads between camps, were indescribable. JF explains that hunger had become so powerful he was willing to risk his life to eat a potato on the road despite a warning by a German guard that such an act would be punished by death. According to JF, "Food at such a time can become more important than family, or friends, or even one's own life."

In order to reach Theresienstadt from Prague, JF and his group were ordered on a death march. The prisoners ate grass along the way. They all became very weak and ill. JF had typhus and his brother contracted tuberculosis.

JF arrived in the United States in 1950 and began his life here in Atlantic City as a dishwasher. After a year, he moved to Newark and eventually to Elizabeth. He has worked as a machinist and locksmith. He married a fellow survivor but is now a wid-ower. He is the father of a son and daughter, both married, and he has two grandchildren. His son works for an investors' service and his daughter is a public school teacher in Manhattan.

PAUL GAST, 1926–

[Holocaust testimony (HRC-1088, videotape: 1 hour, 29 minutes), 23 April 1993; interviewed and indexed by Joseph J. Preil. D804.3/.G261 1993]

Paul Gast in 1945, age nineteen.

Paul Gast [PG] was born in Łódź, an only child, on 16 November 1926. Of his immediate family of three persons, PG is the lone survivor. His extended family in Poland consisted of eighteen to twenty persons, of whom PG is the lone survivor. In addition, four relatives in Germany survived: an uncle, aunt, and two cousins.

PG's father was murdered in a German *Aktion* in Łódź within two weeks of the outbreak of war in 1939. PG and his family were forced to move into the Łódź ghetto in the spring of 1940. He visited the ghetto in 1990 with his American wife: "I, myself, could not believe that we lived there, the condition and the size of the room. . . . It is unbelievable that one could live in such poverty and dirt and filth." This one room was their home for more than four years, from April 1940 until August 1944. PG reports that one day coming home from work, he found, "my grandfather died, sitting in bed." He had starved to death.

The entire extended family lived in one room. In thinking about how he managed to survive more than four years of slave labor in a factory every day, and the primitive, drab housing conditions, PG theorized, "My passive outlook on life may have been the cause of my survival, even from the ghetto to Auschwitz" and the other camps. "I have more or less accepted it for what it was."

By 1942, all of PG's family in Poland had perished except for his mother and one uncle. These three were among the last Łódź ghetto residents to be shipped to Auschwitz in the infamous cattle cars. After Auschwitz, PG was transferred to Braunschweig, Germany, in November 1944, to Wattenstedt in February 1945, to Ravensbrück in March, and, finally, to Ludwigslust in May 1945.

PG reports there was room for only twenty persons in each car; nevertheless eighty to ninety prisoners were squeezed in. The trip from Wattenstedt to Ravensbrück was much worse than the trip to Auschwitz. The former lasted sixteen days and nights; the trip to Auschwitz was measurable in hours. Ludwigslust, the last camp, was the worst of all. "The barracks, the houses, the buildings were all open, except for a roof [unclear; probably "no walls"—*ed.*]. No floors . . . it was all dirty sand. Dead bodies were lying all over the place. . . . Awful starvation. . . . The Russian prisoners of war were cooking human flesh from dead bodies."

PG was liberated by Americans on 2 May 1945. He left Ludwigslust immediately with a friend. Russian-Jewish soldiers were very helpful to survivors. The code word for identification was *Amcha* (Hebrew for the Jewish people).

PG and his friend went to England after the war and he remained there from 1945 to 1952, completing high school and two years of higher education. He arrived in the United States in January 1952 to join German family survivors in New York. He was drafted into the American army in October 1952 and served in Korea. He and his wife have one daughter and two grandchildren.

After working as an accountant and as a leather goods company manager in Oklahoma for twelve years, PG and his family moved to New Jersey in order to provide his daughter with a Jewish education at Bruriah High School in Elizabeth. This change of education for his daughter led to the following thoughts toward the end of the interview.

> I do not understand Hebrew. I feel bad about it and, as a matter of fact, several years ago, I had an interview in London with the *Christian Science Monitor* and I said to them, "No matter whatever I have missed in my life, I was trying and I am going to give it to my daughter." I think, possibly, one of the reasons that I have sent her to the yeshiva. . . . Yes, I blame in a way, at times, my parents, that they did not give me a Jewish education, the knowledge of Hebrew. I cannot read Hebrew today. . . . I enjoy reading it in English. . . . I am conscious of not having the knowledge of the Hebrew language and Hebrew prayers. . . . But I compensate in English.

ELIASZ DAVID GLANZ, 1912–1996

[Holocaust testimony (HRC-2009, videotape: 1 hour, 24 minutes), 2 November 1994; interviewed by Joseph J. Preil and Jeffrey Glanz, indexed by Joseph J. Preil. D804.3/.G556 1994]

David Glanz in his Bronx apartment, 1996.

Eliasz David Glanz [EG] was born in Rozwadów on 12 November 1912. The family moved to Tarnów, a much larger community, in 1926, in the hope of improving their clothing business. EG's immediate family consisted of six persons: his parents, their three sons and one daughter. Only EG and an older brother survived the Holocaust. The others perished in Treblinka or Auschwitz. Of EG's extended family of twenty-three, through first cousins, EG and his brother are the sole survivors.

EG tells how in 1942 he avoided a German roundup of Jews by jumping into a dry canal. Somehow he survived and returned to his home that night. When he entered, his parents cried out, *"Shema Yisrael!"* ("Hear, O Israel!"). They had already begun to observe shiva, the traditional week of mourning, in the certainty that EG had been murdered with all those rounded up during the day.

EG experienced the full impact of the Holocaust in Poland and then in Austria. The Germans allowed him to live after his miraculous escape because they could use his tailoring skills. He describes living in the Tarnów ghetto, which was organized by the Germans; his transfer to the Płaszów concentration camp in Kraków, under the notorious commandant Amon Goeth; being selected by the equally villainous Dr. Mengele for transfer to Auschwitz; the horrible trip to Auschwitz by cattle car; the impossible conditions in the Mauthausen and Melk concentration camps, where he was imprisoned in September 1944; the murderous death march to the Ebensee concentration camp as the war was ending; and the serious illnesses EG and his brother suffer from at the time of their liberation by Americans in Ebensee.

When the ghetto was organized in Tarnów, EG and one brother hid in the home of the family of a former Polish employee in their clothing business. EG had bought the house for the man. When EG's money ran out, he was told to leave. EG understands that he was endangering the man by harboring the two Jewish brothers, and he has no complaints against him. The two brothers were rounded up shortly after leaving their hiding place and were shipped to Płaszów where they were assigned to forced labor as tailors.

During the cattle car trip to Auschwitz, the deportees received salami and water. EG explains the reason for this diet was to cause diarrhea, which would kill many of the deportees on the way to Auschwitz. They "were treated worse than animals." EG remained in Auschwitz three days and nights with no water or food. The Hungarian Jews were being cremated at that time, and the stench of burning flesh was terrible.

EG was then shipped to the Mauthausen concentration camp in Austria. The prisoners were stripped of all clothing and given the flimsy, striped concentration camp uniforms. His next camp was Melk. The conditions were equally miserable in both camps. One day, he walked away from a dangerous assignment. He was the only member of his unit to escape death that day. When he was discovered, however, he was beaten with fifty lashes and became ill.

On the death march from Melk to Ebensee, EG found a potato on the ground and ate it. "It was like a good steak." At night, the marchers went into a pigsty. People ate what they saw there and died. EG ate nothing because he had eaten the potato earlier that day. Only three hundred of the ten thousand who had started out survived the death march to Ebensee.

After liberation, EG and his brother lived in Munich until 1948, when they were able to emigrate to the United States. His brother lives in Israel. EG is married and has one son, one daughter, and six grandchildren. His son was an assistant professor of education at Kean College at the time of this interview; his daughter is an accountant in Florida.

After these experiences, EG seems to summarize his attitude toward his life and his religion.

> Thank God I'm here and I have a nice family. I have a nice wife, a son and a daughter and six grandchildren. I'm proud to see them and I'm happy that I'm alive.
>
> I went back to the religion. Why? . . . If I'm not going to be a Jew, I help Hitler. He wanted to kill the Jews. I have to bring back my Judaism and I didn't do bad. As I told you before, I got my son, my grandchildren, my wife, a nice daughter.

NAT GLASS, 1922–

[Holocaust testimony (HRC-1037, videotape: 3 hours, 16 minutes), 22 May and 6 June 1989; interviewed by Bernard Weinstein and Ruth Harris, indexed by Bernard Weinstein. D804.3/.G563 1989]

Nat Glass [NG] was born on 15 January 1922 in Pabianice, near Łódź, where his father was a successful textile manufacturer. The immediate family consisted of six persons: parents, two daughters, and two sons. NG and his brother survived. His mother and his two sisters perished in Auschwitz. His father was poisoned by a *Kapo* on the very last day of the war.

NG provides a comprehensive description of his Holocaust years, beginning with the Pabianice ghetto from 1939 until its liquidation in 1942, followed by life in the Łódź ghetto until it was liquidated in August 1944, then the concentration camps of Auschwitz, Braunschweig, Ravensbrück, and Wöbbelin. He describes the chaotic, unbelievably inhumane conditions in the camps.

At the beginning of the interview, NG reports his perception of the roles played by many Poles and Germans in the treatment of Jews. In prewar Poland, "Jews were always second-class citizens." Immediately after the Germans occupied Poland, there were to be no more Jewish bakeries or businesses. When Jews joined Poles on the waiting lines at bakeries to buy bread, Poles identified Jews to the German guards in order to have the Jews chased away.

How did the Germans close down every Jewish business? The Germans decreed every Jewish business must have a German *Treuhänder* (trustee). NG's father took an employee of German background for this position in his textile factory. Eventually, this *Treuhänder* told NG's entire family, father and children, to stay away from the factory.

NG then describes the establishment of the Pabianice ghetto for the community's twelve thousand Jews, "within twenty-four hours," as ordered by the Germans. The ghetto existed from 1939 until it was liquidated in 1942 and the city was *judenfrei*. NG was assigned to the cleanup brigade of two hundred on the Sabbath of deportation. In amazement, he describes the discovery of a cholent, a traditional hot Sabbath dish, in every Jewish residence, in a bed to keep the food warm in accordance with Sabbath regulations. The cholent was prepared, somehow, despite a food shortage of famine extent.

NG's brigade was then transferred to the Łódź ghetto. Conditions there were much worse than in Pabianice. In 1944, NG's family was shipped out in the inhumane cattle cars as the Łódź ghetto was liquidated. The journey lasted six or eight days, with no plumbing or sanitary facilities. He describes the effort of several men who worked with a hammer, chisel, and suit jacket (for "privacy") to create a primitive bathroom with minimum privacy for the many people squeezed into their cattle car.

Upon arrival in Auschwitz, men were immediately separated from women. NG never saw his mother and sisters again. One may grasp some of the horror of the Holocaust in the following incident, related by NG, which took place in "Canada" (the location in Auschwitz where the Germans sorted the valuables plundered from the Jews).

One of the "Canadians" came back one night and he said: "You wouldn't believe it. I just burned my father and mother." It sounds awfully tragic. How can a person say that? How can he do it? It's inhuman. It just so happened, he was taken from his little town years before, for the labor force . . . and he went probably to various labor camps. Eventually, he wound up in the Canada in Auschwitz. And when his little town was liquidated, they sent them to Auschwitz. And his father went to the gas chambers, and his mother. And as they were throwing in the bodies, he came across and he saw his father and his mother. But *nothing, nothing, nothing* he could do about it. Sad. It's beyond imagination. Your brain cannot even take it sometimes when you hear the stories. And you hear they just put them in the crematorium. . . . That's the way we live. We weren't any more humans. Even for us listening to the stories, being in Auschwitz. I can go on and on.

NG and his brother were liberated in Wöbbelin by the U.S. Eighty-Second Airborne Division. He and his brother came to the United States in June 1949 and settled in Paterson, New Jersey, in order to be with their American uncle. They worked for him until the brothers developed a partnership in a ladies' coat manufacturing firm in Stanhope, New Jersey. NG married in 1969 and has one daughter, a college student at the time of this interview.

NG believes in the importance of Holocaust education and has lectured extensively, especially in high schools.

It took me quite a few years myself to break down and start talking about it. . . . What made me do it? I think I came to the conclusion after watching a lot of films, and most in the beginning were Hollywood-style . . . that this is not the whole truth. Tell them the way it is. . . . Either you tell them the way it was, how harsh, how sad. But tell them. And then the youth should know about it. . . . It's not only the Jewish question. It's the hatred that's going on all over the world.

GLADYS BRESLER HELFGOTT, 1924–

[Holocaust testimony (HRC-978, videotape: 1 hour, 38 minutes), 10 November 1987; interviewed by Bernard Weinstein and Dan Gover, indexed by Joseph J. Preil. D804.3/.H474 1987]

Gladys Bresler in December 1946.

Gladys Bresler Helfgott [GH] was born in Łódź on 23 January 1924. Her immediate family consisted of four persons: her parents, GH, and a younger sister. Her father and sister perished during the Holocaust; GH and her mother survived together.

The Germans organized the Łódź ghetto in May 1940. "Łódź was the first ghetto to open and the last one to close." She saw a cousin murdered by a German soldier at the beginning of the war. GH reports that the ghetto was lacking in sanitary conditions and social structure. Residents suffered from malnutrition and lack of medical supplies. Unproductive people in the ghetto were deported, destination unknown. People worked in order to survive. Unlike other ghettos, there was no uprising in Łódź.

The ghetto was closed in August 1944. GH and her family hid in an attic for three days to avoid deportation. They then surrendered to the Germans and were shipped to Auschwitz in cattle cars. GH describes their arrival at Auschwitz and how her mother was saved at the introductory selection by a German soldier. Her father died seven months later in Dachau, near the end of the war. After two weeks in Auschwitz, GH and her mother and sister were transferred to Obernheide, a forced labor camp in the Bremen area. She describes the cruelty of the SS women guards. As the Germans were retreating, her mother, sister, and eight hundred other women were marched to Bergen-Belsen in April 1945. Her sister died three weeks later of tuberculosis and malnutrition.

When the war ended, both GH and her mother were ill with typhoid. The Red Cross arranged for them to recuperate in Sweden, where GH met her husband-to-be. They married there, and their first son was born in Sweden. The family of four, including GH's mother, emigrated to the United States in 1952. She has two sons and three grandchildren. A gifted speaker, GH often lectures at Kean University as well as in public and private schools in her admirable effort to teach the Holocaust.

DAVID KATZ, 1920–

[Holocaust testimony (HRC-2000, videotape: 1 hour), 17 February 1994; interviewed and indexed by Bernard Weinstein. D804.3/.K148 1994]

David Katz [DK] was born on 25 August 1920 in Chrzanów, not far from Kraków. DK had four sisters and was the youngest of five brothers. One brother, Yehuda, emigrated to Palestine in 1934. Of the ten family members in Poland in 1939, DK and three siblings survived the Holocaust; his parents and four siblings perished.

DK's father was a shoe manufacturer with a work force of sixty people. When the Germans descended on Chrzanów immediately after the outbreak of war, DK's parents tried to flee to Russia and, as was the experience of many Polish Jews at this time, they returned to their hometown. They were stopped by the Germans, his mother was forced to leave his father, who was brutally murdered together with other innocent victims.

DK's mother, his sister Rachel, and her two-year-old daughter were among the first Jews to be murdered in Auschwitz. The younger members of the family were sent to forced labor camps. DK describes the camps and his ordeal.

The first camp was Faulbrück and suddenly a German soldier talked to me. I didn't really understand what he was talking . . . and this minute he hit me with a gun on the back of my head. I don't know, he broke something, like the doctors explain [to] me here, because I got some wire broken in my head and I got always pain. This pain never goes away. And I'm living still up to now with this pain. [He still takes medication daily to ease the pain—*ed.*]

DK was in Faulbrück with one of his brothers from March 1940 until 1943. Generally, older people were deported to Auschwitz and younger people were taken to forced labor camps. In Faulbrück, they did "regular work, such as building streets." The SS camp commandant said to the prisoners, "If you'll be good, I'll be good." No one who worked in the camp was killed during DK's three years of detention.

His next camp was in Bunzlau, Germany. DK reports the food was better than in Faulbrück and the prisoners in these forced labor camps did not wear the customary striped uniforms. As the German military situation deteriorated, DK was involved in a long death march to Bergen-Belsen. On the way, they passed through the concentration camps in Dora and Ellrich. He saw "still-alive German Jews being burned."

DK tells a remarkable story of this period.

> When we were moving, I was in camp. I don't know the name of this camp. We were staying a few days. . . . I was going around and I came into a room. There was a stove and everybody cooked something for himself by this stove. Suddenly, somebody started to cry.
>
> I asked him, "Why are you crying?" He said, "You don't know me?" I said, "No, who are you?" He said, "I am your brother, I am Avraham. I am your *brother.* You don't recognize me?"
>
> When he started talking, I saw it's my brother.

DK testifies it was impossible for him to save his brother on this death march to Bergen-Belsen. Amazingly, he had a similar experience with a typhus-ridden sister in Bergen-Belsen, at the time of liberation. He did not recognize her because she had lost her hair and her weight was down to forty or fifty pounds. DK and one brother managed to move her to a hospital in Celle and helped nurse her back to health.

DK describes how his father and ten other men were murdered in their town, Chrzanów. The head of their *Judenrat,* a Mr. Zuckerman, shot himself one night after the Germans ordered him to round up "four hundred Jewish kids."

After the war, DK moved to Hamburg, opened two stores where he sold various delicacies, met his wife-to-be, and saved money to leave Germany for the United States. His fiancée arrived in America in 1951 to live with her aunt. DK arrived in March 1952 and they were married in September. Their first residence was in central New Jersey, where they could be with many friends and where DK found employment. They have a daughter who is a speech therapist and a son who is an accountant. Both children are married. DK has three grandchildren.

LUNA FUSS KAUFMAN, 1926–

[Holocaust testimony (HRC-900, videotape: 1 hour, 47 minutes), 29 June 1983; interviewed by Sidney Langer, indexed by Kathy Kosmidor. D804.3/.K21 1983]

The Fuss family survivors, Luna and her mother, in Kraków, 1947.

Luna Fuss Kaufman [LK] was born on 28 November 1926 in Kraków. In 1939, her immediate family consisted of four persons—her parents, one older sister, and LK. Her father perished in Auschwitz. Her sister drowned in Stutthof seaport after leaving Auschwitz during the closing days of the war. LK and her mother survived.

LK has investigated the fate of her extended family and determined that some forty-five family members perished and another forty-five survived the Holocaust decade.

LK describes the entire Holocaust period as experienced by a teenage girl. This covers two years in the Kraków ghetto and four years (1941–1945) in the Płaszów and Skarżysko-Kamienna concentration camps. In her testimony, LK analyzes the psychological strategy of the Germans against the Jews, the role of the *Judenrat,* the futility of resistance by the victims, and the self-assurance of an activist teenager and of the same person later in life.

LK discusses the Germans' psychological warfare against the Jews.

I think that the worst thing that happened was—as you know, the European man was a very proud man, he was always the provider, he was always the one the family depended upon for decisions, and depended upon for income. This was the leader, and the moment the Germans entered, the first thing they did, they did not permit the man to work. . . . As a result, the man immediately was degraded. . . . The man was right away destroyed, his ego was broken, tremendously . . . and to follow that up . . . every morning they would have on street corners people who would capture the Jews and make them work. But they make them work in very humiliating conditions—shoveling snow or coal or sweeping the streets. . . . Those were people who were very highly regarded in the community and, all of a sudden, there they were—sweeping the streets and being jerked by all the people. . . . The class distinction was very strong, and the image of the man who was somebody socially, all of a sudden being destroyed, and the [onlookers] laughing, and seeing the men sweeping the streets, was tremendously destructive.

The importance of education, even under the most dangerous conditions, is described by LK.

Knowing the Jewish interest in education and the importance that education played in Jewish life, immediately the schools were closed. We could not attend schools. And it was illegal to go to school. So, what we did . . . at first, my father organized a school in private homes. The teachers would come, and they would conduct classes. But that became illegal and very dangerous. They had to abandon it after a few weeks. . . . This was a chipping away at the dignity of the community. . . . This was all designed to break the spirit.

After liberation, LK returned to Kraków with her mother. She remained there from 1945 until 1950. She met her husband-to-be in school during this period. She went to Israel in 1950, then to the United States in 1952.

LK studied and made up for her lost educational opportunities by graduating from high school and earning a master's degree in music within five years of arriving. She moved to New Jersey in order to be near her first job. She lived then in Union City and now in central New Jersey. LK has three children. She plays a leadership role in Holocaust education as well as participating in many other community endeavors.

DAVID KEMPINSKI, 1921–

[Holocaust testimony (HRC-937, videotape: 1 hour, 44 minutes), 9 March 1987; interviewed by Bonnie Kind and Bernard Weinstein, indexed by Bonnie Kind. D804.3/.K32 1987]

David Kempinski [DK] was born on 27 July 1921 in Pruszków, not far from Łódź. He was raised in Wielún, where his father owned a flour mill. In 1939, his immediate family in Poland consisted of six persons—his parents, three brothers, and DK. His parents and one brother were gassed in a truck when they were in the Chełmno concentration camp. One brother perished in Kaufering, a subcamp of Dachau, in February 1945. One brother survived and resides in Israel; DK lives in central New Jersey.

DK survived imprisonment in *ten* concentration camps between August 1941 and April 1945: Poznań, Regensburg, Kreising, Reppen, Eberswalde-Brit, Auschwitz-Birkenau, Oranienburg, Sachsenhausen, Flossenbürg, and Dachau. He provides details of life and work in the camps. He worked in the I.G. Farben factory in the Birkenau area from September 1944 until January 1945.

DK describes the hanging of several underground prisoners in November 1944, shortly before the end of the war—a heartbreaking experience. He was in the camp at Dachau when it was liberated on 29 April 1945. DK seems to have experienced the entire brutality of the Holocaust: cattle cars to Auschwitz, death marches in Germany, and constant suffering from painful hunger and lice.

At the time when he was liberated, DK weighed seventy-four pounds. He remained in Germany, in the Feldafing and Landsberg DP camps, between 1945 and 1949. He then emigrated to Israel where he met and married his wife and served in the Israeli army. He moved to Switzerland in 1957 and remained there until 1964. His three children were born in Switzerland.

The family arrived in the United States on 18 October 1964. They settled in New Jersey to be near their friends. Two of his children were married at the time of this interview.

EVA CHAWA HOROWITZ KEMPINSKI, 1925–

[Holocaust testimony (HRC-939, videotape: 1 hour, 24 minutes), 22 March 1987; interviewed by Bernard Weinstein and Irene Katz, indexed by Joseph J. Preil. D804.3/.K321 1987]

Eva Horowitz Kempinski [EK] was born in Wieluń on 25 August 1925. Wieluń had a population of twenty-two thousand, including eight thousand Jews. EK's immediate family consisted of ten persons: her parents, seven girls, and one boy. She is the lone survivor.

EK describes the Hasidic life in her home. The members of her family were loyal followers of the Grand Rabbi of Gur, the largest Hasidic group in Poland and the world.

EK and her family moved to Warsaw from Łódź in December 1939, several months after the outbreak of World War II. EK's father was deported to Treblinka, her mother to Majdanek, and the young people were assigned to forced labor. EK decided to accompany her mother to Majdanek in 1943, although she understood the gravity of the decision. At the time, she was seventeen years old and her mother was forty-three.

She describes the gassing of her mother.

> Sunday, they were telling us to take a shower. And I with mother [was] very close. And . . . we come to the door to go into the shower, SS men on both sides. He took my mother. I screamed, "This is my mother!" Then, he said, "You're so stupid. Your mother go work in the kitchen." And I still keep the mother [gestures with her hands]. Someone take me in [gesture by pushing with hand] and push me into the shower. I no more saw my mother.

After two months in Majdanek, EK was among a small group of inmates transferred to Auschwitz and assigned to forced labor. The others were all murdered. Until this day, EK cannot understand why she alone of her family was able to survive. "Maybe it's a punishment."

In her testimony, EK returns to her time in the Warsaw ghetto and recalls an incident of cruelty.

Across from our door, some Germans stopped into the house, not just to make trouble. . . . He was looking to steal something or to beat up somebody. Once they come in, and we all go down. Next to our apartment was living a young family, with a daughter, maybe six years. And to her comes an old father from a shtetl. . . . The daughter was not a religious Jew. The father was an observant Jew. The German comes. . . . [The father] was standing and davening with tefillin on and can't move in *Shemonah Esreh* [a daily prayer] . . . and she called out "*Tateh! Tateh!* ["Dad! Dad!"] is not here." Meantime, the German beat him up. It was *blood, blood* all over.

And after, he went up, one floor higher was a lady with three small children. And she was just ready to go out from the apartment, and the baby was still in crib. He took this baby, maybe it was a year . . . this was the third floor . . . and we were standing in the back yard and see this child flying from the window. . . . She was so busy with the three small children. She came a little too late. The German come into the apartment before she left, and she's standing, and the child is flying to the ground. And the mother comes with the two children. All three were small. And crying and screaming. . . .

And after, when we went back to the apartment, this old Jew was a wreck with blood. After four or five days, [he] died. [Unclear; probably "This all took place"— *ed.*] in one hour. . . . I see it with my eyes. I was standing in the backyard.

After Auschwitz, EK worked in a munitions factory in Weisswasser, Czechoslovakia, from December 1944 until May 1945. This was a satellite of the Gross-Rosen concentration camp. She was liberated by the Russians. She recalls her friend in camp, Rachel, her neighbors, her misery at the time of liberation, and her return to her hometown in Poland. Her former neighbors were shocked that she had survived. They seemed to be saying, "Why are you alive?"

From Poland, EK went to Slovakia, Austria, Italy and, finally, to Palestine. Her father had been an active member in Agudath Israel, and she was in the first Agudah group to arrive in Palestine in 1946. She married in Israel, moved to Switzerland in 1958, and emigrated to the United States in 1964. The family settled in central New Jersey. She has three children, all married, and four grandchildren.

A dramatic indication of the impact of the Holocaust on this survivor is EK's concluding statement: "One thing I told my children. When it comes the day, and I will be gone, and they make me a stone, I want this number [pointing to her arm] on the stone . . . half of my arm and the number. This I want on my stone."

HALINA GOLDBERG KLEINER, 1929–

[Holocaust testimony (HRC-966, videotape: 3 hours, 45 minutes), 30 March and 23 July 1987; interviewed by Bernard Weinstein and Robyn Rajs, indexed by Anne Kaplan. D804.3/.K532 1987]

Halina Goldberg in Prachatice, Czechoslovakia, June 1945, shortly after liberation. The two men are American liberators. Building in background is the hospital where Halina recovered from her illness.

Halina Goldberg Kleiner [HK] was born on 7 February 1929 in Częstochowa, not far from Kraków. Her father owned a lumber business and the family lived comfortably. She was an only child and the only Holocaust survivor in her family.

HK describes the confusion immediately after the outbreak of war in September 1939. This includes a futile effort to escape from the Germans by fleeing to her grandparents in Będzin. In her testimony, one hears the German persecution evolving in the familiar Polish pattern: family business confiscated, food and clothing shortages, Jewish children expelled from schools, Jews evicted from their homes and forced into ghettos, compulsory wearing of armbands with the Star of David, living in constant fear. This is followed by the terrifying news of the Auschwitz and Treblinka murder camps.

HK continues her testimony by describing her harrowing experience as a young adolescent, her efforts to avoid deportation to murder camps (the fate of her parents and so many others), and finally her decision to volunteer to go to a labor camp. Her first experience was in a small camp, Bolkenhain, with about 150 young women. She was then transferred to Landshut to work in a weaving factory.

HK met two fellow inmates in Landshut, Lily and Halinka. The three girls formed a lasting friendship and remained together throughout the war. This led HK to articulate this profound thought:

> I want you to realize how important it is that the Germans tried to strip us of this humanity, of this ability to think about other people, not only yourself. And they weren't able to do that. We looked out for each other, and we would have risked our lives for each other which, in many cases, people did and helped each other. This was a factor in being able to survive, because you were not an animal. That's what they tried to create. They tried to create this animal instinct in one.

After Landshut, the three girls were transferred to a small weaving factory in Grünberg. They were on a starvation diet in all three camps. Grünberg was designated as a concentration camp. The prisoners lived in terror. As the Russians were approaching in December 1944, HK and the others were commanded to abandon Grünberg and start their death march toward Germany. They reached the devastated city of Dresden. Many died in a typhoid epidemic or because of the generally impossible living conditions. HK was among the survivors who continued the death march, this time to Czechoslovakia. She notes that not a single German came forward to help them on their march through Germany, while many Czechs greeted them with abundant food.

HK was liberated by the Americans in Helmbrechts, Czechoslovakia. Fortunately, she and one friend had succeeded in leaving the death march. She was very ill and was hospitalized for six weeks. The town's mayor took an interest in her progress and visited her in the hospital.

HK met her future husband in the Salzburg DP camp. They arrived in the United States in July 1946 and settled in New Jersey in 1967. She has two children, one in New Jersey and one in Manhattan.

HENRY KOLBER, 1923–

[Holocaust testimony (HRC-924, videotape: 1 hour, 19 minutes), 29 July 1985; interviewed by Sidney Langer, indexed by Joseph J. Preil. D804.3/.K675 1985]

Henry Kolber [HK] was born on 6 June 1923 in Przysietnica, a very small town about forty miles from Kraków. His father owned a lumberyard. The Kolbers were the only Jewish family in town. HK was the oldest of five children and the only person in his family of seven to survive the Holocaust.

HK was enrolled in the second year of gymnasium when the war started in 1939. On the second day of the war, HK's father took the family to the neighboring village of Stary Sącz. All men who were physically fit were assigned to forced labor. In April 1940, HK was included in a group of a hundred men who were transferred to Rapka, a nearby town. Rapka's German commandant, Rosenbaum, was unusually cruel. HK describes instances of Rosenbaum's cruelty. HK was one of four survivors to testify against Rosenbaum in a Hamburg trial in 1967. Rosenbaum was sentenced to life imprisonment.

HK was transferred to Kraków in January 1942. He was assigned to work on the construction of the Płaszów concentration camp. He heard at this time that his parents and siblings had been deported to the Treblinka murder camp. HK was shipped to Auschwitz in early 1944. He describes conditions in Auschwitz and how he managed to survive with the help of a gentile Polish neighbor.

As the Russian military campaign approached Auschwitz, HK was part of a terrible death march to Buchenwald. This is a most effective description. He was in the same Buchenwald bloc as Elie Wiesel. The conditions in Buchenwald, as the war was ending, were increasingly miserable. There was no food. They were liberated by the Americans. Chaplain Herschel Schacter was among the liberators. The chaplain arranged for HK to be on a transport to Switzerland and for young Elie Wiesel to be transferred to France.

HK did not return to Poland after the war. He lived in Geneva and was sponsored by friends of his parents to come to the United States. These friends lived in New Jersey, and HK was able to enter the United States in June 1947. He started to work as a baker's helper. At the time of this interview, he was a construction superintendent. He married an American woman. They have three children and three grandchildren.

EDITH FROHLICH KORNBLUTH, 1929–

[Holocaust testimony (HRC-1035, videotape: 48 minutes), 12 June 1989; interviewed by Bernard Weinstein and Devorah Lichstein, indexed by Bernard Weinstein. D804.3/.K723 1989]

Edith Frohlich Kornbluth [EK] was born on 18 February 1929 in Kupno, where her father was the administrator of a large estate. Her family lived very comfortably. They had two maids. When the war broke out, EK's immediate family consisted of four persons—her parents, EK, and a younger sister. EK is the family's lone Holocaust survivor.

When the war started, EK was expelled from public school because she was Jewish. The Germans evicted her family from their home. They were then moved into a ghetto in Głogów, a nearby town. EK's family was squeezed into one ghetto room together with two other families. EK's father was determined to leave the ghetto. His plan to move in with a Polish family was unacceptable because of the understandable fear of the Polish host. EK's family then lived in the nearby woods. "It was very, very difficult." Obviously, it helped that they were well-to-do.

After EK's younger sister, aunt, and eighteen-month-old cousin had been murdered in prison, her parents convinced eleven-year-old EK to leave the woods and try to move in with a Polish family. The youngster met a Polish couple and asked them if they needed help in their home and with their children. The couple accepted EK's proposal and took her to their home in Rzeszów. She "went to church every Sunday, and even said prayers with their children." Interestingly, this was an antisemitic family. They suspected nothing because EK was blond with a fair complexion. She was able to visit her parents in the woods on two occasions during the war.

After her region had been liberated by the Russians, EK was advised to return to her town. She then learned that her parents had been discovered and murdered by the German SS "two or three months before the war was over." Some distant cousins found EK at this time, and they all lived together. She then moved on to Austria and Germany. She came to the United States in 1947 and lived with an aunt in Brighton

Beach, Brooklyn, until she married a fellow survivor two years later. They have two children.

Toward the end of her testimony, EK made the following statements:

> Life in the woods was a daily struggle, a daily struggle. . . . When I survived, I thought it was a miracle. . . . I am not unique. There were so many that went through a lot more than I did . . . like my husband, for instance. But I am not bitter because I feel that a crazy maniac brainwashed a nation—I'm speaking of the Germans—to do horrible things. And I hope that those who are still alive live with a terrible conscience.

WILLIAM KORNBLUTH, 1922–

[Holocaust testimony (HRC-1036, videotape: 1 hour, 51 minutes), 12 June 1989; interviewed by Bernard Weinstein and Devorah Lichstein, indexed by Bernard Weinstein. D804.3/.K731 1989]

William Kornbluth [WK] was born in Breslau, near the Polish-German border, on 8 January 1922. He was one of five children. Except for a sister who emigrated to Palestine in 1936 to join her husband, the other family members were in Tarnów in September 1939. His parents and younger sister were murdered in *Aktionen* in Tarnów in 1942. WK and his two brothers survived a series of concentration camps. This is the only instance, to his knowledge, where three brothers survived together in the same camps.

In a remarkably detailed description of the savage brutality of the Holocaust, from September 1939 until liberation in May 1945, WK reviews the evolving anti-semitism in Breslau in the 1930s, the savage beatings and random shootings, together with plundering and burning of Jewish property, at the beginning of the war, and the more organized murder system after December 1941. He continues with the tragic year of 1942. In September 1943, WK and others deemed physically fit by the Germans were taken to the Płaszów concentration camp outside Kraków. He worked for a firm called Madrich, where he did sewing.

When Płaszów was liquidated in August 1944, WK and his two brothers were taken by cattle car to Mauthausen, Austria. Conditions in Mauthausen were even worse than at Płaszów. The next camp was St. Valentin, where the ultimate object once again was to kill Jews with maximum cruelty. As the Russians were approaching, the prisoners were moved to Ebensee. They were liberated by the Americans in Ebensee on 6 May 1945.

After the war, WK returned to his new hometown of Tarnów for a short visit. On his return trip to Austria, he and other survivors were injured in a collision with a Russian truck. Three people were killed. As WK was being admitted, reluctantly, to an Austrian hospital, a nurse called him "a dirty Jew."

WK arrived in the United States in December 1947. He met a fellow survivor whom he married in December 1949. He worked as a cutter in the garment industry. In 1956, he bought a poultry farm in New Jersey. At the time of this interview, he had two children, a son and a daughter, and one grandchild. For many years WK refrained from speaking about his Holocaust experiences. He has recently become an active participant in such programs and has accepted invitations to address community and school groups.

ROSE GLUCKSTEIN KRAMER, 1921–

[Holocaust testimony (HRC-934, videotape: 1 hour, 23 minutes), 12 February 1987; interviewed by Bernard Weinstein and Phyllis Ziman Tobin, indexed by Bernard Weinstein. D804.3/.K891 1987]

Rose Gluckstein Kramer [RK] was born on 19 January 1921 in Beuthen, Germany. Her father died before she was born, her mother six years later. The youngest of eight siblings, RK lived in an orphanage for six years until she was twelve years old. She then moved in with one of her married sisters in Będzin, Poland, and one or two years later, she began to work.

Shortly after the war started, RK states that she realized the war was not only against Poland but also against the Jews. There was limited opportunity for work in town, and only for Poles. There was one bakery for the population of 150,000. Jews were forbidden to buy bread. German guards were on duty in the bakery. Several Poles recognized RK on the bakery line, and identified her to the Germans. She was pulled from the line as she was reaching for her bread and was hit by a German guard in the right elbow by the butt of his rifle. Her arm has been crippled ever since.

The Germans ordered the Jews of Będzin into a ghetto. RK lived in the ghetto for three years, 1940–1943. Life was so difficult in the ghetto that her memory is vague on how she managed to survive through those three years.

RK and her sister's family evaded German roundups in the ghetto by hiding in a crawl space near their room. One day during a 1943 roundup, the Polish owner of the house sensed what was happening. He told the Germans to look behind the wall. RK and her family were then taken to the railroad station for deportation.

RK describes two remarkable incidents that occurred in Auschwitz, both involving the selection process. In the first incident, a childless sister of RK sacrificed her life for love of her niece. In the second case, RK escaped death miraculously.

My little niece was very attached to my sister. My sister didn't have any children, so she gave a lot of time to that little girl. And she was very much loved by her. You know very well, when you got to Auschwitz, when they chased you off the train, they divide you. . . . I was young, so they told me to go, let's say, to A or B or whatever. My sister was young, really, she was only thirty-three years old. But the baby started crying . . . and she called my sister. Her name was Marshal, but in Poland, we translate that to Polish, Manya. So the child started calling, and crying, "Manya! Manya!"

So my sister took the child in her hand, and when you have a child, you are doomed. I have seen children thrown away by Jewish mothers, unfortunately, in order to save their life. Piles of kids. And my sister took the little child in her arms and she told her, "Don't worry. I am going with you. You know I love you."

And, of course, they were sent on that truck. My sister saw me on the line A . . . which is for the young and healthy people. And she waved to me, and she was happy that I am the only one who, supposedly, hopefully, is going to survive, to work, or whatever they do there. We had no idea where we are going, and what's going to be with us.

The truck drove to the crematorium. . . . It isn't the burning. . . . Each time, I think of them, the way they died, the way they were gassed, I live through it, time and time again. . . .

We had selections quite often, very often. We were coming back from work, and we were told to go into the shower. . . . And that was late winter. It was quite cold. We were chased out naked, and we were standing outside, just waiting for the selection. . . . In Europe, winters are very, very severe. And we were just huddled together. And then we were led into a barrack. We had Poles with us, too, women.

The man in charge, the officer . . . from the German army, told us to divide the Jews from the Poles. And with a rope, they roped off the Poles, separately, that they are not going to go in there, not going to go through the selection.

And, spontaneously, I don't know how it came about, I only know that the whole Jewish group just tore the rope and went over to the Poles. And at that time, before that, they were already selecting people. And, of course, my number was already selected as to go to the gas chamber.

But after that whole confusion, when we went over to the Poles, the man in charge was very aggravated. How dare we do a thing like that? And he told the woman, the *Blockälteste,* to tear that piece of paper, where she had the numbers already, what he selected to the gas chamber, to tear up, and start all over again. The second time around, he didn't choose my number.

So, how am I to say how I survived? People ask me . . . and I do avoid that, because I have no explanation. I didn't do anything, really, that I deserve any credit. I didn't fight anybody. I didn't try. I don't know how I survived. It happened. I don't know how.

RK tells the story of a young girl who escaped from Auschwitz. The girl was captured and was returned to camp three weeks later. The girl slashed her wrists as she was led to the gallows for a public hanging. The furious German officer in charge then issued an order to burn the girl in the open yard, in front of the prisoners. This occurred in 1944.

One day in 1945, "without any reason," all the prisoners were ordered to start marching out of Auschwitz. This was a death march, a reaction to the Russian advances through Poland. The prisoners marched for days, without food or water. Those who sat down on the ground to rest were shot on the spot. Finally they reached a railroad station where open cars were waiting for them. The trip continued in the cattle cars until they arrived in the Ravensbrück concentration camp in Germany. This camp was disorganized as the war was obviously ending. There was no food or water, but selections were made for the gas chambers, and the crematorium was in operation around the clock.

RK was transferred again, this time to the Neustadt-Glewe concentration camp. She worked in the kitchen until the camp was liberated by Americans and Russians. She and the girls in her group decided to leave the camp quickly because the Russian soldiers behaved improperly, and the girls did not need such attention.

RK discovered that only one brother, in addition to herself, survived the Holocaust. Their six siblings perished. The surviving brother introduced RK to the man who was to become her first husband. They arrived in the United States on 11 April 1949, settled in Brooklyn, and struggled to begin life in this new country. RK and her husband had no children and were divorced. She married a second time and gave birth to a daughter and a son. The family moved to New Jersey in 1969 to be near the husband's construction business. Their son and son-in-law are both stockbrokers. They have seven grandchildren.

ROSE KORCARZ LAITER, 1935–

[Holocaust testimony (HRC-2001, videotape: 1 hour, 28 minutes), 24 February 1994; interviewed and indexed by Bernard Weinstein. D804.3/.L204 1994]

Seven-month-old Rose Korcarz is in the middle of her family.

Rose Korcarz Laiter [RL] was born on 15 May 1935 in Grodzisk Mazowiecki, seventy miles from Warsaw. Her immediate family in 1939 consisted of six persons—her parents and their four daughters. All six family members survived the Holocaust, probably the result of the leadership of RL's father and his instinctive distrust of every German announcement.

Because she was only four years old when the war started, RL does not remember many details of the Holocaust years in the heart of Poland. She does recall the seventy-mile march from her hometown to the Warsaw ghetto, where they saw much German cruelty, including German soldiers beating mothers whose children would not stop crying.

RL describes an interesting disagreement between her father and her grandparents. Her father's work assignment for the Germans was the digging of ditches, evidently for the burial of murdered Jews. Her father felt the family should flee, whereas the grandparents counseled patience. When the Germans announced that Jews should bring their children to a central location for bread and milk, and then leave the children, RL's father suspected a German ruse. Her father and grandfather disagreed once again. Her father was shown to be right—the children left by their parents were taken away and never seen again.

RK believes that this finally convinced her father to flee with his family. They ran toward Russia and hid in the forest and countryside or lived with farmers until that became too dangerous. She and her sisters were not told the names of their protectors so as not to endanger these courageous persons should the girls be captured by Germans.

After liberation by the Russians, RL's father considered emigration to Palestine, but he decided against this when he realized that the children would not live under the same roof as the parents in the kibbutz. They arrived in the United States in 1951 to join RL's sister, who had settled in Pennsylvania. RL's family then moved to Brooklyn. She completed high school and married a fellow survivor, and the young couple moved to New Jersey in 1956.

RL has two children, a daughter who is an occupational therapist, and a son who is a computer scientist. Both are married, and RL has five grandchildren. After marriage and children, RL resumed her higher education. At the time of this testimony, she is a special education teacher in a New Jersey public school system.

Eva Apozdawa, 1945 or 1946.

EVA APOZDAWA LAKS, 1922–

[Holocaust testimony (HRC-1062, videotape: 1 hour, 37 minutes), 2 May 1990; interviewed and indexed by Bernard Weinstein. D804.3/.L21 1990]

Eva Apozdawa Laks [EL] was born on 10 March 1922 in Ryki, not far from Warsaw. Her father was a shochet, a kosher slaughterer. EL was the oldest of seven children. She is the only survivor, the other eight members of her family having perished in the Holocaust.

When EL was three years old, the family moved from Ryki to Janovice, where they remained until the beginning of World War II, the advent of the Holocaust. They suffered from Polish antisemitism in the 1930s. Kosher slaughter was declared illegal, and pogroms and violence broke out, especially on Christian holidays. An early example of German cruelty was the forced shaving of EL's father's beard.

The residents of Janovice were evacuated to Zwoleń in August 1943. Several days later, EL and her parents were taken to the marketplace. The mother was sent home, and EL never saw her mother or siblings again. EL and her father were beaten on trucks during the ensuing ride to Skarżysko. She was assigned to forced labor in a HASAG munitions factory. She received one letter from her father, then never heard from him again. She understands that all members of her family perished in Treblinka.

EL describes her difficult existence in the HASAG factory. In August 1944, all the Skarżysko HASAG prisoners were evacuated to Leipzig, and then evacuated again the day after an Allied bombing attack. During the death march from Leipzig, the prisoners were liberated by the Russians at the Elbe River. EL weighed seventy pounds at that time.

EL then went to Kraków where she met her future husband. They married and went to Prague and Germany. They lived in Landsberg for five years. Her husband, but not EL, wanted to settle in Israel. They arrived in New York in 1950 and were sent to New Orleans. They had no family in the United States and lived the difficult lives of refugee immigrants adjusting to a new country.

After six years in New Orleans, the young family moved to Newark for her husband's employment. She had two sons. The older son is a health economist in Washington, the younger son an ophthalmologist in New Jersey. EL's husband died of a heart attack at a young age. Two years after his death, EL met a survivor-widower who also had two sons. They married and succeeded in combining the two families. EL lives in New Jersey with her husband.

Naftali Laks with his five sisters, their mother, and a little cousin, shortly before the oldest sister (right of Naftali) emigrated to the United States in 1938.

NAFTALI LAKS, 1922–

[Holocaust testimony (HRC-1055, videotape: 3 hours, 45 minutes), 6 December 1989 and 31 January 1990; interviewed by Bernard Weinstein and Patricia Widenhorn, indexed by Bernard Weinstein. D804.3/.L24 1990]

Naftali Laks [NL] was born on 6 June 1922, in Zmigród, near the Czech border and about forty-four miles from Tarnów. His family was very poor and observant in their religious practice. This was generally true of the Jewish population in town. He had four sisters and a mother in Poland at the beginning of World

War II. His father had died of natural causes in 1935, and his oldest sister had emigrated to the United States in 1938. NL and three sisters survived the Holocaust; his mother and one sister perished.

NL provides a detailed description of life for a young Jewish man in prewar and wartime Poland. This includes the antisemitism in Poland of the 1930s, the extreme poverty in Zmigród, and the terrible events perpetrated by the Germans from the first days of the war. He describes the plundering of valuables, the special treatment of Jews, the forced labor, the series of *Aktionen* designed to murder the Jewish population, and his being selected for slave labor in the Płaszów concentration camp in Kraków. NL describes the spiritual desolation of these years.

> People who were doing this [the *Aktionen*] were going around laughing and drinking and making a picnic of the suffering of people. . . . One can never forget this. At night, in the evening, when we came home, from every surrounding house, we heard crying and weeping. . . . Some went home alone. . . . A lot of families were wiped out completely. . . . It was terrible, the crying that was going on, because people realized when they came home to empty houses, then they realized the loss that happened to them.

Three of NL's sisters were also assigned to Płaszów. NL worked on railroads and as a tailor. He and two sisters contracted typhus during a camp epidemic. The third sister took care of them. NL talks about the cruelty of the Ukrainian guards. Płaszów was liquidated in 1943, and NL was sent to the Skarżysko-Kamienna concentration camp to work on munitions for the Germans. Conditions in Skarżysko were worse than those in Płaszów.

In 1944 NL was sent to Sulejow to work on fortifications. He recalls the beatings and being deprived of food, resulting in his physical inability to complete work assignments. After two months in Sulejow, he was sent to Częstochowa to repair tanks. He was then in Buchenwald from December 1944 until March 1945. As the Germans were retreating, NL was moved to Flossenbürg and then to Mauthausen. He describes the emotional effort to celebrate Passover in Mauthausen in 1945, without family and without matzo.

> What I remember is [the] Pesach we spent there. There were a few, I think, two people who were very religious. Polsky, he was from Miechow [in Poland], and there was another one, from Hungary, and they wanted to eat matzo. How did we make matzo? . . . Some got some grains of wheat . . . with a cup, they grind it. Of course, it wasn't flour, it was very coarse.
>
> They mixed it with water, and they make it like, a little more than silver-dollar-size matzos. And they baked it on the pipes of steam which were outside, exposed. And these were the matzos.
>
> And when it came to the seder, we were all sitting and crying, because we knew, we

were wondering, everybody was thinking, "How will we survive?" . . . Of course, we mourned all the dead, all the past. Everybody remembered the seder at home. In a religious home, this was the most festive holiday, the seder. . . .

And those two people decided they wouldn't eat the bread. We used to get, I think, it was like three hundred or two hundred fifty grams [9–11 ounces—*ed.*] of bread for the whole day, and a soup which was water and beets for the cattle. Not those beets that they feed humans. This was our soup.

And they saved their bread. And after a few days, this guy Polsky, this guy apparently got so hungry, he ate up all his saved pieces of bread. And the other, from Hungary, he didn't eat all these eight days, the bread. I couldn't understand how he could survive. I think . . . a willpower like this, not everybody had.

After being liberated by the Americans, NL was hospitalized. He then went to Czechoslovakia and learned that his sisters had survived. He returned to his hometown in Poland and was told that the sisters were in Danzig. They were on a simulated kibbutz preparing for life in Palestine. NL and his sisters arrived in Palestine in 1947 after a very difficult trip. He served in the Israeli army and lived in Haifa from 1952 to 1959.

NL decided to join his sister in the United States because of his physical disabilities. He arrived in New York in 1959 and married a fellow survivor in 1961. The young couple settled in Brooklyn. They had two sons. NL's wife died of cancer in 1969, and he then married another survivor, a widow living in New Jersey with her two sons. NL then moved to New Jersey with his two sons to form a new, expanded family.

Toward the conclusion of his testimony, NL reflected on the significance of religious observance for himself and his family.

In the beginning [after the war], I wasn't religious. . . . I had a feeling about belonging to the Jewish nation. But I got unused to putting on tefillin, and in Israel I felt you could be Jewish without praying . . . twice a day.

But when we had the children, we started to think, with my first wife, what education to give. I insisted I want a Jewish education. . . . I saw that kids who went to elementary school, they get lost. They don't know from Jewishness. And I felt that I'll be closer to them if they're going to have a Jewish education. . . .

Another thing . . . I told my wife, when I remembered in the camps, when I was longing for a home, I didn't remember the four walls. I remembered the Saturday nights, how it was, the holidays, the candlesticks, the food. This always was, for me, the symbol of my home. And I said I want my children should feel like they should be . . . closer to home.

I had the feeling, I saw immigrant children who weren't religious and didn't know anything from Jewish things. They get lost. They intermarry. . . .

And I am very pleased we made this decision, because I think it helped my children grow up without their mother . . . being religious. And I always tell my sons, "I envy you," both of them, I envy them very much. Because they can say, they believe one hundred percent. They are devoted and, morally, they wouldn't do any wrong thing. Not to say, Let's say cheat. . . . Very high standards.

My older son is married, and both he and his wife are the same kind of people. My daughter-in-law works for Dun and Bradstreet . . . a computer programmer. And she wouldn't take off an hour. That's cheating. I admire her very much so. The same [with] my son. He is now working on his Ph.D. in physics. He wouldn't miss a quorum, a minyan, morning or evening [prayer service]. No matter what kind of weather, he always has to learn [Torah] every day. And I'm very proud of them. My younger one . . . he was in Israel for five years, in a yeshiva . . . now he is in Baltimore [in an advanced Talmudic seminary].

HENRY LANDSBERG, 1920–

[Holocaust testimony (HRC-2012, videotape: 1 hour, 59 minutes), 9 and 28 November 1994; interviewed and indexed by Joseph J. Preil. D804.3/.L317 1994]

Henry Landsberg [HL] was born in Warsaw on 3 August 1920. His immediate family of four consisted of his parents, a younger brother, and HL. He and his brother survived the Holocaust. His brother lives in Israel. His extended family, through first cousins, consisted of sixteen people, of whom four survived: HL, his brother, and two cousins.

HL was educated through high school and then had three years of trade school. He was an electrician before World War II and remembers a happy life in a relatively prosperous family. He then describes many details of his experiences during the Holocaust. His family lived at home in Warsaw in 1939. He reports the methods used to gather Jews for shipment by railroad to concentration camps, day after day. He discusses the organization of the Warsaw ghetto, his own work pulling a ricksha, the smuggling of guns and munitions into the ghetto for the underground, and his own forced labor for Germans who were plundering Jewish valuables for shipment to Germany.

HL is impressive in recalling experiences that spell out the horrors of the Holocaust.

That was in the Warsaw ghetto, almost at the end of the ghetto. There was nobody around anymore in the buildings. . . . That was 1943. I was driving the ricksha and one of the officers that I was driving with . . . I usually would wait for him at the entrance to the ghetto.

We had a group of people that went to the houses and took everything valuable . . . furniture or jewelry or whatever they could get out of the houses, they sent to Germany. And that group that I was with used to go to these houses, with a German soldier, and whatever they pointed out, we took it down to the court, and that was picked up later by someone else. But our job was just to bring it down.

Well, we went to a leather factory, and people that owned that factory lived in the same house. And we were told not to take anything. Well, after we were done with the job, the soldier lined us up and searched everybody if they didn't take anything. That time, my ricksha where the officer was sitting, and the soldier was looking at everybody, searching his pocket . . . and he pushed a guy, and the guy was wearing a knapsack. In the knapsack, he had this silver cup, a goblet. Well, without saying anything, the . . . soldier took his gun out and shot the guy in the back of his head. He didn't kill the guy, but the guy was just moving around a little bit on the ground.

So the guy tried to shoot again, but apparently he had no [more] bullets. So he went to this officer that I was standing with, and he asked him for bullets. So he refused to give him anything. He said, "No, I don't have it." . . . So the soldier turned around, he went inside the door, inside the court, and I don't know where he got it from, but he picked up an ax, like a hatchet, and he chopped the guy's head off. . . .

He left him lying there, and just went away. And I took my ricksha with this guy [the officer], and just went away.

When his parents and brother disappeared, HL realized that they had probably been deported to the extermination camps. Finally, in May 1943, HL was also shipped to Treblinka. He describes the trip by cattle car and the arrival at Treblinka. He was among those selected for transfer to Birkenau, where he remained for several months. He then volunteered for transfer to Majdanek and recalls this incident.

I had a very, very tragic experience there. We were carrying stones from place to place. They had to do something with us. In other words, the work. The people were sitting on the ground and cutting stones, big stones, and make them smaller. My job was to take some of the stones from here and bring them somewhere else. So they gave me a partner, and we had this big box, you know, with two handles. . . . He was in the front, I was in the back.

And as we carried that, it was a little downhill . . . and this guy in front of me, he tripped under the weight of the stones, you know, and he fell. He dropped the box, I dropped the box. But I was standing, he was on the ground. . . . There were two soldiers there, and they took his shovel, they put over his neck, and they swing on it, until they chopped him to death. The tongue came out, the eyes popped out.

INTERVIEWER: Because he tripped?

HL: Because he tripped, and I was three feet away from him. They caught somebody else, we had to continue.

HL volunteered for transfer once again, this time to Jaworzno, where he remained until near the end of the war. HL arrived in Mauthausen, Austria, in January 1945, after a death march that was survived by about two hundred of the approximately one thousand people who left Jaworzno. He was then transferred to Gunskirchen, also in Austria. His group was liberated by Americans.

In the Bindermichel DP camp, HL heard that his brother was alive in Poland. He returned to Poland and was told that his brother had just left for Palestine. He returned to Bindermichel and married a fellow survivor in 1948. The couple arrived in the United States in 1949, settled in Newark, and obtained employment quickly. HL established contact with his brother in Israel when his wife's brother visited Israel.

HL is a widower today, living in New Jersey. He is a retired electrician, the father of two married sons, and he has three grandchildren. One son lives in HL's community and is a job consultant, the other son lives in New York and is an advertising executive.

PHILIP LEDERMAN, 1924–

[Holocaust testimony (HRC-2011, videotape: 1 hour, 27 minutes), 23 November 1994; interviewed and indexed by Joseph J. Preil. D804.3/.L558 1994]

Philip Lederman in Feldafing DP camp, Germany, 1946.

Philip Lederman [PL] was born in Zarnowiec ("not far from Kraków") on 12 February 1924. His immediate family consisted of five persons—his parents, two sisters, and PL. He is the family's lone Holocaust survivor. His family perished in Auschwitz. His extended family in Poland in 1939, through first cousins, consisted of thirty-nine people. Only PL and two cousins survived. After the war, the cousins settled in Israel, and PL emigrated to the United States.

PL describes Black Thursday in his town at the beginning of the war, when many innocent Jews and Poles were murdered. In the winter of 1940 he was part of a roundup organized by the Germans. He was judged to be healthy and shipped with about two hundred men to Brande, a camp near Breslau, Germany. For the rest of the war, PL did manual labor for the Germans, mainly in Gabersdorf, Blechhammer, and Swidowa. Toward the end of the war, he was in Reichenbach and Dachau. In these two large, SS- run camps, "they were killing until the last minute. The SS were the worst people."

PL's camps never required the prisoners to wear the striped concentration camp uniforms, and he did not participate in any death march. He has no animosity for Germans—some were bad, such as the SS, and some were good. In terms of survival, he feels that being "zombies," and not thinking, probably helped.

This is a theme repeated throughout PL's testimony. For example: "After a while,

we stopped thinking. . . . We were like zombies. Just go on, go on, go on, go on."
And later in his testimony:

> We were zombies. I think that did us a lot of good. We survived. . . . We didn't think.
>
> *INTERVIEWER:* If you'd think, you'd go out of your mind.
>
> *PL:* Not only your mind. You'd lose hope. This way, you don't think about it, and just keep going. Maybe next day survive, survive.

When asked to compare his experiences in five concentration camps, PL responded:

> First, you had to work twelve hours a day. You had two hours walking. You were fourteen hours. You had twelve hours of work. You never got to eat, no water to drink. If I worked outside, like in ditches, when it used to rain, I would scoop it up [to drink], and make sure I don't pick up the sand. When you got home [the camps], you got a slice of bread, a little soup, and that was it. . . .
>
> All the camps were the same. . . . The camps were different, the people watching. More abusive, or some . . . just didn't care. . . . Whatever you did, as long as you didn't try to run away, that's it. That's the main thing for them. They were responsible. But most of the camps, the same thing. They give so much to eat, and that's it. Just to survive. Nothing else. . . . They killed to the last minute, until the end. . . .
>
> People who did not survive, they started feeling sorry for themselves. Mentally . . . they just collapsed. . . . I realized after the war, you have to be a zombie. . . . If you start to think . . . you are finished. . . . If you didn't think, just keep going.

PL was in Mittenwald, in Bavaria, when he was liberated by the U.S. Third Army. He arrived in the United States in August 1947, became a tailor, and was employed in the garment industry. He married an American woman in 1950. The young couple settled in Brooklyn. As he was preparing to retire, PL and his wife moved to New Jersey in order to live in a suburban community.

PL and his wife have four children, three daughters and one son. All their children are married. The three daughters live in the same community as their parents. PL has seven grandchildren.

ISAK LEVENSTEIN, 1906–1987

[Holocaust testimony (HRC-913, videotape: 1 hour), 14 June 1984; interviewed by Sidney Langer, indexed by Joseph J. Preil. D804.3/.L656 1984]

Sally and Isak Levenstein with daughter, Esther, in Kraków, 1933.

Isak Levenstein [IL] was born on 11 February 1906 in Opole. Both his parents had died of natural causes by the time IL was eleven years old. He then moved to Kraków to live with an uncle. Between the ages of eleven and seventeen, IL was educated in a cheder [study room].

After his years in cheder, IL went to work. He was married when he was twenty-five years old, in 1931. At the time of this interview, he had been married fifty-two years. He was a partner in a factory that manufactured dishes at the time of his marriage. He belonged to two Zionist organizations at the time: Mizrachi and Hechalutz. IL reports that antisemitism was no problem in Kraków until the mid-1930s. He talks about the banning of ritual slaughter of animals and describes the widespread antisemitism in Poland during World War II.

Actually Poland was not so bad. When the war broke out, it started to be bad, because mostly Polish people, you could say 99½ percent, they were working with the Nazis together, to get rid of the Jewish people. Because . . . there are in Poland places which no German stepped in because they were afraid for themselves.

There were villages, there were forests. . . . Maybe there were from the thirty-five million [Poles], maybe there were a few of them . . . would take and save them [Jews]. As a matter of fact, my family and my wife's family . . . my wife's older sister, they had grown-up children . . . in their twenties, and they went to the hideout and gave away all the wealth. They were very wealthy. And a few days later, they [Poles] had everything in their possession . . . and they [Poles] reported them [Jews] to the SS. Otherwise, they would have lived.

This testimony sets the tone for a recurring theme in IL's interview, the antisemitism of the supposedly cultured German people.

Nobody realized, the German people, the most advanced in education in Europe, in those years, . . . nobody realized that the German people . . . could make a Holocaust like that.

Listen, I am not a youngster. . . . I know in Russia there were pogroms. They [Russians] came in, they looted, they killed a few hundred people, but not to wipe out. . . .

Mostly, what they [Germans] wiped out, children, over a million and two hundred thousand children, which they didn't know from any odds and ends, only that they were born from Jewish parents. That's all. Nobody realized that it could happen to a German nation. We were all fooled. . . . Nobody realized that it could happen to a country, the most advanced, educated country.

IL and his family were forced to move into the Kraków ghetto in March 1941. This led to forced labor assignments for which he "was not paid, but . . . was permitted to live." During a comprehensive roundup of Jews in 1943, IL realized the serious nature of the situation. He directed his wife, the children, and her family to hide in a bunker while he was taken to Płaszów, a concentration camp nearby. He studied the situation in Płaszów. Although no children were allowed in Płaszów, he brought his wife and smuggled their children into the camp. The children were among 369 youngsters hidden in Płaszów for a period of fourteen months. IL then recalls his last day in Płaszów with his children.

> There were 369 children. . . . And the big [loudspeaker] on the big field was playing in German . . . "*Mutti, Mutti,*" it means "Mother, Mother, your children go to heaven." . . . This was on Mother's Day, . . . May 14, 1944. . . . This day I will never forget. This was the day when we lost . . . put them on trucks . . . 369 children.
>
> And I'm coming back to you, and I'm saying, the Germans couldn't do it themselves if they wouldn't have any help from the outside. I'm talking from the local authorities. But nobody cared.
>
> It's true that five million Poles got killed. But no children, only men. They revolted. But Jews did not revolt. Children, a year or two, or even six months. They didn't revolt. . . . This is the story.

How was IL able to survive? He qualified at this time to become a metalworker for Oskar Schindler. He went with Schindler's group to the Gross-Rosen concentration camp in Poland and then to Brünnlitz in Czechoslovakia. He has a copy of Schindler's list of 12 May 1944, including his own name as a sheet metal worker. He describes the Oskar Schindler he knew during this period.

IL and his wife were reunited after the war. They decided to come to the United States because IL had an uncle in New York. They arrived in New York with their infant daughter in 1949. He moved to New Jersey in 1954 in order to organize a construction business with two other Schindler survivors—his nephew and the nephew's boyhood friend.

IL became an outstanding community leader in New Jersey and internationally until his death in 1987. His daughter is married and the mother of five. She and her husband continue their families' traditions of community involvement and leadership.

SALLY BANACH LEVENSTEIN, 1909–1991

[Holocaust testimony (HRC-905, videotape: 1 hour, 51 minutes), 21 June 1984; interviewed by Sidney Langer, indexed by Bernard Weinstein. D804.3/.L657 1984]

Sally Banach Levenstein [SL] was born in 1909 in Kazimierza Wielka, not far from Kraków. She was the youngest of nine children. The town was very small. Education was most important in SL's very observant, religious family. She completed gymnasium in 1928, in Kraków, in addition to private Hebrew tutoring. One of her brothers became a rabbi. SL was married in 1931 in Kazimierza Wielka. Thirty of her relatives attended the wedding. Most of these guests perished in the Holocaust. Both her parents died of natural causes before 1939. Of the nine siblings in her family, only SL and two sisters survived.

SL recalls good relations existing between Jews and gentiles in her hometown during the years preceding World War II. A Polish Jew, who had been deported from Germany, told her about the powerful antisemitism then raging in Germany. SL could not believe his stories.

SL and her husband were blessed with two children, a daughter in 1932 and a son in 1937. The family was forced to live in the Kraków ghetto during the war's early years. She was assigned to work in a factory producing stockings for German soldiers. Jews were constantly being deported from the ghetto. When the ghetto was to be completely liquidated and made *judenrein* (free of Jews), SL hid in a bunker with her children and several others.

In the meantime, SL's husband was taken to the Płaszów concentration camp on the outskirts of Kraków. He arranged for the children and SL to be admitted to Płaszów. They then arranged for the children to be hidden for fourteen months in the camp. The pain of losing the children is evident in her voice as SL refers to their last day in camp.

> And this time, they took away all the children, for they made a week before . . . the children to go to a kindergarten home, and all the people who cannot walk. And we were sure that this would stay until the end. . . . But this Sunday, on Mother's Day . . . 1944, all the people, men and women, everyone was outside. . . . We were standing from six o'clock in the morning until seven o'clock in the evening, not to move, twenty-five thousand people.
>
> As a matter of fact, my sister . . . went out, she couldn't take it, she almost fainted. Came an SS man, gave her twenty-five [lashes], and she was swollen and couldn't move for three weeks. . . . And we hear singing and singing, all songs—everything German. . . . Six o'clock, six-thirty, seven o'clock, everybody went out, from home to the bar. I run to the kindergarten. My children went out. Not *my* children, *all* the children went out. . . . This was the end of the concentration camp in Płaszów.

She never saw the children again. SL was then transferred to Auschwitz-Birkenau. She was in Auschwitz three or four months. "It was like years." She participated in a death march to Germany. One thousand to fifteen hundred prisoners were in her group. "We walk day and night, night and day, without food. . . . We walked outside, we saw grass, we took grass in the mouth. Would you believe it? Grass! . . . The whole mind was, Oh, my God, I wish to go to bed today, and tomorrow not to stand up. . . . But it was not God's will. God did not do this to me. I stayed alive." Finally SL and the surviving members of her group arrived at the Bergen-Belsen concentration camp in Germany. She remained there from January 1945 until liberated by the British in April. She remembers the chaos of the war's concluding weeks: "Bergen-Belsen was a death camp. Nobody went to work. Nobody went to the gas chamber. The gas chamber was closed up. Nobody went to showering. Nothing. Just sitting and waiting for death."

After recovering from typhus in a German hospital, SL returned to Poland to look for surviving relatives. Miraculously, she was reunited with her husband in Kraków. She then describes this confrontation.

> We go to our apartment. I knock on the door and put my feet inside.
> "What are you doing here? Why do you want to get in?"
> "This is my apartment. . . . My beds are here; my couch is here."
> "I don't know nothing. You dirty Jew. You go. If not, I'll take a pail of hot water and I put on your face. Go out from here!"
> And I start to cry, and we went out.

SL and her husband left for Austria, for the Bindermichel DP camp. They lived in Austria from 1945 until 1949. Their daughter, Rella, was born in 1948. The family arrived in the United States to join relatives in 1949.

SL's husband began to build homes in New Jersey, where they eventually settled. Their daughter is married, has five children, and is living in New Jersey. The entire family is recognized internationally, as well as in New Jersey, as outstanding community leaders.

HENRY LOWENBRAUN, 1922–

[Holocaust testimony (HRC-1067, videotape: 51 minutes), 16 June 1992; interviewed and indexed by Joseph J. Preil. D804.3/.L917 1992]

Henry Lowenbraun [HL] was born on 1 August 1922 in Łańcut, in southern Poland. There were ten persons in his immediate family in 1939—his parents, four boys, and four girls. Seven perished in the Holocaust; HL, one brother, and one sister survived.

HL experienced the full impact of the Holocaust. After escaping from Łańcut into the woods, he went to the nearby Rzeszów ghetto in the spring of 1942 in order to join his sister there. Although recovering from typhus, HL was selected for forced labor in Rzeszów. His assignments consisted of sweeping streets and assorted tasks at the trains. There was much killing of Jews and a series of *Aktionen* in the ghetto.

After a year, HL was shipped to the Szebnie concentration camp in the spring of 1943. His work in Szebnie was to move manure to the fields. He relates several incidents that demonstrate the brutality of the Szebnie commandant, who was sentenced to death after the war. Several months later, about the fall of 1943, HL was transferred barefoot to Auschwitz-Birkenau. He describes the horrible conditions in Auschwitz. He had to carry stones back and forth every morning. He failed to pick up a stone one morning and was hit with a rifle. He was then taken as a locksmith to work on underground cable in Buna-Monowitz for I.G. Farben Industry.

HL worked in Monowitz until 17 January 1945, when he was assigned to a death march to Gleiwitz, another subcamp of Auschwitz. He was then transferred by cattle car for a twelve-day trip to Czechoslovakia. There was no roof on the train, and it was snowing. The people licked the snow because there was practically no food. His group finally arrived at the Dora-Nordhausen concentration camp in Germany. HL describes the camp in the waning days of the war as "worse than Auschwitz." He caught pneumonia and pleurisy and was in the hospital at the time of liberation. How long did it take to recover? "I'll tell you, I'm not recovered yet."

HL was in the Stuttgart DP camp from 1945 to 1949. He married there in 1946. He came to the United States in 1949 and settled in Brooklyn. He worked for his uncle in a fish market. HL opened his own fish store in Newark in 1955. Although retired, HL continues to live in New Jersey. Of his two surviving siblings, his brother lives in Brooklyn and his sister in Florida. HL has two children, a son and a daughter.

MANYA REICH MANDELBAUM, 1919–

[Holocaust testimony (HRC-1061, videotape: 1 hour, 43 minutes), 19 April 1990; interviewed by Bernard Weinstein, indexed by Joseph J. Preil. D804.3/.M271 1990]

Manya Reich Mandelbaum [MM] was born on 16 August 1919 in Dębica, a small town near Kraków. Her mother was one of nine children, all of whom perished in the Holocaust. MM is the fifth of six children; she is the lone survivor. MM's father sold bakers' needs—everything but flour. She remembers a happy prewar life in a very observant Orthodox family.

> We were an Orthodox family. All the Jewish holidays were strictly observed. And I grew up with that. All my life, I was religious. Even in concentration camp, I was eat-

ing kosher. Oh, I didn't eat any tref food. It was very hard, very hard. But, thank God, I survived, and I'm proud of it.

MM's family lived in Kraków during the years before World War II. She reports a good relationship between the Poles and Jews in Kraków. The difficulty was outside Kraków, with the peasants. Antisemitism throughout Poland increased in the late 1930s. Her husband, Simon, studied engineering in Haifa, Israel, because he was refused admission to Polish universities by the numerus clausus decrees against Jewish enrollment. They were married in 1940.

MM and her husband were interned in the Kraków ghetto from March 1941 until March 1943. Both were assigned to forced labor. MM worked in the Mardarich factory, making shirts for the Wehrmacht. Her husband helped build the barracks for the Płaszów concentration camp.

In August 1944, many of the victims imprisoned in Płaszów were deported to Mauthausen and others to Auschwitz. MM was in Auschwitz for nine days during November 1944. She describes the horror of Auschwitz in personal incidents. Her brother, for example, was killed because he could not join the death march in January 1945, two days after his appendectomy.

MM was in a group of three hundred women who were taken to Hamburg, Germany, and assigned to a plastics factory. The day started at 6 A.M. by marching in groups of one hundred. A German guard struck MM with a rubber truncheon because her group of five women was suspected of talking during the march. During her work in the plastics factory, MM managed to create "candles" for the Friday evening lighting ceremony, a forbidden activity.

MM tells of another religious observance.

I have to tell you one incident [that] happened. It was Pesach [Passover], you know. And as I told you, I didn't eat the soups, I ate only marmalade and bread and margarine. So, during Pesach they gave bread. So, my aunt, what we were together, she worked in the kitchen. Because there are people who worked someplace else, not only in the factory, but whatever they wanted to give them. So, my aunt was working in the kitchen, and every day she brought me potatoes . . . and all eight days, I ate potatoes with the skin. And nothing more. Only water and the potatoes, and I survived. I am proud of that. All during the war, I didn't eat *tref.*

Another incident related during MM's testimony occurred during the cattle car trip from Płaszów to Auschwitz at the end of 1944. When the train stopped:

I asked a peasant woman, "Can you give me a little water?"
So, she smiled, just like in this movie . . . Lanzmann was making, *Shoah.* . . . So she looked at me and she said, "You know where you are going? You don't need a jacket on you. Give me the jacket. I bring you a glass of water."

"Never in your life will you get the jacket!" And I didn't give it.

MM's group was liberated by the Americans in April 1945. She searched for her husband and found him in a hospital in Wels, Austria. She nursed him back to health over a period of several months.

The young couple arrived in the United States in November 1949. MM's husband was able to join Abraham Zuckerman in the construction and real estate business. MM's family lived in Brooklyn for sixteen years. They moved to New Jersey, twenty-six years before this interview, for business, social, and religious reasons. MM has three sons, all university-trained professionals, and grandchildren.

Nine-year-old Jerry Miron in 1945, immediately after the war. Stanislaw and Anna Wrobel, the Polish couple who saved Jerry Miron.

JERRY MIRON, 1936–

[Holocaust testimony (HRC-2007, videotape: 1 hour, 35 minutes), 21 April 1994; interviewed and indexed by Bernard Weinstein. D804.3/.M774 1994]

Jerry Miron [JM] was born in Warsaw on 5 April 1936, the younger of the two children in his family. His father was a chemical engineer. The rising antisemitism in Poland compelled the father to leave his profession and enter the leather business. JM's immediate family survived the Holocaust years in Poland by hiding with Poles.

JM, who was only a youngster, was saved by a family named Wrobel who lived in Dobrowa, a village near Warsaw. JM was visited by his father only once, in June 1943. The father was discovered by Germans and murdered immediately. JM's sister lived with nuns, and his mother moved into the home of one of her sisters who had married a Pole.

Young JM was treated with loving care by the Wrobel family—like one of their own. Mrs. Wrobel had him baptized as a Catholic and, JM reports, he was a "devout Catholic" by the age of nine.

After the war, his mother moved to Lublin with JM, together with his sister and their nanny. JM and his mother remained in Lublin until 1957, when they moved to Israel. By 1957, the sister had married and she remained in Poland with her husband. In 1962, after her divorce, the sister also came to Israel. JM married in Israel and emigrated to the United States in 1964. He earned his doctorate at Brooklyn Polytechnic Institute in 1969 and settled in New Jersey to be near his work. JM is now a chemical consultant, specializing in plastics. He has a son and a daughter; both have college educations.

At the conclusion of his testimony, JM states that he might have become a totally assimilated Pole were it not for the Holocaust. His Jewish identity was confirmed, he says, once he was in Israel.

PAUL MONKA, 1920–

[Holocaust testimony (HRC-1039, videotape: 3 hours, 20 minutes), 17 May and 7 June 1989; interviewed and indexed by Bernard Weinstein. D804.3/.M885 1989]

Paul Monka [PM] was born in Będzin on 23 September 1920. Będzin is in the Katowice district, a relatively large city with a prewar Jewish population of twenty-seven thousand.

In a long, comprehensive, and detailed testimony, PM provides a thorough description of the Holocaust throughout the war, including the confiscation of Jewish businesses by the Germans (such as the textile business of PM's father), the burning of the synagogue, wanton murders, and the hopeless roles of the *Judenrat* and the Jewish police.

PM describes his arrest and beatings by the Gestapo, followed by solitary confinement in prison. He survived this experience miraculously. He decided at this time to join Armia Ludowa, an underground group that accepted Jews. His assignment was to recruit new members. He brought several family members into the organization. His father died in the woods after moving in with PM.

Będzin was being decimated at this time, especially by deportations to nearby Auschwitz. PM's group had to keep moving eastward to avoid capture by the Germans. His group was finally liberated by the Russians near the city of Lublin. PM was appointed to highly responsible positions by the Russians. He met a Russian general named Zavatsky, whose wife was from Będzin. PM was given a position in the security office. He returned to Będzin and found his family in Dąbrowa Górnicza, and they were doing well. He could not recognize Będzin, however. The streets were empty. He found only one family of Jews, who had survived in Będzin by being hidden by Poles. Some Poles were happy to see PM; others said, "Do you still live?" When he checked at city hall to learn what happened to the synagogue, he discovered it had been destroyed by Polish conspirators of German descent.

PM describes what he saw and discovered in Auschwitz after liberation.

When Auschwitz was liberated, I saw with my own eyes what a destruction machine was built in order to destroy the Jewish people. My heart was bleeding; I was crying. My eyes were red all day from seeing the bones and ashes and the broken-up crematoria, because they bombed and dynamited them. And the burnt cabins where the people lived. You had a pretty good picture.

I saw people who wandered around without knowing what happened to them. Some Jews survived Auschwitz all the way until January 23 [1945]. And you saw some of the people who looked like half-people . . . skeletons, walking, with their eyes bulged out. The whole form of a person, you couldn't even look at them. . . . I didn't even meet anybody, I didn't see anybody, of my friends.

I, at that time, understood that a march took place. And some of them, who came back later, a week or two or three weeks later, told us that it was a death march. That 80 percent or 90 percent of the people in Auschwitz were taken out, at the last moment, before the Russian troops came in, and they were walking miles, hundreds of miles, towards Germany. And in the march, many of them were shot, or just dropped dead, because it was winter. Poland has a severe winter, and that winter was a very severe winter, '45.

PM was appointed security chief of Silesia. He was responsible for bringing conspirators to trial, which he did effectively in accordance with strict Russian orders. He also succeeded in providing a decent burial for his father. He was then instrumental in General Zavatsky's appointment as governor of Silesia.

After PM had been injured in a collision with a truck, he decided that he wished to devote more time to his family. He traveled throughout Europe on special assignments and, although only twenty-four years old, gave serious thought to entering the Polish foreign service.

The death of PM's sister in Italy in 1946 changed his life. He and his family decided to leave Poland and the Communist government. Their first choice was Palestine, but this was impossible at the time. The family decided to emigrate to the United States. PM arrived on 21 November 1949. He became the owner of a factory for radar parts. He married a fellow survivor. They have three children.

MURRAY PANTIRER, 1925–

[Holocaust testimony (HRC-2023, videotape: 1 hour, 43 minutes), 23 April 1990; interviewed at United States Holocaust Memorial Museum, indexed by Joseph J. Preil]

Murray and Louise Pantirer, shortly after their wedding in the Linz DP camp, Austria, 1946.

The founding president of the Holocaust Resource Foundation for the Holocaust Resource Center at Kean College, Murray Pantirer [MP] was born on 15 June 1925 in Kraków. He was one of seven children. Of the nine members in his immediate family, MP is the lone Holocaust survivor.

MP's family was poor, as were the Jews generally in Kraków, but he remembers a happy childhood. He tells of the Holocaust details in Kraków: German soldiers pulling out older Jews from synagogues on Rosh Hashanah 1939 and ripping out their beards, the confiscation of valuables, the decree to wear armbands with the Star of David. MP's family joined relatives in Ozarow, near Lublin, in March 1940 and also moved elsewhere. All family members returned to Kraków after the outbreak of the Russian-German war in June 1941.

MP provides a wonderful tribute to his mother.

And we were all nine again together, from 1941, by October. And it was the happiest days of our life. In one room, nothing to eat. . . . I could see, when my mother was cooking some food, and she would say she's not hungry, and she was hungry. But she wouldn't allow herself to have a little food, because she wouldn't take away from her children.

Płaszów was built as a concentration camp on the site of a Jewish cemetery in the Kraków area under Commandant Amon Goeth. MP tells how various members of his family perished and of brutal, senseless murders that he observed. He also recalls Commandant Goeth's inhuman cruelty as head of Płaszów: "And one occasion, I will never forget that the women were coming out and one woman had, in her knapsack, a little baby. The little baby was crying, and the German heard the baby cry. He killed the baby and the mother on the spot."

MP describes how a younger brother perished:

I heard about my younger brother, that he is in Kraków, working at the Visla [River], by those ships, and he is sustaining himself. Till 1944, he was in Kraków, until October/November. In October or November, when the Visla froze up, they had no work for him on the ships. He had no money, and he went to sleep up on the hills where they kept the hay . . . hay for the cows, on the outskirts of Poland.

A Polish peasant caught him, and he said, "If you're sleeping in the winter in that snow outside, you must be Jewish." He [the brother] knew the Catholic prayers better than any Catholic. He said the prayers, but nothing helped him.

He [the peasant] received an award for that—twelve pounds, that's five kilo, sugar. Every time you gave out a Jew in Poland, you have a reward of five kilo sugar.

I know it for a fact because after the war I came to Kraków, and people told me that. I asked him to testify. He said there's no use testifying, the man ran away. I am sure he did not run away, but . . . I couldn't bring him to any justice.

MP was then transferred to the Emalia enamel factory operated by Oskar Schindler. He marvels at Schindler's efforts for his Jews. As the war in Poland was winding down in October 1944 and the Germans were retreating, MP was transferred to the Gross-Rosen concentration camp in Poland. He describes the terrible conditions in Gross-Rosen. Schindler came to Gross-Rosen with a list of essential workers, and MP was on the list, miraculously, to join Schindler. MP joined those on Schindler's list going to Brünnlitz, Czechoslovakia. He describes instances of benevolence by Oskar and Emily Schindler. As for MP's reaction to liberation, he states simply: "I walked out of this camp [Brünnlitz], a healthy boy."

MP then searched in vain for family survivors. He returned to Kraków and registered there with the Jewish community. He was a displaced person hoping to emigrate to Palestine. In this effort, he went to Prague, then to Linz in Austria and, finally, to Italy. Because of British opposition, he gave up the Palestine plan. He returned to Austria, where he met his wife-to-be. They married and emigrated to the United States in 1948. Their three children were all born in the United States. In 1950, MP decided to build homes in New Jersey. MP and his wife, all their children, and their grandchildren live in New Jersey. MP is a strong advocate of Holocaust education. Together with his family and friends, he has played a leading role in this endeavor in New Jersey, as well as nationally and in Israel.

HELEN FAIGENBAUM RAFF, 1921–

[Holocaust testimony (HRC-2004, videotape: 1 hour, 6 minutes), 31 March 1994; interviewed and indexed by Bernard Weinstein. D804.3/.R129 1994]

Helen Faigenbaum Raff [HR] was born on 8 June 1921 in Jędrzejów, between Warsaw and Kraków. Her immediate family consisted of eight persons in 1939: her parents, their five daughters, and one son. Only HR and her brother survived. She estimates that about two hundred relatives were murdered in Treblinka. HR is aware of no family survivors other than herself and her brother.

The Holocaust arrived in Jędrzejów during the very first days of the war.

The minute the [German] army came into the square of the town, they right away picked out three for sure, probably more, prominent Jews, and they simply, in view of everybody, with no specific reason, they shot each and every one of them. This gave us a feeling: Obey me, because you can be next. And this was something that's unbelievable.

From the same moment after this happened, it looks like my father was in the square, and then he ran home, we were probably a block and a half from the square. And coming in, he kept on looking back if the army comes into our street. And they did. He got so scared, that he fell, and had a heart attack. He survived. He survived it.

But it looks like the soldiers or the SS . . . they probably noticed him, too, because they came into our square, where we were living, and took out a religious Jew. And he was with a tallis, praying, and tefillin. He took him out to the middle of the square, where we were living, and cut his beard. And when he objected, he was beaten.

It was repeated in a lot of places, assembling Jews with beards, and cutting their beards, their *payas* [sidecurls]. . . . It was a trying thing for young people to see something like that. That one human can do this to another, with no reason.

Toward the end of her testimony, HR describes an incident that demonstrates how speedily evil can spread.

When the Germans came in, and when we ran away, so we stayed in a small town a few days, in a synagogue, in a bombed-out synagogue, not only ourselves, but filled to capacity. My brother and my father wanted to run away farther, because they said what they do is hunt men. My mother and all the girls stayed in that synagogue. So we stayed for a few days, maybe, the most, a week.

And then my mother said (I cannot even say, "Rest in peace," because she doesn't have a place where she is), "Let's, kids, let's take everything together, and we have to go home. We have to go home, whatever. OK? And let's hope Father and my son are somewhere safe, too."

So we started walking home, just walking. We didn't have any money to pay for transportation . . . because my father ran away. We came back, it took us a day and a half.

When we finally came home, on the outskirts of the city, it was still light, daylight. We were afraid the Germans shouldn't see us. Finally, when it started to get a little bit darker, we came home. We walked into the house, and we lit our kerosene lamp, it shouldn't be too bright, and we went to sleep. All of them in just two beds.

Not even ten minutes later, came a knock on the door. An SS man by the door. And he came in. Now, who sent him? Only the Polacks came. There were no Jews home. They said that somebody came.

HR and several friends decided to run away from the Germans in December 1939. They boarded the train as Poles, not as Jews. SS men on the train ordered them to leave the train in Lzhansk and to begin forced labor. They ran away again, finally reaching Lwów [Lemberg] in the Russian Zone.

The Russian organization of Lwów was so inflexible that people were forced to register to go to Russia to obtain food. HR's group registered and the next day were in cattle cars on the way to the Ural Mountains. In order to obtain four grams of bread and soup daily, she had to move heavy rocks in the process of laying track. She hurt her back. The Russian manager then agreed to assign HR to work on machinery.

HR was married in Russia and bore her first daughter in June 1941. After the German invasion, HR's group was transferred to Siberia. They passed through Tashkent and settled in Bukhara for the duration of the war. She had no knowledge of events in Poland until she returned there after the war. She went then to the Ziegenhain DP camp in Germany. At long last, she met her lone surviving family member, her brother, in Ziegenhain. They went to Landsberg and remained there until 1949, when they were able to leave for the United States. HR's younger daughter was born in Germany.

HR's family settled in Newark with her brother's family. She is now a widow and continues to live in New Jersey. Her daughters are married and both of them have professional positions. HR had three grandchildren at the time of this testimony.

MAURICE RAUCHWELD, 1935–

[Holocaust testimony (HRC-2002, videotape: 1 hour, 38 minutes), 10 March 1994; interviewed and indexed by Joseph J. Preil. D804.3/.R193 1994]

Maurice Rauchweld [MR] was born on 4 May 1935 in Łódź. The family consisted of four, a younger brother having been born in 1941, and all four survived the Holocaust. The extended family, through first cousins, consisted of twenty-three persons, of whom fifteen perished in the Holocaust.

MR recalls that his family lived in relatively comfortable circumstances by Polish standards of the 1930s. They remained in the Łódź ghetto from its inception at the beginning of the war until liberation by the Russians in January 1945. He remembers the ghetto as a state within the state. He describes Chaim Rumkowski as "president of the ghetto." During the war, he never heard anything good about Rumkowski, a "president" who was viewed as a collaborator and who was much disliked by the Jewish population.

When asked what he remembered about life inside the ghetto during the war, MR responded:

> Life, that most always remember it, is hunger. Not only my own hunger, but I have also seen a lot of hungry people. Staying in front of the kitchens. There were soup kitchens, where you could get a soup for a ticket. There were rationings. And there

were people who got no tickets. So they're waiting outside, waiting if somebody will trip and spill some of the soup when he comes out of the kitchen, and they would eat it from the floor. Those are things which I always remember. I remember, myself, I would not be able to fall asleep, because from hunger pains. Those are the most vivid.

Łódź was the last ghetto in Poland to be liquidated. MR believes Hans Biebow, the German commandant, arranged this because ghetto production meant "money in the pocket" of Biebow. MR also heard this from other ghetto survivors. Although he was only seven years old in 1942, MR had a factory job as a general messenger working daily from 8 A.M. until 4 or 5 P.M. His papers were written to make him nine years old.

MR recalls the liquidation of significant groups in the ghetto—the physically strong, the intelligentsia, children, and old people. He describes the decimation of the Jewish population of Łódź:

> After 1942, I started working. But then, there were not many children. I lose all my friends, which I used to play, nobody stays. The building where we lived, it was a big building. There were two courtyards, and nobody stayed for me to play with.
>
> INTERVIEWER: Did everybody understand what happened to the children?
>
> MR: Yes, everybody knew they went with the *Shpera,* with the *Aktion*s. And nothing happened. I see the parents of those children. . . . It was something. . . . Everyone was numb. I saw the parents, they didn't cry anymore. . . . No tears. All my friends. The girl next door to me, she was so smart. . . . Everybody went.
>
> INTERVIEWER: What does *Shpera* mean?
>
> MR: I really don't know what it means. It was a German kind of slang. . . . What it means, I don't know. The *Aktion* was called *Shpera.*

MR was miraculously saved from this deportation *Aktion.* His mother was able to smuggle his younger brother out of the ghetto for a short time. MR's mother refused to believe they could survive relocation in 1944 when those of the Jewish population still alive in the ghetto were promised work elsewhere. In reality, those who agreed to leave were deported to Auschwitz. His mother understood it was inconceivable that MR's brother would be allowed to live outside Łódź.

Thus this family of four, together with another four relatives, hid secretly in Łódź cellars for four months, July through November 1944, "four months of pure torture." When the Russians liberated Łódź, MR's family was among the eight hundred Jews who survived, out of a probable total of one hundred sixty thousand Jews who lived at some time during the war in the Łódź ghetto.

After the war, MR's father and a partner opened a business in Łódź. The two boys joined family members in Paris in 1960. Their parents followed in 1965, and they arrived in the United States in 1966, settling in New Jersey to be near the stepsister of MR's mother. MR is an accountant, is married, and still lives in New Jersey. He has one son who is a consultant in emergency medical services in Idaho.

Toward the conclusion of his testimony, MR talked about the difficulty of communicating with Americans about Holocaust events.

MR: In the United States, I talk about the Holocaust only with my immediate family—my brother, my sister-in-law. . . . Not outside because, really, nobody wants to listen.

INTERVIEWER: Today also?

MR: That's right. I remember one thing which hit me right away when I came to the United States. We were living in Newark . . . and the landlord was a nice lady, Jewish, and she asked me about the Holocaust. So I started to tell her about how we lived and how we *suffered.*

She said, "Yeah, yeah. I remember the war. The war was terrible. We here in America, we got it very bad too. The only thing we could eat, was only chicken."

From then on, I said, "OK. They don't understand. . . . I will not talk with them." The only thing she remembered that she got to eat, there was no beef, no anything, there was only chicken. That is her memories from the war. . . . I noticed a lot of American-born, Jews and non-Jews, they ask you a question, but don't want to hear the story. . . . I don't know why, but they don't want to hear too much about it.

RABBI JACK RING, 1916–

[Holocaust testimony (HRC-1074, videotape: 1 hour, 44 minutes), 19 November 1992; interviewed and indexed by Joseph J. Preil. D804.3/.R581 1992]

Rabbi Jack Ring [JR] was born on 14 September 1916 in Pułtusk, a town near Warsaw. The Ring family in prewar Poland consisted of sixteen members: JR's mother, her five children, the spouses of the four married children, and six grandchildren. Three of the sixteen survived the Holocaust: JR, his oldest sister-in-law, and her oldest son. JR lives in the United States; the other two survivors are in Israel. Thirteen family members perished in the Holocaust.

Shortly after the outbreak of World War II, JR, his mother, and sister fled to the Russian zone, first to Czyzew, then to Białystok. JR then decided to go to Vilna, an independent city in Lithuania that would be safer for a young Talmudic scholar than any place in the atheistic Russian zone. His mother and sister accompanied him to Vilna, where JR rejoined the 350 student-scholars of the internationally renowned Yeshiva of Mir. The yeshiva had moved from Mir in Poland to Vilna, in order to flee from the Communists. Subsequently, JR's mother, sister, and sister's fiancé returned to Białystok, while JR remained with his yeshiva in Vilna.

The Russians then occupied the three Baltic states, including Lithuania. All Mir yeshiva students received permission to leave Russia for Japan when Sempo Sugihara, the Japanese consul in Kovno, Lithuania, defied Japanese government instructions and signed many transit visas in a determined effort to save Jewish lives.

The Mir Yeshiva traveled fourteen thousand miles by train to Vladivostok, then continued their journey by ship to Tsuruga, Japan. They finally arrived in Kōbe in February 1941. All expenses were covered by two historic personalities working indefatigably in New York: Rabbi Abraham Kalmanowitz and Rabbi Aharon Kotler of the Vaad Hatzala, a highly effective rescue organization.

In September 1941, when Japan was preparing the Pearl Harbor attack, the yeshiva was directed to move from Kōbe to Shanghai. The yeshiva remained in Shanghai until 29 August 1946, a total of five years. One student-scholar assumed the responsibility for serving three meals daily to the hundreds of students. Another, Rabbi Leib Blumberg, a postwar resident of New Jersey for many years, was involved in publishing the scholarly texts required by the students.

After the war, practically the entire yeshiva came to the United States on student visas with their inspiring leaders Rabbi Yechezkel Levenstein and Rabbi Chaim Shmuelevitz. These two charismatic personalities then settled in Israel, where they continued to inspire generations of scholars. JR settled in the New York area and took an American bride. He became the manager of a factory in New Jersey. He continues to live in New Jersey where he had been employed until his retirement. He has four daughters, all married, and ten grandchildren.

As he was about to conclude his testimony, JR stated:

> I used to say, I felt that in the course of those years, I felt like somebody took my hand, and guided me how to go, and finally to be saved. Because . . . many times, not anything was my own choosing. It was just something led me from a higher power, led me and saved me.

ARON ROSENBLUM, 1915–

[Holocaust testimony (HRC-1049, videotape: 1 hour, 35 minutes), 12 September 1989; interviewed by Bernard Weinstein and Daniel Gover, indexed by Bernard Weinstein. D804.3/.R807 1989]

Aron Rosenblum [AR] was born in Wieluń on 2 June 1915. His family lived in Pabianice when the war started in 1939. His father died when AR was three years old. His immediate family at the beginning of hostilities consisted of his mother and her six sons. Only AR and his youngest brother survived the Holocaust.

The Jewish population of Pabianice had been liquidated by 1941. AR testifies that Poles helped Germans to identify Jews for deportation. He went to the Łódź ghetto and signed up for work in Dąbrowa, a small town between Łódź and Pabian-ice. He describes the thoroughness of the German effort to plunder Jewish valuables and the difficulty of life for the Jews on starvation diets.

AR and one younger brother were in the Łódź ghetto until its liquidation in August 1944. He tells of being transported by cattle car to Auschwitz and especially of the beginning of his experience there. He says that he "felt dead emotionally but still wanted to eat." He worked in a Krupp brick factory, which meant walking thirty minutes each day from Birkenau to the factory in Buna. "At a minimum, you had to carry thirty bricks at a time, or you were beaten."

The prisoners had no water. AR washed his face with ersatz coffee. He became ill with typhus. Because he was handy, he was able to work at a variety of jobs. A German foreman, who had been a criminal, appreciated AR's ability and provided him with work assignments until AR's group was evacuated from Auschwitz on 14 January 1945. AR started on a death march with ten thousand prisoners. Their destination was Buchenwald, but there was no more work at Buchenwald, so they were moved from there to Dachau, a trip that lasted twenty-three days during the chaos of the war's end. He reports that some victims were so desperate for food they had to resort to cannibalism. He drank contaminated water in Dachau and became desperately ill.

AR knows that two of his brothers perished in Treblinka. His mother was taken to Chełmno and gassed in a van. Many died from the same illness infecting AR as the war was ending. What helped him survive? He "refused to die." He weighed only eighty pounds, with a swollen stomach and swollen legs. An American interviewed him and took him to Linz, Austria, for rehabilitation. He met two women in Linz, sisters from Łódź, one of whom he eventually married.

After recovering somewhat in Linz, AR returned to Łódź with his future wife to check on family and friends who may have survived. He discovered that his youngest brother was in Breslau. When the brothers were united, they all went to Landsberg, near Munich, where AR developed liver problems. This required five weeks of treatment in a spa. After recovery, he returned to Landsberg, took over a store, married in 1946, and a daughter was born in 1947.

Finally, in 1952, AR and his growing family were able to enter the United States. He became a chicken farmer and eventually bought a farm in New Jersey. His son was born in 1954. Both his children are married, and he has five grandchildren. AR concludes by stating that he continues to observe his faith, although he "wonders about God."

CELINA SPIRA ROSENBLUM, 1929–

[Holocaust testimony (HRC-1095, videotape: 1 hour, 30 minutes), 16 December 1993; interviewed and indexed by Joseph J. Preil. D804.3/.R809 1993 (in cooperation with the Holocaust Resource Center of Greater Clifton-Passaic)]

Celina Spira Rosenblum [CR] was born on 23 December 1929 in Kraków. Her immediate family in 1939 consisted of four people: her parents, a younger brother, and CR. Only mother and daughter survived the Holocaust. Her extended family, through first cousins, consisted of twenty-four members, of whom only five survived.

CR's family lived comfortably before the war. In fact, Hans Frank, the Nazi governor-general of Poland from 1939 until 1945, took the Spira home for his residence when he arrived in Kraków. CR's family heard the sounds of German shooting on the first day of the war. Her father decided that the family should escape to Russia, but when they reached Lwów, her parents decided to return to Kraków. This was typical of Polish Jews' desperate movements and the confusion following the German invasion.

The family moved into CR's grandmother's home in Kraków because Frank had already occupied their apartment. When the Kraków ghetto was being organized, they moved to Wieliczka to avoid ghetto existence. By mid-1942, no Jews were permitted in the small towns, and the family had to return to Kraków and move into the ghetto.

Daily living in Wieliczka was "primitive, difficult, sad . . . a boring existence, constantly nerve-wracking." Life in Kraków was "quite horrible," with hunger as their constant companion.

CR tells the following story, an incident that we dare not judge.

> We were very hungry in the ghetto, because we had no money, there was nothing there. And there was a bakery.
>
> It's a terrible thing to say about your mother, what she did. She took us both into the bakery. And it was so crowded. She took a cookie for all of us. Not a cookie. It was like a little bit bigger, a muffin or something, And we ate it and we walked out.
>
> She never paid. She didn't have money. And she knew that she can do it, because it was so crowded, and nobody would even notice. You see, what a mother can do for a child. She did not take it. She did not eat it. I remember that. She gave it to me, and she gave it to my brother. And then we walked out.
>
> INTERVIEWER: But you knew what was going on?
>
> CR: Oh, yes. I knew. My brother didn't. My mother told me, "You know, I would never do such a thing. But I know how hungry you are. I had to do something to help my children." I personally would do exactly the same thing for my children, if I would be in that situation.

INTERVIEWER: You never know until you're there.

CR: That's right. . . . If you are starved, and you see your children are starving, then you will do anything to help those children.

CR's mother was hospitalized with pneumonia in Kraków and at the same time her father was taken to Stalowa Wola, a nearby labor camp, where he perished. Miraculously, thirteen-year-old CR broke into a steel locker one evening and dressed her mother to remove her from the hospital. CR took her home several hours before all of the Jewish patients were murdered. This incident, among others, explains CR's statements: "I never was a child. I was a child until nine years old," and "surviving is an extended series of miracles."

CR's mother had to make a terrible decision at this time—whether to accompany CR into the Płaszów concentration camp or to remain in the Kraków ghetto with her young son. She went to Płaszów and into the hospital. Eventually, a friend brought the son to the camp.

CR decided at this time to leave the Płaszów *Kinderheim,* the special area for children. She decided to act and be treated as an adult, including forced labor assignments. Several days later, all the camp children, including her brother and cousin, were removed from the camp and murdered.

In July 1944, CR and her mother were transported by cattle car from Płaszów to Auschwitz. CR tells of the reactions of mother and daughter to the selection process in Auschwitz.

I had to fight with my mother all the time. Because I always pushed her first. I wanted to know where she was selected to go, so I would follow. And she always screams at me, "No, you don't follow me. You go where there's life, because I'm a little bit older." She was thirty-some years old. And she says, "But you have to survive."

I said, "No, I don't want to survive without you, because there is nobody else left."

Every time we went through a selection, there was this discussion. Constantly, constantly. She said, "No, you have to survive. Somebody will show up after the war. I don't want you to be the last."

I said, "No, I don't want to survive, because I want to be with you." And this was constantly going on.

Several months later, in November 1944, mother and daughter were again transferred by cattle car, this time from Auschwitz to Kratzau, Czechoslovakia, to work in a munitions factory. CR managed to have her work shift in Kratzau changed in order to work with her mother. She also managed to obtain warm coats for her group of eight workers. This is amazing in view of the fact that CR was only fifteen years old at the time.

Upon liberation on 8 May 1945, the Germans suddenly disappeared. CR and a fellow survivor left the barracks and entered an empty home. Obviously, some wealthy Germans had run away and left many costly belongings. What did the two survivors take? "Some cookies!"

Mother and daughter returned to Kraków hoping to meet family members. They remained several months and endured a pogrom by the Poles. After a year in Poland, they went to Linz, Austria, and remained there from 1946 until 1948.

CR married a survivor. Mother, daughter, and new husband arrived in the United States on 19 November 1948, ready to build a new life. CR and her family lived in Cleveland, Vineland, and Canada, and then settled in New Jersey. Mr. R. has been active in real estate construction. They have three children, all married, and six grandchildren. The older son has joined his father as a partner, the younger son is a heart surgeon in Florida, and the daughter is a teacher in New Jersey.

IDEK ROSENBLUM, 1922–

[Holocaust testimony (HRC-1097, videotape: 1 hour), 22 December 1993; interviewed and indexed by Joseph J. Preil. D804.3/.R815 1993 (in cooperation with the Holocaust Resource Center of Greater Clifton-Passaic)]

Idek Rosenblum [IR] was born on 23 July 1922 in Proszowice, a small town near Kraków. His immediate family consisted of seven members: his parents, IR, and four sisters. Only IR and two sisters survived the Holocaust. His extended family, through first cousins, consisted of thirty-five to forty, of whom twelve survived. This was a rather high proportion of survivors for Poland. When asked if he could explain this, IR said simply, "We were healthy . . . and lucky."

In Proszowice, IR was assigned to forced labor, from the spring of 1940 until the spring of 1941. He was then transferred to Kraków, lived in a labor camp (Płaszów Julag), and was assigned to the gas works. Later, he was part of the labor group that constructed the Płaszów concentration camp on the grounds of a destroyed Jewish cemetery in Kraków.

Over twenty thousand prisoners were kept in Płaszów under the infamous commandant, Amon Goeth. IR worked as a plumber in Płaszów until 1944. He describes some of the difficult conditions in the camp. Basically, it was a forced labor camp with much killing, particularly by Goeth. The mood of the prisoners was horrible. The mood of the young people was, "We must survive." In describing Płaszów, IR says, "It was like a big graveyard."

In March 1944, IR volunteered to be transferred to another location in need of plumbers. He was moved to Auschwitz, where his group was treated well because their skills were needed. He remained in Auschwitz from March 1944 until January 1945. He was then part of the death march from Auschwitz to Mauthausen, Austria. He was "lucky" to be among the 25 percent to survive the death march. The

WESTERN POLAND   ■   103

conditions in Mauthausen, the work, and the food were all horrible. People died of typhus.

> The last few months were the most horrible . . . every hour, every hour. I was lucky that I wasn't sick. Because I saw my friends, they got sick, they couldn't walk, they lay down. Those *Kapos*, they saw them lying down, they took a club, and they just killed them. These were facts.
>
> INTERVIEWER: Why did they do that?
>
> IR: Why? Because they were killers, they were killers, those Kapos.
>
> INTERVIEWER: They were supposed to do it or they just wanted to do it?
>
> IR: They wanted to do it. It was a hobby for them. I saw they took a boy out, once, at night, from the bed . . . and they had a barrel of water, and they took his head and put him inside the water, until the night.
>
> INTERVIEWER: No reason?
>
> IR: No reason. Toys. This was going on until April 1945.

IR was taken to Gusen II, where he was liberated by the Americans on 5 May 1945. He then walked with some others to Linz, Austria. In 1948, he married in Austria and emigrated with his wife to the United States. Their first residence was in Cleveland. After several moves, they settled finally in New Jersey as IR developed his real estate construction business. IR and his wife have three children, all married, and six grandchildren. One son is IR's partner in construction, one son is a heart surgeon in Florida, and his daughter is a teacher in New Jersey. At the conclusion of the interview, IR states that he has remained religiously committed and observant, both for himself and for his children. His last statement is that he is very appreciative of his opportunities in the United States.

LILLIAN KRONENBERG ROSS, 1922–

[Holocaust testimony (HRC-981, videotape: 2 hours, 26 minutes), 9 December 1987; interviewed by Bernard Weinstein and Melissa Silverman, indexed by Joseph J. Preil. D804.3/.R817 1987]

Lillian Ross in Stuttgart, 1947.

Lillian Kronenberg Ross [LR] was born in Łódź on 9 August 1922. She was the second of four daughters in a prosperous family. Her maternal grandfather, Rabbi Zvi Perlmutter, was "chief rabbi of Poland" and the first Jewish member of the Seim, the Polish parliament. After the outbreak of the war, the SS ordered her family to move from their homes together with many other prominent Jews. The valuables of these families were confiscated, and the people were packed into a train for a two-day trip to Dębica. Thus the SS aimed to expel the intelligentsia from Łódź.

LR's father took the family to Radom, where he obtained work to support them. In March 1941, the Germans established the Radom ghetto for the community's approximately thirty-five thousand Jews. More than 90 percent of the ghetto's Jews were then transferred by train to Destination Unknown, evidently Treblinka. A man who escaped from the train returned to Radom and reported that he heard from a Treblinka worker the projected fate of the people being deported. Nobody believed the man, and he was ostracized. LR's mother was deported at this time, never to be seen again.

Both LR and her older sister were married in the Radom ghetto in April 1942. She explains the significance of marriage to young couples during the Holocaust.

> My older sister . . . had married. [They went] to Skarżysko. People were married in the ghetto because you had to have somebody. The few people who remained, who had absolutely nobody, they tried to attach themselves to somebody. A friend of mine attached herself to a very old man. You just had to have some solace, someone to think about.
>
> One thing that I have to say about staying alive was, because I was always with, at least, one of my sisters, I have somebody to remind me that I was once a human being, somebody to remind me that there could still be hope. But the people that had nobody, either they adopted somebody, they were just like a family, or if they didn't have the ability to do so, they perished.

They lost the will to live, because there was nothing to live for. But as long as you have a link with humanity, with one other person, you still strive to survive. And that's what happened to me and, I imagine, to anybody else who tried to survive, because you couldn't be alone. Such a terrible, hopeless situation . . . that if you didn't have the warmth of a hand of somebody else, you just couldn't make it.

The final liquidation of the Radom ghetto occurred in November 1943. LR was among the last Jews in the ghetto when she was moved to Szkolna to work in a munitions factory. The treatment there was atrocious. In March 1944, LR was transferred again, this time to Majdanek, and then in April LR's group was moved to Płaszów to avoid the approaching Russians. In July, LR was taken to Wieliczka, together with her father and a younger sister, to work in the salt mines. One month later, in August, the two sisters were returned to Płaszów.

The next move for all four sisters was to Auschwitz-Birkenau. LR had typhus and a boil on her back. Her older sister developed a heart condition. In Auschwitz, LR was forced by the Germans to witness the public hanging of two Jewish girls who had obtained dynamite to destroy the crematoria. Despite their very poor physical condition, LR and her older sister decided to join the Germans and leave Auschwitz in January 1945. The two younger sisters had already left the camp. Thus, they suffered for an additional several months by joining the death march to Ravensbrück, Germany, where they starved. Their group was then taken by train to Neustadt-Glewe. One day the Germans disappeared, and LR's group was liberated by the Russians.

LR and her older sister went to Łódź where they met their paternal aunt, the sole survivor of their father's family who passed as a gentile in Vienna. LR's husband came to Łódź at this time, and then the two sisters and LR's husband went to Stuttgart to join the two younger sisters. In Stuttgart, they were afraid to be seen together—the rarity of four sisters surviving in one family.

The oldest sister died in Stuttgart as a result of various ailments. The three surviving sisters all managed to enter the United States by 1949. LR's first impression of the United States was of shock to see a country so untouched by the war. LR and her husband settled in Newark to be near her husband's uncle. At first, Mr. R. worked as a dental technician. Later, he worked in his uncle's leather jacket factory. They have two sons, one a lawyer in New Jersey and the other a physician in Massachusetts. Both sons are married and each has two children.

In 1975, after both her sons had left home for college, LR enrolled in Kean College. She graduated in 1980, summa cum laude. She continues to live in New Jersey.

DORA LAMPELL ROTH, 1918–1994

[Holocaust testimony (HRC-988, videotape: 1 hour, 12 minutes), 31 May 1988; interviewed by Bernard Weinstein and Selma Dubnick, indexed by Joseph J. Preil. D804.3/.R821 1988]

Dora Roth in Kraków, 1937, the year of her first marriage.

Dora Lampell Roth [DR] was born in Kraków on 5 January 1918. She had one younger sister. DR married her first husband in 1937. The Germans entered Kraków in September 1939. Within three months, DR's grandmother was murdered. Her parents were beaten by the Gestapo. The family was forced to move into the cramped Kraków ghetto. DR's parents were deported three hours before the beginning of Yom Kippur, probably to the Treblinka death camp.

The remaining family members lived in the Kraków ghetto for six or seven months before being moved to Tarnów, a two-and-a-half-hour train ride, where they suffered an equally difficult existence. One day, the Nazis took DR's baby son and threw him on a brick to end his young life. She lost her husband that same day. After less than a year in Tarnów, DR was transported in a two-week cattle train trip to Auschwitz. She saw her sister for the last time in Auschwitz. DR describes Auschwitz—people dying, much typhus, gas chambers, shaving of hair until the inmates were completely bald, selections, numbers tattooed on arms, awful barracks, Dr. Mengele, beatings, the special ingredient in black coffee "to cause sterility in women."

DR was incarcerated in Auschwitz-Birkenau from the summer of 1943 until December 1944. As Auschwitz was being emptied, in an effort to avoid the Russian advance, DR was moved to Bergen-Belsen, Germany, in December 1944, then to Bomlitz in April 1945. She participated in a two-week death march to Potsdam, where she was liberated by the Russians. She weighed seventy-four pounds at the time of liberation. Except for being emaciated, her health was good.

DR returned to Kraków after the war. She found no surviving relatives. In Kraków, she married her second husband, a man who had gone underground with his four-year-old daughter. Father and child were protected by Poles. The new family then went to Linz, Austria. DR gave birth to their son in Munich, Germany. DR's new family of husband, wife, his daughter, and their son arrived in the United States in 1947 to join her husband's relatives. DR was a widow at the time of this interview, still living in New Jersey. The daughter has two sons and lives in California; the son lives in New Jersey and has one daughter. He is a social worker supervisor by profession and a theater and TV critic by avocation.

MORRIS RUBELL, 1930– (DECEASED, DATE OF DEATH UNKNOWN)

[Holocaust testimony (HRC-1031, videotape: 1 hour, 7 minutes), 7 March 1989; interviewed by Bernard Weinstein and Rose Thering, indexed by Bernard Weinstein. D804.3/.R923 1989]

Morris Rubell [MR] was born on 16 January 1930 in Barycz, near the city of Krosno. He was the youngest of five children. MR experienced antisemitism in Poland before the war. He often dreaded school, starting at the age of eight, because rocks were thrown at him and he was called names. Several months after the war began, the Germans organized a ghetto in Krosno, twenty-five miles from Barycz. His family moved into this ghetto after his father had been seized and beaten so badly that he died.

MR and his mother were sent from the Krosno ghetto to the Rzeszów ghetto where they had to sweep streets and sleep in barracks on shelving. There were no beds, no straw. Many Jews were murdered in Rzeszów. He and his mother ran back to Krosno because conditions in Rzeszów were so terrible. They were separated in 1941 and never saw each other again.

In 1942, at the age of twelve, MR was in the Płaszów concentration camp, on the outskirts of Kraków, and his sisters were in Auschwitz. MR describes the German murder process.

INTERVIEWER: When they took you from the ghetto to the death camp, did you know it was a death camp?

MR: We did not know. I don't think we wanted to know. I think that somehow or other, we just could not believe that such a thing could be.

INTERVIEWER: How did you find out?

MR: You found out by seeing it. When they used to pull up trucks, to back up like garbage dumps, they would push them out, and they would fall into the ditches. There was a constant burning of firewood in there. People were falling in. Maybe some of them were shot, and some of them were not shot. So some people were burning alive.

Things like this, people don't really want to believe that these things exist. That this is an isolated case. They can't possibly believe that humanity would allow such a thing. So you try not to see it, you try not to feel it. You try to think that this is just a dream, or an isolated situation.

MR's testimony then focuses on a profound question, "Where did hope come from?" MR's thinking evolves as follows.

INTERVIEWER: What was Płaszów like?

MR: Płaszów was a camp, on a hill. There were terrible beatings by the Kapos and the SS people. The SS had a lot of help, because they had the . . . Black Shirts. They weren't regular Germans, they were more from Ukraine. They took their job with a lot of pleasure. They beat us, and constantly, by marching, by walking, by working, there was never any peace. It was hell, it was hell. But we were alive, and we had hope. We always had hope. That sort of kept us somewhat alive.

INTERVIEWER: Where did the hope come from?

MR: That's a tough question. We, as Jews, always depended on hope.

INTERVIEWER: Did you have one another, to talk it over?

MR: In some cases, there was. There was a sense of humor. I don't know whether we helped each other. I don't think we had this camaraderie. I think everybody was preoccupied by their own survival, by their own misery, by their own sorrows. But, down deep, you wanted to live.

I know, that in my case, I always had that feeling . . . that tomorrow, they'll kill me, but not today. I will survive today. And you kept on repeating, repeating, every day. It wasn't your doing, because everybody had the same feeling. I was just very fortunate. And I believe there was some faith involved, because there really was no reason . . . that a young person or old person would survive, because they were targeted, the first ones to be killed. . . .

You must understand that this whole process did not happen. It was systematically done by, first, they would separate your family. They would cut down your rations. They would make you weak. Physically, mentally, psychologically. You just become a very weak human being.

They were very clever in the way they handled this process. They took away your dignity, they stripped you little by little. They stripped more and more. After a while, there was very little left, except maybe some breath. The soul was still there. And there was that inkling of hope, of surviving another day.

I do remember, in the later years . . . we knew that we are not going to survive. It was sort of hopeless, that's what hurt more. After a while, the pain was not your survival, the pain was not a question of life. The pain was more, of the noncaring people in the outside world, that nobody really cared.

I remember, in retrospect, when we were in the trains, and we looked out and we were passing by fields in Poland and then in Austria. Women, children, passing by in towns. They saw it. They saw us. They saw the hopeless bodies, the crippled bodies, the emaciated bodies, the beaten bodies. They just turned away. In some cases, there was almost a smile. We were in a situation like this, and when we see that there is this kind of feeling of noncaring, you just lose total hope. You just don't care. . . .

But, yet, there is that desire to survive, one more day. Because you really can't believe what you're seeing. The indifference of the outside world. That, I think, was the most painful thing, the indifference. That is something that will stay with me a long time and, I'm sure, with all the other survivors.

Toward the end of 1943, MR was shipped by cattle train to the Mauthausen concentration camp in Austria where he remained one month. He was then transferred to the forced labor camp of Melk, constructing tunnels for ammunition factories. Food rations in Melk were so meager that many people died of hunger.

MR was then shipped to the Ebensee concentration camp, also in Austria. This involved a death march of one week. "There was virtually no food in Ebensee. . . . The German demoralization gave some cause for hope. . . . Still, many Jews died, and this was purposeful." The Germans fled, and the American tanks smashed through the gates. MR did not record the names of the American liberators, but

I'll never forget their faces. This was a long time ago, almost a half-century, but I will not forget their faces. . . . Happy, haggard, dusty. Full of love, caring. Their eyes. Throwing candy, fruits. Giving things to us. And yet they were bewildered. They never saw anything like this before. They wanted to help but they couldn't. They just weren't used to anything like this.

After liberation, MR went to Italy, hoping to proceed to Israel. He learned that his sisters had survived, and he was reunited with his brother in Linz, Austria. Eventually, he was able to enter the United States from France in February 1948. He married in America and had a son and a daughter, both married at the time of this testimony, and two grandchildren. But adjustment to freedom was difficult. The lack of a complete family caused him to have nightmares. "Freedom was not complete because one was not liberated from oneself."

MR was an industrial supplier and lived in New Jersey.

ROSALYN LEISTEN RUEFF, 1932–

[Holocaust testimony (HRC-945, videotape: 50 minutes), 23 April 1987; interviewed by Margaret Dunn and Phyllis Ziman Tobin, indexed by Lou Walker. D804.3/.R942 1987]

Rosalyn Leisten Rueff [RR] was born in Tarnów on 29 September 1932. Her immediate family consisted of four persons: her parents, an older brother, and RR. All four survived the Holocaust.

When the Germans occupied western Poland in 1939, RR's mother decided against leaving her family and Poland, even though she had been born in Newark, New Jersey. Many Jews in Tarnów fled to Lwów [Lemberg], in the Russian zone, in the aftermath of Poland's defeat, but RR's mother refused to walk such a great distance. The family had an apartment near the cemetery when the Tarnów ghetto was established by the Germans. They heard the wailing of the Jews who were forced to dig their own graves before being murdered. RR tells of the deportations of Jews to concentration camps and the dwindling Jewish population in town.

RR describes the efforts of various extended-family members to hide in order to avoid being rounded up. Her family had a hiding place in her uncle's lumber business "for a couple of days." They were also in another hideout for "a couple of days." Her testimony indicates, however, that it was practically impossible to avoid the grasp of the Gestapo.

RR describes the horror of babies being thrown against a wall and murdered, and is asked, "Did your parents shield you from hearing about this?" "There was no way of shielding. This was a daily diet." Finally, the Gestapo notified RR's family that they would be taken to Portugal because her mother was an American citizen. Instead they were taken to Kraków in May 1943 and imprisoned. Conditions in the prison were miserable, "not fit for a dog." Four months later, in September 1943, they were transferred to the Bergen-Belsen concentration camp in Germany. This was the end of the Portugal Plan for the 150 Jews who left Tarnów. RR's family were the only survivors of the 150 people who left Tarnów.

RR recalls several difficult incidents in Bergen-Belsen, especially involving a German daughter who had denounced her mother:

> There was once a woman who came to camp, a German lady. She was German, she came in to be a prisoner like everybody else. Her daughter denounced her because the woman, someplace in generations, there was a mixed marriage. Somebody was Jewish. And the woman wanted to be pure, the daughter.
>
> So she delivered to the gates of Bergen-Belsen. You know, you have room for many children, but one child doesn't have room for mother. So this daughter denounced her, and this is what the lady told us, as we stood there.

And RR continues:

> I think this particular lady had brought many things, many food parcels, along with her. I recall it very vividly. My mother begged her, "Please."
>
> Now, I came from a religious home. She had pork. My mother begged her for this piece of pork. And the woman was melting it, and the grease fell on my mother's leg, that the whole skin just peeled off. She had the third degree burn from this whole thing, because she begged the woman to give me a piece of bacon. I never ate it. But this was part of the reward for begging for food.

As the Allied bombings increased in severity, RR's family was transferred to the Theresienstadt concentration camp in Czechoslovakia. The train stopped along the way, and they were liberated by the Americans.

The family went to Belgium immediately after the war. They arrived in the United States in 1947. RR attended high school in Manhattan and later City College night school. She married a young Swiss man in 1957. They have two children and live in central New Jersey.

At the conclusion of her testimony, RR was asked, If you look back now, do you have any sense of the ways in which your experiences have affected your contemporary life? She responded:

> Yes, I value life immensely. I feel that money doesn't bring you happiness. And I cherish family. I don't have that much of a family. And I think I convey this to my children.

NORMAN SALSITZ, 1920–

[Holocaust testimony (HRC-965, videotape: 10 hours, 20 minutes), 10, 24, 28 April, and 14, 21 July 1987; interviewed and indexed by Bernard Weinstein. D804.3/.S176 1987]

Norman Salsitz [NS] was born on 6 May 1920 in Hindenburg, Silesia, and grew up in Kolbuszowa, where the family lived at the beginning of the war. Both of his parents and four of his siblings were murdered by the Germans. NS and two brothers survived. Thus, only three of nine family members survived the Holocaust.

In a detailed five-part interview, NS describes the pain and anguish experienced by the Jews living in Poland during World War II. He describes the ghettos of Kolbuszowa and Rzeszów, the forced labor camps of Lipie (a stone quarry) and Pustkow (where the first V-2 rockets were tested). He reveals his talent and behavior throughout this era, including escape from Lipie and recovery from an ear infection that forced him to seek medical treatment in Rzeszów and Kraków. Most important for NS's survival were the papers documenting him as a non-Jew, which enabled him to join the Polish underground military organization, the Armia Krajowa, popularly referred to as the AK.

Toward the end of the war, NS met and married a fellow survivor. Both husband and wife worked for the AK and both protected themselves with false identification papers. After the war, NS and his wife lived in Kraków, Breslau [Wrocław], and Liegnitz [Legnica] before they arrived in the United States on 17 January 1947. NS struggled mightily to support his family, starting in the remnants business; he then became a house-to-house peddler in Jersey City; eventually he prospered as a builder. He has one daughter and three grandchildren. NS continues to live in New Jersey.

A comprehensive record of the Holocaust experiences of NS and his wife is available in the book they wrote entitled *Against All Odds: A Tale of Two Holocaust Survivors* (New York: Holocaust Library, 1990).

ROSE PARISER SCHWARTZ, 1925–

[Holocaust testimony (HRC-1043, videotape: 1 hour, 36 minutes), 24 July 1989; interviewed by Bernard Weinstein and Selma Dubnick, indexed by Bernard Weinstein. D804.3/.S399 1989]

Rose Schwartz [RS] was born on 28 December 1925 in Jodlowa, at the foot of the Carpathian Mountains in Galicia. Her father had a lumber business. Her immediate family consisted of her parents, her brother, and RS. All four survived the Holocaust in hiding.

RS recalls an incident when the Germans removed Torah scrolls from the synagogue in town. Her grandfather refused to step on a Torah as ordered by the German invaders; he was beaten mercilessly and thrown into the lake. He never recovered and died shortly afterward.

When RS's family heard of the impending initial German *Aktion,* her family hid in the woods, and RS was sent to warn other Jews. They learned later that other Jews were taken, shot, and thrown into mass graves. This was the town's first large *Aktion* by Germans. RS's family lived in constant danger as the police searched for Jews who had escaped.

RS's father had once forgiven a poor Pole in town who had stolen some wood from him. The Pole now sought RS's father and offered to try to save his family. RS's father initially suspected that the Pole would betray the family and take their clothes, and indeed the Pole's wife had betrayed another Jewish family for their clothing. But the Pole threatened to stab his wife if she talked to the authorities. The family was hidden in a hole in the ground and RS was sent every week to trade some of their hidden possessions for bread from trusted friends among the Poles.

RS recalls a number of incidents when the family was endangered by Polish people who revealed to the authorities that a Jewish family was hiding in town. She describes several events which reflect the family's increasingly precarious situation: fighting with a dog for food, a doctor's opinion that one additional month of hiding would mean the demise of the entire family, and a second woman who was ready to sacrifice the family for their clothes.

After liberation by the Russians, the family went to Czechoslovakia, Austria, and, in June 1948, the United States. Her brother's hips had grown together as a result of the cramped conditions during their period of hiding. He used crutches and learned to walk again in America. Although they had relatives in the United States, the father sought work independently.

The family settled in New Jersey because they had an uncle in Trenton. RS lived in central New Jersey at the time of this testimony. She is married and has one daughter, a college graduate. She is most appreciative of her opportunities in the United States after the horrors of her Holocaust years.

AARON SCHWARZ, 1909–

[Holocaust testimony (HRC-1033, videotape: 3 hours, 49 minutes), 28 March and 5 April 1989; interviewed by Bernard Weinstein and Susanna Rich, indexed by Bernard Weinstein. D804.3/.S409 1989]

Aaron Schwarz in Rzeszów, Poland, 1935.

Aaron Schwarz [AS] was born on 22 February 1909 in Zarowka. His immediate family consisted of his parents and their three sons and three daughters. AS is the lone Holocaust survivor of an extended family that once consisted of forty-six people.

AS was involved in slave labor for the Germans in the ghettos of Radomysl Wielki and Dębica and the concentration camps of Pustkow, Płaszów, Rymanów, Szebnie, and Mielec (Melitz). In 1944, as the Russian offensive forced the Germans to retreat, AS jumped from a cattle train to escape imprisonment and death in Germany. He struggled to survive another six months until liberated by the Russians.

The value of AS's testimony is that he experienced and observed the full fury of the Holocaust in Poland. Three examples in his lengthy testimony illustrate this point. In the first case, AS describes the fate of a young mother and daughter in an *Aktion* in a small Polish town. The reader should bear in mind that countless thousands of Jews were murdered in these *Aktionen* throughout the war.

There was a rebbetzin, as a matter of fact, the rabbi, the husband, survived and he still lives in Boro Park. Just now, Purim, I was there and I visited him. His wife was a beautiful woman, young, maybe twenty-eight years old, with a little girl about six years old. A little blond girl, so beautiful, and they were leading them out to be shot. This little girl was shivering, like a leaf. And [the mother] was crying, *"Shema Yisrael! Shema Yisrael!"* ["Hear, O Israel!"], with such a terrible voice. And this little girl says, "Mommy, don't cry. This is our destination."

When I speak of that, it just cuts my heart. . . . When I remind myself about this little girl, how she went, how she said to her mother, "Don't cry. This is our destination." And so a shot was fired, and this little girl fell. Then they asked [the mother] to turn around, because the SS were never shooting from close range. They were never shooting from in front. Because the victim was falling always to the front, and they were splashed with blood. . . . They asked the victim to turn around. . . .

So, she wouldn't turn around. And she was crying, *"Shema Yisrael!"* Finally, he shot her from in front. . . . Apparently, the bullet did not go through in a place where it should be effective right away. She was moaning so terribly, maybe for fifteen minutes, and this Gestapo wouldn't spare another bullet to finish her. Finally, she didn't die, she was still moaning. So, he put the revolver in his belt.

The Polish policeman who was watching him. . . .He had an electric light, he cut the bra open, he put the light, and he [the SS] looks and he says to him, "Well, the bullet has done its job. It's only a matter of a little time." He wouldn't shoot her again. She was about a half-hour, terrible moaning.

This is how sadistic they were, how life was in their eyes. A Jew was just worse than an animal. If they had only treated us like they treated a dog, it would be heaven.

In describing the work of the Jewish prisoners in clearing the Kraków cemetery to make way for the Płaszów concentration camp, AS tells how the Germans enriched themselves immorally and discusses how the Jews were able to do this inhuman work.

We took a mountain. There were tombstones, old, fifty, sixty years, from famous people. And this mountain was removed. And the reason for it is, every time they opened a grave, there were the jawbones and the teeth, the gold teeth. In Europe, everybody had gold teeth. There were no white teeth, like they do now. So the teeth were always left.

Every day, I have picked up a pail from the cemetery maybe twenty kilos, not pounds. Kilos, that is more than pounds. . . . This was the best gold, twenty-two-karat gold. . . .

INTERVIEWER: Did you actually have to take it from the bodies?

AS: No bodies. This jaw, the jaw and the skull.

INTERVIEWER: Did you have to collect it?

AS: Of course, this was the idea. Buckets full of teeth, every day, gold teeth. And we removed an area, maybe three acres, because it was hilly there. . . . We were loading this by hand . . . And the reason . . . because of the teeth. They knew there was gold. Everyone had gold teeth in Europe.

Even those graves, which were not old, and you opened them, you could still see the tallis, you know, the prayer shawl, and the body was already falling apart, but the teeth were there, in the jaw. We got them out, and this was our job. . . . This is the work we went through there. They gave us this work, and they got the gold.

INTERVIEWER: How did you and your co-workers feel about exhuming these graves?

AS: My dear folks. You were so hardened. There were no feelings for anything. No feeling for a body, no feeling for a child being shot. You had no feeling. You were just like an animal, hardened like a stone. Now, when I remind myself of the cries. . . . There were no feelings. Everyone was numb, numb. That is the word, numb. No feeling for the next person. That's how it was.

Finally, how did individual Germans commit such inhuman crimes? AS addresses this question at the end of the following testimony.

When I came to Płaszów the first day, they put me in a group where we were digging a huge grave. The Kraków ghetto, at that time, was cleared. They brought in trucks, with children, from infant to twelve years old. They were all killed. One group was digging further, about one hundred feet of low grave and about fifty feet wide. When the children were brought in, they were shot, right in that grave. . . .

One group was bringing, with a wheelbarrow, some chlorine powder and putting on, because there was such a tremendous amount of bodies in those graves. They were afraid this would start smelling out. So one group was wheeling with a wheelbarrow some powder, chlorine powder, and spreading with a shovel over. One group was digging further. And one group was just covering up. . . .

A little girl, a beautiful blond girl, sat down in the grave, dressed in an Eskimo white fur coat, was all bloody, and asked for a little bit of water, and asked, "Water, water." But as you know, the heart was sore like a stone, numb, you wouldn't dare go and give that child a little water. And this child swallowed so much blood, because it was shot in the neck. And then it started to vomit so terribly. And then it lay down and it says, "Mother, turn me around, turn me around."

INTERVIEWER: The mother was still alive?

AS: No, no! This child didn't know what happened to it. It was shot, it was half-dead after it was shot. And this child sat down in the grave, among all the corpses, and asked for water. . . . It was still alive. There was no mother, just children brought from the Kraków ghetto.

And, of course, you wouldn't dare move water. . . . As a matter of fact, there were cases when the Germans . . . who were digging and burying those corpses . . . when they finished the work, they were shot, because they didn't want any witnesses to remain alive. . . . We were all shivering, we didn't know what is going to happen to us.

So this little girl lay down, and asked to be turned around. What happened to it? I don't know. It was probably covered, alive, with chlorine. . . . I am sure, because they didn't give another shot to that girl, because they were too busy, going and shooting.

And so things like this, you just cannot forget. It is forty-five years after the war, and this is imbedded in your mind. No matter what you are thinking of, this thing doesn't go out of your mind. . . .

This is the way this highly educated nation became such tremendous, such horrible, murderers, criminals, without any human feeling, without any feeling for a child, for a crying child. It's impossible to comprehend. . . .

INTERVIEWER: Did you ever witness any mercy . . . or compassion shown by the Germans?

AS: No, I did not. As a matter of fact . . . one SS, I got with him so buddy-buddy. He's the one who took me out once from the group, from being shot, because he needed me, and he took me out.

I asked him, "Tell me, are you married, do you have a wife?"

He says, "Yes, I have a wife."

"And do you have children?"

"Yes, I have children."

I ask him, "How can you shoot children here like that?"

He said, "If I would get an order to shoot my mother, I would shoot her."

After the war, AS married a fellow survivor. The young couple and their infant sons were able to emigrate to the United States in 1949. They settled in New Jersey to be near two uncles of AS.

IDA FURST SCHWARZ, 1925–

[Holocaust testimony (HRC-1028, videotape: 1 hour, 56 minutes), 1 February 1989; interviewed by Bernard Weinstein and Ruth Harris, indexed by Bernard Weinstein. D804.3/.S411 1989]

Ida Furst Schwarz [IS] was born in Tarnów on 20 May 1925. Tarnów was a large Jewish city with "at least thirty synagogues." IS's father was a rabbi and a shochet [kosher slaughterer]. Her parents and their large family of ten children lived in a comfortable home. Only IS, one brother, and one sister survived the Holocaust.

IS reports that random killing of Jews by Germans began in December 1941 and the "extermination" program began in June 1942. She describes the *Aktion* that began on 11 June 1942.

The real extermination started in June 1942. I had at that time three brothers, two older and one younger. . . . They had signs placed on the streets, on the houses, that those who did not have working papers . . . have to come and gather in one place. This was the marketplace.

At that time, my brothers, one had a stamp that he could go to work, and the older brother could have saved himself, too. But the youngest one, they didn't want the youngest one to go alone. So they all three went. . . . We figured out that when young boys are called to come on a place, they will probably send them out to work. We were told that we cannot go out, the houses have to be locked, and we cannot look out from the windows, what is going on in the streets. . . .

My three brothers went over there. We did not know where they went. So went hundreds of people that had to go over there. I was left alone in the house. My father, at that time, went into hiding in the attic. And all the other people were afraid to stay in the house. . . .

This was the first day. I was alone in the apartment house. And they even said, "You are not allowed to go to any neighbors." About eleven o'clock, they came into the courtyard, the SS. There were three apartments on the first floor. They went over there and they took out the people, whoever were there. And they started to shoot in the air.

They went to the second floor, and they took out whoever they wanted. We were living on the third floor. Luckily, they didn't come, for they would have taken me, too. They went out and we could see from our house that the next apartment house in the courtyard, they took out almost all old people, and youngsters, and the women. Able-bodied men who had work papers, they left.

In the marketplace, there were about two thousand people gathered there, and they killed on the spot, over there, a couple of hundred. Part of them, they took on wagons, on the trucks, to the cemetery. And killed over there in the cemetery. And the rest they took in a school, until it was dark.

The marketplace was on an incline. We were living on the main road . . . through Germany to Russia. . . . We could see from the window. Of course, we looked what was going on, on the street, and we saw hundreds of those Jews were running. They were not walking, but they just told them to run to the school, about half a mile from where we lived. And the blood was running from the marketplace, right in the gutters of the street.

By the end of the day, we already knew what was happening. I didn't know if my brothers were killed in the marketplace. Probably not, because those people who buried would have known. You know, people knew who they were. They probably went, they took them to Bełżec.

This was on a Monday, June 11 [1942]. It took them three days to bury those killed people. By Thursday, was the same thing again. Another three thousand Jews were either killed or deported. . . . They buried in a mass grave on the cemetery, in Tarnów.

A week later, they started a ghetto, eight square blocks.

IS decided to hide in a sewer pipe with two other girls in August 1942, after the Germans had posted a notice that all Jews must remain at home. IS's older, married sister suggested that she should join the sister's family, hiding in a cellar within a cellar. IS became one of the ghetto people who worked daily and returned to the ghetto each evening. This was her routine from August until November 1942.

The SS came to IS's place of employment in November 1942 and removed her and sixty Jews to join two thousand others who were taken that night to board a cattle car for Destination Unknown. IS and about five others forced the small window open and jumped from the moving train. They all jumped safely and managed, each in his or her own way, to return to Tarnów. They rejoined working groups quietly. This was a miraculous escape.

Announcement was made in September 1943 that Tarnów's ghetto was to be liquidated. IS's group was shipped to the Płaszów concentration camp. She gives an excellent description of the conditions and routines in Płaszów. In October 1943, she was sent to Auschwitz. She mentions that 99 percent of the girls did not menstruate. There was no toilet paper in the camp, all part of the campaign to make the Germans believe that the Jews were subhuman. IS describes a night when four girls were punished with a public hanging, and all the prisoners were compelled to stand and watch.

In January 1945, work in Auschwitz stopped and the prisoners were ordered to walk to the train station. Those who could not walk were shot. Actually, the Germans were fleeing the Russians, who were only twenty miles away. IS and the others were taken to Bergen-Belsen, Germany.

The conditions at Bergen-Belsen were miserable; many prisoners, including IS, were ill with typhoid. There was much Allied bombing of factories. The prisoners were taken by train on a terrible trip through Czechoslovakia and finally arrived in Mauthausen, Austria. This was her worst experience of all, "seeing skeletons who were barely alive." Finally, when the Americans liberated Mauthausen, an American soldier held her as if she were a little girl.

IS recovered gradually from her illness and returned to Tarnów, where it was discovered that she had tuberculosis. She recovered at a resort in the mountains. She met the young man who would become her husband. He had a sister in the United States, and they waited in Heidelberg, Germany, from 1945 until 1949, to enter the United States. They settled in New Jersey where they raised a family of three sons.

BENNETT SILBERSTEIN, 1924–

[Holocaust testimony (HRC-1080, videotape: 1 hour, 31 minutes), 18 February 1993; interviewed and indexed by Joseph J. Preil. D804.3/.S613 1993]

Bennett Silberstein [BS] was born on 6 January 1924 in Biecz, which is in middle Galicia, east of Kraków and near Jasło. His immediate family consisted of six persons: his parents and four children. Only BS survived the Holocaust. His father and an uncle were murdered in an *Aktion* on 14 August 1942. His mother and three siblings were shipped to be murdered in the Bełżec death camp: "This was strictly an extermination camp."

BS learned the fate of his family members "from the Poles. Most locomotive engineers were Poles. We spoke to them." BS testifies that his extended family, through first cousins, consisted of forty-six persons, of whom only BS and two others survived the Holocaust. BS describes the Holocaust from the perspective of a young person in Biecz. This includes the progression from beatings and confiscation of valuables, to wearing of yellow armbands to random disorganized killings and, in the summer of 1942, to the organized campaign. In July 1942, he was shipped to Prokocim, twenty-five miles away, and then to the Płaszów forced labor camp in Kraków. In April 1943, he was taken to Jerozolimska for two days. "There, they shot every tenth person." He was then returned to work in DEF, Oskar Schindler's factory in Płaszów.

BS was transferred by cattle car in May 1944 to Mauthausen, Austria, immediately after reaching Auschwitz. The trip to Mauthausen was an unbearable thirty-six-hour experience. His stay in Mauthausen "were the worst days." He was then moved to Linz, also in Austria, and assigned to the Hermann Göring Works from May 1944 until 5 May 1945, when he was liberated by the U.S. Fifth Army. There was much hunger in Linz and a great deal of Allied bombing of the factory and railroads.

BS went to Italy after the war and then joined relatives in New Jersey in November 1949. He worked as a machinist, married in 1964, and has two daughters. Toward the end of his testimony, BS was asked how the Holocaust has affected his outlook on life and his understanding of human nature.

> Immediately after the war, life was very bleak. I just could not bring myself to think about what happened to all our families and the communities. I felt like an orphan, all alone in the world. It was a terrible feeling. I never forget that minute when I was liberated, the feeling that I had. So, what now? What am I going to do now? They destroyed everything we ever had. Anyway, dark thoughts went through my mind. But, everyone I was with, there was nobody to console us, because everybody was in the same boat. . . .

> The future had no meaning for me. Even though we were supposed to be happy and grateful that . . . after all, we did survive. The only thing I was sure of was that I could never return to that blood-soaked ground, to that place, to my hometown, Biecz, Poland, where I came from.

> I still find this extremely painful to imagine how my family, and all the families, how in the last days of their lives, they spent in those packed cattle cars, going to their horrible death. For me, this is unforgettable and unforgivable. It's still very vivid in my mind. On the surface, life was normal, but in my private thoughts, especially during the holidays or during happy family occasions, I privately mourn for the loss of my family.

> And finally, with the help of my friends in the United States, I came to the United States. I tried, mentally, to close the doors behind me as much as possible and go on from day to day to make the best life for myself and my family. I find it very painful to learn that there are people who are denying the very fact that the Holocaust occurred. And it is difficult for me to forget what I saw with my own eyes. Man's inhumanity to mankind. Antisemitism seems to be flourishing, and I still see atrocities happening in many parts of the world. And it seems mankind has not learned the lesson of the past.

MALA HOFFNUNG SPERLING, 1926–

[Holocaust testimony (HRC-977, videotape: 51 minutes), 12 November 1987; interviewed by Robert Roth and Freda Remmers, indexed by Joseph J. Preil. D804.3/.S72 1987]

Mala Sperling in Linz, Austria, December 1945.

Mala Hoffnung Sperling [MS] was born on 8 April 1926 in Kraków. Her immediate family consisted of her parents, an older sister, an older brother, and MS. She is the lone survivor in her family of five.

MS describes the restrictions imposed by the Germans in Kraków several days after the outbreak of war in September 1939. The new rules and regulations for Jews included armbands, identity cards stamped *Jude,* and German confiscation of such valuables as fur coats, silverware, and jewelry. The Gestapo took charge of her father's thriving lumber business and were especially cruel to Hasidim with beards. MS's family was moved into the Kraków ghetto. MS worked twelve hours a day in a brick factory. Her parents were taken to be murdered in the first selection in June 1942. The rumor at the time identified their destination as the Bełżec death camp.

The food shortage became more severe after her father was gone. MS's grandmother was murdered in a September 1942 selection. MS was then transferred to the Płaszów concentration camp in Kraków, where she describes a fearful incident involving her and Płaszów Commandant Amon Goeth. Her brother was removed at this time, but MS never learned the details of his disappearance from her life.

MS describes the horror of the public hanging of every tenth person. She felt "very alone in a vicious place." One night in the winter of 1943, the Gestapo transferred MS and others on trains, in cattle cars, to the Skarżysko-Kamienna concentration camp.

That was an ammunition factory. They made big bombs over there. When morning came . . . we couldn't believe the sight we saw. This was the worst place I was in, really. We saw really dead people walking, I must say. They were wrapped in paper, from the substance . . . acid, that they put in bombs. That came in big paper . . . sacks. They had no clothing. . . . So they wrapped themselves up in this paper. . . . I cannot describe the sight to you because it's just indescribable. . . .

We used to get a little slice of bread and a soup, that was called a soup. . . . Some water and something swimming in it. And huge barrels. And we all had to line up, and we got one helping of it. We were very hungry. Thus it was really really bad.

There were no sanitary conditions at all. At Płaszów, we could still go and take a shower, whatever. Here, we had no sanitary conditions at all. There was just an outhouse, and one stall shower. So, we had to line up. If we managed before the curfew to take a shower, fine. If not, then you couldn't help it, because there was a curfew. . . .

We all got infected with typhoid fever. . . . I don't know whether I should say it. Huge lice crawling around, all infected . . . from one to one. We all suffered from typhoid fever, including me.

A lot of people died. And there again you see, it was meant for me to survive. Because I don't know how I survived. Typhoid fever is a very severe sickness, very severe. Today, I cannot give blood because there are some antibodies in me that I'm not supposed to. It's a very severe sickness with very high fever.

Now, we had no medication. It was nonexistent. There was nothing. I was lying on the dirty bunk bed, with the lice crawling, and the bed bugs crawling on me. And I came out of it. I don't know how. I just came out of it.

As the Russians kept gaining ground, MS and others were transferred to a factory near Leipzig, and then marched from place to place until at last they were liberated by the Russians. MS returned to Kraków where she found no family survivors. She took a train to Prague and entered the American zone. "The Americans were wonderful."

MS arrived in the United States on 1 April 1949, after her marriage to a fellow survivor in 1946 and the birth of her son in 1949 in Camp Bindermichel in Linz, Austria. Her daughter was born in 1952 in New Jersey. The family settled in New Jersey in order to be near a cousin, also a survivor. Both son and daughter are married and each has two daughters. The son has a doctorate in physics from Princeton University and does computer work in California. The daughter completed her studies in musicology at Rutgers University and does computer work for Merrill Lynch. The daughter and her parents live in New Jersey.

MS concludes her testimony with this comment:

I hope the stories we tell is not only the horrible things we went through, which is bad in itself, but we are here. I hope that people learn a lesson that we are all human beings, that we are on this earth for all the same purpose really. To be aware of leaders that preach hatred against any other people, or single out in a bad way any other people. That's really my message. I think we have to build bridges between people to have more understanding. And we have to tell the story so that it wouldn't happen again.

JACK SPIEGEL, 1918–

[Holocaust testimony (HRC-1089, videotape: 1 hour, 47 minutes), 23 September 1993; interviewed and indexed by Joseph J. Preil. D804.3/.S713 1993]

Jack Spiegel [JS] was born in Łódź on 17 March 1918. His father was in the import-export business and the family lived comfortably. His immediate family consisted of eight people: his parents and six children. JS is the lone survivor. His extended family, through first cousins, consisted of "no less than fifty people." JS, once again, believes he is the only survivor.

JS was incarcerated in an incredible number of concentration camps. He believes that he survived by constantly volunteering for new jobs in different camps. He and his family were in the Warsaw ghetto until October 1942. JS was transferred to Lublin, then to the Bełżec and Opatów concentration camps. He was then able to return to Warsaw to rejoin his family. His father died at that time.

JS was moved to Minsk for a short period and then to Bobruisk, where he remained from October 1942 until March 1944. He remembers "a horrible welcome." The officer said, "If you work, all will be fine. If not. . . ." He took a pistol and killed a person. After two months in Bobruisk, only one hundred of the three hundred men who had been in his bunk remained alive. The others were regularly murdered, especially on Sundays. After a while, JS was given a kitchen job. He found that the food for the dogs was better than the food for the prisoners. In that camp, only ninety-one people were left alive from the original three thousand.

After Bobruisk, JS moved quickly from camp to camp: "Minsk—a very short stay; Majdanek—one week; Będzin—April until November or December 1944; Mielec—two weeks; Wieliczka—two weeks."

By this time, the guards were older people. The "younger kids" were fighting on the Russian front where the Germans were retreating constantly. JS recalls how the Germans would hang "young kids" in Bobruisk to let the prisoners see what could happen to all of them. An SS guard shot at JS one day, and barely missed him, for the "crime" of stretching his arms while working in the field.

JS was then moved from Poland to Germany: "Flossenbürg—two weeks; Hersbruck—summer 1944 until March 1945; Dachau—until liberated by Americans on April 29, 1945." All transfers were in cattle cars except for the move to Dachau. His group was forced to walk there. He weighed eighty-five pounds at the time of liberation.

JS was sent to France for eighteen months to convalesce and to start life again. He was in Israel from 1948 until 1960. He served in the Israeli army. JS married in Israel and his first two children were born there. The family emigrated to the United States in 1960. His third child was born in America. JS has three grandchildren. He lives in New York near the New Jersey border.

MIRIAM SHAPIRO SPIEGEL, 1931–

[Holocaust testimony (HRC-1091, videotape: 1 hour, 29 minutes), 21 October 1993; interviewed and indexed by Joseph J. Preil. D804.3/.S741 1993]

Miriam Shapiro Spiegel [MS] was born on 8 May 1931 in Janów Lubelski, near Lublin. Her immediate family consisted of six persons: her parents and their four children. Her father and three of the children survived the Holocaust. Her extended family, through first cousins, consisted of thirty-one people. Only the four persons in MS's immediate family survived.

Shortly after the war started, the family home was bombed, and MS's father took the family to live in a nearby village. As an eight-year-old, MS was walking one day and met two German soldiers. A Polish boy called out, *"Jude! Jude!"* One of the soldiers punched MS and knocked out two of her teeth. Her father then decided to move the family into the forest.

The family starved in the forest. MS's father and two of her cousins returned to their village to obtain food from the Pole who had been entrusted with all their possessions. They were told never to return, and the Pole betrayed the boys to the Germans for a reward of five pounds of sugar. MS's father heard the screaming, saw what had happened, and returned to the forest to tell MS's uncle of the fate of the two boys. MS's father and cousins then separated to try their luck in different places.

Family members died in the forest because of primitive sanitary conditions, hunger, and murder by Germans and Poles, particularly when they would go to the nearby village of Wola Rasztowska to obtain food. The family moved to a second forest, this one near Zielowiec. The Polish partisans there wanted to kill both Germans and Jews. One night, the Jews heard shots and began to run. MS was left alone when her mother was killed. She ran into Zielowicze and was threatened and attacked by Poles.

The starving girl knocked on the door of a Polish couple's house, begging for bread. The Polish woman said, "Don't worry, child, I'll take care of you." Because of the couple's fear of Germans, MS was provided with food irregularly and lived secretly in the barn for about five years, until Zielowicze was liberated by the Russians.

MS remembers the Polish couple as being very good to her. After the Russian liberation, the Polish woman took MS to church to be baptized and wanted to adopt her. MS met her brother at this time, and the four family survivors were reunited. Until this day, MS can wake up in the middle of the night and scream.

MS was placed in a children's home in Lublin and then sent to Palestine while the other family members emigrated some time later to Canada and to Brooklyn. MS remained in Israel from 1947 until 1959. She married in 1950, gave birth to two children in Israel, and a third child in the United States. Her son is a salesman, her older daughter a teacher, and her younger daughter a legal secretary. She has three grand-children. MS lives in the New Jersey area.

LEO STAHL, 1919–

[Holocaust testimony (HRC-1083, videotape: 1 hour, 54 minutes), 10 March 1993; interviewed and indexed by Joseph J. Preil. D804.3/.S807 1993]

Leo Stahl [LS] was born on 3 September 1919 in Radomsko, a town between War-saw and Kraków. In 1930, the family moved to Częstochowa, a large community about nineteen miles away. His immediate family consisted of ten persons: his par-ents and eight children. Only LS and one brother survived. His extended family, through first cousins, consisted of at least seventy people, of whom only LS and his brother survived.

Two days after the start of the war in September 1939, a German *Aktion* consisted of disorganized, indiscriminate killing. By 1942, the Germans had organized their Holocaust program. Two excerpts from the LS testimony reveal a great deal about the German *Aktion* program. In the first excerpt, we glimpse the motivation of the German guards.

INTERVIEWER: Did anybody ever understand why they hit the older people. In other words, in the beginning, when they were shooting people indiscriminately, you said that was to let the town know they were here, and people should be frightened. Now, they're hitting the older people who don't work. What was the understanding why they were doing that?

LS: They were just enjoying themselves.

INTERVIEWER: That was enjoyment?

LS: For them, this was enjoyment. They were laughing between themselves. You know, "Go up and unload the wagon," and the guy who never worked couldn't do it.

In the second excerpt, we see the thoroughness and efficiency of the German Holocaust in one community, typical of the murder program for all of Polish Jewry.

LS: September 1942, when the *Aktion* started.

INTERVIEWER: What do you mean by *Aktion?*

LS: What I mean, they closed up certain streets. This was the day after Yom Kippur, which was September 22, 1942. They closed up a certain area, three or four streets, where they knew there will be seven thousand people. There was a train. They took out the people and made a selection . . . .

Everybody had to go to the marketplace, and over there they had the head of the police, he was standing with [a pointer] and he went right, left, right, left. People who looked young and healthy were going to the left, and the others were going to the right. That meant just to the train station, loaded up, and they went to Treblinka.

It took about forty-eight hours, until the train came back. They opened up another section of the town, and again. It took about three weeks. I think the last one was, it took about three weeks, until five thousand people remained from over fifty [thousand].

Because, basically, as I said before, Częstochowa, our town, had thirty thousand Jews before the war. During the war, they came in from all the little towns. . . . After three weeks of the transportation, there were only five thousand. . . . These five thousand people went out to work. . . . Three months later . . . they liquidated that ghetto, and all the people went into the HASAG Pelzery.

LS and his brother were moved into the Pelzery barracks and endured forced labor, beatings, and very little food. They remained in the barracks from April 1943 until January 1945, when they were shipped by cattle car to Buchenwald, then to Dora, and finally to Rottleberode.

The incredible cruelty of the SS is illustrated in the following incident. Of the one thousand people from LS's community in Rottleberode as the war was ending, only six survived. The others were murdered. The SS tricked many prisoners into moving to the Gardelegen concentration camp with a promise that soup was available there, but the soup was poisoned and the prisoners were burned to death. LS and five companions were so exhausted they did not wake up in time to accept the invitation for soup.

After liberation by the Americans, LS went to Hanover and then to Zeilitzheim, a DP camp near Frankfurt. He was instrumental in obtaining kosher meat for the camp. LS's brother married a survivor in 1946 and emigrated to the United States in 1949 to join his wife's family.

LS married in 1950 and came to Paterson, New Jersey. He started as a manual laborer, then became a clerk in a large firm, and in 1963 entered the construction business. He lived with his family in northern New Jersey until 1976 when they moved to central New Jersey. He has a son, a daughter, and three grandchildren. His son is a computer analyst, his daughter an editor for *The Economist* of London, working in the New York office.

Seven-year-old Sam Stimler, the lone sur-vivor in his family, with his mother and two of his three sisters.

SAMUEL STIMLER, 1923–

[Holocaust testimony (HRC-2014, videotape: 1 hour, 47 minutes), 29 March 1995; interviewed and indexed by Joseph J. Preil. D804.3/.S872 1995]

Samuel Stimler [SS] was born on 13 September 1923 in Rzeszów, about seventy-five miles east of Kraków. His immediate family of six included his parents and three sisters. There were about thirty-eight persons in his extended family, of whom SS is the only survivor. At this point, SS commented that many families had no survivors at all. SS describes the development of the Holocaust in Poland. There was chaos at the beginning of the war. He was with a group that tried to flee to Russia, but after going some distance, they decided to return to Rzeszów.

The German decrees against Jews began with the confiscation of Jewish business establishments. This was followed by plundering of Jewish valuables by Germans and Poles. A ghetto for all Rzeszów Jews was established in 1941. Very few Poles risked their lives by hiding Jews.

SS was assigned to Nowy Sącz, a forced labor camp, from May until November 1941. This was the first of eight camps for SS. It was a small camp, with a population of 150 men. He returned home in time to rejoin his family as they were about to move into the ghetto in December 1941.

In May 1943, SS was taken to a second forced labor camp, Huta Komarowska, of which he says: "This is my picture of how hell looks." The four hundred prisoners in this camp worked in a forest cutting down trees.

Huta was phased out at the end of the summer of 1943. SS returned home and discovered the ghetto had been emptied. Practically all of Rzeszów's fifteen thousand Jews had been deported to extermination camps. SS was sent to the Pustkow labor camp, near Dębica, in September 1943; this held three hundred prisoners. SS was assigned to work on producing brushes before he was transferred to kitchen duty.

In February 1944, SS was moved to the Płaszów concentration camp, a large camp with twenty thousand prisoners just outside Kraków. He describes the cruelty of Amon Goeth, the infamous commandant of Płaszów. SS was sent to Wieliczka for a short time. This camp was empty. The work assignment for SS and his group was to dismantle the camp and destroy all evidence before the advancing Russians took over.

When he returned to Płaszów, SS was injured while working and was hospitalized. By this time, Płaszów was being evacuated. Prisoners were being sent to Mauthausen and elsewhere. SS was assigned to join Oskar Schindler in Brünnlitz, Czechoslovakia. He passed the Gross-Rosen concentration camp on the way to Brünnlitz. Schindler greeted the group with a speech emphasizing the need to work. SS recalls that Amon Goeth had a supervisory job in Brünnlitz. SS remained in Brünnlitz until liberated by Russians in May 1945.

When asked about his feelings when liberated, SS said that he had a tefillin shel rosh (one of two phylacteries required for morning prayers) in the camp and that he and several men risked their lives to pray. After liberation, he returned to his hometown in Poland. When he was told that Poles were killing Jews, he left for Kraków. He prayed at the early services on Sabbath in the historic Rama synagogue. Later that morning, he heard that Poles wanted to murder Jews at a late service. He returned to the synagogue and felt immediately that his life was in danger. Fortunately, the Russians came and saved them from the Poles.

SS returned to Prague and then moved on to Munich. He reports that the Grand Rabbi of Klausenburg was an inspiration to all survivors in the area. Finally, he went to Belgium, where he remained from 1946 until 1952. He met his future wife in 1948. They were married in 1949.

SS arrived in the United States in 1952. The family settled in Newark to be near relatives. He joined a relative-survivor as a partner in a butcher store. He has two children, a son and a daughter, and eighteen grandchildren. Both children are dedicated to traditional Jewish values and learning. At the time of his testimony, SS was semiretired. He continues to live in New Jersey with his wife.

RABBI ISAAC SUNA, 1930–

[Holocaust testimony (HRC-2019, videotape: 1 hour, 57 minutes), 20 October 1995; interviewed and indexed by Joseph J. Preil. D804.3/.S923 1995]

Sixteen-year-old Isaac Suna, his family's only survivor.

Rabbi Isaac Suna [IS] was born on 3 January 1930 in Końskie, near Łódź. Of the seven persons in his immediate family, IS is the lone survivor. Of at least 120 people in his extended family, through first cousins, in Poland in 1939, only IS and four relatives survived.

Końskie was a community of twelve thousand; seven thousand were Jews. IS's father was a merchant, and the family lived comfortably. IS describes the increasing Polish antisemitism in Poland, beginning in 1936. He feels this "had a lot to do with Nazi Germany. . . . I feel greater animosity toward Poles than to German people."

IS describes the German occupation of Końskie and the organization of the ghetto, and reveals his mother's reaction to the news of the murder of Jews in concentration camps.

They couldn't believe, how could people kill other people? Just to illustrate this. It was 1942, and many things I don't remember. But certain episodes, I do remember. . . . I remember that one day, comes a fellow. . . . My mother says, "This is a cousin of ours." . . . She pushed us aside. Children shouldn't hear. . . . But I have still overheard.

He says that he just came back from Auschwitz, that he killed a *kapo,* and he and two others escaped. We should know that Jews are being exterminated. And my mother [in Hebrew: "of blessed memory"], I don't know, maybe nobody wanted to believe it . . . did not let him sleep over. Because how could one Jew admit that he killed another human being? How can one believe. . . . These are things that, either because they did not want to believe, because they could not fathom such a thing, or it's a question of mechanical protection of oneself. . . .

The human being tries to protect himself and, therefore, does not want to believe that something which, even though it's true, but believes in survival and believes in [in Hebrew: "God"] and, therefore, doesn't want to believe that there is such a thing as extermination camps.

IS describes the German plunder of valuables and the chaos caused by the invading army which replaced the community's sense of law and order. He then continues:

The ghetto. Normalcy wouldn't be the rule of the day. And I tell this to my students. The picture that I see of a young man who was eight years older than me at the time. And all of a sudden, you find the Gestapo, the SS commando, was surrounding this house where we were learning. Breaking up the learning. And then we hear a shot.

What happened? They find this young man, nineteen years old . . . covered his head, wrapped his beard. And since nobody was allowed to have a beard, they shot him on his face. He said that he has a toothache.

That brought, to a certain extent, the reality and the danger, to realize . . . that life is so frail and so fragile. . . .

INTERVIEWER: What did the family do in the ghetto, two years?

IS: It's a very interesting question. I would say the Jewish community, our family tried to have as much normalcy as possible. What do you mean, normalcy? . . . To try, first of all, to get food in, for the children. They tried, if possible, to trade, to do a little business. . . . Not to make any money, however, to get some food for the family. And, as much as possible, to struggle to get wood for heating.

And the children, as much as possible, to continue their education. Either at home, or to send them to a private person. . . . For example, the older ones had to go to the Germans to work. My father had to go . . . he had two days a week to go. My mother, once a week, had to go to work.

The Końskie ghetto was liquidated in 1942 and many Jews were then deported to the Treblinka murder camp. IS and his father were moved to Skarżysko, where they were assigned to shell production. IS testifies:

So, to describe a day [in Skarżysko]. In the morning, there was the *Appell* . . . counting. Even though how cold it was. . . . Everybody in the rags, had to stand outside. In the meantime, if they saw somebody they didn't like, they liquidated. . . . I remember, one of the *Appell*s, all of a sudden, the head of the Gestapo men, comes with two people, who were the foremen . . . and brings them in front of us, and see them pleading in front of him. I suppose he accused them of wanting to run away. And shot them on the spot.

The type of days that are outstanding . . . I don't try to remember them, they are so suppressed. So the typical day is, you got up at an *appell*. And then, if you are lucky, you got a larger piece of bread, some hot water. And if you're not lucky, you got a smaller piece of bread. Then, went to work. And, at work, tried to work as little as possible. We didn't have the strength to work. But, in order to survive, you had to produce. Each one helped the other to get through.

Then the bell rang. You had about a half-hour, there was a soup. Stand in line for the soup, got the soup. This was from eight [A.M.], and at six [P.M.] came back to the camp. And at six, started to again the lineup for supper. What is supper? Also, a little hot water and a piece of bread. And this was almost every day. . . .

I remember that, for the first time, when I was a bar mitzvah, I put on a pair of tefillin for the first time. No wonder when my son was bar mitzvah, that I cried so much, because I felt that I am also bar mitzvah at this point.

In the summer of 1944, IS and his father were transferred to Częstochowa, then to Buchenwald, Germany. Buchenwald meant numbers tattooed on the inmates' arms and flimsy striped uniforms. In September 1944, they were moved once again, this time to Schlieben. IS's father returned to Buchenwald in February 1945, hoping to get medical help. IS participated in a death march, leaving Schlieben in March 1945 and arriving in Theresientstadt in April 1945. His uncle was with him at this time. They were liberated by the Russians in May 1945.

After the war, IS returned to his hometown in Poland with his uncle, hoping to meet other surviving family members. No one appeared. After eight months, they decided "Poland was no place for Jews," and returned to Germany. As a minor, IS's application to enter the United States was processed quickly. He arrived in New York on 12 April 1948, where he was met by his paternal uncle. He enrolled in Yeshiva University High School in September 1948, and he has remained at Yeshiva, enjoying a distinguished career as an educator.

IS is married and the father of three children. All three are pursuing professional careers, are married, and live in Israel. He has twelve grandchildren. In contemplating his experiences during the Holocaust as a youngster, and his successful development, IS states:

> As a survivor, I feel that I have a tremendous [in Hebrew: "responsibility"]. . . . The responsibility is to show, mainly, that Hitler did not succeed. It's the opposite. The fact is that I survived and I continue . . . and [in Hebrew: "thank God"] have a mission, and *Am Yisrael chai* ["the people of Israel live"].

ENOCH TRENCHER, 1926–

[Holocaust testimony (HRC-927, videotape: 2 hours, 10 minutes), 19 June 1985; interviewed by Sidney Langer, indexed by Joseph J. Preil. D804.3/.T792 1985]

Enoch Trencher [ET] was born on 10 March 1926 in Kraków, and raised in Krosno, a small town about sixty miles from Kraków. His immediate family consisted of nine persons: his parents, three boys, and four girls. ET and two brothers survived; six family members perished in the Holocaust.

ET describes Polish antisemitism in the late 1930s. When the Germans invaded Krosno in September 1939, the community's rabbi and ten prominent Jews were taken to the center of town, murdered, and buried by the Germans. In June or July 1941, many Jews were gathered in the marketplace and murdered by the Germans. ET was assigned to a forced labor battalion in Krosno, then transferred to Rzeszów, during 1942–1943. He was sent to a third labor camp, Pustkow, before being moved to three concentration camps and other labor camps: Auschwitz-Birkenau, Oberschlesische, Mauthausen, Düsseldorf, and others.

ET relates many incidents of German cruelty throughout the war. He recalls the time when people in Rzeszów were taken to the forest, commanded to dig their own graves, and murdered. There were no survivors. ET was in a group of six hundred workers who were processed and tattooed in Birkenau: "You had no feeling with all their treatment, you were like an animal."

Perhaps the best illustration of the incredibly inhumane experience of the Holocaust for all participants was their description of prisoners endeavoring to survive in the Oberschlesische labor camp. ET was incarcerated in this camp more than a year, until some time in 1944.

> One episode which cannot be forgotten in that camp: Our commander had a dog. One of the boys, one of us, took care of the dog, a German shepherd. That German shepherd had a booth, almost a small room, and he kept him there. . . . That dog had better food than we did. A pail, full of . . . let us say, a soup, that the spoon could stand in. He used to bring the dog that kind of food.

> That fellow, Yitzchak Silverberg, he survived too. He lives in Florida now. There are only a handful of us alive, and we are still in touch sometimes.

> And I made up with him that he used to take the dog for a walk. That time, we had some things in the factory, that we had to go and throw out the garbage. So the garbage disposal was in the other side of the camp and we had to go by the dog's house.

> In the camps, like anywhere else, you had to find your way to survive. We had some . . . canteens. And while we threw out the garbage and he walked the dog, we jumped in, scooped up a couple canteens of food, put it into the garbage bag, took it back into the factory.

> You never walked alone. You always walked with three, four fellows. So one looked out for the other one. Make sure that the SS don't show up. And it helped. It helped supplement the food.

In the view of the above statement, it is interesting to ponder ET's response to this question.

INTERVIEWER: Did you have any close friends in camp?

ET: No, you never make any close friendships with any of them. Because there was no time. And the time you had, the little time you had, you felt sorry for yourself. You didn't even have time to feel sorry for yourself, to begin with, when you lost your parents. Because you were hungry. You only were thinking about the food that you didn't have.

The war was ending when ET was in the Mauthausen and Düsseldorf concentration camps. Nevertheless, he reports, the Germans tried to murder the Jews with such foods as soft grease on bread and poisoned water. "Half the people fell like flies" during the death march to Theresienstadt. Thirty thousand poisoned loaves of bread were *not* distributed in Theresienstadt. ET expresses the theory that the camp's commandant was protecting himself.

ET was liberated by the Russians in Theresienstadt. After recovering from typhus and diarrhea, he went to the Landsberg and Bergen-Belsen DP camps in Germany. David Ben Gurion came to Bergen-Belsen and spoke in a beautiful Yiddish, encouraging the survivors to make *aliyah* (to emigrate) to Israel. ET visited Poland and returned to Germany, to Regensburg, where he was reunited with his two surviving brothers.

ET arrived in the United States in 1949. He married and has two daughters and one son. He went through a variety of jobs until he became a butcher with his own store in New Jersey in 1962. He is retired and still lives in New Jersey. He concludes with a thought repeated by survivors: "This country is great, the best in the world."

SOL URBACH, 1926–

[Holocaust testimony (HRC-1032, videotape: 1 hour, 38 minutes), 22 February 1989; interviewed by Bernard Weinstein and Marcia Weissberg, indexed by Bernard Weinstein. D804.3/.U651 1989]

Sol Urbach [SU] was born on 25 October 1926 in Kalwaria, near Kraków. His immediate family consisted of eight persons: his parents and six children. SU is the lone survivor.

SU describes the Holocaust in his region from the first days of the war until he was liberated by the Russians in Oskar Schindler's factory in Brünnlitz, Czechoslovakia. It began with a futile effort to flee from the Kraków area, trying to obtain food and essentials, then the organized persecution and torture of Jews by Germans as early as 1940, through forced labor and the decree that Jews must wear armbands bearing the Star of David.

When his family was forced to move into the newly organized Kraków ghetto, SU obtained work in Schindler's enamelware factory and moved into the factory. He learned some time later that another brother was shot and that the remaining members of his family perished in Auschwitz.

SU was in Schindler's factory and in the nearby Płaszów concentration camp from February 1943 until October 1944. At that time, the Germans were fleeing from the Kraków area and Schindler was about to return to his native Czechoslovakia. SU's group was taken to the Gross-Rosen concentration camp in Poland. He remained there only one week, long enough to know how horrible this concentration camp was. As arranged by Schindler, SU was then transferred to Brünnlitz.

Schindler's new factory never produced anything for the German war effort in the closing months of the war. Schindler, however, kept on entertaining the Nazi officers and manipulating events as though he had been operating a productive factory. He also gave guns to a number of his Jewish workers to protect themselves. Schindler had no illusions; he knew the Germans were losing the war. SU comments on Schindler's conduct throughout the war.

> Well, he began to see early on in the war that things are not that great for Germany as he envisioned as a very young man back in Czechoslovakia, that Germany would conquer the world, and he would ride in on that wave and be a big business tycoon. . . . He also recognized that what the Germans were doing was not exactly what he had in mind.
>
> When people were killed in masses, as they were, he began to change his mind as to hanging onto the Germans and helping them. In fact, it turned the other way. But, still, always acting as a loyal German. I mean, he had no way of operating if he did not continue acting as a loyal German.
>
> There was a time during the war that he was jailed, because of suspicions that he was not very loyal. He was kept in jail with another known Nazi concentration camp leader by the name of Goeth, who headed the Kraków/Płaszów concentration camp. But they released him again because of the enormous influence that he had all over the German empire. So they released him, and he came back to the camp and operated again. . . .
>
> From my point of view, he was a fellow who was seeking opportunities, but did not want to join in the ranks of killing people. I have not known him to lift a hand on any inmate or to harm any inmate. So I would have to judge that he was a decent human being, that for a while, was taken by the great anticipation and promise of the German Reich, but certainly did not want to join in and get in on the mass killings and all that.

SU recalls the moment of liberation: "I remember vividly the people crying. How we did that, crying and laughing at the same time, is beyond me. But that's what actually happened. We were crying and laughing at the same time."

After liberation, SU returned to Kraków for the most difficult period of his life. He discovered that he had no surviving relatives. By 1949, he was able to emigrate to the United States to join an uncle and aunt living in Passaic, New Jersey. He obtained a series of jobs and married in 1950. His wife's parents moved to Flemington, New Jersey, together with SU and his wife. He then entered into real estate construction. This was difficult at first, but eventually he was quite successful.

SU has three children. His older son is a cardiologist in New England, his daughter is a lawyer in New Jersey, and his younger son is studying architecture (at the time of this interview) after having completed his undergraduate studies at Princeton University. SU also has five grandchildren.

SU reflects on our post-Holocaust responsibility.

The most important thing of this totally horrible experience, that would seem to be very important at this point, is that this somehow not be written off in history books and be read as one would read any other history book, that that's what happens during a war. But, in fact, that we somehow be able to project it and teach the present generation and future generations of what can happen to a minority group when no one comes to the rescue.

What happened to us is simply, where 90 percent of our people vanished in the European theater, is because the other people did not come to the rescue of us. They simply thought, well, as long as the picking is on the Jews, why not leave it alone? And that's how our people vanished.

So the important lesson to be learned, and in which I would like to help, is to teach the younger people that this really happened. This is not a story as many stories that you find in books, and you tend to disbelieve. This actually happened. People were killed, shot, just because they practiced a different religion, as we did.

LEE LAUFER WEINBERG-ERLICH, 1925–

[Holocaust testimony (HRC-970, videotape: 1 hour, 52 minutes), 28 October 1987; interviewed by Bernard Weinstein and Anne Kaplan, indexed by Anne Kaplan. D804.3/.W42 1987]

Lee Laufer Weinberg-Erlich [LW] was born in Chrzanów, near Kraków, on 1 August 1925. Her immediate family consisted of her parents, a brother, and LW. She is the only survivor. LW presents a very clear, well-organized description of her Holocaust experiences. It begins in 1939 with the German invasion. Intellectuals in the community are rounded up and shot or hanged. It continues with the organization of the ghetto, forced labor, education of Jewish children forbidden (but older children help the younger ones to read), curfews enforced with bullets, confiscation of valuables and especially of jewelry, and the terrifying cattle cars used for transportation to murder camps. Since Auschwitz was only two miles from Chrzanów, that was the destination for many local Jews.

LW then describes the last stage of Chrzanów's becoming *judenfrei* (free of Jews).

That was an extremely difficult experience because, with being experienced already with previous evacuations of Jews from our town, we knew that this was the end of our lives. The whole remaining Jews in the city were brought up again to the same place, which was a square. There was no counting, no nothing. Before there was segregation, from the authority of high officers. Either you go to the right, or to the left. This time, we all stood in one center, and there was a mass of people.

The deportation was a terrible experience. I can still hear the screaming of some small children. They were torn away from the hands, from the breast, of the mothers. You could hear the voice so clearly, even today, "Mommy, mommy, do not [unclear; probably "leave"—*ed.*] me."

After several hours of standing in the same square, we were shifted into a school, to a gymnasium. From the gymnasium, in the middle of the night, we had to walk to the train. With all the people together. We did not know who goes where. . . . My mother and father were hidden again by the Poles. My brother was working. He did not know where I am, and I did not know where he is.

After riding in that particular train from my home to nowhere, we did not know where we are going. The train was extremely slow moving. . . . February—it was bitter cold. We were allowed to take only what we were wearing. Nothing else.

I was working that night, and they took me straight from work. . . . We were traveling at that speed, in that terrible surrounding, day and night, until we came to Markstadt. As we were unloaded from the train, all of a sudden I realized that my brother was there. Now, you can imagine how emotional you get, when you see your only. . . . But we could not talk to each other. We were restricted.

Then we came to a camp, which took several hours, because there were old people with us. They could not walk fast . . . beaten or hurt by the Germans.

As we approached the camp, there was *Appell.* We have to count how many people. And I found that this is almost the city of Chrzanów, which was the total liquidation of Jews.

For the women, we had to go to separate barracks to have some soup. This is what you call it, soup, or coffee. And the men were somewhere else.

The name of the camp was Sosnowiec. LW was relieved that it was not Auschwitz. She describes the diet there: "No food, only soup, dirty hot water with sand, bugs, and a small piece of potato."A few days later, LW's group was transported on a three-day cattle car trip to a second concentration camp in Poland, Klettendorf. Her German supervisor liked her and this was most helpful during her eighteen months of incarceration in Klettendorf. She worked in the kitchen. One day, LW hid a bar of soap for herself and the girls in her barrack. This created turbulence for days as the authorities searched everyone and everywhere for the missing soap. Fortunately, the soap was not discovered and no one was punished.

LW was transferred to another concentration camp in Poland, Ludwigsdorf, in July 1944. She remained there until liberated by the Russians in May 1945. The work of this camp was in a munitions factory, necessitating a walk of eight miles each way, in wooden shoes. The chemicals in the factory caused many illnesses, which, along with the lack of food and the bitter cold, caused much demoralization among the girls and women.

After liberation, LW returned to her hometown only to learn that she was her family's sole survivor except for an uncle who was ill in a hospital. He had been in Mauthausen and two other camps. He looked like a skeleton after the war, and LW did not recognize him. She nursed him back to health. He went to Israel and lived there twenty-five years.

LW married a fellow survivor in August 1945. They arrived in the United States on 8 August 1949. She discovered an aunt in Newark, and the young couple settled there. Eventually, they formed an electrical company which has developed into the family business. They have two sons and, at the time of this interview, two granddaughters. LW recalls the birth of their first child.

> After work, my husband came to see me and [our] son. We were having in the hospital, sitting, a very difficult subject and points, that we were never taught of thinking about it in our lives, due to the fact that we were very young. And right after survival, we had to fight for bread on the table, and decisions where to go and what to do with our lives.
>
> Till now, our life was completely without responsibility, so to say. We did not make an issue for the future. Whatever we had, we were happy. We felt like a bird, free to go wherever we want to.
>
> But when you have a child, you have to think about his future. Friday was his circumcision, his bris milah, in the Beth Israel Hospital. That time, we promised that we would start with our Friday night candles on our Sabbath table, and come back to a strong Judaism.
>
> Our outlook was a very difficult one, but we decided that it would be best for our son to identify himself who he is. And Friday afternoon, I was discharged from the hospital. My first thing was to put a white tablecloth on the table and to light the Sabbath candles, which brought in my feelings, conducting so the tradition that I took out from my own parents' home.
>
> Since then, we are doing it. And my son, who is married and has his own two children, I am very much proud of his conducting now to his children, which would bring us again to the same traditional upbringing for every Jewish daughter or son in the future.

SHLOMO AVRAHAM WEINGLAS, 1924–1997

[Holocaust testimony (HRC-1099, videotape: 1 hour, 58 minutes), 10 February 1994; interviewed and indexed by Joseph J. Preil. D804.3/.W423 1994]

Shlomo A. Weinglas [SW] was born on 15 February 1924 in Ordzywol, not far from Radom. The family moved to Łódź in 1935. Ten members of his immediate family were in Poland at the beginning of World War II. Of these ten, five survived the Holocaust. Two siblings fled to Russia; SW and two brothers managed to survive the Łódź ghetto and the concentration camps. His extended family consisted of more than a hundred people, of whom only SW and his four siblings survived.

SW describes how life deteriorated for the Jews of Łódź immediately after the German invasion in 1939. Jews suffered beatings and inhuman treatment. About March 1940, all Łódź Jews were ordered to move into the ghetto, which existed until August 1944, when the last Jews of Łódź were transferred to the murder camps.

All eight members of SW's family in the ghetto were assigned to forced labor. He recalls meager food allocations, hunger, lice, illnesses, deaths. His father simply "died from hunger." People ate grass and fought for potato peels.

One day living in ghetto, how horrible it was, how subhuman that was. Today, even I can hardly believe it, that it was true, that we survived such a thing.

INTERVIEWER: What was a day like?

SW: OK. You get up in the morning, you have to go to work. There was no food in the house, but you had to get up in the morning, because at work you get a soup. At least, there was nothing in it. If you know the party who gave out the soup, maybe you had a piece of potato in there, inside. Otherwise, you got mostly the leaf with water, and the higher echelons, they had . . . two pieces of potato or three pieces of potato in the soup. If you find a piece of potato, you were lucky. . . . That was the soup.

And, besides, you got paid. You got paid because, otherwise . . . you didn't have money to buy the food rations.

And you came home, and most of the time . . . your feet were swollen from standing or walking. . . . And somehow or other we got experience in ghetto that we became like half-doctors. The swelling gradually went up higher and higher. . . . We knew that if the swelling goes up to here, towards the heart, another day, the person will be dead. One day, I came home with swollen feet, it went up almost to the knees. I tried to sleep. . . . I tried to make as minimum effort as possible. . . .

And somehow or other, the swelling came down a little bit. And Mother sent us down to pick some grass. We chopped it up.

At night we came home, after there was some coffee there, something warm to drink. If we had something to make fire, to warm up a little water, this was lucky. If there was something from the rations left over to make a little soup, with a piece of bread, and that was it.

Cold it was in the house. There was no heat. And it was a terrible experience to live in such a situation. Every day.

Somewhat later in the testimony, the following exchange was recorded.

INTERVIEWER: What kept people going? It was so discouraging.

SW: You go into a prison, what keeps people going? You are there. You cannot help yourself. That's it. That's the situation you live in. And you have to do the best in your situation. . . . You sell your jacket off you to get a piece of bread. . . .

INTERVIEWER: I imagine a lot of people gave up.

SW: A lot of people gave up and they died, yes. A lot of people lay down. . . . They could not go farther, and that's it. We got the food rations, what's just barely enough to survive, not to live and not to die. But you couldn't die from it and you couldn't live with it.

In discussing the role of Chaim Rumkowski, the Jewish king of the Łódź ghetto, SW reports, "Rumkowski was hated by 99 percent of the population." He was in charge of the roundups when Jews were deported to the murder centers. When asked to explain how Łódź evolved as the last major ghetto in Poland to be deported to murder camps, SW responded, "Biebow, the German commandant, wanted the ghetto for his own financial gain."

SW then describes the cattle car transport to Auschwitz in August 1944, the arrival in Auschwitz, and the speedy demise of new arrivals. Only about 815 of 3,500 people survived the initial processing of SW's contingent in Auschwitz. In September 1944, he was in a group transferred in a three-day cattle car trip to Kaufering-Dachau in Germany. SW developed typhoid and was critically ill in March 1945. He was transferred to Allach in April 1945 and was then liberated by the American army.

After the war, SW was in the Feldafing DP camp. He made a quick visit to Łódź and brought out one of his surviving brothers. He moved on to France and then to Israel in 1949. After marrying an American woman in Israel, SW emigrated to the United States in 1953. He has a jewelry business. He moved to New Jersey in 1969 in order to be near two of his surviving brothers. He has three children and eight grandchildren.

DAVID WERDIGER, 1922–

[Holocaust testimony (HRC-1000, videotape: 1 hour, 8 minutes), 26 May 1988; interviewed by Bernard Weinstein and Stanley Friedman, indexed by Jennifer Regan. D804.3/.W473 1988]

David Werdiger [DW] was born on 11 March 1922, in Kraków. His immediate family at the beginning of World War II consisted of five persons: his parents and their three children. DW is the lone survivor.

DW's testimony begins with a description of the antisemitism he experienced as a teenager before the war. After the Germans invaded Poland, he fled toward Russia with his father and older brother. They returned to Kraków after six or seven weeks when they heard conditions in Kraków were "not too bad." As they returned, the Germans started the program of forced labor accompanied by beatings. This prompted DW and several of his friends to flee toward the Russian border a second time, but DW began to fear the Russians and returned to Kraków. This time, in addition to forced labor, Kraków was experiencing German confiscation of valuables belonging to Jews and random murders of Jews.

DW's family moved into the Kraków ghetto together with all the community's Jews in March 1941. He remained in the ghetto for two years, until March 1943 when he was taken to Płaszów, Kraków's concentration camp. His parents were deported to the Bełżec extermination camp and were never again seen by the family. After seventeen months in Płaszów, in August 1944, DW was transferred to the Mauthausen camp in Austria. Many of the six thousand Jews did not survive the cattle car trip from Płaszów to Mauthausen.

In this new camp, DW describes the constant beatings and the meaningless inhuman task of "carrying rocks up and down one hundred steps. . . . It was terrible conditions, terrible conditions. You could wake up in the morning and see dead people with cut-off hands. People were cutting off the hands and feet and eating the flesh. It was normal, every day." After six weeks in Mauthausen, DW told the Germans he was a mechanic. This led to his transfer to work in a factory hidden in the woods. The factory was bombed in November and December 1944. Many of the slave laborers were killed. DW was injured and sent back to Mauthausen.

In May 1945, after participating in a death march to Wels-Gunskirchen, DW was liberated by Americans. He developed typhus and was hospitalized for a month. After recovering, he lived in Hart, a DP camp, where he met his future wife. The young couple moved to the DP camp in Linz.

DW and his wife arrived in the United States in 1949. They lived in Brooklyn until 1973 and then moved to New Jersey where DW became a builder. They have two sons and two grandchildren. The older son is a doctor, the younger son an executive in an architectural firm.

DW describes a return trip to Poland:

In Płaszów, there is a little monument, which I remember about the place, where my brother and his wife were killed. Otherwise, we visited the graves in Kraków, in Auschwitz. That's the only thing we could go and look at. Otherwise, we have no interest whatsoever.

It's true, we went to our birthplace in Kraków; my wife is from Przemyśl. We went to Przemyśl, she saw her house, but she didn't go inside, and I didn't go inside. We just looked from far away.

And then I was walking in Kraków on the streets that I know and I remember very well. The streets are there. The buildings are falling apart. There are no people there.

HENRY YUNGST, 1920–

[Holocaust testimony (HRC-947, videotape: 1 hour, 15 minutes), 18 May 1987; interviewed and indexed by Bernard Weinstein. D804.3/.Y94 1987]

Henry Yungst [HY] was born on 7 October 1920 in Ozorków, not far from Łódź, where his father owned a textile factory. His family consisted of six persons: his parents, their three sons, and one daughter. HY is the lone survivor.

On 1 April 1940, the Jews in town were rounded up at a theater where they were treated civilly, then brutally. HY was sent to Danzig for forced labor. His father and older brother were sent to a concentration camp in Poznań, where they died of starvation. His mother, sister, and younger brother were sent to the Łódź ghetto, then to the Chełmno murder camp, where they were gassed and cremated. HY describes a camp in Lithuania.

In Lithuania, we were there, there was a nice camp. They sent the Jewish people from Vilna. That was mothers, with children, the fathers with families. That was the first time, in a year or two, we saw families together. It was very nice and peaceful. That *Lagerfuehrer,* the commandant of that camp, he was a reasonable man too. There was not SS.

All of a sudden, the SS started to take it over. Come big huge trucks in front of the camp. All the kids. The women should give the kids up. So surely no one would like to give the kids up. Some kids were small, little babies. Some hide the babies. So the baby was crying, because all of them, all of us, have to go out from the barracks.

Then, they come in and check. . . . Then, they throw them, just like that [he gestures], onto the trucks, open trucks. That means the kids are going to be dead. We know it already. You don't treat little babies like that. . . .

So one woman, I remember, she begged that SS man, tall guy with heavy boots, "Please leave my kid." The kid was maybe three years old, a cute, little boy. He said, "No. Do you want to go with?" She said, "Yeah, I want to be with my son." They took her too. A half-hour from there, or an hour, there was Ponary woods. . . . They killed them, they dug holes.

Then it was quiet. After two, three days, they looking for sick people, because there were no more children. And while that was going on, we had to sing. Because I was entertaining us, when we had good time. You know, we sing . . . nice old songs from the hometown. And here we had to stay and sing for the crying women, what they took the children away. Do you know how that feels? They force you to do something but your heart was beating. They were so stupid. What do you want to prove to those women, what their hearts are beating, they took their babies away? Our singing is going to help them? Is going to comfort them?

HY was then sent to Polemonas, a concentration camp in Lithuania, where prisoners were forced to view dead bodies before eating. HY's next camp was Riga-Kaiserwald, where he remained six months. He was then moved to the Stutthof concentration camp near Danzig, then to Buchenwald in Germany, to Bochum-Verein, and back to Buchenwald.

Finally HY was taken to Flossenbürg for a very short period and was about to be moved to Dachau when he was liberated by the Americans. He was so weak and sick by that time that he could not reach out for the food tossed out by the American soldiers. He became ill with typhus and was sent to a hospital in Straubing. While recovering, he went into a depression. He was helped out of his depression, began to work, and met his future wife, who was visiting in Straubing.

HY searched for his sister, even visiting Israel, but it was a futile endeavor. He and his wife arrived in the United States in 1954. Their first residence was in Newark, with his wife's sister. Eventually, they bought a house in New Jersey and operated a delicatessen. They have three children, a son and two daughters. The son is a physician in Florida. Their daughters live in New Jersey. One is a surgical assistant; the other is a hostess for the New Jersey Lottery. HY has five grandchildren.

ABRAHAM ZUCKERMAN, 1925–

[Holocaust testimony (HRC-906, videotape: 1 hour, 20 minutes), 1983; interviewed by Sidney Langer, indexed by Bernard Weinstein. D804.3/.Z94 1983]

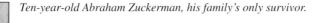

Ten-year-old Abraham Zuckerman, his family's only survivor.

Abraham Zuckerman [AZ] was born in 1925 in Kraków. His immediate family consisted of five persons: his parents, two sisters, and AZ. Only AZ survived the Holocaust.

AZ describes the unexpected violence that accompanied the German occupation of Poland. This involved the German seizure of people in Kraków, followed by their disappearance, food shortages, the decree that Jews must wear armbands, the beginning of forced labor, the plundering of Jewish valuables, and the establishment of the Kraków ghetto. AZ's father decided to flee to his father's town, Dukla. The family was then deported to Biała Podlaska, near the Russian border, where AZ was assigned to forced labor at the military base. The father returned to Dukla and his family followed.

Six months later, all the Jews were rounded up in the center of town. AZ was selected for labor, the other family members were removed on trucks. AZ never saw his family again. The Jewish population of Dukla was liquidated; AZ and some others were sent to the Rzeszów ghetto. When Rzeszów was being liquidated, AZ hid under a blanket. The Germans sent him to the Płaszów concentration camp in

Kraków. He was then selected by Oskar Schindler to work and live in Schindler's enamel factory.

> They were making pots and pans, you know, and dipping them in porcelain. Besides that, we were making shells. . . . Whatever happened with these things, I don't know. He, Schindler, used to take loads of these pots and pans, and sell them to the farmers, and bring food to his people.
>
> We were never hungry there. There were always piles of potatoes. Pots you had, because there were always plenty of pots. Put it at the edge of the stove which always used to be red hot. In a half-hour you had a meal, if you were really hungry. But he really made sure that his people were fed right.
>
> There used to be inspections and he never let them in. The Germans who came to inspect to see what he's doing. Somehow, they got into his office, and they drank, and whatever else they did. And they forgot about him.
>
> He always used to tell us that they're coming, so that we'll be on guard, and everybody kept busy. The word has it that never did anything go out of his factory. It was just an item that was done over and over, just to keep his people. There, I was, for about a year, by Schindler. I regained my strength . . . I became human again.
>
> After a while, I don't know what happened, an order came, and they split up this camp. . . . I was among the people who was sent out from this camp.

In the heat of August 1944, AZ was shipped to the Mauthausen concentration camp in Austria. He describes the cattle car trip: "No food or water . . . People actually drank urine. . . . Many died en route." They were shaven completely and they were given the thin, striped camp uniforms. Their work in the quarry consisted of the futile exercise of carting a load of rocks up and down 186 steps all day, every day, for several weeks. He was then transferred to Gusen II, a concentration camp in the Mauthausen region.

AZ worked as an electrician in Gusen, building German airplanes. He saw mountains of corpses every morning on the way to work. The corpses were cremated during the day and were gone by evening when the slave laborers returned to camp. He describes the cold camp showers of January 1945 and running back wet to the barracks. Food was sparse, and prisoners had to struggle for part of a single loaf of bread to be shared by twenty-four men. AZ then decided to remain hungry in order to stay alive. In general, "life was really without hope."

AZ was liberated by Americans at Gusen. He went to the Linz and Bindermichel DP camps. He describes the feeling of dependency. The survivors "lived like five-year-olds." But it was essential for him to learn the fate of his family. He returned to Kraków with a friend but found no one. In essence, he says, "we were liberated, and didn't have where to go."

Upon his return to Bindermichel, AZ met the young woman who would become his wife. They were married in camp and were finally allowed to enter the United

States in May 1949. They lived in Passaic, New Jersey, where an aunt of his wife had settled. They moved to central New Jersey, where they continue to live to be near business associates and friends. They have three children, all married, and, at the time of this testimony, four grandchildren.

AZ has become a successful builder and, together with his partners who are also survivors saved by Schindler, they are committed to the cause of Holocaust education, especially the Holocaust Resource Center of Kean College. Their appreciation of Schindler's conduct remains alive and fresh, as indicated by AZ at the conclusion of his interview.

> The first thing we did is when we went into the building business, we went and we got these subdivisions to do streets and houses, we remembered Schindler. Even though we didn't know where he was. We met him after the war. He was in Binder- michel a couple of times. But then . . . we lost contact with him. We didn't know where he was.

> The first thing we did, we named streets after him. We did that in many, many towns. Today, I would say a dozen streets are named for him in New Jersey, after Schindler. Then, later on, he came here in 1957, for the first time. We met him and we took him to the streets. . . . He was like a little baby, when he saw the name on the streets. He was very, very grateful.

> He was a man who devoted his life, really, to humanity. He was not interested in business, or in money. He always used to come here, and he used to count his children. He said, "These are my children." Because what he did for us, you know, saved us. That gave us a chance to have a family, and he called them "*meine Kinder*" ["my children"]. He was a very humble man. Too bad that he died that young.

> We also arranged to have a scholarship in Schindler's name in Hebrew University [Jerusalem], because he was very, very involved with Hebrew University. He loved Israel, and he used to come six months out of the year.

In 1991, AZ published a book in which he recounts his and his wife's Holocaust stories: *A Voice in the Chorus: Life as a Teenager in the Holocaust* (Ktav). When the new Holocaust Resource Center was dedicated in Kean College in December 1996, AZ and his partner, Murray Pantirer, commissioned a bust of Schindler to be displayed in the center.

MILLIE MARK ZUCKERMAN, 1925–

[Holocaust testimony (HRC-908, videotape: 1 hour, 48 minutes), 14 February 1984; interviewed by Sidney Langer, indexed by Joseph J. Preil. D804.3/.Z941 1984]

Eight-year-old Millie Zuckerman.

Millie Mark Zuckerman [MZ] was born in September 1925 in Humniska, near Brzozów. The immediate family consisted of four persons: her parents, her older sister, and MZ. Her father was a grocer and was well liked in the small village with a population of only two thousand.

When Hitler invaded Poland, MZ recalls, Jewish children could no longer attend public school and Jews had to wear armbands. From 1939 until 1942, the family continued to live at home. MZ, her father, and sister were assigned to meaningless forced labor. In 1942, all Jews in Humniska were ordered to move to Brzozów.

The family was moved to a third small town and assigned to forced labor. MZ's father decided they should return to Brzozów when he sensed the Jewish population in their new town was being liquidated. In Brzozów, in September 1942, the Germans ordered all Jews to assemble in the stadium for the purpose of being moved to work elsewhere. MZ's father again decided he did not want his family to be moved from the stadium under German orders.

MZ's father recalled a former customer of his, Michalina Kedra, who had once told him, "If ever you need help, call on me." Mr. M decided to return to Humniska and ask Mrs. Kedra for her assistance for one or two days.

INTERVIEWER: Did you have any trouble going back to that city [Humniska]?

MZ: Who thought about it? You were so involved, how to save yourself, that they shouldn't find you, that you really didn't think of anything. I don't remember thinking anything, just that we should be hidden someplace, that they shouldn't find us.

INTERVIEWER: I mean, physically, you were able to leave, to get back, to the town. . . . How was it that you were able to escape from the town [Brzozów]?

MS: You know, it was just one of those things. You just didn't think about it, I guess. We just said, "We're leaving, we're going." We left everything behind and we just started running away. We ran away. Because we did go during the night. Because during the day, first of all, you had to wear the armbands, so they would know right away that we are running away. . . .

So, we knocked at her [Mrs. Kedra's] door, and she said, "Who is it?" And my father said, "Mark. This is Mark." She said, "Sh! Don't say loud." And she opened the door and said, "What do you want?"

My father said, "You know, we came from Brzozów, and I think tomorrow is going to be this liquidation of Jews. Can you hold us for a day? Two?"

She said, "OK. Let me see what I can do." Quiet, very quiet, she put us all in the attic. And it was true. Next day she came up and she said, "You were lucky. You escaped. They did liquidate the whole town."

Of course, my mother was crying, we were all crying, because we figured we lost everybody. So, now we said to her, "What are you going to do with us?" She said, "What can I do? I have four of my own children. I'm going to try to see if I can keep you all here."

It wasn't easy for her because . . . she was a widow, she had no husband, she had those four of her own children. We were four. There were all eight of us. And from day to day it was very dangerous to live there. . . . She was probably scared because in the beginning they were looking for Jews. They were looking, not particularly for us, but they were looking for Jews.

INTERVIEWER: So you were not able ever to go outside the house?

MZ: Not at all, not at all.

MZ's family remained in the Kedra home "maybe a couple of months," but then her father's money ran out. Mrs. Kedra was very poor and could not afford to feed four guests indefinitely. MZ's father went to a Polish acquaintance in the dark of night to ask him for help. Everyone realized that such contacts could mean death for Poles and well as Jews, but the Pole agreed to provide money from time to time to assure food for MZ's family. This arrangement continued until August 1944 when Humniska and the Mark family were liberated by the Russians.

In contemplating the fact that her family of four were the only Jews in Humniska to survive the Holocaust, MZ says, "It's unbelievable how we survived. I guess Somebody up there wanted us to survive."

After liberation, MZ's father returned to the family home in town. The Pole living there threatened him and forced him to leave. The family then went to Brzozów, where they confirmed that all their local relatives had perished the night they escaped to Humniska.

Why did Mrs. Kedra risk her life to save MZ's family? MZ struggled with this question near the end of her testimony.

You know, I always think why, why did she do it? And I even talked to her daughter, why did your mother do it?

"We really didn't give you anything," she says, "I don't know. . . .She was a religious woman. She always said, 'God is going to pay me back.'"

I don't know why. We're always asked, "Why? Why her?" I really don't know. . . . She always said my father always gave her credit in the store. Because she became a widow very young, I think thirty-four. And my father always said to her, "Michalina, when you have money, you'll pay me. Don't worry. Your children have to live."

And that was very big for somebody. I guess she remembered that. . . . But I really don't know why she did it. She was just a good person.

Mrs. Kedra's daughter, Helen Bocon, visited MZ recently on a trip from Poland. She confirmed everything described by MZ. At the conclusion of her interview, Mrs. Bocon said:

> The Jews were people too, and we should have helped them to save them. A lot of them came, but she could only take so many. But the message is that Jews are human beings too, that we should take care if [we] can.

TEDDY ZWEIG, 1923–

[Holocaust testimony (HRC-1073, videotape: 53 minutes), 13 November 1992; interviewed and indexed by Joseph J. Preil. D804.3/.Z965 1992]

Teddy Zweig [TZ] was born on 2 March 1923 in Opatów, which is near Kielce and Częstochowa. At the outbreak of the war, his immediate family consisted of five persons: his mother, one sister, two brothers, and TZ. His mother and sister perished in the Holocaust. TZ lives in the United States; both his brothers live in Israel.

From 1939 until 1941, TZ lived in his town's ghetto and was assigned to forced labor for the Germans under cruel conditions. He was in a group that was then shipped to Skarżysko, a labor camp, to work in a munitions factory. He provides details of the living conditions that included lice, typhus, and the same miserable work routine every day for three years, 365 days a year.

The German head of the Skarżysko camp "was a hunchback who walked every day with a dog and whip and hit people twenty-five, thirty times on their body." He also shipped many people to murder camps. TZ describes how he learned the fate of his mother and sister.

> There was a time when they needed people to work in labor camps. They took out the young kids. We were sitting on a field to go on trucks. They would ship us out to factories or camps. . . . I had a cousin. He was a policeman in the ghetto. He told me and my brother [about] my sister and my mother. My sister was hiding, she didn't want to leave my mother alone, she was hiding in a basement. Somebody went out. There were fifty-nine people in the basement. Somebody had to go out for air. A Polak called the SS, and they came. They took all the fifty-nine people on the spot. They gunned them down. . . . They killed them all.

INTERVIEWER: Why did the Pole do that? . . .

TZ: Yes, yes, they got rewards. There were a lot of cases like this.

In 1944, as the Germans were retreating in Poland, TZ was transferred for several months to the Częstochowa concentration camp. He describes the constant killing of prisoners.

INTERVIEWER: They shot people in all the camps?

TZ: Sure. If they didn't do anything, they took them out, not in front of you. But we know, they took them out to the woods. Oh, we know, this guy out, they took five people out, they took six people out. They heard the shots in the woods. Every camp was in the woods.

INTERVIEWER: And this was going on all the time?

TZ: All the time.

INTERVIEWER: Could you figure out why certain people were being pulled out?

TZ: Some people, if they run away, some people went close to the wires, . . . just going close. You had to be away. If you went close, they shot you.

INTERVIEWER: On the spot?

TZ: On the spot.

INTERVIEWER: And this was a daily occurrence?

TZ: Daily occurrence. Sometime two, sometime nothing, sometime three. . . . They took them out in the woods, and then we heard shots. . . . If you're going to the wire, you'll be shot. If you don't stay in the line good, when you're getting your portion or something like this, you'll be shot. . . . If you have to go across a street, and you don't stay in line, if you just move like you're going to run away, you'll be shot.

TZ reports that in his first two camps, "you had a quota for your work. If not filled, you received beatings, [the] first two or three times. After that, you were shot." TZ was an electrician. He did not have a quota. By the time TZ arrived in Buchenwald, the Germans were quite disorganized and conditions in the camp were chaotic. Prisoners would die in the barracks and their corpses could remain there for two or three weeks.

After liberation by the Americans, TZ worked in a kitchen in Frankfurt. Through an American uncle, he was able to enter the United States on 2 February 1949. He married, became a baker, and had one son. He lives in New York State. His son is a police lieutenant in the United States Park Service and lives in New Jersey. TZ has two grandchildren.

Toward the conclusion of his testimony, TZ tells of the continuing impact of the Holocaust experience on many survivors. When asked when he started to talk about the Holocaust, he said:

> Since I came here, I always try to talk about the camp. I sleep with the camp, I dream with the camp, I always talk about the camp. In one way, I can never forget. I try to forget, I can never forget.
>
> I [have been] sleeping on tranquilizers since I came here. Six tranquilizers a day . . . headaches every day. And I think, even now, and I think, probably it comes from this.
>
> I'm a crier, I always cry, I don't laugh. I like to be alone. Death doesn't bother me. I can see hundreds of dead, I wouldn't cry. . . . You can die only once. But if I see a story, on television . . . or movies, or something in the paper, I crack down. I can't control myself.
>
> INTERVIEWER: When you see something, you're talking, that's related to the Holocaust?
>
> TZ: No, anything. But death doesn't bother me.

The next question was, How has the Holocaust affected your outlook on life and your understanding of human nature? TZ's response:

> I don't get excited. I'm not a happy man. I don't care if I live or I go today. . . . I'm not excited. The first time I went to see my brother after he went from Germany . . . to Israel. He was in a kibbutz. I didn't see him for twenty-five years. Right? I went to see him, I wasn't excited. . . . I didn't kiss him.
>
> INTERVIEWER: How do you view human nature, that human beings did what they did in the Holocaust? How do you view that?
>
> TZ: They're not human. They're not human. As a beast, as a tiger. If they're hungry, they eat you up. Why? . . . My mother . . . didn't hurt anybody, my sister didn't hurt anybody, I didn't hurt anybody. . . . How can you believe in a human being?

Chapter Three
Eastern Poland

~~~~~~

In August 1939, Germany and the Soviet Union signed two treaties enabling Hitler's Germany to invade Poland in September 1939 without fear that Russia would join England and France as World War II started.

Map 3 shows the division of Poland between Germany and Russia. The Russian section of Poland contained a significant number of yeshivas. Rabbis Alter Pekier, Jack Ring (whose story is in the preceding chapter), and Abraham Shlomowitz discuss the impact of the Holocaust on yeshivas and how one among many yeshivas was saved by the actions of a single Japanese consul.

Hitler revealed in December 1940 how meaningless his treaties were when he initiated planning for war against Russia. Germany invaded the Soviet Union in June 1941. The Holocaust was now being conducted in all of Poland. The German bureaucracy had perfected the details of Holocaust organization by this time. Most of Polish Jewry had been murdered by 1943, and the four murder camps—Bełżec, Chełmno, Sobibór, and Treblinka—were dismantled. Chełmno was reopened as the war was ending to enable the Germans to murder the remaining Jews of the Łódź ghetto, the last Polish ghetto to be destroyed.

The reader should note that Clara Kramer based her testimony on the diary she wrote as a teenager during the Holocaust.

Thirty-one Survivors from Russian-Occupied Eastern Poland, 1939–1941, and Subsequently Occupied by Germany until Evicted by the Russians, 1944–1945

Julia Waldman Altholz	Miriam Link Fisch	Edward Harvitt
Pola Bilinska-Jasphy	Pepa Sternberg Gold	Dina Weinreb Jacoud
Aida Chaja Czerczewsky Brydbord	Zygmunt Gottlieb	Clara Schwarz Kramer
	Roney Wiener Haliczer	Rae Kushner
Martha Zeidner Eckstein	Arie Halpern	Mayer Lief
Lillian Landau Ettinger	Sam Halpern	Ann Stolowitz Monka
Erwin Fisch	Gladys Landau Halpern	Sarah Snowski Osak

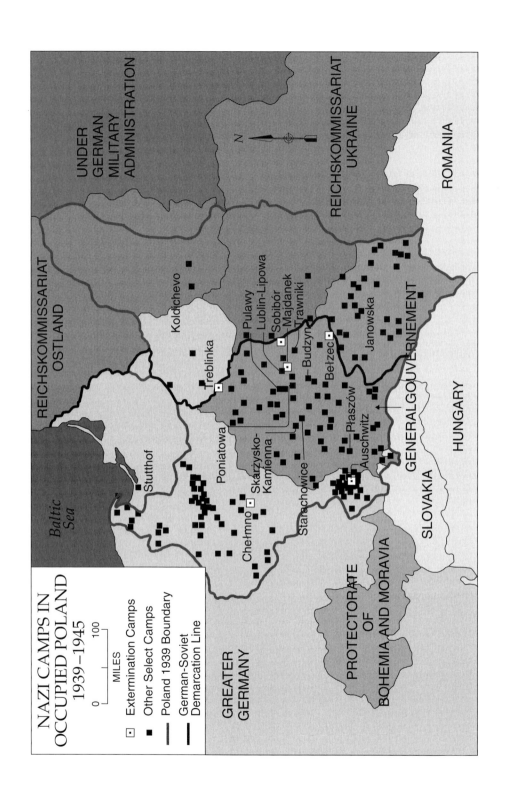

NAZI CAMPS IN
OCCUPIED POLAND
1939–1945

☐ Extermination Camps
■ Other Select Camps
━━ Poland 1939 Boundary
━━ German-Soviet
　　Demarcation Line

MILES
0　　　100

N

REICHSKOMMISSARIAT
OSTLAND

UNDER
GERMAN
MILITARY
ADMINISTRATION

REICHSKOMMISSARIAT
UKRAINE

ROMANIA

Baltic
Sea

Stutthof

Koldichevo

Treblinka

Poniatowa

Chełmno

Skarżysko-
Kamienna

Starachowice

Pulawy

Lublin-Lipowa

Sobibór

Majdanek

Trawniki

Budzyń

Bełzec

Janowska

Płaszów

Auschwitz

GENERALGOUVERNEMENT

GREATER
GERMANY

PROTECTORATE
OF
BOHEMIA AND MORAVIA

SLOVAKIA

HUNGARY

Sonya Gorodynski Oshman

Rabbi Alter Pekier

Lisa Kushner Reibel

Ann Charasch Schatz

Paul Schmelzer

Susan Fleischer Schmelzer

Rabbi Abraham Shlomowitz

Adela (Ulka) Spitzer Sommer

Julius Sommer

Ilona Mandel Werdiger

Elizabeth (Suzie) Fisch Wilf

JULIA WALDMAN ALTHOLZ, 1932–

[Holocaust testimony (HRC-1072, videotape: 1 hour, 58 minutes), 12 November 1992; interviewed and indexed by Joseph J. Preil. D804.3/.A469 1992]

Julia Waldman Altholz [JA] was born in Lwów [Lemberg] on 18 August 1932. She was an only child. At the beginning of her testimony, JA showed two photographs, one of her maternal family and the other of her paternal family. Of the fourteen persons in the photograph of her maternal family, one uncle survived the Holocaust, and of the thirteen persons in the photograph of her paternal family, four survived.

JA spent her earliest childhood years in Szereszniowce, a small village where her father had a farm. This was in the Russian zone of Poland at the beginning of the war, 1939–1941. As a landowner, Mr. W. feared the Russians would consider him an enemy of the state and ship him to Siberia. So he moved his family to Lwów, the large city in the region, "to get lost in the crowd." Father took a job as a bookkeeper. As for her education, JA reports, "I never went to school until after the war."

The Germans invaded Russian Poland and Russia in June 1941. The deadly danger of the Holocaust spread throughout the land. Seeing the Germans indiscriminately killing the Jews, JA's family moved back to the farm. They then moved in with the maternal grandmother in Jezierzani, a small village nearby. Grandmother was murdered in a German *Aktion,* when she would not hide in a cellar with JA because JA did not look Jewish. Grandmother did not want to endanger JA should they be discovered together by the Germans. JA's parents then arranged to have her live with a Christian family for her safety. She entered the family of Andrew Surowice, a widower, and his two nieces, who accepted her because she did not look Jewish. JA understood Surowice's action as follows:

> He was a true human being. He was a Christian. I guess he was a true Christian. He was a man who believed in God, and he was a man who believed in the goodness of people. So when he took me, he didn't love me, he didn't know me. And he did it, first, because he thought it was the right thing to do. He did protect himself as much as he could. The way I look. They needed pictures. He didn't want to endanger me or himself. He did endanger himself plenty. But he was just an extraordinary human being who had some financial arrangements, some. By that time, my father didn't have anything to give him. But he was just an extraordinary human being. . . .

Apparently, there was a pact between Mr. Surowice and my parents, and I admired my parents for it and I will continue to admire them for it. They said they felt, although they were Jews—obviously Judaism was very important—but to them the love of their child was more important. It was above everything. And they felt that after the war, if no one remains from our immediate families, rather than being a Jewish orphan, they would have preferred for me to be a loved, beloved Christian child that would have family. It took me many years to understand it. I understood it only when I had my own children. My parents' love for their child was more than the love for their religion, their background. And every person has to do their own thinking about it. I'm not saying they were right or wrong. I'm saying they were my parents.

JA remained with the Surowice family for three and a half years, from June 1941 until early 1945. The Surowices decided she should not attend public school for safety reasons, so instead she went to a church school.

JA's father was determined that he and his wife should not be shipped to a concentration camp. They moved from hiding place to hiding place, but JA's mother was murdered by the Germans one day while her father was away seeking a new hiding place.

JA describes Mr. Surowice's disappointment after the war when her father did not agree to have his family (father, uncle, and JA) move in with the Surowice family. Instead they returned to Lwów, then went on to Bratislava, and finally to Germany. Father married a second time. They lived in Germany from 1946 until 1952, when they emigrated to the United States.

JA had studied English in Germany, which enabled her to enter Hunter College of the City University of New York upon arriving in New York at the age of twenty. She married a fellow survivor and has two children, a son and a daughter. The son is a lawyer, the daughter an arts editor. The family moved to central New Jersey to a community with an excellent school system for the children. When JA's father invited her husband to join the father's firm as a builder, it was "an offer that could not be refused."

JA relates that she has always been in touch with Mr. Surowice and his nieces. They correspond, and she has sent gifts and visited them in Poland. "We felt it was an extended family. . . . We planted a tree in Yad Vashem [in Jerusalem] in their honor on the Avenue of the Righteous."

At the end of her testimony, JA considers the question why it took so long for the survivors to tell their story or for the audience to listen.

I had many different feelings but my final observation. . . . I would like to feel this way . . . maybe it was too painful and too difficult. And it wasn't, maybe, a lack of interest. I do not believe that was so. That it was just such an unbelievable, inhuman thing that happened in human history, that people just couldn't talk about it and couldn't listen. Maybe that's what took so long. At times it was surprising that other Jews weren't, maybe, more interested. But maybe it was just too painful. In any event . . . my comfort level comes from thinking that it was too traumatic, too painful, and people simply wanted to protect themselves. I don't feel—I wish maybe, it would be . . . different—but I think that was their reason. It was just too painful. And I just couldn't broach the subject.

POLA BILINSKA-JASPHY, 1927–

[Holocaust testimony (HRC-1092, videotape: 1 hour, 40 minutes), 11 November 1993; interviewed and indexed by Joseph J. Preil. D804.3/.B554 1993]

Pola Bilinska-Jasphy [PB] was born in Rovno, Ukraine, in 1927. Rovno was in Poland at that time but was incorporated into the Soviet Union at the beginning of the war. She is the lone survivor of a family of four: her parents, PB, and a younger brother. In 1939 her extended family, through first cousins, consisted of more than two hundred people, of whom only four cousins and PB survived the Holocaust.

When the war started, PB's family was living in the small farming community of Antonovka. Life was rather normal under the Russian occupation until 1941 when the Germans invaded eastern Poland and Russia. PB describes the full fury of the Holocaust as experienced in her region of Poland, starting in June 1941.

> First day, when the Germans came in, the first German came into our house. . . . "Damn Jew, give us bread!" And they immediately started to plunder. And the Ukrainian bandits came along with them, looking through the house. We immediately felt that we had no rights. Nothing had to be said. They immediately took out people, and forty people they took out, and they said they are going to burn down the barn if we don't give them a certain amount of coffee, chocolates, all kinds. So people collected whatever foods they had.

Among their various hiding places, PB's group lived in a hut built to store potatoes and in a pigsty. Plumbing facilities were nonexistent during the years of hiding. Hunger was a constant companion. PB remembers one day when she and her thirty-one-year-old aunt ate sour grass to assuage their hunger.

Her group kept losing members as Ukrainians in the area murdered Jews. PB's small group of survivors was liberated by the Russians on 13 January 1944. She and several family members had been hiding in a barn for eight days, unable to move from their prone positions for safety considerations. She was so stiff, she could not move. Her attitude at the time of liberation:

> I just prayed to God that I should fall asleep and not get up. I did not want to be killed by a pitchfork, but a bullet I would not have minded at that point. It didn't mean anything. You were tired of life, tired of this kind of life.

INTERVIEWER: You were all of about fifteen, sixteen at this time?

PB: Sixteen, yes.

Although the Jews had been liberated, the Ukrainians continued to murder them. PB went to Nova Huta, Mezherichi, and Rovno in a futile effort to find relatives. PB was in Łódź when the war ended in May 1945. Eventually, she arrived in Linz, Austria, where she married her first husband, who was the only survivor in a family of six. Shortly after their marriage, he was murdered by a robber in Poland. PB arrived in the United States in February 1950. She married an American, bore three children who are now all college-educated professionals, and she has four grandchildren. She herself attended evening high school, continued in Brooklyn College, and is now retired from her position as a public high school librarian. PB lives in New Jersey.

AIDA CHAJA CZERCZEWSKY BRYDBORD, 1919–

[Holocaust testimony (HRC-1094, videotape: 3 hours, 25 minutes), 28 October and 22 November 1993; interviewed and indexed by Bernard Weinstein. D804.3/.B917 1993]

Aida Brydbord in Berlin, 1947.

Aida Czerczewsky Brydbord [AB] was born in Pruzhany in 1919, the youngest of six daughters. Her father was a respected religious leader, shochet, teacher, and grocer in a very active Jewish community. Her parents were murdered in Auschwitz. One married sister was murdered with her family in Linevo, a nearby community. Two sisters had emigrated to Israel and two to the United States before the war. Thus, of the family members in Poland in 1939, AB is the lone survivor.

During the 1939–1941 period, living conditions in Pruzhany deteriorated under Russian occupation. Because of Russian influence, the young people began to "walk away" from religious observance although they still attended synagogue services regularly, celebrated religious holidays, and ate only kosher food. This testimony reflects the deep commitment to religious observance, which would be destroyed by both the Russians and the Germans.

The Jewish condition in AB's region of Poland changed radically when the Germans replaced the Russians in June 1941. "Misery began when the Germans walked in." AB describes the organization of the ghetto by the Germans, the role of the *Judenrat* in town and, in general, the miserable and dangerous condition of the Jews under the Germans. AB discusses ghetto life.

First of all, you were taken out to work. Working today they are coming, and they say they need twenty people to go some place. They don't tell you where. Twenty boys, young age, they want them to have. They can take only fifteen. Why? He didn't like the look of him, or he didn't look good at him, or he didn't walk so fast as the German wanted him. Bing! Bing! Without regret! What? Is it a big deal? He's killing a *Juden-schwein*. That means a Jew pig.

What is it, a Jew? A Jew is worth anything? They take away from you the pride, they take away from you to be a human being. They're putting up a yellow star from the front and in the back. God forbid, if he's walking, and he sees you from the back, he should recognize that you are a Jew.

You couldn't walk on the sidewalk, you had to walk in the street. Your friends, with whom you went to school, cannot talk to you. They forbid any gentile friends, with whom I grew up together, we stop talking to each other. They made you feel like you're nothing.

Sometimes you felt . . . let them kill me. I cannot take this any more. But you're young. . . . In the evenings . . . we still try to get together with other young people in the evening.

In a remarkably detailed description of events, AB recalls the deportation of her parents to Auschwitz at the same time that her father ordered her to marry her fiancé, Feivel (Paul), and to accompany him as he joined the partisans. Their group was called Ostrad Kirowa. AB describes the difficulties and assignments of the partisans' daily life: the bitter cold in the woods, the lack of food, the carrying of a rifle, pistol, and grenade, the satisfaction of working with Russians to sabotage the German war effort and help surviving Jews in the area whenever possible.

AB and her partisan group were liberated by the Russians in June 1944. She and her husband returned to Pruzhany, which was now part of the Soviet Union. The oldest of their three children, a daughter, was born in Pruzhany in 1944. The young family was allowed to leave for Poland. They went to Łódź and then managed to move on to Szczecin and Berlin. After the Berlin Blockade, they went to Rosenheim and then to the Feldafing and Förenwald refugee camps. AB wrote to her sisters in the United States and, in 1951, the three surviving members of the family arrived in New York after a difficult voyage.

Toward the end of the interview, AB expresses her appreciation for her life in America and her hope for this testimony.

The journey here was worth it. It's a beautiful country. I gave birth to two more children. My husband worked for only one year and then we went on our own. We made a nice living. If and when I'm sitting here and talking about . . . everything will reach one person and will enlighten that we Jews, that not everyone was going to the slaughter. We were trying to fight, but not every time was possible. If within our means to fight, [we did]. But it's worth it to sit here and tell everything for one person who's going to listen and see.

AB is a widow today, with three children and three grandchildren. She lives in New Jersey and is active in Holocaust education. She has lectured to numerous groups, particularly to students.

MARTHA ZEIDNER ECKSTEIN, 1937–

[Holocaust testimony (HRC-1008, videotape: 55 minutes), 14 January 1988; interviewed by Selma Wasserman and Phyllis Ziman Tobin, indexed by Jennifer Regan. D804.3/.E19 1988]

Three-year-old Martha Zeidner in Siberia, ca. 1940–1941, with her parents and an uncle.

Martha Zeidner Eckstein [ME], born in Kazimierz in 1937, was only two years old at the beginning of World War II. She was an only child when her parents fled with her into the depths of Russia. They remained in Siberia for a short time, then moved to Bukhara in Asia where they remained until the war ended. Almost none of their family in Poland during the war survived the Holocaust.

ME's father had been a businessman and her mother a pharmacist. Although she was a very young child during the war, ME is able to describe some of her family's sufferings. She feels her mother's profession as a pharmacist, so essential in Russia, saved the entire family.

After the war, ME and her parents returned to Kazimierz and found complete destruction. They lived for short periods in Warsaw, then in Munich and Bremen, and finally emigrated to the United States in 1947. They moved to the Bronx and took whatever employment they could find. Her mother became a housekeeper, her father worked in a sheet metal factory, and then drove a truck for a delicatessen. Her parents then opened a grocery store and continued to rise in the world of business until he entered real estate development in New Jersey.

ME and her husband have three children. Two of the children had married by the time of this interview. All the family members live in New Jersey.

At the conclusion of her testimony, ME discussed the importance of religious values and family relationships, which, it seems, were strengthened by their Holocaust experiences.

And, of course, we went back to keeping kosher. It [the Holocaust] was a tremendous experience, a tremendous experience. But my mother never did go back to being a pharmacist. She found it too difficult. And, again, it was a case of the two of them working together, one helping the other. And they did very well, they were very successful in everything they did. They worked very, very hard. A lot of responsibilities fell on me, and there was just never any question about it. You had to clean house, cook, iron. And that was it. No back talk about it, nothing.

INTERVIEWER: How did these experiences affect who you are today?

ME: I think it made me a stronger person. I think I can cope with a lot. . . .

INTERVIEWER: What about your own children? Did this affect the way you brought up your own children?

ME: In a lot of ways, yes. My husband, who is a survivor also, as soon as we met, one of the first things he said was: "I'm going to marry you. You don't know this yet, but I'm going to marry you, and our children are going to yeshiva, and that's that. There's no question about it." . . . And that's the way it was. There was no question ever, in that my father and my husband, that they must have a Hebrew education, so they know who they are, where they come from, what we have all gone through all the years, all the generations.

INTERVIEWER: Was that difficult for you?

ME: No, not at all, not at all. We've always kept a kosher home and there were times when I said, "Oh, I want them to have a good American education so they can get into the finest schools." It didn't take very long, ten minutes later, that OK, OK. And they all went through yeshiva. None of them are sorry about it. Two of them are married now, and I know they plan to do the very same thing with their children. . . . And our daughter, likewise, I am sure, will continue with it.

It's made me a stronger person. It's made our family stronger persons. . . . Family ties are very important. . . . I don't think anyone reading about it, no matter how much is written, and how many movies are made, can truly understand what people went through.

LILLIAN LANDAU ETTINGER, 1929–

[Holocaust testimony (HRC-942, videotape: 1 hour, 57 minutes), 11 May 1987; interviewed by Bernard Weinstein and Ruth Harris, indexed by Joseph J. Preil. D804.3/.E87 1987]

Lillian Landau Ettinger [LE] was born in Przemyśl in April 1929. Her only sibling, a sister, was born eight months before the outbreak of war in 1939. Their father was a lawyer for the government and army and a translator of seven languages. The family was wealthy and highly cultured.

Przemyśl was in the Russian zone before the Germans invaded eastern Poland and Russia in June 1941. In July 1942, LE's family was forced to move into the ghetto in town. Her father was imprisoned, then murdered in the Jewish cemetery after competing lawyers lied to the Germans that he was forging identification papers in an effort to save the Jews. LE then became the head of the family in accordance with her father's directive.

At this point in her testimony, she says:

> It's many, many years later. And I'm not a very religious person. I do believe in God. I still don't understand why I survived, because many times I cheated death. There must be some purpose for it. I did not achieve anything. But maybe through my children, one day there may be an answer, why God spared me.

LE's mother was transported to Auschwitz and murdered there. LE and her sister were saved by Polish families until liberated by Russians. She met her future husband in Przemyśl as the war was ending. She relates the amazing story of her successful search for her younger sister. Her sister emigrated to Israel, LE and husband to the United States. LE worked with her husband in their leather factory in New Jersey. They continue to live in New Jersey and have two sons, a doctor and a diplomat.

MIRIAM LINK FISCH, 1902–1999
ERWIN FISCH, 1934–
ELIZABETH (SUZIE) FISCH WILF, 1932–

[Holocaust testimony (HRC-2025, videotape: 1 hour, 52 minutes), 3 February and 8 March 2000; interviewed and indexed by Joseph J. Preil. D804.3/.F57 2000]

Left: *Markus and Miriam Fisch (ca. 1948–1949) in Augsburg, Germany.* Below: *Erwin and Elizabeth Fisch, DP camp 1947.*

The description of the remarkable escape of the four members of the Fisch family from the Lwów ghetto is based on the written memoirs of Miriam Link Fisch [MF], in addition to the Kean University interviews of her daughter, Elizabeth (Suzie) Fisch Wilf [SW], and her son, Erwin Fisch [EF].

Miriam Link Fisch was born in Lwów [Lemberg] in 1902 and died in New Jersey in 1999. She was an active, alert, and involved person until the last day of her life at the age of ninety-seven. Her husband, Markus Fisch, was born in Stanisławów in 1900 and died in New Jersey in 1959. He suffered for many years from kidney disease caused by eighteen months of hiding beneath the ground during the Holocaust. Before World War II, Markus owned a lumber business in Lwów.

In 1939, the total population of Lwów was 340,000; the Jewish population was 110,000. It was the third largest Jewish community in Poland.[1]

Markus Fisch had one sister and one brother. His sister, her husband, and their two children escaped to Russia. His brother, sister-in-law, and their children perished.

MF was one of six siblings. Her sister Dina survived with her husband and their daughter. The other four siblings all perished with their spouses and all their children.

SW was born in Lwów in 1932; her brother, EF, was born in 1934. They remember Lwów as a modern city for the Poland of the 1930s. The family lumberyard was quite successful. Life in school and at home was pleasant and comfortable.

SW: The Russian takeover was not a threat to our lives. The Germans came and that was it.

EF: Antisemistism reared its ugly head when the Germans came in.

The Jewish situation in Lwów was exacerbated by the neighboring Poles and Ukrainians, who were pleased to cooperate with the antisemitic Germans. Shortly after their arrival, the Germans formed a ghetto for all the Jews. Brother and sister recall ghetto life and "the shortages of food, medicine, everything." Their mother left the ghetto occasionally, passed as a gentile, and bought food for the family. MF succeeded because of her general appearance and her ability to speak Ukrainian. The fear, though, was that she would be seen by a Pole who knew her and who would inform the Germans.

Father was assigned to forced labor by the Germans. Once, when he was injured in an accident at work, he had to recuperate in the ghetto for two or three weeks. The parents then decided to formulate a plan to escape from the ghetto.

MF obtained false identification papers for herself and the two children. There would be no papers for the father. As a Jewish man, they decided, he would have to remain in hiding. MF explained their reason for wanting to escape: "Here, we have no chance to survive; outside, it's fifty-fifty. I'll take the fifty-fifty."

SW: Yes, [it was her decision]. . . . She was very strong. Never came to our mind before the war, how strong and how decisive she was until the occasion came, in emergency. . . .

EF: In those moments of crisis, of course, she discussed it with our father, I am sure. But she really was the strong force in getting things accomplished that had to be done to survive.

SW reports that her mother had told her through the years that her parents spoke to each other every day about the family's difficult situation. MF said that she "had the strength from him."

EF: First of all, she didn't look Jewish . . . and, being a woman, it was easier to get around than for a man, which could be for a Jewish man . . . could be proven immediately. . . . So mother had the ability, of course, the strength that she could maneuver easier than a man, which was my father.

SW and EF discussed the partnership of their parents throughout the Holocaust as follows:

SW: Father was supportive, encouraging, and gave her the will to fight. . . . She had to talk things out with him. . . . The guidance he gave her helped her tremendously.

EF: Some of the people who helped us, eventually, to get out of the ghetto, and survive. . . . As far as we know, he and my mother made some of the arrangements with them to set it all in place.

EF does not know of others who escaped, and he hopes there were others. They both say they had a lot of help in planning. A member of the Jewish militia advised them of the specific time when he would be on guard. He shielded them and told them when to flee.

At this point in the interview, EF agreed to read his mother's writing. The following seven incidents that took place during the Holocaust are part of memoirs that EF's mother wrote several years ago in Polish for the family, which EF translated into English and his mother edited.

Incident #1

In the ghetto, they had a kitchen for children who came with their own containers to receive a little soup and bread. My nephew Marcel, six years old, went one day to this kitchen with other children, and never returned or was ever seen again. Tears are swelling in my eyes and I cannot write any more. [Marcel was the youngest child of my mother's oldest sister, Zenia. Her family needed the soup kitchen. This is what could happen in the public kitchen. MF, however, purchased food for her family outside the ghetto and did not line up in the public kitchen.—*EF*]

Incident #2

They announced "AKCJA" [*Aktion*], that means to take the hundreds of people to the camps and thereby shrinking the ghetto. I took my daughter "Zuzia" [Elizabeth] to my former neighbor, who lived in my former neighborhood in Lemberg [Lwów]. She hid Zuzia in the basement so that her father, who was of German origin, should not find out that she was hiding a Jewish child. My little son, Erwin, remained with me in the ghetto.

Next to the house where we lived was a barn, so me and my son, Erwin, climbed into the attic of that barn to hide from the Ukrainian militia. We covered ourselves with straw and lay still, barely breathing. The Ukrainian militia came and were taking people away. My husband, who had working papers for railway work (essential work) was outside. Some Ukrainian men raised a ladder to go up and look into the attic where I and my son were hiding. Erwin was seven years old at that time. As one militiaman was climbing the ladder, another one said to him, "Can't you see there is roofing up there?" He climbed down, and my husband took fast the ladder away, and we were saved.

From the same hiding place, I saw through a little opening, how they took my older sister, Zenia, and her daughter Lily, and how the brutal Ukrainians took them for the last walk. I can't write further; tears are swelling in my eyes.

Incident #3

You could hear screaming and crying to the heavens, and we knew that someone was being tortured and murdered. It was then that my husband and I decided that I, with my son, Erwin, would leave the ghetto and try to go to the outside, because if they came to our house they would take us.

I was able to obtain a passport from a Ukrainian woman acquaintance and that of her small boy, which fit my son Erwin's description. With my knowledge of the Ukrainian language, we set out of the ghetto, for the time of the raids which lasted one or two days. I held Erwin by the hand and we started walking toward the outside gate, but before we could cross this large field, a band of eight to ten Ukrainian youths, with sticks and razors, along with one Ukrainian militia[man] and one Gestapo officer, approached us.

My fear was unbelievable, because all they were interested in was beating and killing Jews. One the youths shouted, "No! No! No!" meaning that we might not be Jews. I showed my passport to the Ukrainian militia[man], conversing with him in Ukrainian. He looked it over, returned the passport to me, and told us we could proceed. I held my son Erwin's hand tightly, so he would feel secure, and that is how we left the ghetto this time. A few days later, when the situation in the ghetto was calmer, I returned with both my children, Erwin and Zuzia. I picked up my daughter, Zuzia, from the woman who hid her in the basement. Upon my return to the ghetto, my beloved mother, Brania, was gone. They took her away during those two days of raids.

Incident #4

One evening, my husband and the children and I were home in the ghetto, and my brother-in-law came to visit. I wondered why he came so late, and I asked him where is Minka, my younger sister. He told us that she and her four-year-old son are far away. Upon hearing that, I had a premonition and started crying out her name, "Minka! Minka! And now I lost you too!" My brother-in-law didn't say anything upon seeing my despair, but looking at him I knew what had happened to her. We said good-bye to each other, and he left.

Incident #5

My neighbor, a widow, lived with her daughter Rivka for many years. Rivka worked as a bookkeeper in the ghetto, and they lived in a small apartment not far from me. One day when they announced "AKCJA," raid, which meant that they would come and take many people to the Janowska camp, from which no one ever returned. Rivka took a few neighbors and her mother and locked them up in a separate room, and stood watch herself.

When the Gestapo came, she showed them her working papers, which were in order. When they asked her, "Was there any people here?" she said, "No." Unfortunately, someone in the hidden room coughed and, of course, they pushed her aside, broke down the door and pulled out all these people, among them Rivka's mother. One of the Gestapo pulled out his pistol and shot Rivka on the spot. Rivka's mother begged them to shoot her too. They refused her, and took all of them to the Janowska camp of no return.

Incident #6

Another raid was announced. Me and my children, along with many other people, some of whom I didn't know, went into a cellar to wait and hide until the raid was over. There were between ten and fifteen people all huddled together in the pitch dark. There was one mother with her child, who I did not know. When the Gestapo came together with some Jewish militia, we could hear the opening and closing doors, and lots of banging going on. At this moment, we could hear the child cry out in the cellar and, at that same time, one Jewish militia[man] in Polish said loud, "I hear a child's cry." The mother in the cellar fearing . . . the lives of many people were in danger, did put her hand over the child's mouth, and the child never cried again, ever.

Incident #7

We realized that no one would ever leave this ghetto alive. As time went on, everyone knew that on a given day, they would close down the ghetto and take all the people out. That will be the end. I feverishly thought about how to get out and leave certain death behind. We waited for an opportunity, but this was easier said than done. On the other side, we had no one.

One incident that befell my husband helped our decision on how to get out. One morning, my husband was packed into a truck with other men who went to work on the railroad. One of the truck's side racks opened, and some men fell out with my husband on the bottom. They took him to a drugstore and treated him for his injuries. A militiaman came to my house and told me about the accident and told me to have a few zlotys to pay for treatment. So we went to the drugstore to pay for his treatment and to take my husband home. The militiaman told us that my husband didn't have to report for work for two or three weeks.

It was during this time that we prepared our plan to escape from the ghetto. The accident turned out to be a blessing in disguise. I told my husband not to return to work afterward, as they will probably shut the gates to this working camp, with all the people in it including my husband, and that will be the end. At this time, there were less people left in the ghetto, and we came up with our escape plan.

My husband met with a Gentile fellow who used to work for him in the lumberyard business before the war on Krolowej Jadwigi Street. This fellow agreed to hide us for two days, a short period of time, if we got out of the ghetto, until we located elsewhere. When my husband recuperated from his accident, we decided to leave. By now, the gates were completely under the control of the Jewish militia. We could leave in the early morning, together with the workers who went outside the ghetto every day to work. They were checking everyone's working papers, and it was not easy to leave. We had a good friend who was not afraid of the militia, and he told us to meet him by the gate on a certain morning.

On a cold, rainy, freezing day in December, I went to the gate with my son in my arms, as he just got over an illness, and my daughter holding my other hand. We were at the gate when a Jewish militiaman said to me, "Where are you going with the children? They don't have any working papers. Children don't go to work." Our friend went up to the militiaman and said, "Look away to the other side and let them by, because if you don't, you will never be able to look again."

This is how we left the Lemberg, Lwów, ghetto to a new location and eventual survival and life. Our friend wished us good luck in saving ourselves. Unfortunately, this friend was not saved. He perished with all his family together. One of his sisters was here in America.

SW now describes the family's life after their escape from the ghetto.

SW: Mother took an apartment, a boarding room. . . . We stayed in that apartment for a very short time, until Mother could get more secure papers for the family, not for my father. And transportation to another part of Poland, because in Lwów she could not walk around. There was always someone that she met, that followed her, that wanted to extract money from her. . . . There were a few incidents that a neighbor, or a Polish acquaintance, saw her and they followed her. It took her sometimes hours to lose them, running away.

INTERVIEWER: Her ability to escape is very impressive. How did she get away?

SW: She walked from door to door, the person followed her, and she made . . . faster walking, until she went to an attic and lost sight of that woman, and stayed in that abandoned building until nightfall. Then she came back to the apartment.

INTERVIEWER: And this happened about how many times?

SW: A few times, a few times.

INTERVIEWER: This is frightening.

SW: Very frightening, because Erwin and I and Father were in that apartment, we did not go out. . . . If Mother does not come back, that's the end of us. But finally she came back. Then we had the story. . . . It took a whole day, not to come to the apartment, otherwise the woman would follow us.

SW explains that Mother feared being recognized by Poles because the Poles might report her to the Germans and receive a small reward or would demand something of value from Jews. The plan was for the family to use their remaining money to move to a safer region of Poland.

Mother developed a plan with her brother, who lived in Warsaw, to approach an elderly peasant widow who lived alone on a farm near Kraków, in Lipnitza. The family had spent all of its money to escape from the ghetto and reach Lipnitza. It was agreed that the woman, already in her mid-seventies, would provide food and lodging in exchange for the work of Mother and children, both in the fields and indoors. Father was not to be seen by anyone in the hamlet because Polish identification papers could not save Jewish men. He hid under the barn floor. Even the peasant widow did not know that Father had accompanied the family.

When asked to describe their daily routine during their year and a half in Lipnitza, the responses were:

SW: We tended the farm animals, and we gathered wood, firewood, in the forest.

INTERVIEWER: You had responsibility?

SW: Whatever Mother told us to do every day, that morning, that was it. For the farm woman, that needed to be done. . . .

EF: I remember that my kind of small chore was getting water almost every day . . . out of the well, which was about a thousand yards down the hill. I used to get two buckets on my shoulders. . . . Sometimes, during those trips, that I would have to go down by the well, which was right near the barn, where my father was hidden, my mother would put in some food, or something in the bucket . . . and I would drop it off to him. And that's how we would get food to him sometimes. Other times, she would take it down. . . . It was very primitive.

INTERVIEWER: How did you feel when you were there?

SW: We had to get through the day. I don't think we worried for the next day. But that day had to be taken care of. Whatever that day had to be done. . . . The parents did all the worries, the arranging. For us children, we just obeyed what we were supposed to do.

With all the difficulties in Lipnitza, how did the two children understand their lives at this time? What kept them going?

SW: There was always hope.

EF: Our parents would always say, "Hopefully soon, soon." . . . Every day, it was important to keep going. Nobody knew, nobody knew, they would last five years in the war. . . . There was hope, there was hope. . . . Maybe they were saying it as encouragement.

Some people in the hamlet of Lipnitza developed suspicions regarding the Fisch family background. Were they Jewish? EF tells how some men wanted to examine him physically. EF ran home. Mother went to the men and explained that EF was embarrassed by the plan. This ended the problem. The next rumor was that Mother was not Jewish, but she was saving Jewish children.

The family remained in Lipnitza from the summer of 1943 until liberation by the Russians in early 1945, approximately eighteen months. After liberation, some neighbors wanted to kill them as Jews. They were forewarned, so Mother decided to leave that night. They walked to the next town, where a Russian truck took them to Tarnów.

Obviously, the Fisch family was confronted with serious challenges during their eighteen months in Lipnitza. Mother and children could never reveal their Jewish background. With their false identification papers, SF became Ursula Osowski and EF became Kazimierz Osowski. Their most serious problem, of course, was feeding and caring for Father every single day and trying not to be seen in this endeavor by any resident of the hamlet, not even their widowed landlady. This was achieved but, sadly, at the cost of Father's health. Father had developed kidney disease after lying so many months in the damp ground. In Tarnów, he received medication and entered the hospital. The family was dissuaded from returning to Lwów. They went to Katowice, still in Poland. Mother decided to wait until her sister and family returned from Russia, then both families went to Germany, to the American zone. The sister's family emigrated to Palestine. In Germany, SW met and married her husband, Joseph Wilf, and gave birth to the first of their three sons.

The Wilf-Fisch families arrived in the United States in 1950 and lived in Birmingham, Alabama, for a year. They moved to Forest Hills, New York, where they lived until the mid-1950s, when they settled in central New Jersey for business reasons and to become part of a dynamic Jewish community. EF married an American bride. All the sons of SW and EF are lawyers and builders in New Jersey.

Father continued to suffer from his kidney ailment, which caused his death in 1959 at the age of fifty-nine. Mother remained active and alert until October 1999, when she died at the age of ninety-seven.

The conclusion of the interview is especially significant.

INTERVIEWER: She lived a remarkable life, and did a beautiful job saving the family. The sad part is there were so few people who were able to do it.

SW and *EF:* That's true. . . .

SW: From the whole history of Lwów, that my parents were telling us, that after the war they were talking to other people, or documentaries, we are the only intact family that lived through the ghetto [in Lwów]. . . . Of course, there are many that went to Russia, they made it. . . .

INTERVIEWER: It's a remarkable story that is a tribute to a remarkable woman.

EF: We are very grateful that although she saw a lot of bad times, she also had a lot of *nachas* ["pleasure"] in her years after the war, and she saw *nachas* from my sister's family and myself. She saw happy occasions. Five grandchildren, thirteen great-grandchildren she had, and weddings, bar mitzvahs. So she had a lot of *nachas.* And we're grateful for that.

PEPA STERNBERG GOLD, 1924–

[Holocaust testimony (HRC-946, videotape: 35 minutes), 26 March 1987; interviewed by Bernard Weinstein and Frances Farber, indexed by Helene Walker. D804.3/.G618 1987]

Pepa Sternberg Gold [PG] was born in Buczacz in January 1924. Her father was a candy manufacturer. PG's immediate family consisted of seven persons: her parents, four sons, and PG, the only daughter. She and two brothers survived the Holocaust. One brother fled to Russia and was mobilized. PG and one brother hid and managed to evade the Germans. The other four family members perished in the Holocaust.

When Buczacz was under Russian occupation from 1939 to 1941, life may have been difficult economically, but it was not physically dangerous. PG reports that life under the Russians was "like paradise" when compared with the German experience. All this changed after June 1941 when Germany invaded the Soviet Union. The very day of the Germans' arrival in town, a German soldier spotted PG's father at a second-story window and entered the house looking for "the Jew" in order to rip out his beard.

PG tells of the changes and new regulations under the Germans that were designed to make the Jews lower-class people and less-than-worthy neighbors for the townspeople. There were five German *Aktionen* in which the Jews of Buczacz were murdered, including PG's parents and two brothers. A German *Aktion* in February 1942 led to the deportation of a thousand Jews.

Young PG hid in a series of Polish homes to avoid capture. A former maid helped her. In general, Poles would give food but were afraid to provide shelter since hiding Jews could incur a death penalty. PG was liberated in the Russian advance on 24 March 1944. The Germans fought back and the Russians retreated. PG joined a family fleeing town to the side of the retreating Russians. Three months later, in July 1944, she was liberated a second time.

After liberation and the war's end, PG went to Kraków, then to Breslau [Wrocław] (1945–1946), Berlin (1946–1948), Munich (1948–1951), and finally to the United States in March 1951. She met her husband-to-be in Breslau. He had survived by fleeing to Russia. The young couple arrived in the United States under the sponsorship of her American uncle.

PG tries to explain how she survived the Holocaust.

PG: I'm not afraid.

INTERVIEWER: So that helped?

PG: I don't think . . . I don't know what helped. It helped. . . . Luck! It's just luck. Not that you're so smart, not that you're intelligent, not that you're rich helped you. It's just luck. Because you think of places where you were, and those people were with you and they're not here and you are here. You don't know why. It's just your luck. I had a lot of girlfriends; I had a lot of neighbors. And nobody's here. . . . We had a lot of smart people, a lot of professionals and big businessmen, and nobody survived. And I was a girl, and I survived. Luck!

PG and her husband live in New Jersey. His business is in building construction. They have a son and a daughter. They play leadership roles in community affairs and are active members of the Holocaust Resource Foundation for Kean University.

ZYGMUNT GOTTLIEB, 1923–

[Holocaust testimony (HRC-1021, videotape: 59 minutes), 21 February 1989; interviewed by Bernard Weinstein and Sidney Krueger, indexed by Bernard Weinstein. D804.3/.G696 1989]

Zygmunt Gottlieb [ZG] was born in Kopyczynce on 9 December 1923. He was an only child. His father was a prominent businessman and leader in town affairs.

Kopyczynce was in the Russian zone from 1939 to 1941. The Holocaust came to ZG's area with the Germans in June 1941, when ZG was selected with the young men in town to work on the railroad in Tarnopol from the end of 1941 until the summer of 1942.

ZG and the other young men were assigned to forced labor in Kamionka during the winter of 1942–1943. He ran away from the Germans and the labor camp and joined his father and other relatives who were being hidden by a Polish farmer, endangering his own life. In fact, the farmer's wife told the Jews one day, "You have to die, but why should I die?" The farmer insisted that he would protect the Jews hiding in his barn and overruled his wife.

ZG and his relatives remained in hiding for some time from the summer of 1943 until March 1944 when the Russians liberated the surviving Jews of Kopyczynce.

ZG finds it incredible that only sixty-five Jews out of a population of between five thousand and six thousand survived the Holocaust. His mother did not survive.

ZG was in the Russian army until March 1945. He was released on the claim that he was a teacher. He went to Vienna and Munich and, finally, emigrated to the United States in 1951. He met his wife in Cuba seven years later. They have two sons, one a doctor and the other a lawyer, and two grandchildren. ZG is in real estate construction and lives with his wife in New Jersey.

Several themes appear forcefully in his testimony. "How can you forget it?" he says, referring to the Holocaust and to those involved in ZG's own experiences. When asked whether he thought he would survive, he replies "Never! Everyone has a different story." He says of the Poles who risked their lives to save Jews, as was the case of the Polish farmer who saved him and members of his family, "I think there's no money in this world to do something for those guys."

RONEY WIENER HALICZER, 1928–

[Holocaust testimony (HRC-943, videotape: 58 minutes), 16 March 1987; interviewed by Bernard Weinstein and Robert Roth, indexed by Bernard Weinstein. D804.3/.H155 1987]

Roney Wiener shortly after the war, 1945.

Roney Wiener Haliczer [RH] was born on 21 June 1928, in Borysław. She had one brother who was eight years younger. Roney's father was a builder, and the family lived comfortably.

Borysław was under Russian occupation from 1939 to 1941. This meant economic hardship, but the Jews were able to live relatively safely. The fury of the Holocaust began in 1941 with the arrival of the Germans. RH tells of six *Aktionen* in Borysław during which the Jews suffered beatings and killings and their valuables were plundered. In the sixth *Aktion,* her eight-year-old brother and two-year-old cousin were among the six hundred children taken to the slaughterhouse and killed. "The soil moved for days."

People were then sent to concentration camps. "Nobody really knew what was being done." RH talks about the role of Ukrainians and Poles in the Holocaust, the forced labor camp where she and her father worked, the *Judenrat,* the Jewish police, and the hiding places that saved her and her parents. The Germans and their accomplices were so effective that only about five hundred Jews survived out of a prewar population of fifteen thousand in Borysław: 97 percent of the community's Jews were murdered in the Holocaust. After the war, RH and her parents moved through Poland, Germany, Czechoslovakia, and Austria until they were able to emigrate to the United States in July 1949. They settled in Newark. RH got married to a jewelry store owner. Their business and home are both in New Jersey. They have two sons, a dentist and a physician, and two grandchildren.

ARIE HALPERN, 1918–

[Holocaust testimony (HRC-910, videotape: 2 hours), 1983; interviewed by Sidney Langer, indexed by Joseph J. Preil. D804.3/.H194 1983]

Arie (left) and Sam Halpern with Michael Gorniak (center), son of farmer Jan Gorniak, who saved the two brothers.

Arie Halpern [AH] was born in 1918 in Chorostkow, a small town in Galicia in eastern Poland. His father was a Hasidic Jew, "like 80 percent of the [Polish] Jews at the time." AH describes the culture and religious life of Poland in the early decades of the twentieth century. He discusses the role of Hasidism, of Zionism, and especially of the education program in the Polish cheder and the financial commitment of Jewish parents to cheder tuition for their children.

AH started to attend cheder at the age of three, public school at the age of six. His schedule had him in public school all morning until 1 P.M., then cheder until 8 P.M. During his school years, he confronted the challenge of juggling the religious, secular, and Zionist strands of his development.

He entered the family business before World War II. Chorostkow was in the Russian zone from 1939 to 1941. The Germans invaded in July 1941. AH describes the development of the Holocaust in Chorostkow through several *Aktionen,* the *Judenrat,* and forced labor. The murder program was especially brutal and thorough.

During the Sukkoth holiday, October 1942, the Germans surrounded the town and caught 850 people. The remaining Jews built bunkers to hide in during the next *Aktion,* but the Germans returned with bombs and killed many. They then took 900 people ("60 to 70 percent of the population") and shipped them to Lwów or Bełżeć. AH's father was murdered in this *Aktion.*

When a Pole warned AH of the next *Aktion,* he escaped to the ghetto in Trembowla, and found his mother was there also. AH became ill, was hospitalized, and was thus saved from being sent to a concentration camp. AH believes this was one of several instances of divine intervention for his survival so he would tell the Holocaust story. In April 1943, AH's mother, many relatives, and most of the ghetto were murdered. Five weeks later, the Germans liquidated the ghetto of Trembowla.

AH managed to escape and join his brother Sam in the Kamionka labor camp outside of town. Realizing the terrible danger in camp for the remaining Jews, AH wrote to a Polish farmer, Jan Gorniak, a business friend of the family. On 8 July 1943, he and his bother and many inmates sensed the time to move had come. There was German shooting all around the Kamionka area. AH and his brother ran away from the camp; each ran separately to the Gorniak farm. AH's original plan was to remain on the farm one night, but they stayed from 8 July 1943 until 22 March 1944, when they were liberated by the advancing Russians. Even when Gorniak was murdered as a Pole by surrounding Ukrainians, his wife and her teenage son continued to care for the two brothers.

After liberation, AH was hospitalized with typhus. He remained in Russian Poland until the war ended in May 1945, then moved on to western Poland and to Germany. He emigrated to the United States in 1950. He married a fellow survivor. They have three daughters and ten grandchildren. After his first wife had died of cancer, he once again married a fellow survivor. After residing several years in New York, AH moved to New Jersey to enter the home construction business. He is a leader in many community activities. In fact, the founding of the Holocaust Resource Center at Kean College began with a plan proposed by AH.

SAM HALPERN, 1920–

[Holocaust testimony (HRC-904, videotape: 1 hour, 44 minutes), 1983; interviewed by Sidney Langer, indexed by Helene Walker. D804.3/.H196 1983]

Sam Halpern [SH] was born on 20 July 1920 in Chorostkow, a small town in eastern Poland near the Russian border. His story is really the story of the Holocaust. In 1939, his immediate family consisted of five persons (parents and three sons), of whom only SH and his brother Arie survived. His father was a successful businessman and a Hasid. SH went to cheder for religious studies, to public school for secular studies, and was very active in the Zionist movement.

During 1939–1941, Chorostkow was under Russian domination and most business owners gave up their companies under communist rule. The Holocaust was felt in the town immediately upon the German invasion in June 1941. The Germans bombed the area in July. In August, two German soldiers, "probably storm troopers," asked where the Jews lived and proceeded to murder thirty-four of them without any preliminaries. Yitzhak Goldflies, a late resident of Elizabeth, lost his parents, wife, son, and daughter before he managed to run away from the carnage.

SH describes the brutal treatment of Jews in those first days of German occupation, followed by the organization of a ghetto, antisemitic decrees, establishment of a *Judenrat* and Jewish police, forced labor for the young people, and murder for the rest of the Jewish population. The father of SH and others organized a soup kitchen. Jews continued to conduct religious services secretly despite the German ban.

SH describes the brutal treatment of eighty-four young men, including himself, in the snow during the winter of 1942. The Germans squeezed the entire group into a small room in prison and kept them there for three days without food or water. Finally they were transported by cattle car to the Kamionka labor camp, not far from Chorostkow.

The Chorostkow ghetto was liquidated in October 1942 during the Sukkoth holiday. On the night of the final *Aktion,* SH's father, mother, and brother Arie all hid in different locations. The father was discovered by the Germans and was shipped immediately with a thousand other Jews to the Bełżec murder camp. Mother and brother Arie escaped and fled to the ghetto in Trembowla, a nearby town. Mother was murdered in an *Aktion* about six months later together with about twelve hundred Jews. Brother Arie managed to escape and joined SH in the Kamionka labor camp.

The Kamionka camp was scheduled to be liquidated in the summer of 1943. The two brothers joined a large group of prisoners in a plan to escape from the camp on 9 July 1943. Many were caught and murdered. The brothers hid in the nearby fields where they heard the sounds of German guns. "This day was one thousand years long." The brothers finally managed to run away. Four days later, SH arrived at the farm of Jan Gorniak, who said nothing but simply pointed to the attic in the barn. There in the dark SH found his brother Arie. Unwittingly, both had arrived at the same place. Gorniak was a business friend of their family, and the Gorniaks cared for the brothers for more than eight months, until the area was liberated by the Russians on 22 March 1944.

SH has been in constant contact with the surviving Gorniak family members. They exchange visits in Poland and in America. "We feel like one family." A tree has been planted in honor of Jan Gorniak in Yad Vashem, Jerusalem, on the Avenue of Righteous Gentiles.

When the war ended in May 1945, SH went to Germany. He and his wife were married in Bayreuth, and their oldest son was born there. SH was successful in business during their four years in Germany. He and his family emigrated to the United States in 1949 with the help of an uncle who lived in New York. He took a job in a supermarket and eventually owned four of them. His family continued to grow. He gave up the supermarket business and moved to New Jersey to involve himself in real estate development and to become part of a dynamic Jewish community.

At the present time, SH has four sons and five grandchildren. He is a recognized leader in many general and Jewish community organizations. In addition to being a founder of the Holocaust Resource Center at Kean College, he is also a member of the board of trustees of the United States Holocaust Memorial Museum in Washington, D.C. Toward the end of the interview, SH explains his concern for teaching the events of the Holocaust.

I am very happy that I lived to see this day . . . in 1983 . . . so that I can tell the story. Hopefully, some other people will be able to listen to the story, to watch the story on tape. . . . I remember the days in camp and ghetto, when people were going to their death. They told us, "If you are alive, please tell the story." And I personally had many times, when it was very dark, when everybody was being killed, I thought, "Who knows if somebody will be alive to tell the story?" And I am happy that I am among the ones who are telling the story. I wish there would be more. And I think anyone who is alive should tell the story, because we owe it to them, the ones who didn't have the *zchus* ["privilege"] to be here, to tell the story.

GLADYS LANDAU HALPERN, 1928–

[Holocaust testimony (HRC-1066, videotape: 1 hour, 20 minutes), 11 February 1988; interviewed by Bernard Weinstein and Joan Bang, indexed by Joseph J. Preil. D804.3/.H195 1988]

Gladys Landau Halpern [GH] was born in Zólkiew on 30 October 1928. Zólkiew was in the Russian zone from 1939 to 1941 and is part of Ukraine today. GH is a direct descendant of Rabbi Ezekiel Landau, the eighteenth-century Talmudic scholar and rabbi of Prague and all of Bohemia whose responsa, published in *Noda BiYehuda,* continue to be studied today in yeshivas throughout the world.

GH is the only survivor among thirteen grandchildren on her father's side. GH, her mother, and two of her mother's sisters are the only survivors on the maternal side of her family. In 1939, Zólkiew had a population of fifty-five hundred Jews in a total population of twelve thousand. Only fifty-two Zólkiew Jews survived the Holocaust. Both GH and her cousin, Clara Kramer, are among this small group of Zólkiew survivors.

When the Germans invaded Russian Poland and Zólkiew in June 1941, the pogroms, murders, selections, and general brutality began immediately. Many in town were shipped to Bełzeć and murdered there. When GH and her parents were rounded up in this early German *Aktion,* her mother, who spoke German, asked a soldier if they were taking children. The soldier told her to take GH away, and when her mother indicated that Father was in the roundup, he was also excused. As they were leaving, someone spat in GH's thirteen-year-old face. "That was my introduction to the German army."

In 1942 their town experienced the first *Aktionen* and plundering of valuables, and GH's father made arrangements for the family to hide in Lwów, a nearby city. GH was the first to go, followed by her mother and two aunts. A Pole by the name of Halitsky hid them with eight other Jews in his house on the outskirts of Lwów. Halitsky sent his wife and daughter to live in town. GH remembers Halitsky as "a very good-natured man." GH's father never managed to flee to Lwów and was murdered in the last Zólkiew *Aktion* on 25 March 1943, together with the entire Jewish population left in the ghetto. These last Jews were then buried in three mass graves outside the town.

In Lwów, the situation was becoming desperate for GH and those in hiding. There was no money, no food, and hiding Jews was becoming increasingly dangerous. Finally, after eighteen months of hiding, the advancing Russians liberated Lwów in July 1944, and the Jews in hiding were free at last. GH and her mother returned home to Zólkiew and obtained employment. A sense of tragedy lingered in the air. GH tells a terrible story.

> A young woman . . . was saved by a widower, a Ukrainian widower, with eleven children. He was a shoemaker. He saved her in the house. When anyone would come, they had a hole under the table, and she would crawl into a hole. It would be covered up, they would put the table on top and all the children would sit around the table. . . . When the war ended, the next day, out of gratitude and wanting to be a mother to the children, she married this man in the church. That night, they came . . . the Ukrainian National Revolutionary Organization . . . and they killed all of them, the man, this girl, and all the children except one who crawled someplace under the bed. And being there were so many of them, and they lost count, so they missed one.

GH met her future husband in Poland. They became engaged and went to Germany when the war ended in May 1945. They lived in Bayreuth from 1946 to 1949. Their oldest son was born during this period. The family emigrated to the United States in 1949 to join an uncle of her husband. They settled in New York City where Mr. H. went into the supermarket business. The family moved to New Jersey in 1958 after her husband transferred to home construction and in order to raise their four sons in a vibrant Orthodox Jewish community. GH and her husband play dynamic leadership roles in the general and Jewish communities, locally, nationally, and internationally. They have five grandchildren.

EDWARD HARVITT, 1929–

[Holocaust Testimony (HRC-990, videotape: 1 hour, 33 minutes), 3 March 1988; interviewed by Bernard Weinstein and Joan Bang, indexed by Joseph J. Preil. D804.3/.H278 1988]

Young Edward Harvitt (left), and classmates at a Purim party in Hebrew school in Stanisławów, 1938.

Edward Harvitt [EH] was an only child, born on 29 June 1929 into a middle-class family in Stanisławów, which is now part of Ukraine and called Ivano-Frankovsk. Since Stanisławów was in the Russian zone from 1939 to 1941, the real problems for Jews began in June 1941 when the Germans invaded Russian Poland.

EH describes the German *Aktionen* to eliminate the Jewish population. He provides an excellent comprehensive description of German and Ukrainian cruelty in the ghetto, including the murder program which took the lives of EH's father and three grandparents by the end of 1942. Of his entire family, including many cousins, uncles and aunts, EH and his mother are the only survivors.

EH tells the incredible story of his mother's simply walking out of the ghetto with EH, being directed to Lwów, where the Catholic archbishop Andre Szeptycki was helpful. Mother and son were baptized and received authentic papers. Poles were understandably afraid to help them until finally a woman teacher, divorced and with a daughter of her own, told Mrs. H. it was too dangerous for her to work because she was Jewish and hid them in her house. The Russians liberated this area in March 1944. The mother then married a widower who was also a survivor.

After the war ended in May 1945, EH moved with his mother and stepfather to Liegnitz [Legnica], to Vienna, to a DP camp, and finally, to Munich. They lived in Munich from 1946 to 1951. EH attended and graduated from an engineering school where he was the only Jew in an all-German class. He remains in touch with one of his German classmates who continues to live in Dachau, and they have exchanged visits in Germany and New Jersey. EH feels that Ukrainians and Poles were more involved in murdering Jews than were the Germans. He recognizes, nonetheless, that he was saved by Ukrainians.

EH and his family emigrated to the United States in 1951. He married a survivor from Holland. EH has become a real estate developer. He and his wife have two sons and one daughter.

DINA WEINREB JACOUD, 1925–

[Holocaust testimony (HRC-955, videotape: 2 hours, 26 minutes), 9 and 27 April, and 1 June 1987; interviewed by Phyllis Ziman Tobin, Henry Kaplowitz, and Bernard Weinstein, indexed by Anne Kaplan. D804.3/.W424 1987]

Dina Weinreb Jacoud [DJ] was born to a middle-class family on 7 June 1925 in Lawoczne, near the Hungarian border and thirty-five miles from Lwów. She was the middle child, with two brothers and two sisters. DJ is the sole survivor in her family.

DJ describes the hardships of living as Jews, first under the Russians and, especially later, under the Germans. Her mother decided that each member of the family should try to survive independently. DJ, her father, and one brother fled to Hungary and obtained papers certifying they were Christians. Germans occupied Hungary in 1944. The three fled to Budapest, were imprisoned despite possessing Christian papers, and shipped to Auschwitz by cattle car. Her father and brother perished in Auschwitz, while DJ was sent to Plauen, a labor camp in Saxony, where she worked in a bulb factory. She was liberated in Plauen and then went to Feldafing, Bavaria. She traveled to Hungary, Vienna, and back to Feldafing, where she married a fellow survivor who was studying dentistry.

The young couple arrived in New Orleans in August 1949 and settled in Miami where their son was born. Unfortunately, her husband's German dental degree was not recognized in the United States. They moved to the New York area and opened a business in Newark. They have two children. Their son is chief of staff in neurology in a Veterans Administration hospital; their daughter has a Rutgers degree in biology and works on quality control for Johnson and Johnson.

DJ's first husband died in 1967. She has remarried and lives with her current husband in central New Jersey.

CLARA SCHWARZ KRAMER, 1927–

[Holocaust testimony (HRC-907, videotape: 2 hours, 16 minutes), 26 October 1994; interviewed and indexed by Joseph J. Preil. D804.3/.K89 1994]

Fifteen-year-old Clara Schwarz in Zólkiew, 1942.

Clara Schwarz Kramer [CK] was born in Zólkiew in April 1927. Her immediate family in Poland in 1939 consisted of four persons: her parents, a younger sister, and CK. She and her parents survived by hiding in a bunker in Zólkiew. Her extended family, through first cousins, consisted of thirty-six persons. Five survived in the bunker; seven fled to Russia and survived; twenty-four perished in the Holocaust.

CK describes her pleasant childhood before the war, including her outstanding education in public school and afternoon Hebrew school. Life began to change under the Russian occupation of 1939–1941 with its Soviet antireligious regulations. Tremendous changes took place in June 1941 when the Germans invaded the area. She describes the Russian occupation.

> Every school had a political commissar. He came into the class and announced, on this and this dates, which was two days Rosh Hashanah and one day Yom Kippur, if we don't come to school and don't bring a letter from a doctor, our parents will be responsible. That meant I went to school Rosh Hashanah and Yom Kippur. It was terrible. But I was afraid they would arrest my parents. And a doctor wouldn't give you a letter because he was afraid. But that's the only thing I remember before they took away my grandfather and grandmother. . . . But all this paled when it came to 1941.

In describing her happy childhood, CK tells of the personal impact of the German invasion.

> I had a lot of friends, considered them friends. But when the Germans came, they were friends no more. I cannot remember one instance—after all, we were already by that time fifteen years old—I don't remember *one* of my friends meeting me in the street, stopping and saying, "Clara, I am so sorry [about] what is happening now." *Never.* They nodded their heads that they know me, some of them crossed the street when they saw me. . . . And for a teenager, it hurt!

CK describes the organization of the Holocaust as experienced in her region of Poland: the plunder of Jewish valuables, the division of Jews into three categories, the antisemitic regulations, the *Judenrat,* the cattle cars for transporting Jews to extermination camps and forced labor camps. Only fifty-two Jews survived in Zólkiew out of a Jewish population of fifty-five hundred, less than one percent of the community's Jews.

CK then describes her twenty months of life in the underground bunker, from November 1942 until July 1944. The bunker was under the home of a Mr. Beck, his wife, and daughter. Originally, ten people from three families moved in. They were eventually joined by others, including two of CK's young cousins after the children's parents had been murdered in an *Aktion* in the Zólkiew ghetto. Ultimately, eighteen people were saved in the bunker.

CK reports how the town was made *judenrein* by means of three German *Aktionen* during the spring of 1943, how Mr. Beck decided the two young children must be saved in the bunker, how her sister was murdered by the Germans when a fire threatened the entire Beck neighborhood, and how the retreating German army often requisitioned living quarters in the Beck house directly above the bunker. At her mother's insistence, CK kept a diary of all these events.

A sensitive illustration of the impact of bunker existence on CK is contained in this testimony.

> Once, Mrs. Beck brought flowers. I cried when I saw the flowers. There are flowers out there . . . but not for me. . . . Many times, before the soldiers moved in, Mrs. Beck called [me] upstairs, locked the house, the windows, and everything, and I was helping her to clean. I once saw a dog outside, and I thought to myself: He can walk, and I can't.

The group in hiding was finally liberated by the Russians in July 1944. When asked what freedom meant to her, CK responds:

> Being free? We slept in the house, on the floor. We didn't go down there, to the bunker. I ran to the well, I drank water. But when I looked out the window . . . here was my aunt, and here was my friend—cemetery! Then, when I went to the cemetery, because somebody told me that my sister is buried on the Jewish cemetery, that's where they took her to shoot her, I saw cows!

After the war, CK met her future husband, and the young couple married in Austria. CK, her husband, and her parents kept moving and reached Israel in 1948. CK's two sons were born in Israel. The family emigrated to the United States in 1957 to be near her husband's relatives. The family moved to New Jersey in 1964 when Mr. K. joined a home building corporation.

CK's two sons are married and live in New Jersey. They are partners in their father's business. CK has five grandchildren. All the adult family members are outstanding community leaders. Among her many endeavors, CK is president of the Holocaust Resource Foundation of Kean College.

RAE KUSHNER, 1923–

[Holocaust testimony (HRC-911, videotape: 1 hour, 57 minutes), 29 November 1983; interviewed by Sidney Langer, indexed by Joseph J. Preil. D804.3/.K97 1983]

Rae Kushner in Italy after the war, 1945.

Rae Kushner [RK] was born in Novogrudok on 27 February 1923. Her father had two fur stores, and the family lived comfortably. Her immediate family in 1939 consisted of six persons: her parents, their three daughters, and one son. RK, her father, and one sister survived the Holocaust. Her mother, brother, and one sister perished. Her father was one of eight children, her mother one of four. Of her large extended family of approximately two hundred, RK reports, "I have two cousins after the war. . . . Nobody is left from them."

Novogrudok, in the Russian zone from 1939 to 1941, had a population of approximately seven thousand Jews. The Germans attacked the Soviet Union in 1941 and occupied all of Poland. They brought in Jews from many surrounding communities and created a ghetto in Novogrudok of approximately thirty thousand Jews. RK reports that perhaps eleven hundred, or less than 4 percent, survived the Holocaust.

RK describes several brutal *Aktionen* of the Germans, designed to wipe out the Jewish population in town. This includes the murder of 150 of the community's intelligentsia to the sound of music in the town square. The girls were directed to wash the blood away while the Germans danced.

Another incident involved RK's brother. The Germans rounded up twenty boys to hold flames under the outside water pipes to provide hot running water in the governor's mansion while the Germans caroused. Then Germans murdered all the boys. RK's parents found her brother close to death and were able to extricate him. The Germans counted the bodies the next day and discovered one missing.

RK then describes *Aktionen* in which the Germans slaughtered many thousands of Jews, including her mother and second sister. The climate of fear created by the Germans is apparent in this testimony.

> You see, the panic was like this. If they caught somebody, they were so punishable, that a human being could not understand how people could do this to people. Or they shoot them in front of all the people or they hang them on a tree in front of all the people.
>
> And mostly, when somebody went out. I know, a lot of friends of ours tried to break out, in the daytime, when they worked. . . . And so they caught them. They came and

took out the family. . . . You were punished for your daughter, [that] she went out. So the panic . . . it was not easy. And the scare . . . your responsibility for the other Jews. If they caught you, they can come tomorrow and kill everybody. So we were locked in.

Finally, only 350 of the original 30,000 Jews remained in the Novogrudok ghetto. These survivors devised a plan to dig a tunnel, one and a half miles long, to escape from the ghetto. For three months they worked for the Germans by day and dug the tunnel at night. RK tells the story of the tense escape through the completely dark tunnel, while a thunderstorm raged outside. Many of the heroic 350 were picked up by the Germans the next day and were immediately executed. RK, her father, and her sister Lisa survived that night and, after several harrowing experiences, met members of a partisan group led by the legendary Tuvia Bielski. RK describes how they hid, before meeting the partisans, between Rosh Hashanah and Yom Kippur: "Ten days we were sitting under bushes. And rain was pouring like God was crying for us. We were soaked, and we were wet, we didn't have any food."

RK, her father, and sister joined Bielski's group of approximately a thousand partisans in the forest. RK's brother also escaped through the tunnel that night, but was never heard from again.

After liberation, the three surviving family members lived in DP camps in Czechoslovakia, Austria, Hungary, and, for three and a half years, Italy. RK married in Hungary and, during the course of these travels, gave birth to the first of her four children.

The family arrived in New York in 1949 and moved to New Jersey in 1955 to be near her husband's business. Her children are all highly educated. RK and her family are active community leaders. All the children are married and living in New Jersey. At the time of this interview, RK had seventeen grandchildren and one great-grandchild.

MAYER LIEF, 1908–

[Holocaust testimony (HRC-914, videotape: 1 hour, 40 minutes), 8 July 1985; interviewed by Sidney Langer, indexed by Joseph J. Preil. D804.3/.L719 1985]

Mayer Lief [ML] was born on 18 August 1908 in Lemberg (Lwów). He estimates the population of the city at a quarter-million, of whom 30 percent were Jewish. ML was the third of seven brothers. He attended public school, and then a cheder for religious instruction after school hours. He began to learn a trade at the age of thirteen. When he was twenty years old, he was drafted into the Polish army for two years. ML's father died of natural causes before World War II; his mother then emigrated to the United States.

Lemberg was in the Russian zone of Poland between 1939 and 1941. ML's family felt no particular danger until the Germans invaded Russian Poland on 22 June

1941. ML was captured that very day. He was forced to dig graves for Jews being murdered. He refused to return to work the second day and hid in the family's cellar.

The Germans organized a ghetto in Lemberg in November 1941. Jews were ordered to leave their homes and squeeze into the ghetto. For the next nineteen months, ML's talent as a locksmith provided him with a relatively privileged existence.

> I was able to survive. I was allowed also to go outside the ghetto without permission. I was allowed to walk around. . . . When I was going from one place to the other, freely, the one place was here and one place was twenty streets away. They used to lend me out, one institution to the other. . . .
>
> INTERVIEWER: What were you doing? I understand you were a locksmith.
>
> ML: The Russians left safes, locked up. I was able to open them and to set up keys. . . . That was my most privileged profession. . . . I was living in the facilities of the *Oberfelder* Kommander. . . . They treated me very well . . . until about June 1943. . . . Later . . . they made it like *judenfrei,* so they shipped us out. . . .
>
> INTERVIEWER: How many people were privileged like you?
>
> ML: They had a group of about thirty-five people, for all kinds of services . . . [for example] to put up signs. . . . Except I was the one that I could walk freely, and they . . . were under escort as a group.

In June 1943, ML and his group were taken from the ghetto to Janowska, the Lemberg concentration camp. He describes the *Aktion* to slaughter the Lemberg Jewish population.

> INTERVIEWER: How did they decide when to kill?
>
> ML: They killed everybody. Blood was flowing like a river. A German officer said he was honorable and asked to be killed. The German officer in charge responded, "Why not? Let him pick a grave and kill him." This was done.

ML then tells how he obtained false papers that gave him a Polish name and he was able to escape the decree. They made him a Pole, with a Polish name and saved his life. He had no contact with any family members during the period that he spent in hiding.

The Russians liberated Lwów in July 1944. ML went to a DP camp in Germany in 1946. He emigrated to the United States in 1949 and joined his mother in New Jersey. He married in 1954. He has two sons. His first job was in construction and later he bought a farm. At the time of this interview, ML was retired.

ANN STOLOWITZ MONKA, 1929–

[Holocaust testimony (HRC-1038, videotape: 1 hour, 44 minutes), 17 May 1989; interviewed and indexed by Bernard Weinstein. D804.3/.M883 1989]

Ann Stolowitz Monka [AM] was born on 27 August 1929 in Lida. She was the youngest of three children. Her father was an accountant in a brewery. AM recalls a happy childhood in a comfortable home.

Lida was a city in the Novogrudok district, with a population of thirty thousand, including approximately ten thousand Jews. Of these, perhaps a hundred, or one percent, survived the Holocaust. Lida was in the Russian zone from September 1939 until June 1941. The Russians made life difficult for the well-to-do, but the situation became dangerous when the Germans invaded in 1941. At first, her father and family were protected by the German director of the brewery, but when the deportations to murder camps were instituted, AM's family hid in forests, homes, and bunkers. Finally, they joined Tuvia Bielski's band of Jewish partisans, eleven hundred people living together in the forest. Her family was with the Bielski group for nearly two years. They lived on watery soup and one slice of bread daily, but they survived as a family until liberated by the Russians in 1944.

During this period of turmoil, the Germans methodically conducted *Aktionen* designed to wipe out the Jewish population of Lida. AM's description of these years is truly masterful and conveys the terror involved in struggling to survive during the Holocaust.

When the family returned to Lida after liberation, they discovered their home had been destroyed by fire. No one else among their circle in Lida had survived the Holocaust.

In concluding the interview, AM describes the family's difficulties after the war. Her father's dream was Palestine, but that proved unrealistic. Finally in 1949 they were able to enter the United States with the help of relatives who had emigrated from Poland between the wars. They settled in Boston, where AM worked as a milliner.

AM married a fellow survivor in 1952. They have three children and one grandchild. Their daughter is a teacher, the older son is a doctor, and the younger son has assumed a leading role in the radar parts factory built by his father.

SARAH SNOWSKI OSAK, 1917–

[Holocaust testimony (HRC-1071, videotape: 1 hour, 41 minutes), 29 October 1992; interviewed and indexed by Joseph J. Preil. D804.3/.O752 1992]

Sarah Snowski Osak [SO] was born in Slonim on 6 May 1917. Slonim was in the Russian zone from 1939 to 1941. SO's immediate family in 1941, prior to the German invasion, consisted of eight persons: SO, her husband, their two children, her parents, and her two brothers. All were murdered by the Germans except for SO and her husband. Of approximately fifty people in her extended family at that time, all perished except for SO, her husband, and one cousin who escaped to Russia.

When her parents and children were murdered in a German *Aktion* in August 1942, SO and her husband joined Partisan Group No. 51 outside Slonim. When they left Slonim, she and her husband were among the last of the twenty-two thousand Jews in Slonim before the German *Aktionen*. SO's children were murdered in Slonim; her brothers were murdered as partisan soldiers.

Wasila was the commander of the almost eight hundred partisans in her area; SO's unit consisted of a hundred fifty. Originally, the partisans did not want to accept SO and her husband, two volunteer members who came with no guns or ammunition. They were accepted, finally, because they had a friend with influence in the group. SO's first assignment was to wash clothes and sew buttons; she was then transferred to the kitchen to cook. SO reports it was very cold living in the woods during the bitter Polish winter, and she cried a great deal, thinking about her children and parents.

After liberation by the Russians, SO and her husband went to Pinsk, where her husband opened a tailoring establishment with twelve employees. NKVD spying activity unnerved the young couple, and they moved to Łódź, then to Nuremberg, Germany, and finally to the United States in 1948. They settled in Trenton, New Jersey, where a friend from Slonim helped them adjust to their new country.

SO and her husband discovered that "nobody wanted to listen to our stories." People told them it was not true, so their stories were not believed. SO reports that she was very observant in her religious practice in Slonim, but she has been struggling theologically since the Holocaust. "To kill kids, to kill babies, how could it be?" She attends synagogue regularly now, but she has questions.

SO has two American sons and two grandchildren. She is a widow and lives with the family of her older son, who has a position with the New Jersey State Department of Education. Her younger son is an electrician.

Sonya and Aaron Oshman with their older son, Matthew, in Italy, 1945. Shaul Gorodynski, Sonya's brother, is standing behind them.

SONYA GORODYNSKI OSHMAN, 1922–

[Holocaust testimony (HRC-991, videotape: 3 hours, 15 minutes), 17 February and 4 May 1988; interviewed by Bernard Weinstein and José Quiles, indexed by Joseph J. Preil. D804.3/.O82 1988]

Sonya Gorodynski Oshman [SO] was born on 17 December 1922 in Novogrudok. She was one of five children, of whom only SO and one brother survived the Holocaust. The other five family members perished.

SO describes her beautiful, traditional prewar family life on Sabbaths and holidays. She is a gymnasium graduate. There were some helpful Poles in her community, but most were antisemitic and did the Germans' work. By contrast, she is very appreciative of her opportunities and neighbors in the United States.

Between 1939 and June 1941, Novogrudok was in the Russian zone, but then the Germans invaded. The first German activity in town was to round up and murder the Jewish intelligentsia. SO describes when the Germans ordered all Jews, approximately eighteen thousand, into the Novogrudok courthouse. The young people were separated from the older people and children. Trucks then arrived to remove the older people and children, supposedly to work. "Kids were thrown like rocks into the trucks." Her grandparents were removed at this time. "When the rabbi stood up and protested these atrocities, he was murdered on the spot. The others were taken to open graves and slaughtered."

SO, her family, and others were assigned to live in the ghetto and employed in forced labor. They were given a very sparse diet. In 1942 the Germans decided they did not need all the younger Jews for labor and began to murder the ghetto population. In 1943 the surviving three hundred fifty Jews began to dig an escape tunnel.

SO tells the harrowing story of the stormy night of escape and of the following day when a large majority of the escapees were hunted down and killed. SO was among the one hundred tunnel survivors.

After about six or eight difficult weeks, SO's group finally met Tuvia Bielski's partisans. "This was a miracle." The Bielski group started with one hundred fifty partisans in 1941 and numbered a thousand fighters in 1943. SO and her friends remained with Bielski from September 1943 until July 1944 and liberation. She compares the liberation of the Bielski partisans to the story of the Israelites being freed from bondage in Egypt.

By the time of liberation, SO and her brother were the only surviving family members. Her brother went to Palestine, married, and has three children. Upon medical advice for a Holocaust-related illness, SO and her new husband did not go to Palestine. In 1950, after five years in an Italian DP camp, the family came to the United States. Eventually, Mr. O. worked in real estate management.

SO and her husband have two sons, both lawyers. At the time of this interview, they also had two grandchildren.

RABBI ALTER PEKIER, 1917–

[Holocaust testimony (HRC-1078, videotape: 1 hour, 30 minutes), 16 December 1992; interviewed and indexed by Joseph J. Preil. D804.3/.P537 1992]

Rabbi Alter Pekier [AP] was born in October 1917 in Slutsk, a town near the Russian border. He was the oldest of five children. The Germans invaded the Russian zone in June 1941. By October 1941, AP's parents and three siblings had been murdered in German *Aktionen.* Germans murdered groups of fifty Jews in Slutsk until forty-five hundred had been slaughtered.

AP and his brother, Rabbi Berel Peker, were on their way to Siberia at the time of this massacre. The yeshiva in Slutsk had been founded by the community's chief rabbi, Isser Zalman Meltzer. Rabbi Meltzer's son-in-law, Rabbi Aharon Kotler, joined his father-in-law in leading the yeshiva at the time of his marriage in 1914. When the Russians occupied Slutsk, Rabbi Kotler fled from the antireligious communists and established the yeshiva in Kletsk, a nearby community on the Polish side of the border. Rabbi Meltzer stayed in Slutsk for a period of time, however, in order to provide leadership in his community. He was compelled to flee when warned that his life was in danger if he remained in communist territory.

In 1939, the Kletsk Yeshiva and several other world-famous yeshivas in the Russian zone of Poland fled to Vilna, Lithuania, upon the urgent summons of Rabbi Chaim Ozer Grodzinski, the leading rabbinic personality of that era. The purpose of the summons was to ensure their escape from the antireligious Communist government of Soviet Russia. Lithuania was an independent country in 1939.

AP reports the dramatic circumstances of the yeshiva's escape from Kletsk. Reb Aharon Kotler had wired an urgent message from Vilna to Kletsk that all the yeshiva people should travel to Vilna immediately. This was done, and all the students and staff arrived by train in Baranowice on a Friday morning. In order to avoid Sabbath travel, the several hundred members of the Kletsk group arranged to remain in Baranowice for the Sabbath day. This arrangement was communicated to Rabbi Kotler in Vilna, who responded immediately that all his people must continue their trip to Vilna, even if this meant Sabbath travel. The group followed their revered leader's instruction, of course, and they arrived in Vilna on the Sabbath day.

The Kletsk Yeshiva remained in Vilna from October 1939 until March 1940 when they moved to Jonava, a small town nearby. The Russians occupied Lithuania in June 1940. The Kletsk students were then dispersed into three neighboring communities: Salakas, Dusetos, and Dukstos.

Many Kletsk students escaped during this Russian period. In June 1941, a year after the Russian occupation began, the Soviets moved the remaining Kletsk students, including the Pekier brothers, to Reshoti in Siberia, at the same time their parents and three younger siblings were murdered in their hometown of Slutsk.

Earlier, in January 1941, Rabbi Kotler had managed to leave for Japan and to enter the United States in an effort to save his yeshiva. He founded the American branch of Kletsk in 1943 in Lakewood, New Jersey. The Lakewood Yeshiva today is recognized as the largest yeshiva in the world for advanced Talmudic study and research.

AP describes the labor programs assigned to his group of fifteen students in Siberia. Living conditions were primitive and food in short supply. They worked in a forest and in swamps to clear the area for railroad travel.

After four harsh months, the brothers found their names on a list to be freed from the camp. In order to survive, their small group moved to Chymkent in south Kazakhstan where the climate was relatively warm. The brothers wrote a letter to Rabbi Kotler in the United States, and were helped by food packages sent from America by Reb Aharon Kotler and from Jerusalem by Reb Shneur Kotler, the son of the yeshiva's leader. Fourteen of the fifteen students survived.

After the war, the brothers returned to Poland, to the city of Łódź. The Kielce pogrom in July 1946 convinced them to leave Poland. They arrived in the United States in November 1946 and were reunited with Rabbi Kotler in the Lakewood Yeshiva in January 1947.

Both brothers had married in Chymkent in May 1945. Through the years, their families grew to five children each and numerous grandchildren. Rabbi Alter Pekier served for many years, until his retirement, as assistant rabbi of the prestigious West Side Institutional Synagogue in New York City. He is the author of two books: *From Kletzk to Siberia* (Mesorah, 1985), and *Reb Aharon* (C.I.S. Publishers, 1995). The late Rabbi Berel Peker was for many years the distinguished instructor of Talmud in the high school of the Jewish Educational Center in Elizabeth, New Jersey.

Toward the end of his testimony, AP responded to two questions.

INTERVIEWER: What . . . happened with Reb Aharon Kotler and with the yeshiva during the years that you've been watching it develop here in the United States?

AP: Well, Reb Aharon, as in Kletsk, he was a leader in Kletsk, even. When he came to America, of course, I would call him *the* leader. Such people . . . once in generations. . . . As a matter of fact, I'm writing a book about Reb Aharon. . . . I describe his leadership, besides his learning, one of the greatest [talents]. His leadership, his kindness, his love for people, especially his [students].

INTERVIEWER: How has the Holocaust affected your outlook on life and your understanding of human nature?

AP: For us, the yeshiva students, Talmudical students, which were taught, always, to have faith in God, and whatever happens, is God's will. We have to accept it. It's not too hard to understand, but *hard,* but not too hard. God's will. Why? Why did He do it? Such religious thoughts. Great people, they perished. We don't understand everything. God is leading the world the way He sees it, and the way He sees it is correct. That's always our belief, and that made it much easier to go through with it, with that problem of How? How?

INTERVIEWER: What about your understanding of human nature?

AP: That was a real surprise. We realized, we knew, that a human being without . . . working on himself, to be good-natured, to be full of love, compassion, he can be bad. But so bad, we didn't realize that. That he can be worse than an animal. . . . They killed people for no reason whatsoever. . . . For no reason. You are a Jew, you've got to be killed. *That* we couldn't realize, how important it is to work on your . . . [in Hebrew: "character traits"]. To work on yourself. To realize that you are a human being . . . to think about good, not bad; to think about love, not hatred. And to realize more than ever how important it is.

LISA KUSHNER REIBEL, 1930–

[Holocaust testimony (HRC-982, videotape: 57 minutes), 17 December 1987; interviewed by Nancy Kislin and Marcia Weissberg, indexed by Joseph J. Preil. D804.3/.R347 1987]

Lisa Kushner Reibel [LR] was born in Novogrudok on 8 March 1930. Her immediate family, in 1939, consisted of six persons: her parents, three girls, and one boy. LR, her father, and one sister survived the Holocaust; her mother, brother, and one sister perished.

LR's father was in the fur business. She remembers life, and Jewish life, as having been wonderful. What were her fondest memories? "School, camp, summer resort, and family." When World War II started, Novogrudok was under Russian control. The Germans took over in 1941 when they invaded eastern Poland and Russia. She describes a scene of horror when the Germans assembled fifty Jewish professionals, placed them face to face, and murdered them. Children stood at windows in their homes and watched in order to see whether their fathers had been killed.

In 1941 alone, five thousand of the town's six thousand Jews were murdered by the Germans. LR with her father, brother, and one sister were moved into the Novogrudok ghetto. At one time, there were only five hundred Jews left alive. This remnant of Novogrudok's Jewish population secretly built a narrow escape tunnel at night. Understandably, it was primitive, requiring great effort to crawl through. The project was organized and implemented by 250 young people. As the time to escape neared, some of the young leaders of the tunnel project approached LR and her sister.

> They told us, "Listen, Tuesday, they want to kill us. We are leaving tonight through the tunnel." . . . They explained, "We're not going to die any more like this. We're going to *run*. We're going to save ourselves."
>
> And they put a line, you know, who should go first . . . because it's very dangerous, it's a very small tunnel. . . .

INTERVIEWER: It might collapse?

LR: It might collapse is nothing. But if somebody becomes dead, and he stops there, then nobody can go out farther. So they came to me and my sister, Rae, and they said, "Listen, your brother is going from the first ones, because they dug the tunnel. But you and your sister can also go from the first ones" because we are young. "But your father cannot go. So either you remain and go with your father, with the last ones, or you go alone."

> So we said, "No, we're going to go with our father" So we were going with the last from the tunnel.

LR, her father, and sister escaped through the tunnel and joined a Jewish partisan group in the surrounding forest. When LR's family returned home after liberation by the Russians, only two or three Jews remained in Novogrudok, in what had been a thriving Jewish community. Their former neighbors greeted them with surprise, "Are you still alive?"

The family wished to settle in Palestine. They spent four years in a DP camp in Italy and then moved to Rome. Finally, they received permits to enter the United States. Their first residence was in Brooklyn, and then they moved to New Jersey to be near the family's developing business interests. LR is married and has two daughters and four grandchildren.

The strength of her family is obvious throughout LR's testimony. As the interview is drawing to a close, LR is asked, "What was your worst experience?"

She responds, "Everything was. The worst thing was when I lost my mother, sister, and my brother."

ANN CHARASCH SCHATZ, 1922–

[Holocaust testimony (HRC-915, videotape: 1 hour, 13 minutes), 18 July 1985; interviewed by Sidney Langer, indexed by Joseph J. Preil. D804.3/.S533 1985]

Ann Charasch Schatz [AS] was born on 3 March 1922 in Brody in the Galician region of Poland. Her father, a merchant, was a highly respected, pious member of the community. Her brothers were Talmudic scholars who joined the Mizrachi, the religious Zionist movement. AS is the lone survivor of her immediate family of seven and of her extended family of about fifty.

Brody was under Russian occupation between 1939 and 1941. Terrible danger for the Jewish population began in June 1941 when the Germans attacked Russia and occupied all of Poland. AS's father was murdered in bed when he was ill with typhus. Her mother and brother were taken to the train "supposedly to Majdanek." AS, two of her sisters, and about eight others hid in the cellar for two days. A Polish fireman discovered them, confiscated AS's jewelry, and arranged for the group to be sent to a forced labor camp "because [I] owe it to your father to help."

AS was liberated by the Russians in 1944. She lived in small Galician towns (Dubno, Gleiwitz) for about a year and was married at the end of 1944. She and her husband went to Córdoba, to DP camps in Germany, and to Frankfurt. Her husband had a brother in the United States and the young couple was able to join him in 1948. They lived in New York until 1955 when they moved to New Jersey, where they had a number of friends.

AS concludes her testimony as follows:

> In 1948, we arrived in this country, in June. I remember it was Shavuot [Feast of Weeks]. My brother-in-law and sister-in-law took us down [from] the boat. It was a very heartbreaking reunion for my husband to tell his brother that he was the only one left from his big family. He had a nice, wonderful family life. They adored their sister, who had such a hard time to have a baby, and she had it two years before the war. The mother, that was like a queen for them, died too in the ghetto.
>
> Then my relatives start to pour in, which I incidentally found. And, in a way, it was one of the hardest times in my life too. That, I always thought, would be one of the happiest. But all of a sudden, you wind up in a country. It's not envious that you see full families together, living normally. . . . And here you find yourself, all alone. Every one you had. Our family consisted of around forty to fifty cousins, from both sides, my father's and my mother's. All of them brutally killed, not till right now, I have no idea.
>
> If I would want to go back, like people go back, to see the grave, you feel it will

give you a relief. There is no place, where to go. There are no graves. All Poland is covered with Jewish blood. But somehow, you adjust.

In 1950, my daughter was born. And I think that was the turning point in my life. I think that was one of the happiest moments, when Sue was born. All of a sudden, I felt so strong. I felt like I am now in charge, and responsible for my daughter's well-being. I just prayed she should never have to go through, half of one minute, what we went through, the war.

She could not understand why she does not have any grandfather, any grandmother, any aunts, uncles, cousins. And I just could not make myself tell my children. I thought it was not fair, they should be told about all the suffering. I thought it would give them a harsh outlook of life. But, somehow, I survived.

Pleasant things have been coming. Little birthday parties, little celebrations. I really think that my children brought back life to me.

We both work hard here. But we gave our children a good education, what was pounded into me from home. My daughter graduated Boston University as an art major. She was working later for a publishing company. My younger daughter graduated college as a teacher, is considered a very good and caring teacher when she taught. . . . I guess I had to live to give life to my children, or to tell you the story.

PAUL SCHMELZER, 1916–

[Holocaust testimony (HRC-998, videotape: 57 minutes), 10 February 1988; interviewed by Marcia Weissberg and Ruth Harris, indexed by Joseph J. Preil. D804.3/.S347 1988]

Paul Schmelzer [PS] was born in Gwozdziec on 3 September 1916. He was the youngest of nine children. His parents had a wholesale-retail grocery. PS is the lone Holocaust survivor in his family of eleven.

PS served in the Polish army from 1937 until September 1939. After the German invasion, all the Jews in Gwozdziec were herded into a two-block ghetto. The entire ghetto was transferred to the ghetto in Kolomyya and then to a slave camp of the Wehrmacht. The German plan was to send all the Jews to the Bełżeć death camp after the summer of 1941. PS managed to escape to Horodenka and then to Tluste, where he met his future wife in 1941. In April 1942, they were taken to another slave camp. When they heard that all the Jews of Tluste were to be murdered, PS escaped with his future wife.

PS testifies that he escaped "at least twenty-five times." They remained for short periods with various Polish farmers. With his name and wits, he presented himself as a German or Pole, not as a Jew. He wandered about the region with a group of about twenty-five others, of whom six were Jews. He describes how he bought guns and ammunition for himself and his companions. One of his brothers was killed just before liberation. Most of his siblings were murdered in their hometown. The other family members were shipped to the Bełżec death camp.

After liberation by the Russians and the end of the war, PS and his fiancée went to a DP camp in Czernowitz. They were married there, moved on to Munich, and finally to a DP camp near Nuremberg. Their son was born in a DP camp; their daughter was born in the United States in May 1949. PS started life in the United States as a butcher and then became a builder. The family moved to New Jersey in 1970, where PS was able to establish his own business. He and his wife consider the United States to be the best country in the world.

SUSAN FLEISCHER SCHMELZER, 1923–

[Holocaust testimony (HRC-987, videotape: 58 minutes), 1 December 1987; interviewed by Bernard Weinstein and Jeanne Miller, indexed by Joseph J. Preil. D804.3/.S348 1987]

Susan Fleischer Schmelzer [SS], the oldest of three children, was born on 23 February 1923 in Zaleszczyki, a town on the Romanian border. Her father owned property, including a flour mill, and the family lived comfortably. Their region was occupied by the Russians from 1939 to 1941. They did not experience persecution under the Russians.

The Germans occupied Zaleszczyki in 1941 and immediately began to murder Jews. In an *Aktion* in November 1941, two thousand Jews were murdered on one day. A girlfriend of SS's survived on top of many people who were murdered. The Germans then deported Jews to the Bełżec death camp. The Fleischer family saved themselves by hiding in the basement and then moved to a nearby town. The Germans sent the Jews from this new town to the ghetto in Tluste. The young people were assigned to slave labor. SS met her future husband in Tluste.

While working one day in May 1943, SS and others heard shots. Upon returning to the ghetto, SS discovered that a terrible *Aktion* had taken place. Three thousand Jews were murdered, including her parents and eleven-year-old sister.

> That day, when they killed my parents, they killed three thousand Jews. My father had to dig himself his grave. They put a board on top of the grave, and they were killing people. They took off jewelry, clothes, just naked men and women. They had a guy, with a violin, with instruments, to play. This is what they did.
>
> INTERVIEWER: What was the purpose of having somebody play the violin? Just to be sadistic?
>
> SS: Yes . . . I didn't know what goes on there. We just . . . while we were hidden in the fields, you know . . . out of the town . . . And we were lying there, like a whole day, till about six o'clock in the afternoon, quieted down.
>
> So I went to town to see my parents. We were stepping on dead bodies, because

people were still lying in the streets. . . . I came to the house, where my parents were there. . . . A gentile neighbor says that my sister was yelling and saying, "*Ich bin so jung. Lass mich leben,*" which means, "I am so young. Let me live." But they killed her. . . . How they were killed, my parents, somebody told me that my father dug his grave himself. He was lying up on the cemetery. They rounded up the Jews, with the arms behind the head, and they were sitting, waiting, and one after one, they were killing them.

Later, they spread . . . you know, some people were still alive. You know, when you go on that grave, the soil was still moving. So they spread something . . . should be no disease. Because the soil was still moving from that grave.

INTERVIEWER: Was your sister with your parents at the time?

SS: Yes. She was killed with my parents. My mother was forty years old, my father was forty-five, and my sister was eleven years old. Three thousand Jews were killed that day.

SS describes several of the miraculous escapes that she, her girlfriend, and future husband made:

We were in attics . . . in a chicken coop with the chickens. In the nighttime, we were in the fields. I used to watch, every bird has a nest, where to go in. Every little ant has a thing, where to crawl in. And we didn't have no place where to go.

Finally, in October 1943, the girlfriend took them to a farmer she knew who agreed to hide the three young Jews. They remained at this farm until they were liberated by Russians in March 1944.

After liberation, the three friends went to Czernowitz for about a year. SS married her husband in religious and civil ceremonies. The young couple arrived in the United States in 1949, where they were reunited with SS's brother. She, her brother, and husband are the only survivors of their two families.

SS and her husband lived in the Bronx and in Queens before moving to New Jersey. They have a son, who is in business with his father, a daughter, and four grandchildren.

RABBI ABRAHAM SHLOMOWITZ, 1923–

[Holocaust testimony (HRC-1087, videotape: 1 hour, 24 minutes), 20 April 1993; interviewed and indexed by Joseph J. Preil. D804.3/.S564 1993]

Rabbi Abraham Shlomowitz [AS] was born in 1923 in Amstiwowa, a village near Wołkowysk, between Baranowicze and Białystok. His father was the rabbi of the community. His immediate family consisted of ten persons: his parents and their eight sons and daughters. Only three family members survived the Holocaust. AS and his twin brother were able to escape to Shanghai with the Yeshiva of Mir; one sister had emigrated to Canada before the war to join her husband's family. This Canadian brother-in-law, Rabbi Nosson Wachtfogel, served as dean of students for more than forty years in the Yeshiva of Lakewood, New Jersey. Of AS's extended family of fifty to sixty persons, only six have survived: the three mentioned above, two cousins in Palestine, and one in Russia.

In 1939, AS and his twin brother were students in the Yeshiva of Mir, a major institution of Talmudic study with an enrollment of more than four hundred students. Mir was in the Russian zone in 1939. The outstanding yeshivas in that area—the yeshivas of Kletsk, Baranowicze, Kamenets, Navaredok, and Mir—decided they could not remain under the antireligious communist regime and moved to Vilna, Lithuania, an independent state at that time.

The leaders of the Mir Yeshiva were rabbis Eliezer Yehuda Finkel, Chaim Shmuelewitz, and Ezekiel Levenstein. The Mir Yeshiva community realized quickly that Vilna did not offer a permanent solution for them, as Soviet Russia had assumed power in Lithuania. Through incredibly good fortune, and the humane cooperation of Japanese consul Sempo Sugihara, the entire yeshiva received authorization to leave Russian Lithuania for Japan. This was arranged by student Jacob Ederman, who became a well-known cantor in Brooklyn after the war.

Three hundred eighty Mir Yeshiva students were transported by train on an eleven-day trip to Vladivostok, then by boat to the port of Tsuruga, Japan, and finally to Kōbe. Thirty students remained in Lithuania. Rabbi Abraham Kalmanowitz of Vaad Hatzala, a rescue organization based in New York, paid the expenses. Rabbi Finkel's intention was to transfer the entire yeshiva to Palestine and for the remaining war years he was in Palestine while the Mir Yeshiva was in Shanghai under the leadership of rabbis Levenstein and Shmulewitz.

When the yeshiva arrived in Kōbe, Japan had already begun to prepare for war and wanted all foreigners to leave. Thus, after eight months in Kōbe, the yeshiva moved to Shanghai.

The level of study in Shanghai was high despite the obvious stress. Rabbi Levenstein in particular played a key role in comforting and inspiring the students.

After the war, by January 1947, the entire yeshiva had left Shanghai. Practically all of its students settled in the United States. The yeshiva reorganized itself and is now a major institution in Flatbush, Brooklyn. The successful transfer was accomplished under the leadership of Rabbi Kalmanowitz. Rabbis Shmulewitz and Levenstein moved to Israel; the former became the head of the Mir Yeshiva in Jerusalem and the latter became dean of students of the Ponovezh yeshiva in Bnei Brak, the two largest yeshivas in Israel.

AS married and settled in Brooklyn. He is the father of four daughters and one son. His son and all his sons-in-law are involved in advanced Talmudic research in the internationally famous Yeshiva of Lakewood. AS has been a Talmud instructor for the past twenty-five years in the high school of the Jewish Educational Center in Elizabeth, New Jersey.

ADELA (ULKA) SPITZER SOMMER, 1923–

[Holocaust testimony (HRC-909, videotape: 1 hour, 48 minutes), 19 September 1983; interviewed by Sidney Langer, indexed by Bernard Weinstein. D804.3/.S697 1983]

Adela (Ulka) Spitzer Sommer [AS] was born in 1923 in Tluste, a small town in eastern Galicia. Her parents, older sister, brother-in-law, and baby nephew all perished in the Holocaust. The only other member of her extended family to survive was a cousin who served in the Russian army.

AS's father was in the lumber business, and their family lived comfortably. AS lauds a book, *Sefer Tluste* (published in Tel Aviv in 1965 and edited by Gavriel Lindenberg), which depicts the history of Tluste through the Holocaust. Tluste was home to many ideologically different Jewish groups, and education was crucially important for all the Jews in town—everyone was literate.

The German invasion of the Tluste region of Poland revealed much Polish antisemitism. Two priests in town, however, a Ukrainian and a Pole, provided the moral leadership to save a number of Jews from being murdered.

> The war started June 22 [1941]. For ten days, in our town, you did not see a German. The Christian population, in the villages around, killed all the Jews in the villages. And they were going to our town to do the job on the Jewish population. . . .
>
> The Ukrainian priest, I just want to tell you how important a small leader [can be]. . . . Here, you have an example. He called his . . . people together. He told them he wants a Ukrainian [state] . . . but not on Jewish blood, not on blood of God's children. We're all God's children.
>
> He sent young Ukrainian boys that he had an influence on, around the town. He would not let in the murderers from the villages. . . . And the Polish priest, also, kept the people from committing murder. If not for those two priests . . . I would not be here today. . . .
>
> So one person can have an influence. . . . Our maid used to tell us all the sermons. Every Sunday, he [the Ukrainian priest] used to give sermons and tell them that we are all children of the same God. If we don't take care of each other, if we kill one, tomorrow they will come and kill us. . . . And they listened to him.

The Germans organized a ghetto in Tluste where AS lived from 1942 until 1944 when she was liberated by the Russians. She describes a German *Aktion* when she hid in an attic with a group of thirty-two Jews, including a young mother with her crying infant. She was so desperate that she was ready to have her baby killed in order to avoid betraying the entire group. When the *Aktion* was concluded, the group was criticized by the Hungarian soldiers stationed there for having a baby. The soldiers said they whistled and sang loudly in order to muffle the baby's noise. AS concludes by commenting that the soldiers may have been approached for help by the father of her future husband. Evidently, he knew these soldiers. The father himself, however, was murdered in this same *Aktion.*

AS then discusses the moral disintegration she observed among young Poles as compared with older people. She illustrates this conclusion with two unforgettable incidents.

It seems the older people . . . knew life better. . . . And once they wanted to take me into their home, they were already good. I mean, not everybody did it. . . .

The Jewish people were killed, but the Poles and Ukrainians were shipped to Germany to work. There were few able-bodied men to work the fields. . . . A young boy, from the hillbillies, worked for one of the families there. . . .

One day, I was sitting, and it was dark, and the son of the family I was knitting for came back from town. [He reported hearing that an *Aktion* would take place shortly in the locality of AS's future husband.—*ed.*] He didn't see me in the dark. When I heard that, I started crying. He tried to calm me down and the mother. Of course, I was very upset.

So that night . . . they were sitting and playing cards, and I would sit and knit. . . . That night I didn't feel like knitting because my boyfriend probably is dead already. . . .

That young hillbilly [a man who worked for the family—*ed.*] comes in and says, "Hey, what's the matter with her? She's not knitting tonight?" So they said, "Leave her alone. You know, Ivan came. . . . So she's worried." . . .

All the time he used to bother me I should make gloves for him. I said, "As soon as I finish this sweater, I'll make you gloves." So he says, "I hope they don't kill her until she makes the gloves."

I have to give credit to the people. They start yelling at him, he's not a human being and I'm a young child, and I'm younger than he is and he should stop talking like that.

The second story involves the daughter of the family protecting AS.

The young people, they were stupid, some of them. Just seeing the way the world treats us they thought that our life didn't mean anything. And the story I want to tell you, just one incident, there were a few, but this incident is a story I call "The Story of My Dress."

I had a dusty rose woolen dress. It was a beautiful dress. From before the war yet, before the Russians came. . . . It was the only thing I owned. . . . That family had a daughter about my age. She probably liked that dress very much. In order to get it, she put up a scheme. She was going to ask a girlfriend to foretell my future. You didn't have to be a genius to foretell a Jewish girl's future at that time.

Nevertheless, she told the girl to foretell my future, and of course she told me that in two weeks I will be killed. I said, "I will be killed. What can I do?" After a while, she comes with an old dress of hers, a rag, and she tells me, "Why don't we trade?" I said, "Why should we trade?" And she says, "I want your dress. What do you need it for? In two weeks, you will be dead, anyway."

I said, "Well, in two weeks, you will have my dress." She said, "By then it will be full of blood. And it's a pity, such a pretty dress."

The members of AS's family were murdered during the years of German occupation. When her mother died in February 1944, her entire family had perished. AS was liberated by the Russians one month later. The Germans bombed Tluste on the day of liberation, killing a hundred fifty Jews.

After the Russian liberation, in order to avoid being arrested on the grounds of vagrancy, AS became a bookkeeper in a brewery. In the fall of 1945 she moved to Katowice, then to Austria and Germany.

She was married in Austria. The young couple lived in the Ulm DP camp for three years and also in Ebensee and Förenwald. Their twins were born in 1947.

Finally, the family was cleared to enter the United States, arriving in New York on 13 March 1951. They lived in Queens and Brooklyn before moving to New Jersey where AS's husband had a home construction business. AS and her husband are active leaders in many community endeavors, including the Holocaust Resource Foundation for Kean University.

JULIUS SOMMER, 1918–

[Holocaust testimony (HRC-3006, videotape: 1 hour), 1 July 1997; interviewed and indexed by Joseph J. Preil. D804.3/.S699 1997]

Julius Sommer [JS] was born in Tluste in eastern Galicia on 26 May 1918. Tluste was under Russian occupation between 1939 and 1941 and is now in western Ukraine.

JS's family had provided the shochet for eight consecutive generations, father to son, until JS's father decided to end this tradition by opening a textile store in the center of town.

Before World War II, the population of Tluste was three thousand, of whom two thousand were Jews. JS's immediate family consisted of four persons in 1939: his parents, an older brother, and JS. JS is the lone survivor. The extended family, through first cousins, consisted of twenty persons, of whom fifteen perished in the Holocaust.

JS's education through seventh grade involved a short period of cheder studies immediately after the morning religious services, followed by a full program of public school studies from 8 A.M. until approximately 2 P.M., concluding with a cheder program again until the evening. He continued his general studies until tenth grade, when he transferred to the larger community of Lwów, where he lived with an uncle and aunt. Success in his studies qualified him for acceptance to medical school.

JS never attended medical school, however, because this was June 1941 and the German invasion of eastern Poland and Russia had just begun. He was able to convince a Ukrainian guard to allow him to return to Tluste. "That was my first miracle."

Tluste had more Holocaust survivors (five hundred, out of the Jewish population of two thousand) than any other community in eastern Galicia. The two Germans assigned to administer the town saved many by claiming that they required cheap labor. In 1943 his father managed to have JS transferred to the nearby community of Lisowce, a desirable placement since the two humane German administrators had been transferred there.

JS describes the systematic decimation of the Jewish population of Tluste, including those Jews sent to Tluste from other villages. The first *Aktion* took place in 1942 when a thousand Jews were deported to the Bełzeć murder camp. JS's father was among the three thousand Jews murdered in the *Aktion* of May 1943, the "big *Aktion*." Ten days later, JS's mother was murdered in a mop-up *Aktion*.

In discussing these *Aktionen,* JS speaks of when he knew that his father had been murdered.

> I blame myself, and I'll blame myself the rest of my life, how I could . . . not take care of my father and mother. I did not have even any inclination to go. What Hitler succeeded, more than destroying us physically, is the gradual degradation of our people, to lower them to a level of primitive creatures. There was only one drive, to survive. Nothing else mattered. There were no morals. There was no consideration.

JS reports, "We were hungry many times." But it was not as bad as in many other places.

> I cannot compare myself to those who were in Auschwitz and in concentration camps . . . or the big cities. No, their misery was above and beyond. It's indescribable, how they survived.
>
> Tluste, whoever survived, owes a lot of gratitude to the two priests in our town, the Ukrainian and the Polish priests.

JS's brother joined the Russian army after liberation and was killed in Latvia several months later when the Russians were liberating Riga.

After liberation by the Russians in 1944, JS and his future bride, Ulka, went to Katowice where they were married. They remained in Katowice until 1946, when they went to Austria, Czechoslovakia, and Hungary, all in the hope of emigrating to

Palestine. Their two daughters were born in the Ulm DP camp. They were also in Foerenwald and succeeded, finally, in emigrating to the United States in 1951.

JS found what he wanted in the Elizabeth community: "modern Hebrew, modern Orthodoxy, love of Israel, and tolerant. I'll never forget that regal couple, the rabbi and the rebbetzin." (See the Epilogue for more about JS by his wife.)

ILONA MANDEL WERDIGER, 1925–

[Holocaust testimony (HRC–1001, videotape: 1 hour, 53 minutes), 11 February 1988; interviewed by Bernard Weinstein and Naomi Gelb, indexed by Bernard Weinstein. D804.3/.W478 1988]

Ilona Mandel Werdiger [IW] was born on 16 December 1925 in Przemyśl, which was in the Russian zone of occupation from 1939 to 1941. Her father was a Talmudic and secular scholar. Her family consisted of five persons: her parents, two brothers, and IW. She is the only survivor; all the others perished in the Bełżec murder camp.

At the outset of World War II, IW's family fled from Przemyśl because they did not want to live under the Russians, but they found Lwów unsatisfactory and returned to their hometown. The Russians mistreated the family, confiscated valuables, and cut off her father's beard.

The situation was much worse after the Germans invaded eastern Poland in June 1941. IW recalls that many Poles joined the Germans in carrying out their antisemitic murder program. There were *Aktionen* every few months in town, including the tearing of children away from parents. Young, handsome people were selected for slave labor. IW was assigned to work as a servant.

In 1943 IW's family was living secretly in a bunker, but their hiding place was revealed to the Germans and the family was shipped to the Bełżec murder camp. IW saved herself miraculously by jumping from the moving cattle car and returning to Przemyśl.

IW speaks of her Holocaust experiences.

I wanted to kill myself. I did not want to face the future because I knew that I'm going to die. I knew it. I had the feeling. I knew it. . . .

When they discovered us in the bunker, and when they took us to that place, it was a gathering place, when they gathered together about two hundred people, they would come with trucks, they would load us on trucks, and bring us to the trains. While we were coming out of the bunkers, they were hitting us, we should run, we should run. They always did that, we should run. They were hitting, and we had to run.

I left my mother with my two brothers, because my father went with the men. Men were separated from the women. My mother went with my two little brothers, because they were still children, so they were permitted to go with my mother. But my father went with men.

So we left each other. And then, you know, when they brought us to the trains, while I was going up the stairs, because those were cattle trains, so . . . the stairs were quite high. . . . On each car, there was a Gestapo, so I told him he should shoot me right away, because I know that I'm going to die. I said, "I don't want to suffer. Why do you make me suffer longer?"

He told me, "Oh, you are so pretty, and you are so young, and nothing will happen to you." And he pushed me into the car. So I was in the car and people were coming. So I just happened to stay by the window, which was wired.

We were sitting there. At first, the laments were crying and asking for water and standing there for a few hours. But nobody cared, nobody did anything to us. After a while, everybody got tired, and got used to the thought that we are going to die. . . .

When I was in the train . . . we stayed there for a few hours. They called us about twelve o'clock noontime, and the train left at seven o'clock. It was in autumn, and it was raining a little bit. When the train started to roll, people started to cry again.

When I heard that, I couldn't take it any more. So I said to the women, "Please push me up. I want to jump out." They wouldn't do it. They said, "You are going to kill yourself. You are too young." I said, "That's what I want to do." I was so desperate for them to lift me up, that they lift me, I sat on the window and I jumped out.

The train left. I was lying there on the ground. I don't know for how long. Then I came down. . . .

INTERVIEWER: You were able to pull the bars of of the window apart?

IW: Those were not bars. Those were wires. And I really don't know how I did it. I pushed it away. And cattle windows, if you are familiar with them, they are not very huge. They're like little squares. I don't know how I did it.

In a way, I believe in destiny. You know, because I was not that smart. I was not shrewd at all. . . . I don't come from a family like this, I should know how to help myself, you know, how I should act in certain situations. I don't know, I think it was destiny.

But I don't know why I was destined to live and not my family. That I cannot understand.

My father, who was such a pure person, such a wonderful, kind, and civilized. But it has to be destiny with me, because I wasn't smart to do a thing like this. But I did it. I want you to know, I did not do it because I wanted to go on with life. . . . I did not care to live, and I did not believe that I am going to live. I just didn't want to witness all this. I knew I am going to die, so I wanted to do it as fast as possible. . . .

When I jumped out of the train, I was crying for six months. I was crying. I was young. You know a young person takes life differently. But I was crying. I had spasms for six months. It was difficult to be without them [parents]. And then, always before my eyes, when I was thinking what happened to them, to my little brothers. You know, until now, when I think about what death they died. . . .

After jumping from the train, IW managed to return to Przemyśl. The Jewish population was now "down to six hundred" from its prewar population of twenty-four thousand. The factories were being liquidated. IW joined a group of women whose assignment was to dig graves for the Jews being murdered. She was then shipped to the Płaszów concentration camp. "There were always *Aktionen* in Płaszów." She was transferred to Auschwitz, arriving there on 6 August 1944, on one of the last transports.

After describing Auschwitz and Birkenau, IW tells how a group of two thousand girls were sent to the Stutthof concentration camp in Germany. They were put on barges and drowned en route. IW was in a much smaller group being sent to Villi Stahl, Saxony, Germany, where they worked in a munitions factory. This camp was "paradise" after her Auschwitz experience.

IW's next camp was Theresienstadt, which was "horrible," as the war was ending. She was liberated by the Russians. After the war, she went to Austria, where she met and married her husband.

The young couple could not arrange travel to Israel. They emigrated to the United States in February 1949. They lived in Brooklyn until 1973 when they moved to New Jersey to be near her husband's business. IW has two sons, a physician and an executive in an architectural firm. Both sons are married, and IW has two grandchildren. IW continues to live in New Jersey.

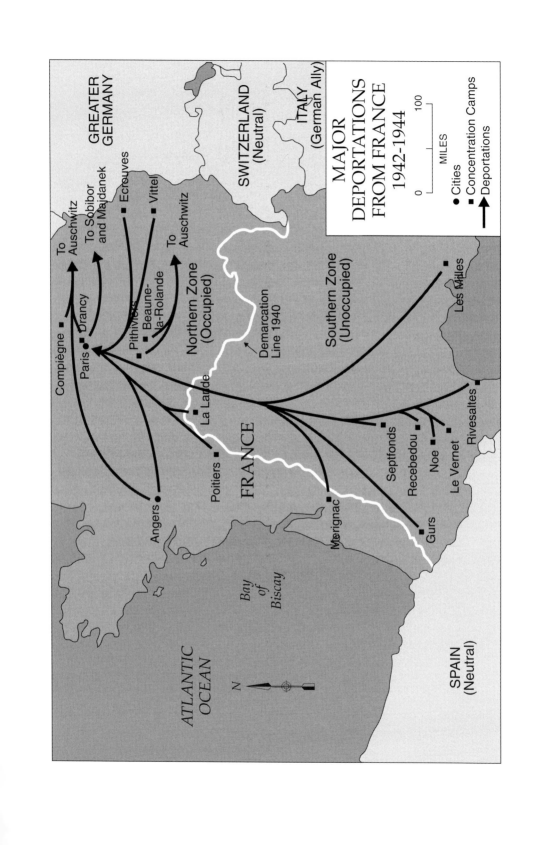

MAJOR
DEPORTATIONS
FROM FRANCE
1942–1944

0   100
MILES

• Cities
■ Concentration Camps
→ Deportations

ATLANTIC
OCEAN

N

Bay
of
Biscay

SPAIN
(Neutral)

FRANCE

GREATER
GERMANY

SWITZERLAND
(Neutral)

ITALY
(German Ally)

Northern Zone
(Occupied)

Southern Zone
(Unoccupied)

Demarcation
Line 1940

To Auschwitz
To Sobibor
and Majdanek
To Auschwitz

Ecrouves
Vittel

Compiègne
Drancy
Paris
Pithiviers
Beaune-
la-Rolande

La Lande
Poitiers
Angers

Merignac
Gurs

Septfonds
Recebedou
Noe
Le Vernet
Rivesaltes

Les Milles

Chapter Four
Western Europe: Belgium, Netherlands, France, and Italy

W E have only six survivors from these countries represented in *Holocaust Testimonies*. Nevertheless, their testimonies confirm much of what is reported in histories of the Holocaust. Twenty-nine thousand Jews perished in Belgium, 44 percent of the Jewish population. On the other hand, a hundred thousand Jews, or 71 percent of the Jewish population, succumbed in Holland. Lien Con refers to differences among the Dutch. Con, her husband, and his daughter were saved by several people, but almost all the relatives in their two large families were sacrificed during these eventful years.

The Anne Frank story may be *the* Dutch Holocaust story. Miep Gies, an employee of Anne's father, Otto Frank, worked diligently to save the Frank family. On the other hand, an anonymous phone call to the German authorities revealed the Franks' hiding place. Anne died in Bergen-Belsen, a German concentration camp, in March 1945, a few short weeks before the end of the war.

The French Holocaust experience is also discouraging: seventy-seven thousand Jews, 22 percent of the Jewish population, were killed. Most of these victims met their fate in Auschwitz. The French proclaimed the principles of liberty, equality, and fraternity; Michel Thomas testifies that he saw French bureaucrats cooperate with the Germans in organizing the deportation of French Jews to Polish concentration camps.

Nella Bergen's story speaks for the Italian experience. She and her five siblings were all saved by Italian families. Under Mussolini and, later, under German occupation, Italians generally did not obey German orders, and 82 percent of Italian Jews survived the Holocaust.

Six Survivors from Western Europe

Nella Anguillara Bergen (Italy)	Lauryann Uray Friedman (France)	Cecile Holzmann Seiden (Belgium)
Lien Cohen Con (Netherlands)	Robert J. Mansfeld (Netherlands)	Michel Thomas (France)

NELLA ANGUILLARA BERGEN, 1921–

[Holocaust testimony (HRC-2013, videotape: 1 hour, 53 minutes), 22 February 1995; interviewed and indexed by Joseph J. Preil. D804.3/.B459 1995]

Nella Anguillara Bergen [NB] was born in Rome on 21 March 1921, the youngest of six children. Her father's family had been in Italy for generations. He owned a fabric store. During the Holocaust, all members of her immediate family were saved by hiding in several Italian homes. She knows of three Italian cousins who perished during the Holocaust. Her parents died of natural causes during the first two years of the war.

As far as the Italian Jewish population was concerned, major changes were decreed in 1938. The racial laws affected employment and business. During the period from 1939 to 1943, however, many Italian people ignored the authorities. NB's family lived in their own apartment, in "almost normal" circumstances, until 1943.

When Italy withdrew from the war in 1943, Germany asserted authority in northern Italy and the situation for Jews became much more precarious. People were taken to Germany to work, especially young men. NB describes the deportation process to transfer Italian Jews to concentration camps in Poland. She knew "some" Jews who were deported. No members of her family were deported.

NB testifies that she "was fortunate. God bless this family"—a lawyer and his wife who saved her, her sister, brother-in-law, and their two children. She responds to a question about what motivated him to assume this risk.

> When I was in Rome this summer, I went in to visit Giorgio [the lawyer's son] and his wife. I said, "I think, if I recall, that your father saved also some Fascists when the war ended."
>
> Giorgio said, "But, of course." He meant that they helped anybody in trouble. . . . He was very moral, very ethical. He was shocked one day. He came to lunch and he was very shocked, very upset. I said, "What's the matter?"
>
> He said, "I was talking with another lawyer and I said, 'How are you doing?' You know, because of the food [costs]. And the other lawyer said, 'Oh, we found a way.'"
>
> "Yes? What do you do?" And he said, "I denounce one Jew a month, five thousand liras."

NB and those in hiding with her were forced to leave Rome for a short period because someone had spied on them and notified the authorities. She fled to Milan for one or two months.

After the war, NB's family resumed their prewar lives. Everything had been removed from their father's store, but she and a brother reopened the store for business. She met a concentration camp survivor from Poland, and they married in 1946. NB wanted to remain in Rome with her family and store, but her husband wanted to emigrate to the United States. They arrived in the United States in April 1951. They settled in New Jersey in order to be near NB's brother and his family.

NB and her husband were divorced in 1973. She graduated from St. Peter's College that year and earned a master's degree at Trenton State College in 1975. She has retired from her position as a social worker with elderly people. She has two children, a son and a daughter. Her son is a lawyer in New York, her daughter a restaurant manager and consultant in San Francisco. She has two grandchildren.

LIEN COHEN CON, 1915–

[Holocaust testimony (HRC-989, videotape: 1 hour, 43 minutes), 20 April 1988; interviewed by Bernard Weinstein, indexed by Joseph J. Preil. D804.3/.C787 1988]

Lien Cohen Con [LC] was born in Amsterdam, on 18 January 1915. She was the youngest of three sisters. LC studied nursing, and in 1939 she married a widower who was the father of a baby girl.

LC describes the antisemitic decrees following the German invasion of Holland in May 1940, including the plundering of valuables and furniture, the requirement to wear the identifying Jewish star at all times, and the enforced removal of all Jews to a ghetto. The critical question became, "Whom can you trust among the Dutch?"

In October 1942, LC and her husband hid in order to avoid deportation to a concentration camp. Her husband's four-year-old daughter was given to a Dutch family for safekeeping. Other Dutch non-Jews who helped LC and her husband included Irma Saltens, a member of the Resistance who was a good friend of LC; Cory Bukiet, a boardinghouse proprietor who made her entire house available for Jews in hiding; and a young family in Naarden, a suburb of Amsterdam, with whom LC and her husband lived for three months when they had to leave Cory for fear of the Gestapo.

LC describes the life-threatening dangers encountered by Jews in Holland, especially during the last year of the war, which included food shortages and visits by the Gestapo, who had been notified by a Dutch informant that Jews were hiding in Cory's boardinghouse. Through it all, LC testifies that "Cory was great." The Con family was liberated on 5 May 1945, just three days before the war's end.

After liberation, LC and her husband were reunited immediately with his daughter. Then they tried to retrieve family valuables entrusted to Dutch friends and neighbors. This effort led to the following conclusion by LC.

> You had three kinds of people. People who said, "We never got it." You had people who said, "We were hungry. We bought food for it." . . . And there were people who said, "Your mother said, 'When I do not come back, you can keep it.'" But there were also people who gave everything back.

LC reports that after the war, the critical question was, "Who comes back?" Her husband's family in 1939 consisted of twelve brothers and sisters, most of them married with children. The only survivors are her husband, his daughter, and two of his cousins. LC is the only survivor in her family. After the war, she and her husband had a second daughter. At the time of this interview, LC lived in New Jersey.

LC concludes her testimony by paying tribute to non-Jews who saved Jews during the Holocaust at the risk of their own lives.

> And I want to conclude with this, saying, "Let us never, ever, forget." For it does not take that long anymore, that no survivors are alive anymore. And let the younger people know and never, ever, forget it. For the expression, "They were like animals." No, the animal is much better. It was terrible.

LAURYANN URAY FRIEDMAN, 1928–1990

[Holocaust testimony (HRC-1003, videotape: 2 hours, 33 minutes), 14 and 28 April 1988; interviewed by Bernard Weinstein and Nancy Kislin, indexed by Bernard Weinstein. D804.3/.F762 1988]

Lauryann Uray in Hungary, March 1944, at time of Nazi invasion.

Lauryann Uray Friedman [LF] was born in Strasbourg, France, on 2 March 1928. She was the only child of a Hungarian mother and French father. The family moved to Hungary, and LF grew up in Gyulahaza, later in Újpest, in the northeastern part of the country. Her father was an engineer who worked for French automobile manufacturers. Although her family was strictly Orthodox, LF attended a Catholic school because there were no other educational facilities for the handful of Jewish families in their small town.

Life at home and in school was pleasant and joyful for LF and her family until March 1944 when the Germans occupied the country. Shortly after the German arrival, LF's family moved into the newly established ghetto where they remained for two or three weeks. Jews were not allowed to walk on sidewalks, could not leave their quarters after 5 P.M., and were subject to many new decrees as well as the plundering of their valuables. In addition, Jews could not enroll in universities, so LF attended a private art school. Her continuing education exempted her from public service jobs, such as cleaning streets.

This almost normal existence did not last long. The Jews in town were assembled in a brick factory, for deportation, ostensibly to a labor camp but actually to Auschwitz. The conditions in the brick factory were miserable. There were no sanitary facilities and no food. When the family entered the cattle cars for the trip to Auschwitz, they were completely unaware of what awaited them, incredible in the last year of the war.

Some Catholic priests entered the cattle cars to convert Jews in order to save them from deportation. This was a "false promise"; none of these Jews could have been saved from the German determination to destroy them. LF could have avoided deportation because she had a French birth certificate with no indication of religious affiliation. When given a choice by her father, she refused to be separated from her parents and was "almost insulted" by the offer.

LF describes the horrible two- or three-day trip to Auschwitz in the cattle cars. Many died on the way. Immediately upon arrival at Auschwitz, men were separated from women, old were separated from young, and LF never saw her parents again. She was with a group of girls assigned to an empty barracks where they had to sleep on the bare floor after being totally shaved and dehumanized. There were no bathroom facilities. There was absolute chaos that first night

LF remained in Auschwitz from March until October 1944. Her description of her existence there during these seven months is masterful. On 16 October 1944, she was among five hundred prisoners who were shipped for forced labor to the Siemens factory in Nuremberg. Actually, the five hundred had been lined up for extermination, but the error was discovered at the last minute and they were transferred to Germany.

The group remained at Siemens from October 1944 until March 1945 when they were liberated by Yugoslav partisans. The Germans had fled the preceding night. Suddenly, they were "challenged by freedom." The next day, the Americans came. An American GI stood on a tank and announced in Yiddish, "I am Moshe from Brooklyn." LF reacts, "If he was Moshe, we were OK."

LF returned to Hungary after the war, but her life there had been destroyed. She went to Paris, attended art school for two years at Strasbourg, and in 1950 moved to Chicago to live with her mother's cousin. She later moved to New York and was employed as a textile designer for a New Jersey firm. She met and married her husband. They have two daughters and five granddaughters in Manhattan.

Did LF discuss her Holocaust experiences with her children?

As for my children, I have never talked about anything. I have decided quite early that I will talk to them when they will ask questions, and always find out what was the motivation . . . and how much they want to know. I did not want to give them any of the reality, which were really horror stories. I felt I myself did not cultivate hatred because I felt if I let myself be eaten by hate, it will eat me up and not change anything of what happened, and I did not want to infect my children with hatred. I felt whenever they will be old enough to ask questions, I'll tell them about it factually what happened. . . . One of my daughters went automatically to a lot of the literature . . . and my other daughter could never cope with it.

It is interesting to note, as this testimony ends, that one daughter encouraged her mother to participate in this interview and the other daughter studied the Holocaust in college.

ROBERT J. MANSFELD, 1927–

[Holocaust testimony (HRC-949, videotape: 1 hour, 23 minutes), 15 May 1987; interviewed by Bernard Weinstein and Selma Dubnick, indexed by Bernard Weinstein. D804.3/.M287 1987]

Robert Mansfeld [RM], a retired quality control manager, was born on 13 February 1927 in Amsterdam. His father was a prosperous manufacturer of high-fashion clothing. As a very young child, RM and his family lived for several years in Berlin. The family returned to Amsterdam in 1936 when the situation in Germany became dangerous for Jews. Subsequently, the parents were divorced and RM and his sister then lived with their father.

After the German occupation in 1940, RM was sent to a Jewish school. Many children from the school were sent to the concentration camp at Westerbork, a transfer point to the death camps in Poland. RM's father, meanwhile, had studied economics, and he became a prominent figure in the Dutch government. He was arrested in 1940 and imprisoned for six months in the Orange House. By 1942, all Dutch Jews were concentrated in Amsterdam and roundups began. RM was arrested at that time, but was released later in the day while many others were incarcerated.

Some time later, RM's father was warned by the underground that his family was destined for the next German roundup. His father arranged for RM and his sister to be sheltered separately by Dutch Christian farmers. RM became the "cousin" from Amsterdam. He did farm work for the sheltering family on their property in Ureterp, Friesland. Until the end of the war, his only real "deprivation" was not seeing his family. He did find his sister, though, who was also being sheltered in Friesland. When German soldiers came to the farm, they never suspected RM's real identity.

RM was liberated in 1945 by Canadian soldiers, as were his sister and father. Thus, these three members of his immediate family survived the Holocaust with relative ease. Most members of the extended family on both sides, however, perished during the war.

After the war, RM's family returned to Amsterdam. RM completed high school and enlisted in the Dutch army, but he did not care to enroll in officer training. His father, meanwhile, became an economic advisor to the Dutch textile industry and was knighted by the queen for Jewish philanthropic work. RM emigrated to Canada in 1952 to join family members there. He studied in George William College in Montreal and married the daughter of a U.S. Army officer in Canada.

The young couple came to the United States in 1955. They have one son, an engineering student at the time of this interview.

CECILE HOLZMANN SEIDEN, 1937–

[Holocaust testimony (HRC-1013, videotape: 58 minutes), 25 October 1988; interviewed by Bernard Weinstein and Selma Dubnick, indexed by Bernard Weinstein. D804.3/.S472 1988]

Cecile Holzmann Seiden [CS] was born on 25 November 1937 in Antwerp. Her father was a jeweler. CS was an only child. Her parents had moved to Belgium in the 1920s. Her father was Romanian, her mother Polish.

The family's problems began in 1940 when the Germans invaded and occupied the Low Countries and France. Her parents were unsuccessful in their effort to flee to England. The Germans raided their home and terrorized them. One time, her father was arrested and beaten but was allowed to return home. Her father was arrested a second time and shipped to Auschwitz. After six weeks in Auschwitz, he was transferred to a forced labor camp.

After her father's deportation, CS and her mother were not welcome in the neighborhood. Some gentiles helped mother and daughter escape to a farm owned by a Christian family in Boom, about forty-five minutes from Amsterdam, where they pretended to be relatives of their protectors.

CS attended a Catholic church and prepared for First Communion. Once, the woman sheltering CS heard a nun make an antisemitic remark and withdrew from the church. This aroused suspicions about CS, her mother, and her protector.

Some friends promised to help them flee to Switzerland, part of a group of thirty on a dangerous trip. Avoiding German border guards was most difficult. When they finally crossed into Switzerland, CS's mother was hospitalized with a gall bladder attack, and CS was so upset that, for several days, she did not even know where they were.

CS's mother was released from the hospital and entered a refugee camp for adults. CS moved in with foster parents. Her first placement was a terrible experience, but her second foster home was satisfactory.

In the meantime, CS's father had survived three years in forced labor camps. He weighed eighty-five pounds when liberated by the Russians. His lungs were punctured from malnutrition and beatings. He returned to Antwerp, heard his family was in Switzerland, and parents and daughter were reunited. They emigrated to Australia, where they remained until 1954, when they were finally allowed to enter the United States and begin their lives here.

CS's parents will not speak about the Holocaust. CS, on the other hand, "cannot speak enough." She is a college graduate, married, and has two daughters. She is the educational director of a religious school. She resides and works in New Jersey.

MICHEL THOMAS, 1914–

[Holocaust testimony (HRC-1054, videotape: 3 hours, 43 minutes), 28 November 1989 and 14 March 1990; interviewed by Bernard Weinstein and Patricia Widenhorn, indexed by Bernard Weinstein. D804.3/.T463 1990]

Michel Thomas [MT] was born on 3 February 1914 in Łódź, Poland. He was an only child. After an unpleasant antisemitic incident involving Łódź neighbors when MT was seven years old, he was sent to Breslau to be raised by an aunt and uncle. MT remembers his parents were often in touch with him.

He was in France from 1933 until 1937, enrolled at the University of Bordeaux. He returned to Poland in 1937 to visit his family, actively opposing the trend of European events. He was in Austria at the time of the *Anschluss* in 1938, and had to give up his Polish passport and flee to France. When war broke out in September 1939, he was offered a passport by the Polish consul but refused it.

MT expresses his thoughts about the perpetrators of the Holocaust.

> We try to talk about what the Nazis did, but who were the Nazis? It was the German nation. . . . Whatever was done was done by the Germans, and with the knowledge, with the knowledge of all Germany. Whatever was done, and one chose Poland as a country, as a place of extermination camps and death camps, was not by accident.
>
> But the Germans, not the Nazis, but the Germans knew that . . . collaboration, and the proper climate, to build death camps, to round up Jews, millions of Jews, men, women, and children, with the help, either the active help or, at least, the passive, of the whole population. And, again . . . one can always find those righteous ones, and count them on your fingers.

MT was in several detention camps in Vichy France, including Le Vernet, Gardanne, Les Mes, and Les Milles. He managed to escape being deported to a death camp in Poland, probably Auschwitz, and joined the French secret army, the Maquis, in August 1942. He is bitter when recalling this period.

> They were rounded up by the French, in a neutral country [that is, unoccupied France — *ed.*], thrown in a so-called deportation camp, Les Milles, right next to Aix-en-Provence, it's practically part of Aix-en-Provence now, near Marseilles. I was brought in there at that time in chains, in chains, to that camp.
>
> And there, cattle cars were brought in, and they were . . . deported to Drancy and Auschwitz, never to come back. Carried out by the French, and only by the French. There was not one German there. In a neutral country.
>
> The only ones, remember, who tried, tried, and showed some human interest in what was going on were the representatives of the American Friends Society, the

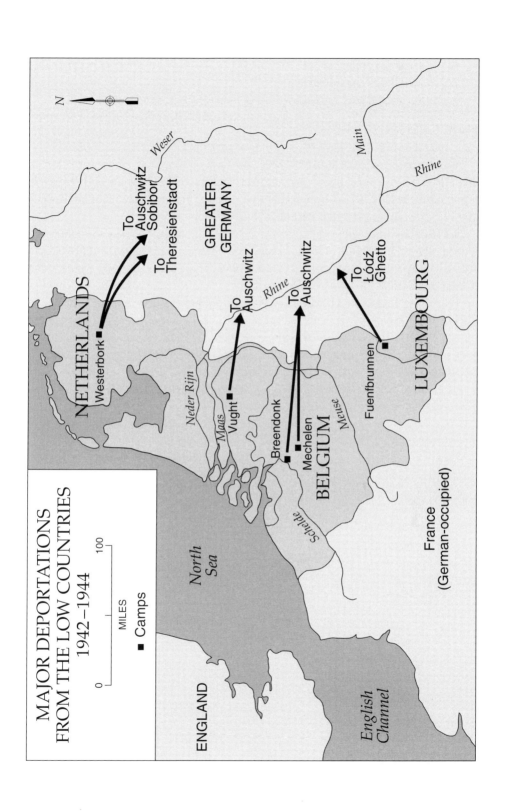

MAJOR DEPORTATIONS
FROM THE LOW COUNTRIES
1942–1944

MILES
0   100

■ Camps

ENGLAND

North
Sea

English
Channel

NETHERLANDS

Westerbork ■

To
Auschwitz
Sobibor

To
Theresienstadt

GREATER
GERMANY

Weser

Main

Rhine

Neder Rijn

Maas

Vught ■

To
Auschwitz

Rhine

Breendonk

Mechelen ■

To
Auschwitz

BELGIUM

Meuse

Schelde

Fuenfbrunnen ■

To
Łódź
Ghetto

LUXEMBOURG

France
(German-occupied)

N

Quakers, in Marseilles. . . . There was no reaction on the part of the United States or other countries, in a neutral country.

MT describes his perilous experience when brought before Klaus Barbie, "the butcher of Lyons." He managed to convince Barbie that he was being detained erroneously. This incident and MT's testimony were important in Barbie's indictment.

In 1943, MT was captured by the Milice, the French Gestapo, and tortured for six and a half hours. Once again, MT escaped and joined the U.S. Seventh Army in Grenoble in 1944, enabling him to enter the Ebensee concentration camp in Austria as a liberator, followed by his assignment to Dachau until 1947.

MT tried constantly during these years to learn the fate of his parents and his extended family in Europe. He has concluded that his parents were murdered in Auschwitz and that he, MT, is the lone survivor of those of his family who resided in Europe in 1939.

MT arrived in the United States in 1947 and settled in Los Angeles to be near an uncle. He had maternal cousins in Los Angeles and paternal cousins in Israel. He opened the first of his schools of language instruction in Los Angeles. He concludes his testimony by presenting his thoughts on his philosophy of education and his philosophy of life.

At the time of this interview, MT's permanent residence was in Tel Aviv, Israel. He is married and the father of two children, an eleven-year-old son and a nine-year-old daughter.

Chapter Five
Lithuania and Russia

~~~~~~

In depicting Holocaust events in Russia and Lithuania, we have to contend with both the dictatorship of Joseph Stalin and the relentless murder program of Adolf Hitler. Consequently, few Lithuanian Jews survived the Holocaust, and Russian Jews were not permitted to leave the country so long as the communist government exercised dictatorial control. This may explain why we have so few Lithuanian and Russian testimonies.

Lithuanian Jewry, during its long and productive history, had established a number of outstanding yeshivas. As a result, this small state became an important religious and cultural center for the two centuries prior to World War II. The vibrant Jewish life in this region ended with the Holocaust: 140,000 of 168,000 Lithuanian Jews (nearly 85 percent) perished.

One million of the Soviet Union's three million Jews were murdered during the war. The surviving Jews endured the increasing antisemitism that permeated the country under Stalin after the war, resulting in a considerable Jewish emigration from the Soviet Union as communist control disintegrated at the end of the twentieth century.

Quite a few Jews now living in New Jersey fled from Poland to Russia to escape the Germans. During the war, they moved into the interior of the Soviet Union, far removed from the killings. While living conditions were certainly difficult for them in Russia, these survivors feel they did not experience the horrors of the Holocaust to such an extent that they should volunteer their testimonies. Consequently, we have families in which the wife, for example, survived the war years in Poland. The husband, on the other hand, was in Russia, which by comparison to Poland was a veritable Garden of Eden and does not warrant his testimony.

Three Survivors from Lithuania and Russia

Miriam Lichtenstein Gershwin (Lithuania)

Jack L. Chevlin (Russia)

Pearl Lucy Gorman Shames (Lithuania)

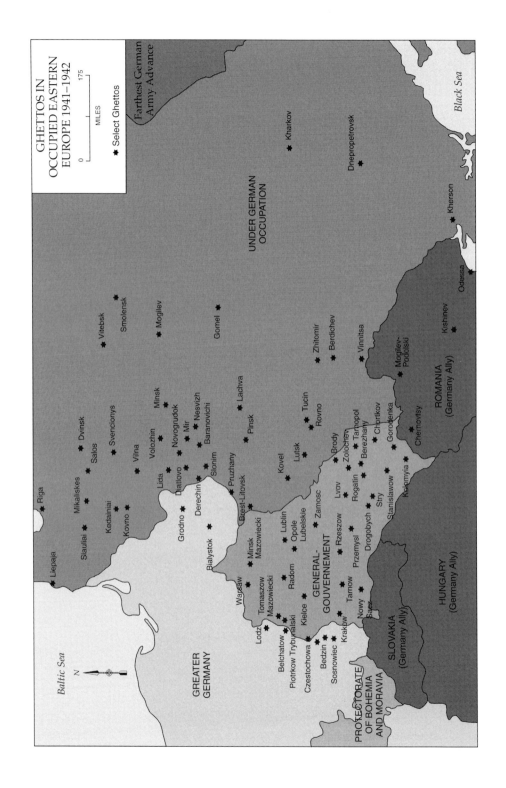

GHETTOS IN
OCCUPIED EASTERN
EUROPE 1941–1942

★ Select Ghettos

0   175

MILES

Farthest German
Army Advance

Baltic Sea

N

GREATER
GERMANY

PROTECTORATE
OF BOHEMIA
AND MORAVIA

GENERAL-
GOUVERNEMENT

SLOVAKIA
(Germany Ally)

HUNGARY
(Germany Ally)

ROMANIA
(Germany Ally)

UNDER GERMAN
OCCUPATION

Black Sea

Liepaja
Riga
Siauliai
Mikaliskes
Kedainiai
Salos
Dvinsk
Kovno
Svencionys
Vitebsk
Smolensk
Vilna
Volozhin
Minsk
Mogilev
Lida
Diatlovo
Novogrudok
Mir
Nesvizh
Baranovichi
Gomel
Grodno
Derechin
Slonim
Pruzhany
Lachva
Pinsk
Bialystok
Brest-Litovsk
Minsk
Mazowiecki
Kovel
Lutsk
Tucin
Rovno
Zhitomir
Berdichev
Warsaw
Lublin
Opole
Lubelskie
Zamosc
Brody
Zolochev
Tarnopol
Berezhany
Chortkov
Vinnitsa
Lodz
Tomaszow
Mazowiecki
Radom
Rzeszow
Lvov
Rogatin
Stry
Gorodenka
Mogilev-
Podolski
Belchatow
Kielce
Przemysl
Drogobych
Stanislawow
Kolomyia
Chernovtsy
Piotrkow Trybunalski
Czestochowa
Bedzin
Tarnow
Nowy
Sacz
Kishinev
Sosnowiec
Krakow
Odessa
Kherson
Kharkov
Dnepropetrovsk

MIRIAM LICHTENSTEIN GERSHWIN, 1923–

[Holocaust testimony (HRC-2021, videotape: 1 hour, 50 minutes), 28 February 1996; interviewed and indexed by Joseph J. Preil. D804.3/.G391 1996]

Miriam Lichtenstein Gershwin [MG] was born in Memel, the second largest Lithuanian city, on 13 August 1923. In addition to herself, her immediate family in 1939 consisted of her parents and an older brother. Her mother perished in Kaiserwald, Latvia. Her brother was murdered in the Kovno ghetto. She and her father survived. Her husband, whom she married during the war, also survived. MG's extended family consisted of thirty to thirty-five persons, of whom she, her husband, and her father are the only survivors.

MG's father was the director of a textile factory. MG recalls a happy childhood in which religious practice was most important and her family lived well. Rabbi Selig Reuben Bengis, her maternal grandfather, was one of the outstanding rabbis of the first half of the century. His career began in Lithuania and continued in Jerusalem, and his biography appears in the *Encyclopedia Judaica.* MG's father was also a descendant of a rabbinical family.

To avoid the deteriorating situation in Memel at the beginning of the war, MG's family moved to Schaulen (Schawel in Yiddish) and then to Ponevezh. When MG's brother became ill with pleurisy, the family moved to Kovno for medical consultation and care. The economic changes under the Russians (1939–1941) made life difficult for those who had been reasonably successful in the Lithuanian economy.

After the Germans invaded in June 1941, the Kovno ghetto was organized. The German commandant of Kovno offered MG the position of maid in his apartment, perhaps because of her ability to speak German fluently. MG worked hard as a maid, and the commandant treated her well. She was in a position, at times, to help other Jews (for example, she saved her aunt from liquidation). During this period, she met and married her husband.

MG remained in the ghetto until it was liquidated in June 1944. She and her parents were deported in cattle cars. Women were taken to the Stutthof concentration camp near Danzig, and women with children were separated from those without children. The food situation was very bad, and they were reduced to eating the flesh of dead horses. The mood in camp was profoundly demoralizing. When asked what kept people going, MG replied, "Probably the will to live. Some, probably, the religion."

In October 1944 MG agreed to have an abortion. "This saved my life," because Jewish women were not allowed to give birth.

MG's work was to dig trenches. After Stutthof, she worked for two months in Torun, two months in Trunz, and two months in Lubicz. The work remained the same, digging trenches.

On 17 or 18 January 1945, the Germans announced that they were liquidating Lubicz and would return to Stutthof; then the Germans fled. MG and her fellow prisoners were liberated by the Russians on 22 January 1945, before reaching Stutthof.

After liberation, MG and many others had to recover physically and regain their strength. The women in her group helped nurse one another back to health. A Polish Jewish soldier warned them not to return to Lithuania. His argument? The Russians will always allow you to enter the country, but not to leave. His advice? Go to Lublin.

Eventually, she went to Berlin where she recognized and was reunited with a friend from Kovno. Later she was reunited with her husband and father. Her husband had received a letter notifying him that MG had perished. She has the letter today. Her description of her surprise arrival in Munich to meet the two men in her family is a dramatic high point in MG's story.

The three survivors arrived in the United States in 1949. During their first month in America, they lived with cousins in Baltimore, in a rabbinical home. Then her New Jersey uncle convinced them to settle in central New Jersey. MG's father lived with his daughter and son-in-law until his death in 1963. She has two children and four grandchildren.

Toward the end of the interview, MG responded to a question in a manner that revealed the significant impact of the Holocaust, even on a person who is determined "to emphasize the positive, not grim, aspects of the experience."

INTERVIEWER: How has the Holocaust affected your outlook on life and your understanding of human nature?

MG: My outlook on life is that nothing matters except your family and your health, because other things are all minor things. You have good things, and one day or in one hour, you don't have them. Now we, for instance, like our family, lost twice. We went out of Memel, only with a little suitcase, we left everything. We went to the ghetto, only with a little package. And, thank God, we came here, and God was good to us. We educated our children. They both went to college. . . . That's what we felt, that nothing matters, only that we are a very close family, that only those things matter to me.

INTERVIEWER: What about your understanding of human nature?

MG: Well . . . I take them as they come. I don't . . . trust too much. I look for the good things but, for instance, to have a very, very close friend, what I could tell all my intimate things, and this I can't. Because, as I said, I don't trust people.

INTERVIEWER: You don't trust people?

MG: No, it's not a good thing.

INTERVIEWER: You don't trust all people?

MG: No. In a way, I trust them, because otherwise I couldn't function. But I take it only to a point, that I shouldn't be again . . . disappointed, or let down, so it's only up till a point.

PEARL LUCY GORMAN SHAMES, 1921–

[Holocaust testimony (HRC-1056, videotape: 1 hour, 55 minutes), 19 December 1989; interviewed by Bernard Weinstein and Marcia Weissberg, indexed by Bernard Weinstein. D804.3/.S522 1989]

Pearl Lucy Gorman in Vilna, September 1933, age twelve.

Pearl L. Gorman Shames [PS] was born in Vilna on 6 January 1921. Her father, who was in the lumber business, died in 1927 when PS was six years old. PS's mother then assumed responsibility for the family. It was difficult for Jews to be accepted in the gymnasium of Vilna, but PS achieved high scores on the entrance examinations and was accepted together with several other Jewish girls. This may have saved her life in the Holocaust. She studied German and was a university student when World War II started.

The Germans invaded Russian Poland and Russia in June 1941. All the Jews were compelled to move into a ghetto in Vilna. Then, "a miracle happened." A German officer asked PS if she spoke German. When she confirmed that she did indeed speak German, PS was taken to the guardhouse and assigned to darning socks for the German soldiers. She was given privileges and treated well. She arranged for her sister to be given the same work. Several months later, the German soldiers were moved to the front. PS and her sister were sent to the labor camp Heereskraftfahrzeug Park outside Vilna. Once again, PS's fluency in German impressed the camp administrator, and she was given special privileges and food.

There was an active cultural life in the ghetto. The Jews organized libraries, a theater, and conducted Yom Kippur services. PS fasted on Yom Kippur even though the Jews were near starvation. In the meantime, Vilna's Jewish population had declined precipitously, from seventy thousand to twenty thousand. The ghetto was being liquidated. Only those Jews considered "useful" by the Germans would be allowed to live. There was a *Kinderaktion* on 27 March 1944. Evidently, children were not useful.

When the SS replaced the German army in Vilna, they were determined to wipe out all of Vilna's remaining Jews, but the Russians liberated Vilna before the last Jews were murdered. PS returned to the university to complete her studies. She married in 1947. Her dissertation on sickness in the camps so impressed her professor that he recommended her for doctoral studies. Her application was turned down by the Soviet authorities because she was Jewish, and she was not allowed to take the entrance examinations.

PS, her husband, and daughter worked their way to freedom by leaving Vilna and moving through Łódź, Warsaw, and Stettin. They arrived in the United States in 1959 and settled in New Jersey.

Jack Chevlin and relatives in Dohlinow, ca. 1933–1934. His mother stands at extreme left. Jack, in cap, stands in back row near his mother. Others in picture include his grandparents, an aunt, three siblings, and five cousins.

JACK L. CHEVLIN, 1931–

[Holocaust testimony (HRC-2006, videotape: 1 hour, 25 minutes), 14 April 1994; interviewed and indexed by Bernard Weinstein. D804.3/.C492 1994]

The youngest of four children, Jack Chevlin [JC] was born in 1931 in Dolhinow, White Russia (Belarus). His father was a prominent businessman and enjoyed good relationships with his Christian customers. Dolhinow was occupied by the Russians from 1939 to 1941, then the Germans invaded Russian-held territory. JC's family remained in town for a year and experienced the developing Holocaust in Eastern Europe—confiscation of valuables, roundups, and murders. His family was hidden and assisted by several Gentile customers. When warning came of a major German campaign against the Jews in town, the family began a perilous escape into Russia.

JC's father's family perished at this time, but the immediate family, after walking "hundreds of miles," crossed the border into Russia and arrived in Torapetz. They managed to take a train deeper into Russia and arrived at a cooperative village where they lived until the end of the war. The father worked; the children went to school. The oldest brother volunteered to serve in the Russian army, and the family assumes that he died a soldier's death. As the Russians advanced into Poland, JC's family was able to return to Dolhinow. Polish citizens were permitted by the Russians to leave for Poland. JC's family took advantage of this opportunity and continued to Bratislava in Czechoslovakia, Linz in Austria, and then to West Germany. A fantastic development was the survival of JC's grandmother with partisans in Poland.

The family intended to emigrate to Israel, but after arriving in Germany, JC's father located and communicated with his brother, a dentist in New York. The family arrived in the United States in 1949 and settled in the Bronx. JC completed high school, went on to Hunter College of City University for undergraduate and graduate degrees in music and became a music teacher. JC's wife is from Montreal. They lived in Montreal four years before coming to live and teach in New Jersey. They have three children, all of whom have begun professional careers.

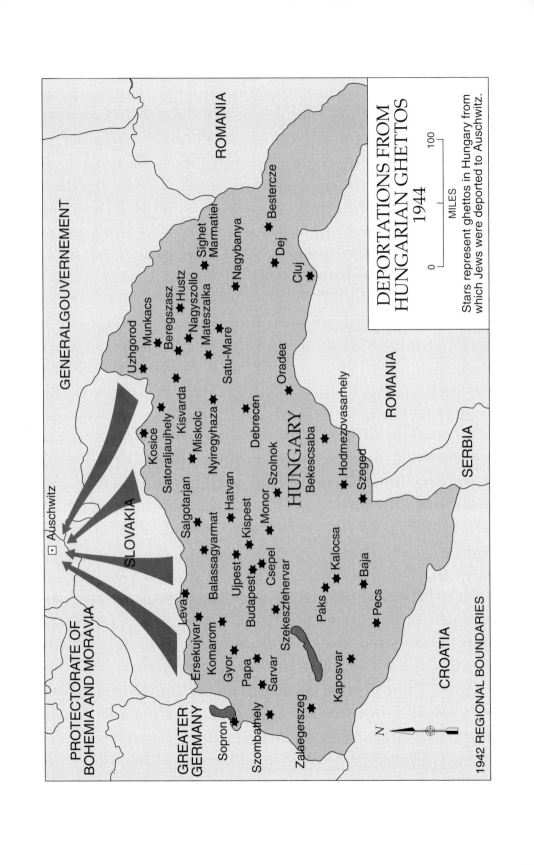

DEPORTATIONS FROM
HUNGARIAN GHETTOS
1944

MILES

0   100

Stars represent ghettos in Hungary from
which Jews were deported to Auschwitz.

GENERALGOUVERNEMENT

ROMANIA

PROTECTORATE OF
BOHEMIA AND MORAVIA

SLOVAKIA

Auschwitz

GREATER
GERMANY

HUNGARY

ROMANIA

SERBIA

CROATIA

1942 REGIONAL BOUNDARIES

N

Uzhgorod
Munkacs
Beregszasz
Hustz
Nagyszollo
Sighet
Mateszalka
Marmatiel
Satu-Mare
Nagybanya
Dej
Bestercze
Cluj
Oradea

Kosice
Kisvarda
Satoraljaujhely
Miskolc
Salgotarjan
Nyiregyhaza
Hatvan
Debrecen
Szolnok
Monor
Kispest
Bekescsaba
Hodmezovasarhely
Szeged

Leva
Ersekujvar
Komarom
Balassagyarmat
Ujpest
Budapest
Csepel
Szekeszfehervar
Paks
Kalocsa
Baja
Pecs

Gyor
Papa
Sarvar
Kaposvar
Zalaegerszeg

Sopron
Szombathely

Chapter Six
Central Europe: Czechoslovakia, Hungary, Romania, and Yugoslavia

$\mathbf{T}_{\text{HE}}$ Holocaust in Central Europe reveals the extreme dedication of the Germans to this crime and tragedy. After all, by the spring and summer of 1944, it was obvious that Germany had lost the war; nevertheless, it was during these months that Hitler's army moved in and Eichmann initiated the program of uprooting the Jewish population and transporting the victims to the murder camps in Poland, primarily to Auschwitz. What must be remembered is that in a few short months in 1944, with the Russians advancing from the east and the Allied forces having opened the second front in the west, the Germans under Eichmann worked unceasingly. In Hungary, for example, 525,000 of a Jewish population of 825,000 (two-thirds of Hungary's Jews) were wiped out after the outcome of the war had been determined.

The twenty-eight testimonies in this section provide firsthand descriptions of the organization of the Holocaust: the gathering of Jews into ghettos in larger communities, the plundering of Jewish valuables, the cattle car transportation to Auschwitz, the arrival at Auschwitz-Birkenau, the death marches from Auschwitz as the Germans fled the advancing Russians, the utter chaos in the camps during the closing days of the war, and finally the bitterness of liberation for the small number of victims who managed to survive.

As we read these testimonies, we marvel at the ability of the survivors to recover—physically, emotionally, and spiritually—to resume their lives, and to build new families. At the same time, we must always remember the millions of their relatives who perished and the many other millions who were never born.

Twenty-eight Survivors from Central Europe

CZECHOSLOVAKIA

Margie Gottesman Appel	Edith Muller Farben	Pearl Katz Gruenberg
Ernest Bokor	Eugene Fried	Helen Stern Herman
Helena Lebovitz Bokor	Frieda Stern Fried	Michael Hersh
Pearl Davis	Mike Goldberger	Fanny Schachter Katz

Benjamin Katzwer	Allen Moskowitz	Saul Weinberger
Rose Feig Lazarus	Hugo Princz	Harold Zelmanovics
Susan Sturc Lederman	Otto Salamon	

HUNGARY

| Margit Buchhalter Feld-man | Ernest Gottdiener | Martha Seiler Klein |
| | Judit Tauszky Gottdiener | |

ROMANIA

| Musia Luttinger Gross | Dora Basch Schoen | Sylvia Blau Wirtzbaum |

YUGOSLAVIA

Zvi Stern

Czechoslovakia

MARGIE GOTTESMAN APPEL, 1928–

[Holocaust testimony (HRC-952, videotape: 1 hour, 54 minutes), 30 March 1987; interviewed by Bernard Weinstein and Phyllis Ziman Tobin, indexed by Bernard Weinstein. D804.3/.A646 1987]

Margie Gottesman Appel [MA] was born in Klecenov on 13 August 1928. She was the eighth of nine children (seven boys, two girls). In addition to MA, three brothers and her sister survived the Holocaust; her parents and four other brothers perished. The family was middle class; her father was in the cattle business. There were forty-five Jewish families in their small town.

Klecenov was in the region taken over by Hungary in 1938. "That's when the trouble started. . . . Jewish kids stopped going to school." MA's education stopped in the sixth grade. While Jewish men and boys were taken for forced labor through 1943, the most dangerous time began in 1944.

MA's family was moved to the Munkács ghetto in April 1944.The town sheriff and his son approached MA's father and offered to hide MA and her younger brother. Her father refused; he wanted the entire family to remain together. They lived under horrible conditions in a Munkács brick factory for about four weeks. The men had to cut off their beards; MA had her braids cut off. A curfew was decreed; torture awaited those who returned late. MA's grandfather was ninety-four years old. He refused to go to the ghetto and was beaten by Hungarians and Ukrainians. In general, MA reports, the attitude of their neighbors was very disappointing.

They laughed at the forced departure of the Jews and seemed to enjoy the scene. MA gives powerful descriptions of the cattle car trip to Auschwitz, the arrival at the camp, and the trauma of existence during her six weeks in Auschwitz.

The railroad trip, as is well known, meant no bathroom facilities and no water in incredibly crowded conditions for endless days. "It was terrible, horrible." In a poetic vein, MA continues:

> One day in the morning, it was about four o'clock, or four-thirty, I woke up and I look out the window. I see the beautiful sunrise, which I never saw in my life. I never got up so early. And I said, "Isn't that beautiful! I never saw anything like that!" And I said to myself, "Look how nice it is. Why is it for us so heavy on our hearts that we cannot enjoy this?" And I started to cry. My mother woke up. She said, "What's going on? Why are you crying?" And I said, "Nothing, nothing." I'll never forget that sunrise, how I felt, the heart was so heavy. We knew it was no good. And this is so beautiful.

On arrival at Auschwitz, Polish Jews were assigned to confiscate all the belongings of the new arrivals for the Germans. MA describes the mumbling of these workers.

> Kids who are young, say you are older. Women who have children, give the children to older women. And he didn't stop, he kept on talking. . . . To this day, I am so angry at myself that I didn't look back [to see] which way my mother went. But later, far away, I saw the women walking. You couldn't, because they hit you, they kept pushing you. . . . Fast! Fast! . . . I come to Mengele's table. And Mengele said to me, I'll never forget those eyes. He said, "Turn around." And just to me he says, "How old are you?" Then I started to think what the man said.
> I said "I am eighteen."
> "Do you know how to work?"
> "Yes."
> "Do you want to work?"
> "Yes."
> "Okay."
> So I was saved. And my sister also. And I knew my three brothers, I knew, they were also at work.

MA then describes her six weeks in Auschwitz. She and her sister were among the five hundred girls selected for transfer to forced labor in Gelsenkirchen, Germany. They loaded bricks, worked with cement, lived in tents, and had toilets. "It was good."

The sisters were transferred to Essen to work in the Krupp munitions factory. After six months in Essen, the sisters were taken to the Bergen-Belsen concentration camp in March 1945. MA reports they were treated relatively well in Essen because of the Germans' desperate need for labor as the war was ending. Bergen-Belsen, however, was worse than any other camp during the chaos of the war's closing weeks. There were mounds of corpses all over the camp, and in describing the survivors, a British soldier said he "thought the dead got up and were walking." Bergen-Belsen was liberated by the British in April 1945. When MA arrived at the camp, she was greeted by three of her brothers through the barbed wire separating the men from the women. They had survived until that time. She looked for these brothers after liberation only to discover they had perished as the war was ending.

In referring to the impact of the strong religious upbringing of herself and many others during the war, MA relates how they fasted and prayed on Yom Kippur, and recalls that she recited prayers and blessings every morning and every night. MA spoke with Eleanor Roosevelt during Mrs. Roosevelt's visit to Celle, a town near Bergen-Belsen, shortly after the war.

MA met a fellow survivor while visiting Czechoslovakia in 1945. They were married in 1946 in Gabersee, Germany. They had twin boys but only one lived. The family arrived in the United States in 1949 and settled in New Jersey in order to be near MA's brother. Another son was born in 1952. MA's husband had several jobs and finally in 1954 bought his own grocery store. In December 1970, shortly after returning from their first and only trip to Israel, her forty-five-year old husband was murdered in the store. She married a second time, a fellow survivor again. Her sons both work with emotionally disturbed children. She has two grandchildren.

ERNEST BOKOR, 1920–

[Holocaust testimony (HRC-960, videotape: 1 hour, 27 minutes), 17 September 1987; interviewed and indexed by Bernard Weinstein. D804.3/.B686 1987]

Ernest Bokor [EB] was born on 21 August 1920 in Debrad. He was the oldest of three siblings. His father died of natural causes in the 1930s, his mother perished in Auschwitz, and his brother died within the first week after liberation. EB and his sister are the family's only Holocaust survivors.

When he was three years old, EB's family moved to Dubovec, about eighty miles from Debrad. Dubovec was a largely Catholic community where EB experienced much antisemitism. He was enrolled in a Roman Catholic school for four years because there was no other school in town. Consequently, he received practically no Jewish education. The closest synagogue was four miles from home.

At the beginning of the interview, EB describes an incident that had a powerful impact on him all his life.

One time I came home with a little blood on my face from a fight, crying. My father was a merchant and also a butcher. He was a very strong guy. And he gave me, through my behind, and he said, "Never come home crying. Fight back." And this made me a fighter and a hard kid. Sooner or later, I became the leader between the kids, like a small gang. We weren't afraid of anybody. They respected me. . . . And this way I grew up.

The family moved to Rimavska Sobota in 1938, at the time of the Hungarian occupation. He moved to Budapest in 1939. When he was called up for forced labor in 1940, his mother pleaded that he was the lone family breadwinner. A one-year deferment was granted. He was recruited for forced labor, in textiles, in 1943, and in 1944 the Germans took over in Hungary. The Holocaust was now in full swing.

EB tried to save himself by leading a double life. He met an old friend, a Catholic who had become a Nazi. This friend recommended EB for membership in the Nazi party in Budapest. With appropriate false papers, EB became a Catholic Nazi during the day and a Jew working in forced labor at night. In October 1944, when Eichmann was deporting masses of Hungarian Jews to Auschwitz, EB forsook his night factory job to devote all his time playing the Nazi role to save Jews. He also joined Raoul Wallenberg in his rescue efforts.

EB found his young brother in a Budapest synagogue. Both brothers were captured by the Germans and deported to the Mauthausen and Gunskirchen concentration camps as the war was ending. His brother became ill and died several days after liberation.

After the war, EB met and married his wife. They went to Israel in 1949, where the older of their two daughters was born. They emigrated to the United States in 1958 to be near EB's cousins in New Jersey. The daughters are married, and EB has four grandchildren.

That's it. That is the story. What came out from me after so many years. And I had to relieve myself about these terrible things that happened to us in that death generation. Not to give up. Today is much better, much stronger, than we were at that time. To fight back. Don't give up. Because if they want to kill you, they will anyway kill you. But if you're going to fight back, you have [a] chance.

INTERVIEWER: Did you always believe you would survive?

EB: No, No! . . . First of all the bombardments. I wasn't safe from the bombs, the same like the Germans. The bomb could hit me too. That was me. The other part, I was always afraid from my friends. I never was afraid of the Nazis. I was afraid of my friends. Someone might recognize me and would say, Oh. . . those days, you had to have guts, but more, luck. Guts to do it and luck to survive it. I was one of them.

HELENA LEBOVITZ BOKOR, 1925–

[Holocaust testimony (HRC-1009, videotape: 1 hour, 29 minutes), 18 October 1988; interviewed by Bernard Weinstein and Carole Shaffer-Koros, indexed by Bernard Weinstein. D804.3/.B689 1988]

Helena Lebovitz Bokor [HB] was born in Košice in 1925. She had one older brother and two younger sisters. Her parents and one sister perished in Auschwitz. HB, her brother, and one sister survived the Holocaust.

In a remarkably detailed and comprehensive testimony, HB describes her family's experiences during the war, especially the last years under German occupation. Jews did not really feel antisemitism when their country enjoyed independence as Czechoslovakia. Of course, she says, coming from school "there were fights every day. This we were used to. It really didn't mean too much to us." But they never had pogroms, and Jews appreciated living in a safe, democratic country.

This relatively calm life changed when Hungary took over this region of Czechoslovakia in 1938.

> First of all, the young men were taken to forced labor camps. So when they say that we didn't fight against the Germans, we didn't have young people. We had old people, with children, and the young girls and young boys, because they took everybody to forced labor.

The Hungarians promulgated a number of anti-Jewish decrees within weeks of entering the region. As a result, HB's brother went to Budapest because he could no longer obtain employment or matriculate in a university in his native region.

On 19 March 1944, the Germans marched into the Košice region. Jews had to wear armbands indicating their Jewish identity, and all Jewish homes were emptied to be plundered systematically by the Germans. Within two weeks, all the Jews were rounded up and marched into the cinder block factories.

> In two weeks [after the Jews entered the cinder block factories—*ed.*], cattle cars arrived. We thought they came to pick up the cinder blocks. I don't know how they did this but they just managed. . . . The whole train was loaded with Jews, as many as they could push in, they did. They told them, "Leave everything and we take you to working camps." . . . The transport left and in a few days, another arrived. Again they took Jews. Because this was a big city. We had about twenty thousand Jews in our city. And all the area around Košice, the little villages and little towns, they all concentrated in Košice.

HB reports that she and her family were taken from Košice on the holiday of Shevuoth on 28 May 1944. The ages of the family members were father, forty-six; mother, forty-two; HB, nineteen; sisters, fourteen and sixteen.

In the train, it was horrible . . . for the three days, I couldn't move my leg. . . . Hysterical women, children crying. No water. Food—bread we had enough, but who needed to eat? Water, they didn't let us have. . . . A Polish couple was in the train [some Polish people tried to escape to Hungary—*ed.*]. They thought they will escape, they will be safe. But it didn't happen. Fate caught up with them. . . . [The Polish man told HB's father the critical time would be when the train arrived in Kraków. Would the train remain there, or would it move beyond Kraków?—*ed.*] This was the third day, the train started to move. The Polish man, as he couldn't move, managed to find his talis and tefillin, and he put it on, and he started to pray. All the way to Auschwitz he prayed. And people already sensed something, it was something terrible.

Upon arrival in Auschwitz, men were immediately separated from women and children. The two sisters were directed to one line, for work, and the mother was directed to another line, for immediate entry into the gas chamber and crematorium.

My father came to me and wanted to hug me. I loved my father very, very much. And the German pushed him away. I will miss that hug forever. I have never seen them again. So my mother vanished, my sister, my father, never to see them again.

HB's detailed testimony continues. She describes the assignment of identifying numbers, the shaving of all hair, showers, barracks, the miserable bread which she refused to eat, the lack of any drinking water. A German woman guard had informed HB that she has no parents or younger sister, that they are in the smoke coming out of the chimneys. "The smell of Auschwitz, you can never forget."

Several times, HB was selected for work while her frail sister, Naomi, was selected for the crematorium. This required HB to desert her line, destined for life temporarily, in order to remain with her sister.

One day, a selection. Again, they select me to work; Naomi to the crematorium. Again, I had to escape. I had to go back to her. They were beating me. They were beating me terribly. So I went there again, to Naomi, and we started out. We saw we are going to the crematorium. This was a miracle. As we are going, the woman who was our *Blockälteste* . . . who counted us and everything. She came after me, and she grabbed me, and she said, "Where are you going?" I said, "With my sister." She hollered at me. She knew where they are going. They are going to the crematorium. You can go to work. I don't care. I have nobody in the world. I go with my sister. My sister was crying. She begged me, "Go! . . ." No! I went with her. We came to the crematorium, near the crematorium. And they pushed me into a big, big building. We were in the gas chamber. Naomi started to holler, screaming, beating on the door. Let my sister out, she doesn't have to die! I remember seeing the shower heads of the gas. . . . Miracle of miracles, the door opened, and they let us out. Today, if I think about it, what happened, I think there were not enough people to waste the gas, because they

had to have a certain amount of people to gas them. So why use for only a few? . . .
They let us all out. It was not too many, maybe fifty or a hundred, I don't remember.

HB was moved to the Stutthof concentration camp where the beatings were
worse than those in Auschwitz. A terrible sadist there, Max, went around beating
the girls.

> There, really, if I can express myself, hell broke loose. A gang of Ukrainian SS wel-
> comed us. Terrible sadists. They were beating and beating. . . . Our job there was to
> dig trenches. They assigned the amount which we have to dig.

Stutthof was probably HB's most horrible experience: twenty-eight hundred
girls left Auschwitz; a thousand of them perished in Stutthof in less than a month
of horrible labor and beatings. As the war was ending, HB was moved constantly,
from Stutthof to Botten and, finally, to tents on a baron's estate in Grodno. She and
a friend escaped from the death march from Grodno and miraculously survived several harrowing events in the war's final days. She and her friend finally crossed into
Russian territory and arrived in Kraków. After walking what she estimates as a thousand kilometers, she arrived in her hometown in Czechoslovakia. There, to her joy
and amazement, she discovered her surviving brother and sister. HB had concluded
that she could not hope for her sister's survival in Auschwitz after HB left that camp.

HB met and married a fellow survivor. They went to Israel in 1949, the older of
their two daughters was born there. The young family emigrated to the United States
in 1958 to join her husband's relatives. The family lives in New Jersey.

PEARL DAVIS, 1929–

*[Holocaust testimony (HRC-963, videotape: 1 hour, 6 minutes), 14 October 1987; interviewed
by Bernard Weinstein and Robin McHugh, indexed by Bernard Weinstein. D804.3/.D207 1987]*

Pearl Davis [PD] was born in 1929 in Nizni Verecky, a very small town with only
ten Jewish families. Her family was very religious with a great deal of love for one
another. They were never uncomfortable about being different. The family consisted
of six persons: her parents, three girls, and one boy. All but PD perished during the
Holocaust.

The Hungarians occupied their territory in 1938, and the family experienced the
developing antisemitism. Under the Germans in 1944, they were herded into the
ghetto of Sátoraljaújhely. The four children refused their parents' request to hide because they did not want to leave their parents. Consequently, all were shipped to
Auschwitz in a three-day, three-night cattle train ride. PD describes the arrival at
Auschwitz at four o'clock in the morning. The family was separated in three direc-

tions: PD's mother and younger sister perished immediately, her father and brother were taken to a forced labor camp, PD and her older sister remained in Auschwitz.

PD's sister pulled her off the crematorium truck on three occasions before they were transferred from Auschwitz to nearby Milchausen, where they worked in a factory for airplane parts from August 1944 until March 1945.

The sisters were moved to Bergen-Belsen, Germany, in March 1945. The conditions were horrible: no food and no water but much illness, typhus, and lice. They were liberated by the British. PD was stunned at this time by her sister's death from typhus exacerbated by tainted canned meat supplied by the British. PD was too sick to eat the meat, and she survived. She was surrounded by death, however; she did not care to live.

> We didn't care anymore. There wasn't enough energy to care what's going to happen. At that point, we were so weak that we really didn't care. The only thing, we were happy that they brought us something to drink and to eat. But most of us couldn't eat it. There were plenty of people who died after the war, after it was over. . . . It was very rich food, and who knew it, that you are not allowed to eat it?

She returned to Czechoslovakia, and "had a very bad time." Her mother's "best friend" would not return the bedspread made by her mother's hands. Other Czech neighbors would not return any of the family belongings confiscated during the war. She worked in a factory with a cousin with whom she shared an apartment. "It was nonstop troubles since I was fourteen years old."

PD married in 1949 in Prague's famous, historic Alt-Neu Shul. She and her husband moved to Israel and then emigrated to Canada in 1953, to Ohio in 1954 to be near her husband's brother, and, after six years, to New Jersey where they owned a restaurant in Linden. PD had three sons and three grandchildren at the time of this interview.

EDITH MULLER FARBEN, 1925–

[Holocaust testimony (HRC-951, videotape: 1 hour, 12 minutes), 7 May 1987; interviewed by Bernard Weinstein and Charles DeFanti, indexed by Bernard Weinstein. D804.3/.F219 1987]

Seventeen-year-old Edith Muller, 1942.

Edith Muller Farben [EF] was born on 7 May 1925 in Polana. She was one of four children. Her older brother emigrated to the United States in 1938 "on the last boat." Of the five members of her immediate family living in Europe when the war broke out, EF, her mother, and younger brother survived the Holocaust. Her father perished in Auschwitz, her sister in Bergen-Belsen.

During the early years of the war, EF's region was occupied by the Hungarians. Jews had to wear yellow stars. Less food was available for Jews than for non-Jews. They had to produce family documents proving their citizenship. For older people, such as EF's eighty-seven-year-old grandfather, there were no papers, and thus he had to report to the gendarmes every Sunday despite his venerable age.

The Germans took over in 1944, and the full horror of the Holocaust began. In April, the family was directed to the ghetto in Mukachevo for one month. The beards of pious Jews were shaved off. "Grandfather looked dead. Two weeks later, he died." EF and the family were then deported to Auschwitz in cattle cars. "During May, all the ghettos were liquidated." EF describes her arrival in the Birkenau camp of Auschwitz. Polish Jewish inmates advised them: "Young mothers with children, give them to your mothers. Young girls, say you are older than your age." (Men and women had already been separated.) These suggestions were offered surreptitiously to avoid being overheard by the German guards. Children should be given to grandmothers to save the mothers for forced labor while the grandmothers and children would be gassed.

EF worked in "Canada," sorting clothes and doing rather "light" work. She was in Birkenau for seven months and in "Canada" for five or six of these. From her work she could observe older people being trucked in from the railroad station and dumped directly into the incinerator for cremation. During her last month in Birkenau, EF was assigned to a factory that produced parachutes. The inmates were able to calculate the day of Yom Kippur, but the guards did not allow them "to goof off in observance of the day." She reports, "Whenever we went to showers, we never knew who would return and who would be sent away never to return."

The Russians were advancing in Poland. EF was transferred to Weisswasser in the Sudentenland. This was a small camp for three hundred or four hundred women and girls. "Nobody died in that camp. The Czech workers treated the Jews nicely, despite its illegality." The Jewish girls took care of one another, as in the case of the girl who could not see well and was assigned to the night shift. EF remembers the remarkable speech by the SS woman guard at the time of liberation, in which much helpful advice was given to the inmates.

EF was liberated by the Russians. "The Russian soldiers were a problem for the girls." She describes the dramatic and emotional meeting with her mother and brother when she left the train at Bratislava as she was making her way home. She appreciates that she was not assigned to the difficult physical labor in the camps, which was the fate of so many others. "Yet," she remarks, "it was a nightmare." The family returned to Mukachevo and she met the man who would become her husband in October 1945. The family was then reunited with EF's older brother, an American G.I. at this time.

EF and her husband arrived in the United States in July 1947. They settled in New Jersey to be near her mother, who had arrived six months earlier, and her brother's family. EF worked in a dress factory, her husband in a lumber mill. She has one daughter and three grandchildren. Her husband died in 1980, and EF continues to live in New Jersey.

EUGENE FRIED, 1926–

[Holocaust testimony (HRC-2015, videotape: 1 hour, 30 minutes), 23 March and 8 May, 1995; interviewed and indexed by Joseph J. Preil. D804.3/.F73 1995]

Eugene Fried in 1945, shortly after liberation.

Eugene Fried [EF] was born in Munkács on 18 August 1926. His immediate family in 1939 consisted of eight persons: his parents and six children. His parents and two of his siblings perished in the Holocaust. His extended family, through first cousins, consisted of twenty-six persons. In addition to EF and his siblings, two other relatives survived. Thus, twenty members of EF's family perished in the Holocaust.

The Hungarians occupied the Munkács region of Czechoslovakia in 1938. Jews suffered economically and physically under the Hungarians. In school, EF and his classmates were taken from class and forced to dig ditches in the fields. Many boys suffered beatings. Pious men and boys were compelled to perform such work especially on Sabbaths. The Germans replaced the Hungarians in the Munkács region during the spring of 1944, just before Passover. EF and his family were evicted from their home immediately to make room for a kindergarten. He recalls the kindergarten teacher telling the Gestapo guard on eviction day, "Check the attic; there may be children hiding there."

EF and his family were taken to a brick factory and remained there for one or two weeks. His father and one brother had been sent by the Hungarians to a forced labor camp. EF and the other family members were transported to Birkenau in cattle cars. He describes their arrival. The older people who could not walk were thrown into a pit and burned alive. He tells of the selection process of extermination or forced labor and the scene of a baby being murdered. His group was told to take showers after all their hair had been shaved. He saw mountains of hair and jewelry. He managed to keep his shoes until they were taken from him in Buchenwald about nine months later. The new prisoners received no food during their few days in Birkenau.

EF was then moved to Auschwitz for a few days. On the first night, bread was brought to their barrack, exactly one slice for each prisoner. One slice was missing. When the Germans discovered the person with two slices, he was subjected to twenty-five lashes. "He never got up from there." EF was tattooed in Auschwitz: "A4310, that was my name." After three days in Auschwitz, EF and his group were marched to a satellite camp, Jawischowitz, about sixty miles away, where they worked in a coal mine. They were awakened at four or five A.M. daily to stand at *Appell* for about two hours. After black coffee, they walked two or three miles to the coal mine where they worked for ten or twelve hours continuously under the severe pressure of, "Fast, fast, fast!" On returning to camp at night, they were given miserable soup and blutwurst.

EF remained in Jawischowitz until 15 January 1945, when he was sent with a group of three thousand prisoners on a cruel death march to Buchenwald. "Buchenwald was hell." They stood at *Appell* in the bitter winter cold for hours, both morning and evening, in their thin, striped uniform pajamas.

After several weeks in Buchenwald, EF was transferred to Rehmsdorf, a satellite camp. He worked there several weeks in a factory for lenses. Pushcarts picked up corpses daily in Rehmsdorf, but there were mountains of dead bodies remaining around the camp. EF's next death march was to Theresienstadt, Czechoslovakia. Many were too weak to walk; he estimates that perhaps two hundred of the original four thousand prisoners actually reached Theresienstadt. He was liberated there by the Russians.

EF was hospitalized immediately after liberation. Upon recovery, he returned to Munkács and was reunited with his surviving brother and one of his sisters. These three siblings went to Budapest where they met their second surviving sister.

EF arrived in the United States on 12 December 1947. He served in the U.S. Army during the Korean War. He moved to New Jersey, where he met his future wife, and they were married in November 1957. They have three children. All are married and, at the time of this interview, the three have one child each.

FRIEDA STERN FRIED, 1928–

[Holocaust testimony (HRC-972, videotape: 1 hour, 30 minutes), 4 November 1987; interviewed by Henry Kaplowitz and Selma Dubnick, indexed by Bernard Weinstein. D804.3/.F732 1987]

Frieda Stern Fried [FF] was born on 10 October 1928 in Polana. Her immediate family before the war consisted of six persons: her parents and four children. FF was the youngest in the family. Her father was in the timber business.

The Polana region was taken over by the Hungarians until 1944 when the Germans occupied the country. FF reports the Jews suffered serious persecution under the Hungarians; for example, Jewish children were not accepted in Hungarian schools and were compelled to attend Russian schools. The situation became infinitely more dangerous with the arrival of the Germans in 1944.

FF's entire family was sequestered in the Munkács ghetto for a period of four to six weeks. She describes how the beards of pious Jews were ripped out, including that of her grandfather. She relates that she became ill in the ghetto because she was too embarrassed to use the open bathroom in the ghetto house, which was assigned to hers and other families. After their short stay in the ghetto, FF's family and many others were transferred in cattle cars to Auschwitz. Referring to the cruel treatment in the ghetto and the roundup for the trip, FF states, "I did not see a Nazi, an SS, until Auschwitz. The Hungarians did it to us."

She provides a comprehensive report of their arrival and conditions in Auschwitz. Upon arrival, Polish Jews advised surreptitiously, "Give the kids to the older people." Her father and the children were assigned to forced labor while her mother was taken for gassing and cremation. FF kept on asking her oldest sister, "Where's mother?" The consistent response was, "Tomorrow." Finally, a Polish girl said, "You see that chimney there? . . . That's your mother." FF: "That's impossible." Polish girl: "No, my child. Try to survive." They remained in Auschwitz for a period of five months, beginning in June 1944.

FF and the others were tattooed with numbers and given the flimsy, striped concentration camp uniforms. She was assigned to sorting clothes of prisoners for the Germans. She was once beaten for the "crime" of giving a kerchief to one of the girls in camp. Another time, she was "selected for a medical experiment." Margaret, the sister who was with her in all the camps, was certain that FF would be cremated that day. Margaret fasted all day for FF and volunteered to carry heavy stones to be near the crematorium. Fortunately, the "experiment" consisted of two young SS boys injecting needles many times into FF in order to draw blood. FF returned to her barrack with swollen black arms.

FF was moved to several concentration camps, including Bergen-Belsen, Weinsberg, and Mauthausen, as the Germans tried to avoid the advancing Russians and Allies. Her descriptions reveal Auschwitz as a death machine geared up for mass destruction of Hungarian Jews. Bergen-Belsen, by comparison, was chaotic and messy. They actually took showers (with water) once a week in Auschwitz, something not available in Bergen-Belsen. Her memory of Mauthausen is "mountains of bodies, just mountains." She was liberated in Mauthausen by Americans on 5 May 1945.

When asked what she felt at liberation, FF replies, "I can't say what I felt. I was too young to think. . . . I was a frightened little girl." The sisters learned that in addition to losing their mother at Auschwitz, their father perished in the Flossenbürg concentration camp three weeks before liberation. Some two hundred to three hundred members of their extended family perished in the Holocaust.

FF and all her siblings emigrated to the United States. She arrived here in September 1947 to join an uncle in New York. She married a fellow survivor in 1951 and has three children. Her two sons are accountants and her daughter has a responsible position at the Contemporary Resort in Disney World. To conclude her interview, FF states, "It's beautiful to live. It's terrible to hate . . . and it makes no difference what nationality."

MIKE GOLDBERGER, 1921–

[Holocaust testimony (HRC-959, videotape: 1 hour, 17 minutes), 28 July 1987; interviewed and indexed by Bernard Weinstein. D804.3/.G619 1987]

Mike Goldberger [MG] was born on 13 February 1921 in Nové Město, near the Hungarian border and later part of Hungary. His immediate family consisted of five persons at the beginning of World War II: mother, three sons, and one daughter. MG and his sister survived the Holocaust; he never learned the fate of his mother and two brothers. MG's father had died of natural causes when MG was nine years old.

The family struggled, especially after the father died. Nevertheless, MG continued with his education until the age of eighteen. Evidently, he was a brilliant student, and significant people in his life helped to ensure the continuation of his studies, including secular education at the high school level and yeshiva education for three years between the ages of fifteen and eighteen.

MG comments on the extent of antisemitism in Hungary during this era: "Antisemitism was part of life . . . like the air you breathe. . . . They threw stones at us, especially on Shabbos. They knew we couldn't throw back." MG was in the Third Battalion, Second Company of the Hungarian army between 1942 and 1944. They were stationed in Köszeg, Hungary. It was not really an army unit but an all-Jewish forced labor unit serving under Hungarian military officers. MG's unit was given no uniforms or weapons; it was assigned to manual labor.

As the Russians were advancing through Hungary in September 1944, MG and two friends walked away and escaped from their unit. They hid in Varhomog until liberated by the Russians. MG was reunited with his girlfriend, Lily, and they were married on 26 March 1946. He decided that postwar Hungary was not for them.

They managed to move to Austria, then to Sweden, and finally arrived in the United States on 20 January 1952. Obviously capable and creative, he started his American life as a tool and die worker, became manager of the company, and then organized his own company. Their son is a graduate of the University of Chicago and a physician, their daughter is a Harvard graduate. Both son and daughter were National Merit finalists in high school. At the time of this interview, MG and his wife lived in Manhattan.

PEARL KATZ GRUENBERG, 1925–

[Holocaust testimony (HRC-968, videotape: 3 hours, 38 minutes), 17 and 30 September 1987; interviewed and indexed by Bernard Weinstein. D804.3/.G86 1987]

Pearl Katz Gruenberg [PG] was born on 28 October 1925 in Okrouhla. Her immediate family in 1939 consisted of eight persons: mother, four daughters, and three sons. Her father had died in 1934. Of the eight family members, PG, one sister, and two brothers survived the Holocaust.

The situation began to deteriorate for Jews under Hungarian occupation during the early years of the war and became deadly under the Germans beginning in the spring of 1944. All members of PG's family were ordered to the Tyachev ghetto and four weeks later were transported by cattle car to Auschwitz. She recalls the ordeal of marching to the cattle cars with her young nieces.

> And my sister's little girls . . . I cannot forget those words from those kids. . . . They were dragging bundles . . . because everybody had to carry. And the older one, she was six years old, and she said to her mother, "Mommy, dear, where are they taking us, what's going to be with us? . . . I cannot carry these bundles anymore, they're pulling me down to the floor." My sister started to cry. She said, "Just a little bit longer. We'll be there soon, wherever we'll be going." . . . Those words from a six-year-old, I will never forget.

The terrible train trip to Auschwitz lasted five days. PG remained in Auschwitz for two months. They were sent to the showers twice a week. They "never knew if [they] were going to the shower or to the crematoriums."

In July 1944, PG was selected with other young girls for transfer to the Unterluss labor camp. The cruelty was indescribable, both at selection by Dr. Mengele and supervision by a twenty-two-year old German woman guard, "the meanest person I ever knew."

They were assigned to work in a munitions factory in Unterluss. The foreman saved her life each time she collapsed at work, even when the SS guard was ready to send her back "to the crematorium." When the munitions factory was destroyed by Allied bombing, PG was assigned to construction work with cement, once again under the cruel SS guard. She collapsed again and was then assigned to digging graves. She refers again and again to the inhuman conduct of the SS woman, especially in the bitter cold, rain, hail, and snow of December 1944 and January 1945.

As the Russians were advancing, PG and the other prisoners were transferred by truck to Bergen-Belsen in January 1945. People kept on dying. "I was surrounded by dead bodies. . . . People were dying like flies." Diarrhea became a problem. PG "was lucky. Everyone had diarrhea. I was constipated."

PG's sister, Sarah the mother of the two little girls, died one night in bed lying next to PG, who was also very sick. She was so sick, in fact, that after liberation she was evacuated by the British (or possibly the Red Cross), and she "woke up in Sweden." Three months after liberation, it was determined that PG had tuberculosis. She was hospitalized for an additional two months, sent to a sanitarium for six months, and then spent a full year in a convalescent home.

In 1947, PG learned that one sister and one brother had survived the Holocaust and were living in Czechoslovakia. It was decided that she would join her uncle's family in Newark, New Jersey, while her siblings would emigrate to Israel. PG arrived in the United States in February 1949. She worked in a factory in Newark, became an American citizen, and then traveled to Israel in 1955 to visit with her family. She met and married her husband in Israel and returned to the United States.

In discussing marriage, PG says:

> I never wanted to get married, I'll be honest. I didn't want to bring children into this world . . . [so] they should suffer like I did. I just wanted to be free. I just was afraid. I was afraid. I was afraid. And when I was here, those five years, every night I was dreaming, waking up in the middle of the night, crying, dreaming. Every night I had nightmares. I used to call my aunt. . . . I used to call in the middle of the night. I was shivering, in the middle of the night, waking up with such fright. . . . That was going on night after night, I'm still dreaming. I'm still crying . . . my husband wakes me. And when my son used to be home, he used to say, "Ma, you're always crying at night." I constantly have bad nightmares, and I'm always dreaming. They're taking me. They're coming for us. They're taking us away. Or I'm running. Never a dull moment since then.

PG has one son, a physician, and two grandchildren. She has lived in New Jersey ever since her arrival in the United States.

HELEN STERN HERMAN, 1924–

[Holocaust testimony (HRC-976, videotape: 1 hour, 14 minutes), 17 November 1987; interviewed by Daniel Gover and Jodi Frank, indexed by Jodi Frank. D804.3/.H545 1987]

Helen Stern, ca. 1942–1943, prior to the German occupation of Hungary.

Helen Stern Herman [HH] was born on 8 March 1924 in Polana, a summer resort town where her father was a self-employed contractor. HH had one older brother and two younger sisters. They were "not rich but comfortable." Her mother was murdered on their first day in Auschwitz, her father perished at the end of the war, and all four children survived the Holocaust.

HH lists the antisemitic decrees introduced during the Hungarian occupation that began in 1938. Their worst problems began in 1944 when the Germans occupied the country. They were moved to Mukachevo, a neighboring town, which served as a way station before they were taken by cattle cars to Auschwitz.

HH delivers her testimony very effectively. She begins with the ghetto in Mukachevo and proceeds to the cattle cars, the arrival and then the difficult existence in Auschwitz, the work in the Weisswasser concentration camp in Czechoslovakia, the experience of liberation, and the renewal of her life in the Gabersee DP camp after the war.

HH reacts to her entire experience as she describes the routine in Weisswasser for the five hundred Jewish girls who had been assigned to forced labor in the camp.

My foreman, he was in the Wehrmacht [German army]. He was an engineer. He was a little bit human. He used to ask questions, and he couldn't believe what I was telling him. He had asked me, "Where are your family? Where is your mother? Father?" He didn't believe that five hundred girls lived alone in the camp. . . . I says, "Hitler killed my mother. Don't you know?" He says, "No, we are not told these things." And . . . he asked me, "Where is your Moses?" That, he asked me. I had no answer. He says, "Our Moses is Hitler. What he promises, he delivers."

But he was human. As I said, he used to leave a little salt for us there. That we should have that little extra salt. And if he would have been caught, I'm sure they wouldn't be too kind to him—the Germans, the SS.

But other than that, they were all very, very brutal. The experience is indescribable. The fear, the fear. Especially in Auschwitz, where every week to stay naked and go through the selections. . . . Mengele was the one that selected. . . . Every week, as I said, we had to stay in front of him and . . . I wasn't fearing for myself so much, because I felt pretty strong then yet. But my sister Frieda, [I] always feared for her that we were going to lose her one day. Every time before the selection came, we used to take some rouge paper and make her cheeks red . . . because the one that they didn't like, they went the other way. That was the last time you've seen them. There were no explanations.

As long as someone was sickly looking, or they didn't like the way your body looks, or the way your hair looks, he looked the other way. There was nothing you could have done . . . and every week we were going through that. I'm not talking no more about the humiliation, of standing in front of them naked. Eventually, probably, it was part of life. But the fear was unbelievable.

After liberation, HH returned to her region of Czechoslovakia and remained in Munkács for a short stay. She was reunited with her sisters, and they accepted the fact that their father had perished at the end of the war. She went to the Gabersee DP camp and met her future husband. They waited in Gabersee from 1946 until 1949, when they received papers to enter the United States. They married in the United States in 1949 and settled in New Jersey. They have one daughter and one son, an accountant. They were expecting their first grandchild at the time of this interview.

MICHAEL HERSH, 1929–

[Holocaust testimony (HRC-1068, videotape: 1 hour, 21 minutes), 18 June 1992; interviewed and indexed by Joseph J. Preil. D804.3/.H572 1992]

Michael Hersh (left) with his brother, Albert in Žatec, Czechoslovakia, late 1945.

Michael Hersh [MH] was born in Rakosin on 25 June 1929. The family moved to a neighboring town, Velikiyé Luki, near Munkács, where MH's father was a struggling grocer. This region became part of Hungary during World War II. MH's family consisted of seven persons: his parents, three boys, two girls. The mother and two sisters were murdered upon arrival at Auschwitz; the father perished, apparently, during MH's two weeks in Auschwitz; the three brothers survived the Holocaust.

After describing the antisemitism in this region of Czechoslovakia-Hungary before 1944, MH reports that the full fury of the Holocaust descended on the country with the arrival of the German army and Eichmann. MH provides remarkably detailed and effective descriptions, beginning with the decree to assemble in the central plaza of town in April 1944, the transfer to the ghetto in nearby Munkács, the trip by cattle train to Auschwitz several weeks later, the arrival at Auschwitz, and their experiences there. The trip from Munkács to Auschwitz lasted about two weeks.

> The conditions inside those trains were probably the worst thing that can happen to a human being, although the Nazis found things that were worse than that. The smell from the waste that was there, no one was bathing, constant crying, crying from babies and children, from other people that just couldn't stop crying.

MH describes the chaotic scene on arrival at Auschwitz. Polish Jews assigned to greet the new arrivals advised the youngsters under eighteen to claim they were eighteen years old. This could be lifesaving for those who would be selected for slave labor for the German war effort, and the Polish Jews endangered themselves by providing such counsel.

> That was the last time I saw my mother and my two sisters. . . . [The Germans] gave us our new clothes, which consisted of wooden-soled shoes, a pair of slacks, a jacket, and a cap. We also had to have our hair done, our hair clipped. There were people who sat there with clippers and clipped your hair short. Then there were other people there with razors and they shaved your head about two-inch stripes, going from the back, then to the front. This, they said, in the event anyone would escape, they would be easily detected. There was no way anyone could possibly escape from these situations. . . .
>
> They gave us soup. The soup itself, the only way I can describe it, it looked and smelled like vomit. There's no way you could eat it. So there was a man there, who was there before we got there, and he looks at me and says, "Are you going to eat your soup?" And I said, "No." He said, "Can I have it?" He took and put it in his cup. So he told me, "Tomorrow, you will not give it away." And I never did.

During the two weeks in Auschwitz, all prisoners became numbers and were no longer addressed by name. He describes the *Appellplatz,* where they were counted over and over again. He describes the inedible "daily menu" they were "served." One day his father was taken on a work detail, and MH reports, "That was the last time I saw my father." He believes his father was part of the group that blew up a crematorium in Auschwitz.

In May or June 1944, MH was transferred by truck to Mauthausen in Austria and then to Ebensee. Many perished doing the construction work in Ebensee. "When a group marched out, let's say a group of a hundred, at least twenty-five were not coming back . . . every day."

As the war was ending, MH was returned to Mauthausen and was sent from there to Wien Schwechat, a suburb of Vienna, where MH worked in the Heinkel factory making the first jet planes. In the closing days of the war, he returned to Mauthausen on one of the infamous death marches, which featured absolutely no food but a great deal of cold weather. The prisoners dug for worms and snails to eat. Finally they arrived at Wels near Linz. Again, absolutely no food was provided; they saw human flesh being eaten.

Wels was liberated by one American soldier in a jeep. Immediately after liberation, MH became ill with typhus and was totally blind. He was hospitalized and is unaware of how he recovered.

MH returned to Czechoslovakia and was reunited with his two brothers. Relatives in the United States made it possible for the three brothers to be among the first survivors to emigrate there in June 1946. MH joined the United States Army and later became an interior designer, married, and had three children. He also has one grandchild. MH lives on Long Island, and was brought to this interview by a New Jersey relative whose family was instrumental in bringing the three brothers to this country.

FANNY SCHACHTER KATZ, 1922–

[Holocaust testimony (HRC-1010, videotape: 1 hour, six minutes), 30 November 1988; interviewed by Bernard Weinstein and Devorah Lichstein, indexed by Bernard Weinstein. D804.3/.K15 1989]

Fanny Schachter Katz [FK] was born on 22 September 1922 in Pilipec where her father was a shochet. She remembers a happy childhood as one of the youngest children in a family with seven siblings. Only FK and her brother Eleazer, the oldest, survived the Holocaust.

Hitler annexed a major part of Czechoslovakia before the outbreak of World War II. FK's experience began with brutal persecution and plundering, and it continued with hiding, ghettoization, and deportation to murder camps. FK was deported to Auschwitz with her parents and several other family members. As was true in so many cases, the old and the very young were murdered upon arrival. The young, strong people were assigned to forced labor until they lost their strength.

FK reveals her state of mind in Auschwitz.

> I was relieved to know that my mother and father are not alive, or the small children, to see the torturing what they do to us. That they don't have to live in the hunger, and stay in *Zählappell* half of the night, and go . . . to work. . . . I was relieved that they are in heaven, and they are not in torture any more.

FK gives a very effective description of all her experiences and of her remarkable determination to adhere to the tenets of religious observance. She was in Auschwitz from late spring 1943 at the time of Shavuot until February 1945. She then participated in the death march to Bergen-Belsen in Germany, where she was liberated by the British in May 1945. She articulates her values and recalls her feelings in Bergen-Belsen.

> When I was there, I was just praying. If I survive and if I have a loaf of bread, a pitcher of water, changing of clothing, two sets of underwear and two dresses, and a coat, I'll be always very happy. That remained with me. I never, ever looked at what other people have. I'm always very happy with what I have. And especially my children, my family. Because I always have it on my mind that I said it to myself. I don't go for jewelry, I don't go for nothing. I always am very satisfied with what living my husband makes and with whatever we have. And I'm grateful to *Hashem* ["God"] that we live in America and it's a free country and we can do what we want. And we pray as much as we want. And be recognized as people and not chased with dogs.

After liberation, FK moved to Sweden and remained there for several years. She entered a hospital for treatment, followed by a period of recuperation. She took up residence with a religiously observant German-Jewish family. She returned to Czechoslovakia after receiving a telegram from her brother, the only other family survivor. The new communist government in Czechoslovakia did not allow her to return to Sweden. This enabled her to meet her husband-to-be in 1948, and they arrived in the United States on 14 June 1949.

FK lives in central New Jersey, in the same community as her son and his family of five children. She has one daughter who lives in New York state with her husband and six children.

BENJAMIN KATZWER, 1929– [1994]

[Holocaust testimony (HRC-1069, videotape: 1 hour, 21 minutes), 22 October 1992; interviewed and indexed by Joseph J. Preil. D804.3/.K159 1992]

Benjamin Katzwer [BK] was born on 16 January 1929 in Yablonov, a small town near Munkács. He was the youngest of eight siblings when the war began in 1939. His immediate family, including his parents, consisted of ten persons at the beginning of World War II. Four of the siblings survived the Holocaust; his parents and four siblings perished.

The family's difficulties began with the increasing antisemitism in 1938 after the Germans annexed the Sudentenland. BK describes the worsening situation after the Hungarians occupied Yablonov and the surrounding region as World War II started. The family remained in Yablonov until 1944, when the Jews in town were directed to walk to the Munkács ghetto. They remained in Munkács for one month; then BK was shipped to Auschwitz on the first day of Shevuoth, 28 May 1944. His mother and three siblings were in the cattle car with him.

BK was the only member of his family to survive Auschwitz. He became very ill, however, as a result of beatings by the SS combined with the nature of his forced labor and typhus.

During the last year of the war, BK was transferred to Mauthausen, then to Gusen I, Gusen II, back to Mauthausen, and finally to Gunskirchen, where he was liberated by the Americans on 5 May 1945. He tells how he "miraculously" escaped death on several occasions.

After the war, BK returned to his home in Yablonov, where he found his two sisters and a brother. The brother, who had become a hero of the Russian army, advised the family to leave Czechoslovakia immediately in order to avoid Russian Communist rule. BK was the only family member to emigrate to Palestine. He lived there from 1945 until 1958. He married, and the first two of his five children were born in Israel.

BK and his young family arrived in the United States in November 1958. Their first residence was in Pennsylvania in order to be near his family there. He and his family moved several times, from job to job and from place to place. Finally he settled in New Jersey where he found a job, and his children were enrolled in a fine Hebrew day school. He was compelled to retire in 1984 because of a physical disability. One brother and one sister live in New York state and one sister lives in Pennsylvania. At the time of this interview, BK had eleven grandchildren.

ROSE FEIG LAZARUS, 1922–

[Holocaust testimony (HRC-931, videotape: 1 hour, 46 minutes), 19 June 1985; interviewed by Sidney Langer, indexed by Joseph J. Preil. D804.3/.L463 1985]

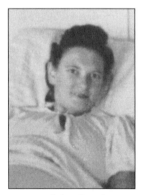

Rose Feig recovering in a hospital, 1946.

Rose Feig Lazarus [RL] was born on 15 February 1922 in Yasinya, a resort town in the Carpathian Mountains. She provides a vivid description of life in a middle-class Jewish family in prewar Carpathia. RL's family consisted of her parents and their eleven children. Practically the entire family perished during the Holocaust. RL's community was surprised by the ruthlessness of the Hungarians who occupied their region in the spring of 1943. Her family was modern; the men were clean-shaven. RL reports the more pious Jews were treated terribly. On the second day of Passover, in April 1944, all the community's Jews were rounded up in an open field for shipment by cattle car to the ghetto in Mátészalka, Hungary. She describes the brutality of the Gestapo guards. Three weeks later, they were shipped to Auschwitz by cattle car.

Incredibly, RL's community had never heard of Auschwitz before the spring of

1944. RL says that she "cannot believe" now that she survived the trip by cattle car. She reports the chaos of arrival at Auschwitz, her separation from her mother and the young children, and how a female German guard pointed to the smoke from a crematorium and announced they were burning there.

RL returns to Auschwitz in her imagination.

I'm going to see my parents! . . . But unfortunately, she was not lying because that was the last day, the last time, when I saw my family. You see, we all really thought that the world will come and save us. The world will save us. No, nothing can happen to us. But, unfortunately, nobody saved us.

RL finds it difficult to leave her Auschwitz experience.

Auschwitz is something that I don't believe a human being could really describe it, because it's undescribable. I will never forget that. They were feeding us . . . like for the animals, when they give the food, everybody was given one plate of that big thing, and I always felt this was cooked with some human flesh. I swear, I could not eat anything and I wished myself daily, I begged God to take me and let me not suffer, let me not see what's going on. And for a young child, it was a lot of suffering . . . that you want to die, daily. . . . It was not a very good life. . . . There was no life. I still have nightmares, believe it or not.

Toward the end of her Auschwitz testimony, RL tries to connect this experience with her life today.

I'm very strong. . . . I must be very strong, because I survived the Holocaust, I survived many other things. It was not easy to return and not finding anybody. . . . I'm not very healthy mentally, really not healthy. And I'm surprised . . . because I brought up two beautiful children. . . . I brought them up with all my love. . . . I got plenty of love from my family, but after that, I was alone, all alone. And I really had to fight for my life, and fight for everything. So, my kids, surprisingly, are normal. And I say surprisingly, because I didn't think I could bear a normal child. . . . And I don't know. My son is a doctor. My daughter has a very good position. She's the director of a research firm. So, they turned out OK. . . . So, it's really unforgettable.

After a month in Auschwitz, RL was in a group of six hundred victims being transferred to Gelsenkirchen. Four hundred of the six hundred were killed by American bombs. RL worked in a munitions factory. She describes the awful conditions and routines in Gelsenkirchen. As the Russians advanced, RL's group was moved to the Sommerda munitions factory, where they remained four or five months, and finally to Altenburg, where her group was liberated. RL's group of a thousand women marched constantly during the last four weeks of the war. The conditions were unbearable. Food was practically nonexistent, and the Gestapo women guards were worse than the men.

RL's description of liberation is very meaningful. She was in a group of twenty that hid in a bunker for an entire week with just one loaf of bread. They were afraid to leave the bunker; they could not believe they were free. When the Americans arrived, one soldier was able to speak Yiddish, and hesitantly and fearfully RL's group left the bunker.

After liberation, RL searched for her family. She spent three weeks in Budapest and was disappointed that the citizens there were nasty to survivors. She went to Czechoslovakia where she found one surviving brother. They emigrated to the United States in 1948. RL moved to New Jersey and married a New Jersey resident.

The impact of Auschwitz on RL was so compelling that she returned to that period toward the end of her testimony in order to recall several of her experiences.

> I'd like to tell you many things. With all telling you, the way it was and the way it is, you cannot tell this story in a lifetime. And if you tell it daily, a little bit, this was just a tiny little bit that I'm telling. . . .
>
> I came in to Auschwitz and a kid, she was fifteen years old, and this woman . . . you may not believe this, I wouldn't believe and you may not believe it, this woman said that your parents and sisters and brother are burning. You would not believe it that this kid, within a half-hour, she turned gray, completely gray. . . . You would think that only happens in a picture, in a movie, but we were all standing, and I said, "Oh, my God, look, her whole face got white and the head . . . got gray, completely gray. How could that happen?" You know, within one day, that girl was gone. She died. I mean she didn't want to live, and she was gone. . . . We tried to pour into her some liquid. . . . It didn't do a bit of good. "I want to die. I want to die." And she went.
>
> There was another woman in Auschwitz. . . . She was standing around and praying, "My children, my children, my children. I want to die." They took away her kids. They left her alive and took away her kids. She died, she died in Auschwitz . . . without being killed. . . . She just wanted to die and she made up her mind she's going to die. And you know, she suffered, she was saying *Tehillim* [that is, reciting from the Book of Psalms—ed.]. . . . She wouldn't take anything, she wouldn't do anything. She said, "I'm going to die. I want to die, and they're not going to kill me. I'm going to die." She did. . . .
>
> Believe me, these are not made-up stories. These are really stories that I had seen with my own eyes. How could you really have a peaceful night, and not have nightmares, of all those things that happened?

SUSAN STURC LEDERMAN, 1937–

[Holocaust testimony (HRC-901, videotape: 1 hour, 10 minutes), 22 November 1983; interviewed by Sidney Langer, indexed by Joseph J. Preil. D804.3/.L559 1983]

Susan Sturc Lederman [SL] was born in Bratislava on 28 May 1937. German was the mother tongue in her cosmopolitan family. Her father owned a printing shop. Her parents each had a good Jewish education in addition to a university education. Her mother had also attended finishing school in Germany. Her parents observed the Sabbath and kept a kosher home during the prewar years.

SL was an only child. She and her parents survived the Holocaust. Aunts, uncles, cousins, and grandparents, however, perished in concentration camps or fighting as partisans.

SL reports she could not have been saved without gentile help. In the spring of 1943, she was in Trnava, at her grandparents', which was an hour away from her own home. She was taken by a German nurse to the priest in the local church in order to be "converted" for her safety. Although only six years old at the time, SL "understood the sham."

SL's parents made several unsuccessful attempts to find a safe haven for the family during the Nazi period of terror. SL was finally accepted by a Hungarian family living in Bratislava, who were willing to accept this little Jewish girl because she had blond hair, blue eyes, and spoke Hungarian. As a seven-year-old child, SL had to play a role, and she never "blew the cover." When neighbors visited unannounced while her parents were in the house, SL acted as though she did not know them.

SL's parents survived by renting a room for her mother and aunt, who were also able to pass as non-Jews, and her father moved into the room secretly. The landlord never knew that SL's father was in the house; he rarely left the room. Her parents visited SL about once a month.

SL knew Jews were being deported to concentration camps. Her father was spared deportation so that he could keep his printing plant operating for the Germans. During two parts of her testimony, SL reflects on the essential components of her family's survival.

> That I survived, obviously depended on many courageous acts on the part of the gentile community. I could not have survived without that kind of help. And that help came partly because my father had good friends who were not Jewish. Much of that help dealt with information, forging papers, as well as actual help in finding safe houses and surviving.

Toward the end of her testimony, SL adds this factor necessary for survival.

> So much of the little survival that there was depended not just on the goodwill and heroic efforts really of gentiles, but also a lot of luck and courage. My father was particularly concerned with trying to communicate to family members about potential danger because of some contact he had. He sometimes did get warnings of potential roundups earlier. In one case, he and my mother traveled to Trnava, that neighboring city where my grandparents lived, to warn them of an approaching roundup, and were stopped by some Nazis . . . and before they even had a chance to ask my parents for

their identification, my father pulled out a Bible, which had been printed in our shop, a Christian Bible full of beautiful color illustrations. I have a copy of that Bible now, very beautifully printed, and with a lot of loose, holy pictures. . . . My grandparents' home was right next to the archbishop in Trnava. And my father said, "I'm going to see the archbishop . . . to show him this new Bible that we've just printed." He started distributing the pictures and managed to sort of weave his way out that difficult spot.

Bratislava was liberated by the Russians in April 1944, and SL's family was able to move into an apartment, not their home or a DP camp. SL's father decided in 1948 that he wanted his family to emigrate to the United States. Czechoslovakia was becoming uncomfortable under Communist domination. Her father's brother in the United States helped them move. SL's father, a printer and publisher by trade, worked for Czech newspapers in New York and then became a clerk in the United Nations Postal Administration. The family lived in Bayonne, New Jersey, and later moved to Woodside, Queens. SL adjusted well to her new country and to public school. She was graduated from the University of Michigan and earned a doctorate in political science at Rutgers University. SL and her husband live in New Jersey, where they are both professors in New Jersey colleges. They have two children, a son who is a lawyer in New Jersey and a daughter who works for J. P. Morgan in London. SL has served as president of the New Jersey League of Women Voters (1985–1989) and as president of the United States League of Women Voters, (1990–1992).

ALLEN MOSKOWITZ, 1923–

[Holocaust testimony (HRC-1065, videotape: 1 hour, 20 minutes), 25 March 1992; interviewed by Joseph J. Preil and Mark Lender, indexed by Joseph J. Preil. D804.3/.M911 1992]

Allen Moskowitz, 1946.

Allen Moskowitz [AM] was born in Brusnica on 27 March 1923. His family moved to Svidník in 1937. Of the six persons in AM's immediate family before the Holocaust, AM's father perished in Mauthausen, a fourteen-year-old brother was murdered in Auschwitz, one brother and one sister survived Auschwitz, and his mother survived in hiding.

AM himself survived a total of seven concentration camps between October 1944 and May 1945: Sered-Slovakia, Sachsenhausen, Heinkel, Siemensstadt, Ohrdruf ("the worst of all the camps"), Kräwinkel, and Buchenwald. He was not shipped to any of the notorious camps in Poland because by this time (late 1944) the Germans were fleeing from the advancing Russians.

AM's father came from a family of twelve, all of whom and their children (except for two) were murdered during the Holocaust. All thirteen relatives in his mother's family also perished.

AM's parents did not trust the Germans. The increasing antisemitism in Czechoslovakia and Hitler's threats on the radio convinced his parents not to trust the authorities and to go into hiding. AM testifies that Czechoslovakia collaborated with the Germans between 1939 and 1943. Young Jews were taken to forced labor camps in 1942; entire families were being deported in mid-1943. The full fury of the Holocaust descended on AM's community when the German SS units arrived.

AM's mother managed to hide with a gentile family who accepted payment for their cooperation. She had to leave this family when funding was no longer available, and accept work as cook at an inn. Her piety meant that she ate none of the food, she did not work on the Sabbath, and observed her religion meticulously.

AM describes his experiences in seven concentration camps during the concluding eight months of World War II. When asked why the Germans moved the victims so often (since the forced labor in these camps was similar), AM answered, "Perhaps it saved the Germans from the Russian front."

A very interesting response was provided by AM to the following question.

INTERVIEWER: You said Ohrdruf was the worst camp. You were there, you were the only member of your family there, and you were a young boy. What kept you going?

AM: What kept me going is, I tell you, if I did not believe in God, I would commit suicide. Suicide was very easy to commit. A lot of them committed suicide. In fact, a lot of them gave away a piece of bread, and asked the fellow, "I give you my bread, if you kill me, if you choke me."

And the only reason I didn't commit suicide, because I knew it is against my religion. . . . because the work was so heavy and it was so discouraging in the morning to see when they lined us up for the count, and you saw all the dead lined up.

As the war was ending and AM's last camp, Buchenwald, was being liberated by the Americans, he fell ill with typhus and was completely unaware of his surroundings for three weeks. After recovering, he returned to his hometown and was reunited with his mother and surviving brother. His sister then returned from Sweden, and the four family members were together for a short time.

AM describes a legendary hero of the Holocaust.

The real hero was . . . Rabbi Michael Ber Weissmandel, who was working very hard to save the few thousand Jews, . . . about twenty thousand Jews, left in Slovakia in 1944. He was doing the negotiating with Wisliceny [Eichmann's deputy in Slovakia— ed.]. Gisi Fleischmann was also active and, you know, they were paying off as much money as they could get out of the committee, or the few people left with money, and to postpone the transports as far as they could. But it didn't work, because they stopped for a few months and, at the end, we all went.

INTERVIEWER: How would you describe Rabbi Weissmandel?

AM: He was a brilliant man. He had a wild look in his eyes, and he was so devoted to the cause of saving people that he, many times, at the complete disregard of his own safety—He was the one who jumped off a moving train, and got into a bunker in Bratislava. And even from the bunker, he was working, trying to find out where all the Jews were hidden, if they have any needs to help them.

INTERVIEWER: He was the one who demanded that the Allies bomb the tracks and the camp, Auschwitz?

AM: I was carrying letters between Nitra and Pressburg.

This statement referred to the fact that Rabbi Weissmandel knew AM as the brother of one of his students in the Yeshiva of Nitra, a highly advanced Talmudical seminary. Rabbi Weissmandel worked indefatigably to save Jews during the war years, and he corresponded with many individuals in this effort. He requested AM to deliver letters to Pressburg, an important community in the region.

AM remained in Czechoslovakia in order to liquidate the family possessions while the other three family members left for Palestine via France. When AM arrived in France, he heard from Palestine that he should emigrate to the United States in order to render financial assistance to his family in Palestine.

AM arrived in the United States in 1948. He moved to New Jersey because of a business opportunity and married an American woman. They have three children, all educated professionals living in New Jersey, and eight grandchildren.

HUGO PRINCZ, 1922–

[Holocaust testimony (HRC-936, videotape: 1 hour, 24 minutes), 17 February 1987; interviewed by Bernard Weinstein and Carole Shaffer-Koros, indexed by Bernard Weinstein. D804.3/.P956 1987]

Hugo Princz [HP] was born on 20 November 1922 in Silvas [Slivnk]. His family was comfortable financially. He remembers a happy childhood in his small town, in a prosperous and democratic Czechoslovakia, where all the Jews he knew were observant and Orthodox. His immediate family consisted of his parents and eight children. All perished in the Holocaust except for HP.

Antisemitism was no problem in Czechoslovakia before 1938. The Slovakian government was established that year by the Nazis, and anti-Jewish laws were enacted, kosher slaughter was banned, businesses were confiscated, and former friends turned against Jews. HP provides testimony of how speedily a friendly country and community can become antisemitic when it becomes government and church policy.

> Our own priest—our town . . . was 95 percent Catholic. The priest in town, the sermons every Sunday were taken up, every time, talking against Jews. And this is unbelievable. You know, a priest says something, well, this is holy, you know. Because we had a couple of people who discreetly told us, you know, what the sermon the priest had this Sunday.
>
> But the whole town would be empty. Everybody was in church. That's how religious those people were. These are religious bigots, I call them. How can you be religious and be antihuman? I mean, take people and kick them out of their homes? This is people who go to church, run to church, rain or shine, rain or shine! You couldn't see a person. If you came Sunday morning, everybody was in church. That's how holy those people were!
>
> When it came to ship the Jews, one policeman came, one policeman, and about forty of this fascist group from the town. My friends who went to school [where] my brother went, and they guarded the house. They gave us . . . about a half-hour, or an hour, to pack forty pounds per person.

HP's father had American citizenship, and he tried to save the family by emigrating to the United States. The American embassy and the Roosevelt administration refused to help. HP remains bitter about this treatment to the present day.

HP's family was deported to Poland in March 1942. Their first stop was the Majdanek concentration camp in Lublin. The parents were then sent to the Treblinka murder camp; the children were sent to Auschwitz. HP was assigned to Buna and worked for I.G. Farben on road construction. He recalls being subjected to twenty-five lashes for the "crime" of picking up potato peels to assuage his hunger. He reports that most people were worked to death. Birkenau was his worst experience. People were beaten to death there for wanting additional food. He worked at the crematoria and describes gassing a thousand people jammed together. He saw people thrown into the ovens after being gassed while some of the victims were still alive. From HP's perspective, all the guards were cruel. "I was in, how many camps, eight or nine camps, I haven't come across one decent guard, SS or even Wehrmacht." HP does not know how he remained alive. There were times when he admired those who had the courage to commit suicide on the electrified wires in the camp. He thought all Jews would be destroyed before the war ended. In April 1945, as the war was concluding, HP was in a group being transferred to the Austrian Alps to be murdered. In Poing, Germany, a railway station, they were liberated by the Americans.

HP went to the Feldafing DP camp. He then returned to Czechoslovakia and learned that his large family had all perished. He succeeded in entering the United States on 31 December 1946. He moved to New Jersey in 1957, after a cousin convinced him to open a business there. He is married and has three children.

OTTO SALAMON, 1934 –

[Holocaust testimony (HRC-2022, videotape: 59 minutes), 30 April 1996; interviewed and indexed by Joseph J. Preil. D804.3/.S168 1996]

Otto Salamon [OS] was born on 23 July 1934, in Leitmeritz in the Sudetenland. An only child, he fled with his parents to Beregovo in 1938, when his father sensed imminent danger for Czech Jews as Hitler had become a powerful threat. They then moved to Prague and, in 1940, the family fled to Budapest to escape the German menace. OS's extended family consisted of about fifty people. OS, his parents, and a few others survived the war; the overwhelming majority perished in the Holocaust.

When the Hungarian secret police imprisoned him and other children in an internment camp, his mother managed to have him freed. OS was a young boy at this time and could never bear to hear the entire story of how his mother arranged for his freedom. He understands that the other children perished and, according to his mother, OS is the only survivor. What is OS's reaction? "I'm not so sure of that."

His mother was able to save herself by behaving as a non-Jew. Both his parents struggled in a series of menial jobs, and they lived in a flat with no heat and little food. OS's father was taken to a forced labor camp and trained to be a fireman in the expectation of enemy bombing. Budapest did experience much bombing, both Russian and Allied. OS attended school for about two or three years. By 1943, at the age of nine, there was no more schooling for him. "We were in hiding, trying to survive." He wore the Star of David at one time, but he and his mother discarded these armbands when they tried to pass as non-Jews with their false papers.

Finally, mother and son received papers from Raoul Wallenberg and moved "into his house." The Germans arrived in Budapest in April 1944, "when everything culminated, and my father was taken away to Bergen-Belsen." OS watched as his father was driven away in a truck from a square in Budapest. OS describes the dangers he and his mother lived through, "Every day . . . from the bombings, and from the people. . . . The Hungarians were just as bad as the Germans." After several false leads, OS and his mother learned that his father was still alive. This was confirmed on 23 July 1945, OS's birthday. The family went to Torino, Italy, after they were reunited. His mother's sister emigrated to the United States, and OS and his parents followed in August 1949, after visiting Paris and then living in Brussels for three years. OS attended high school in New York, graduated from City College of New York, went into show business, and became a film producer. Among his films was *The People against Jean Harris,* which was nominated for awards.

OS married an American woman who was raised in Brooklyn. They moved to New Jersey after visiting a friend and falling in love with the idea of settling there. OS has two children, a daughter who teaches in central New Jersey and a son who works in computers.

OS did not talk to other survivors about his Holocaust experiences for many years. He felt his "story is painful, others' stories are horrendous." He spoke for the first time on a recent Kean College trip for educators to the United States Holocaust Memorial Museum in Washington. He will now tell his story to his daughter's class.

SAUL WEINBERGER, 1926–

[Holocaust testimony (HRC-2008, videotape: 1 hour, 12 minutes), 12 October 1994; interviewed and indexed by Joseph J. Preil. D804.3/.W421 1994]

Saul Weinberger (right) and his two surviving siblings in the Braunau, Austria, DP camp, 1946.

Saul Weinberger [SW] was born on 25 January 1926 in Munkács. Of nine members of his immediate family in Europe in 1939, three survived the Holocaust: SW, a brother who lives in Israel, and a sister who died in the United States in 1975. Six family members perished in the Holocaust: his father, step-mother, and four brothers. He had a large ex-tended family including first cousins from the families of ten uncles and aunts. Of this extended family, only two cousins survived in addition to SW and his two siblings. He also had one sister in the United States before 1939.

SW's father was a small manufacturer of kerosene lamps. Life in general was hard for them and most others, but they enjoyed a beautiful family life. SW describes anti-Jewish laws and antisemitism when Hungarian forces entered the community in 1939 and the Munkács region became part of Hungary. In 1944, the Germans occupied all of Hungary, and SW felt the full impact of the Holocaust. He describes the German organization of the Munkács ghetto at Passover 1944; the "eerie march" to the railroad cars under the silent, watchful eyes of the townspeople; the cattle car journey and arrival at Auschwitz; and the selection process when most Jews were designated for gassing.

SW was selected for forced labor and was transferred to Jaworzno, followed by the death march to Leitmeritz in Czechoslovakia. "This was worse than the train. . . . The worst thing that could happen."

SW arrived in Leitmeritz with typhus and "was practically dead." He was then transferred to Theresienstadt. A cousin met him in this camp and helped him recover miraculously. He returned to Munkács after being liberated by the Russians and met his surviving brother and sister. With the help of his American sister, he came to the United States in January 1947, became a cabinet-maker, and served in the American army, 1950–1952. After army service, SW married an American woman. The young couple moved to New Jersey to be near SW's sister who had moved there from the Bronx. He has a son who works in telecommunications, a daughter who works in a day care center, and four grandchildren. SW continues to live in New Jersey, as do his two children and their families.

Toward the end of his testimony, SW tells a dramatic, personal story that reveals the severe pain of the Holocaust for survivors, even decades after the event.

I had nightmares for thirty years, from 1945 until about 1975. I remember waking up at night in a sweat, and my wife used to calm me and talk to me when she saw me yelling and screaming in my dreams. She knew what it was. And it was always the same dream, it was always the same dream. It took me thirty years. I no longer dream, thank God . . . about those things. But nevertheless, there was a day ahead of me. I had commitments. I had to provide for my family. I had to work. I had to succeed. And that drove me on.

INTERVIEWER: You said it was always the same dream?

SW: Always the same dream. I used to wake up screaming. . . . My wife was the only one who understood that. . . . The SS man was chasing me and shooting at me, and I was constantly hiding and resisting arrest. . . .

The whole experience was just haunting me. . . . I remember, in 1954, that my daughter was to be born. I had a nightmare that she was born and she had a number . . . on her arm. That fantasy took over. I actually was afraid that something like this happened. I know it's outrageous. And I remember going to the hospital and my wife giving birth. And the first that I looked at the arm, you know. And I was relieved, actually, that she didn't have a number. But these things worked on you. Everything worked on you.

So, finally, when my daughter was expecting her first child, I had my tattoo removed surgically. So I didn't have to tell my grandchild what that number is. I remember lying to my children when they asked me. . . . And I just didn't want to go through the same thing with my grandchildren.

HAROLD ZELMANOVICS, 1921–

[Holocaust testimony (HRC-1077, videotape: 1 hour), 4 December 1992; interviewed and indexed by Joseph J. Preil. D804.3/.Z511 1992]

Harold Zelmanovics [HZ] was born on 11 June 1921 in Svalava. His immediate family consisted of nine persons: his parents, four sons, and three daughters. HZ, one brother, and two sisters survived the Holocaust; the other five family members perished.

Hungarians occupied the Svalava region after the outbreak of war in 1939. Thus began the restrictions and hardships for the Jewish population, including confiscation of properties and food shortages, especially for Jews.

HZ became an electrician at the age of seventeen. He did much work in his hometown during the following four years, until October 1942 when he was shipped by cattle car on an eight-hour trip to Komárom, Hungary. His forced labor assignment in Komárom was based on his ability as an electrician. About five months later, in March 1943, HZ was transferred to Budapest for similar work. He remained in Budapest until November 1944.

HZ's "worst experience of the war" was the eighteen-day cattle car trip from Budapest to the Buchenwald concentration camp in Germany. His train arrived on 24 December 1944, and he was assigned to repairing cattle cars, in which his group worked and slept for four or five months. They did good work and had to cooperate "in order to survive."

In April 1945, HZ was attached to a group of Buchenwald prisoners assigned to a death march to Dachau that lasted eight or ten days. After liberation by the Americans, he was taken to Prague, became ill, and was hospitalized for two or three weeks. HZ recovered, lived in Czechoslovakia for a year, then for three years in Bavaria in the American zone, where he worked as an electrical instructor for UNRRA. HZ married in Czechoslovakia in 1945, arrived in the United States in 1949, and has since lived in New Jersey near relatives and fellow survivors. He has one son, a computer programmer.

Hungary

MARGIT BUCHHALTER FELDMAN, 1929–

[Holocaust testimony (HRC-1057, videotape: 1 hour, 21 minutes), 30 January 1990; interviewed by Bernard Weinstein and Daniel Gover, indexed by Joseph J. Preil. D804.3/.F312 1990]

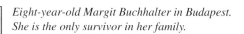

Eight-year-old Margit Buchhalter in Budapest. She is the only survivor in her family.

Margit Buchhalter Feldman [MF] was born in Budapest on 12 June 1929. She was the only surviving child in her family by the time the war started in 1939, when her family was living in Tolcsva near the Czech border. She recalls that Jewish men were taken to forced labor camps in neighboring cities in 1943.

The Germans occupied Hungary in 1944. "My world really stopped one day in 1944 when Hungarian gendarmes came knocking to inform us that we have to pack all our belongings. . . . It was in April. . . . The next day we assembled in the town hall." They walked to a ghetto in Sátoraljaújhely, a nearby town. Quite a few people committed suicide. Fifteen thousand Jews were then transported to a labor camp in railroad cars. Of these, only two hundred fifty survived the Holocaust. Of the sixty-eight members in MF's extended family in Hungary, only two survived, and of the three persons in MF's immediate family, only MF survived.

MF saw her first German SS men at the railroad station where they went for deportation by cattle cars to Auschwitz. "More than one-third did not make it to Auschwitz alive." In Auschwitz, "once you went through that iron gate [with the words *Arbeit Macht Frei*], you really entered into hell itself. . . . My father risked his life, received a tremendous beating. . . . He ran over to the women's line from the men's line . . . and said his last blessing over me. . . . My mother went straight to the crematorium" with other family members. MF remembers "the horrible, horrible fumes coming out of the gas chambers. . . . The furnaces were going day and night, day and night."

In the camp MF claimed she was eighteen years old, making her eligible for forced labor and, in her case, this meant eventual survival. She was transferred to Kraków to work in a quarry. She describes the German game there of counting the Jews and murdering every tenth person. After working six to eight weeks in Kraków, MF was moved back to the horrible conditions of Auschwitz, which she once again describes in vivid detail.

MF's next camp was Grünberg where she worked in a munitions factory. "Life was much more bearable there because they needed you. . . . Some of their people risked their lives by following us to the bathroom and slipping us some bread." She met Gerda Weiss Klein, a well-known author today, who was also imprisoned at Grünberg.

MF participated in the horrible death march to Bergen-Belsen, which she describes as being "really the pits. . . . Diphtheria, typhus, mounds of corpses. . . . We had no strength." By the time she was liberated by the British on the eve of her sixteenth birthday, MF was sick and without a family. She had also been injured by a German explosion intended to destroy the camp.

MF was sent to Sweden after the war. The Swedes were wonderful to her. She discovered that she had an aunt and uncle in the United States and arrived there in August 1947 to live with them. She worked and studied, married in 1953, and had two children. MF is active in Holocaust education and is a member of the New Jersey Commission for Holocaust Education. As a central New Jersey resident, she is also active in community endeavors.

ERNEST GOTTDIENER, 1920–

[Holocaust testimony (HRC-1070, videotape: 1 hour, 36 minutes), 27 October 1992; interviewed and indexed by Joseph J. Preil. D804.3/.G684 1992]

Ernest Gottdiener [EG] was born on 13 October 1920 in Hajdunánás, a small town near Debrecen. His family's experience during the Holocaust provides much insight into the Holocaust for Hungarian Jewry.

EG was the youngest of twelve children. Of thirty-three family members in Hungary in 1939, including EG's mother, her children and their spouses, and the grandchildren, twelve survived the Holocaust and twenty-one perished, nineteen in Auschwitz. No member of his family survived Auschwitz.

EG describes his education in several yeshivas. The plight of the Jews became especially critical after 19 March 1944, when Germany marched into Hungary and Eichmann arrived to deal with the Jews. The women and children were in greater danger than the men because, by 1944, the Holocaust was efficiently organized for those Jews who continued to reside in their own communities and most men were in the Hungarian army, serving in segregated all-Jewish forced labor units. Consequently, the men were in a better position to move about and evade the Nazi dragnet.

Throughout this testimony, EG describes the several miraculous escapes aiding his survival, and he recalls living in Raoul Wallenberg's Swedish House. The miracles were necessary even though the full brunt of the Holocaust was not felt in Hungary until the final year of a long war. He describes the chaos in Budapest as the war was ending, including "mountains and mountains of dead bodies."

EG returned to Debrecen and Hajdunánás after liberation and made an effort with several family members to resume their lives and family business. They left Hungary in 1948 because the Communists had become dominant.

EG married a fellow Hungarian survivor in Budapest in 1948. The young couple moved to Vienna with several other members of EG's family. Some of his relatives emigrated to the United States in 1947. EG and his wife made their final decision to move to the United States, to central New Jersey, because of the educational opportunities available for their son and daughter in the vibrant Jewish community of their choice. EG and one of his brothers became partners in a New Jersey construction firm. His son is a rabbi in Maryland; his daughter is a social worker and lives in New Jersey, where EG and his wife continue to reside. He has ten grandchildren and one great-grandson.

The following exchange toward the end of the interview reflects the attitude of many survivors.

INTERVIEWER: So you feel more strongly about talking and teaching the Holocaust today than you did right after the war?

EG: I certainly do. After the war, I was busy with physical and emotional problems, and this has now been put in a distance. Now we can see it more clearly.

JUDIT TAUSZKY GOTTDIENER, 1930–

[Holocaust testimony (HRC-994, videotape: 1 hour, 40 minutes), 9 March and 6 June 1988; interviewed by Bernard Weinstein and Robyn Rajs, indexed by Joseph J. Preil. D804.3/.G685 1988]

Judit Tauszky Gottdiener [JG] was born on 11 November 1930, in Budapest. In 1939, her immediate family consisted of five persons: her parents, JG, her older sister, and a younger brother. All five survived the Holocaust because they were included in the group of seventeen hundred Jews to be transported to Palestine via Switzerland as a result of negotiations between the Nazis and Rudolf Kastner.

JG's family were and remain deeply observant Orthodox Jews. Her father was a wholesale-retail dealer in tobacco and smoking accessories. The Germans occupied Hungary during the spring of 1944, and anti-Jewish decrees began immediately: wearing a yellow star, daily curfew, the closing of Jewish business establishments, and the expulsion of Jewish students from schools. The situation became deadly when the Germans searched for Jews in massive numbers for deportation to Auschwitz.

JG's father heard that Rudolf Kastner, a leading Hungarian Zionist, was involved in a plan to save Jews who would be sent to Palestine. The cost per individual was prohibitive. Her father took all the family jewelry and valuables to the *Judenrat,* and her family members were included among those selected by Kastner to be saved. Kastner also selected prominent Jews from all over Hungary, including leading rabbis and professionals. The Grand Rabbi of Satmar and the Rabbi of Debrecen were saved in this manner. Kastner also chose to save members of his own family and community, and he remains a controversial personality. Some feel "he sold his soul to the devil," others believe he deserves credit for saving seventeen hundred Jews. Kastner was assassinated during his 1954 trial in Jerusalem. The court then exonerated Kastner of all charges except that of helping some Nazis escape from justice.

JG relates the saga of the group organized by Kastner. The first part of the trip, by cattle car, was confusing even to the Germans because they did not know how to proceed. Finally, the group arrived at Bergen-Belsen where they suffered from hunger because their diet of "soup, bread, and margarine was just enough not to die." Unlike others in the camp, JG's group was not assigned to forced labor. The group was in the camp during the 1944 High Holiday season. JG describes the Yom Kippur prayer service with the Rabbi of Debrecen. The impact of the dramatic prayer *"Unesaneh Tokef"* was so powerful that it still affects her every year. Another indication of the preferred treatment provided for this group was the fact that her father participated daily in prayer services with the Grand Rabbi of Satmar and others. JG's family was among those endeavoring to avoid nonkosher food, including the "junk" tossed into the soup. After six months in Bergen-Belsen, the Kastner detainees were transported by "regular" train to Switzerland. Arrival there is described by JG as "from hell to paradise." When the war ended, seven hundred members of the group moved to Palestine. JG's family returned to Budapest, where they learned that one grandfather had died quickly of pneumonia in the ghetto. Her other grandparents died of starvation at the end of the war and were buried in a common grave.

JG's parents joined her brother in Israel in 1950. She met her future husband at a European resort in 1948. They were married in Budapest and moved with several members of his family to Vienna. The couple and their two children moved to the United States in 1961. JG's husband became a real estate developer in New Jersey, where they still live. Their son is a rabbi in Maryland, their daughter is a social worker and lives in New Jersey with her lawyer husband. JG has ten grandchildren and one great-grandson.

JG's commitment to her religious values is encapsulated in this statement, in which she explains the reasoning for moving from Vienna to her community in New Jersey.

There we wouldn't give in on that, not to give our children a Jewish education. So it would mean to send them always to another country. So when we came to America, and we settled and then my children were registered in the Jewish school, in the JEC [Jewish Educational Center] when I went in there, I was so happy. It was for me a great feeling. And they were all very nice to us—the principal and the teachers—because, for the children, it was very hard. They didn't know English; they were backwards in Hebrew education. And they were very helpful. . . . I am very, very thankful that my children are both observant. They have a Torah-observant life. And my grandchildren are all in very good Jewish schools. I hope they will go on and just stay on this path all their lives, because there is nothing better.

MARTHA SEILER KLEIN, 1922–

[Holocaust testimony (HRC-1096, videotape: 1 hour, 41 minutes), 13 December 1993; interviewed and indexed by Bernard Weinstein. D804.3/.K525 1993]

Martha Seiler Klein [MK] was born on 6 August 1922, in Nagyvárad in the Transylvania region of Hungary. While she managed to survive, as did her parents and brother, MK identifies eight close relatives who were murdered in Auschwitz. MK's parents had a comfortable home. Her father had an excellent job as a lithographer. Her mother's family was modern Orthodox, while her father and his family were assimilated Jews.

MK received a fine education, including one year at the university, but rising antisemitism meant the end of her formal education. The persecution of the Jews in Hungary began in 1944 when the Germans occupied the country. Her parents were moved into the Budapest ghetto; MK was in a group taken on a forced march to Germany in the summer of 1944. The German part of this trip was by train. Her group arrived in the Ravensbrück concentration camp in September 1944. MK's parents were both saved by Raoul Wallenberg.

She gives a comprehensive description of her brutal experience in Ravensbrück. In December 1944, she was transferred to Venusberg to work in a Messerschmitt aircraft factory. As the Russians were surrounding Venusberg, MK was one of over a hundred prisoners sent by cattle car to the Mauthausen concentration camp in Austria. Only ten survived the harrowing journey. Finally, on 6 May, the camp was liberated by the Americans.

MK was extremely ill at the time of liberation, but was miraculously able to inform her parents of her location. She provides this poignant description of her reunion with her father.

> I was [in bed] . . . because I couldn't walk. My bed was across from . . . the window. I was lying there and to see my father . . . obviously walking very fast. . . . I see a man going there, going by the window. . . . I say, "This is my father."
>
> You know what I did? I rolled down from the bed, I crawled to the window, I pulled myself up, and I *screamed* with all my strength, "Father! Father!" . . . He heard me, and he turned back. He did not recognize me. . . . I was bald, I was bones, I was nothing. Only my glasses, I still had my glasses on. I cannot tell you this feeling what I had, this was unbelievable. That what I prayed for, what I imagined, it happened. And he came. . . . First he said, "Look, maybe you can stay here, and I can bring . . . Mother and brother and we can all go." He did not want to stay there. I said, "Father, if you leave me here, I won't survive."

The doctor agreed with MK. Her father nursed her; he cooked chicken soup. They went to Vienna and then home to Budapest, where she entered a hospital and remained for six months. Even then, she was not completely cured. "My father saved my life."

MK married a man who had lost his first family in the Holocaust. Two years later, she finally recovered and was able to bear children. They emigrated to the United States in 1948 and settled in Connecticut where her husband accepted a position as a rabbi and shochet. Her husband died in 1957. He had kidney problems caused by the beatings he endured in Buchenwald.

MK has two married daughters, both Barnard graduates, and seven grandchildren. MK now lives in New Jersey to be near her daughters and their families.

Romania

MUSIA LUTTINGER GROSS, 1920–

[Holocaust testimony (HRC-2005, videotape: 1 hour, 44 minutes), 7 April 1994; interviewed and indexed by Joseph J. Preil. D804.3/.G841 1994]

Musia Luttinger Gross [MG] was born on 29 January 1920 in Sadagura, a small town near Czernowitz. Her immediate family consisted of five persons: her parents, two daughters, and one son. Only two of the five survived the Holocaust—MG and her sister. Her extended family, through first cousins, consisted of fifty-eight people, of whom twelve survived; forty-six perished.

MG's father was a grain merchant and dealt in currency. The family lived comfortably. Her area was occupied by the Russians for a year, June 1940 to June 1941, with the German invasion of the Soviet Union, began also the beatings and murder program against the Jews. She describes the confiscation of valuables and the relocation of her family to Verchovka in Russia as decreed by the Romanian dictator, Ion Antonescu, who was cooperating closely with the Germans at this time.

The trip to the Transnistria region of Russia began in cattle cars to Bessarabia, then by foot, and finally by boat on the Dniester River in the Ukraine. She and her family arrived in Verchovka in December 1941.

MG's own words vividly describe the trip and the horrors of their first year in Russia.

> It [the cattle car trip] was a nightmare. The rain was beating down on us. The people who accompanied us beat up on us. It was a nightmare. I don't know, whether one day or two days, until we came to the border of Bessarabia in Russia, the Ukraine, the Dniester. . . . Finally, we came to Yampol . . . then to Verchovka . . . a little before Hanukkah . . . 1941. . . . When we came there, it was chaos. . . . No place to lie down. . . . People were dying. . . . You were worse than an animal. . . . Typhus, lice, vomiting, diarrhea.

The first year in Verchovka was her worst experience in the war, worse even than the cattle car, where the family was still together. MG describes her mother's deathbed scene; her mother was in her mid-forties. MG's brother died a few weeks later, incoherent with typhus. His final words were, "Mother, I am coming." MG's father died in the spring, shortly before Passover 1942. At this point, MG said with great emotion, "I don't know where my parents are buried. They are in a mass grave. That's why I want to make this tape. They died for *Kiddush Hashem* ["sanctification of the Lord's name"]. . . . I named my children for my parents."

MG and her sister were liberated by the Russians in May 1944. When asked what they did during this long period, MG replied, "Absolutely nothing. It was a self-destroying camp. . . . There was no program of activity. You sat and you waited. You waited to be destroyed."

The men, it seems, did have work. MG and other women knitted sweaters for farmers in the area, and in return some of the farmers would pass food to the prisoners surreptitiously on market days.

After liberation, MG walked back to her hometown, a distance "of one thousand miles." The peasants along the way gave them food. Her family's home had been plundered. She and her sister finally went to Vienna where MG met her husband-to-be. They could not go to Palestine because of the restrictions then in effect. Finally they arrived in the United States in 1951. She has two daughters, one in Brooklyn and one in New Jersey, as well as two grandchildren in New Jersey.

At the conclusion of the interview, MG was asked, "What should be taught about the Holocaust to your grandchildren, to American students?" MG, a really gentle person, responded.

> Fight for your right! Never again! Never again! Imagine with your eyes what we went through. It's not a percentage that anyone can imagine. The misery, the hunger, the rumbling of your stomach. Getting up in the morning, taking a piece of board, and scraping all the lice from you. Asking yourself: Why? Why? Is that person different from me? We came the same way into this world. We die the same way. We ache the same way. Why? Why?

MG, who lives in Brooklyn, was brought to this interview by her daughter who resides in New Jersey.

DORA BASCH SCHOEN, 1919–

[Holocaust testimony (HRC-999, videotape: 56 minutes), 23 March 1988; interviewed by Selma Dubnick and Henry Kaplowitz, indexed by Joseph J. Preil. D804.3/.S365 1988]

Dora Basch Schoen [DS] was born in Sighet on 10 July 1919. Her family consisted of eight persons: her parents, their three sons, and three daughters. Five family members perished in the Holocaust; DS survived with one sister and one brother. Her father was a butcher. Her family lived three blocks from Elie Wiesel's family and the Wiesel grocery.

Sighet's difficulties began with the Hungarian occupation in August 1940, when kosher slaughter was forbidden. The Jewish situation became perilous when the Germans occupied the country in March 1944, and the Jews were gathered in ghettos one month later. The Germans lost no time in confiscating Jewish jewelry and valuables and then announced that the Jews were to be transferred to work on farms. Actually, the transfer was a two-day train trip to Auschwitz.

At Auschwitz, DS's parents were taken away forever. DS witnessed the hanging of a young girl as the victim's eyes were being pulled out. When the war was ending in Poland in November 1944, DS was moved to Germany, to Bergen-Belsen, Bendorf, Braunschweig, and Buchenwald.

In her testimony, DS remembers the day she left Auschwitz when she heard the voice of a girl calling out to her sister, "You are going on a transport; I'm going to the crematorium." As the war was ending in April 1945, DS and her group were transferred to Denmark, and then to Sweden. The Swedes were especially kind.

DS returns once again to her Auschwitz experience. She recalls the arrival one Saturday of a new group that included DS's younger sister, but the guards did not allow the sisters to embrace. DS traveled to Israel in 1948 in response to a letter from a cousin in Haifa. She married this cousin and remained in Israel until 1956. The couple then moved to the United States. She obtained employment as an office worker until she retired. She lives in New Jersey and does volunteer work, which includes speaking to groups about her Holocaust experiences.

SYLVIA BLAU WIRTZBAUM, 1928–

[Holocaust testimony (HRC-2010, videotape: 1 hour, 16 minutes), 30 November 1994; interviewed and indexed by Joseph J. Preil. D804.3/.W673 1994]

Sylvia Blau Wirtzbaum [SW] was born on 12 September 1928 in Borod. Her immediate family consisted of six persons: her parents, their two sons, and two daughters. Only SW survived the Holocaust. The extended family in Romania, through first cousins, consisted of sixteen persons, of whom SW was the lone survivor.

SW recalls a happy home and childhood in Borod. The Germans turned over their region of Romania to Hungary from 1940 to 1944. SW speaks favorably of the Romanians, but not of the Hungarians, under whom life was difficult economically, although they were relatively safe physically.

This feeling of safety ended with the entry of the Germans in 1944. The Jews were moved into the town ghetto in Borod, then to the ghetto in Oradea, for shipment to Auschwitz in cattle cars. The trip lasted about one week, but SW cannot "remember" the details. She does describe in detail their arrival in Auschwitz in May 1944. Dr. Mengele came to her barrack daily. She was selected to join a group on a truck to be murdered but on her own she returned to the barrack and thus saved her life.

SW then describes the barbaric details of life in Auschwitz.

The constant *Zählappell* . . . the miserable food. . . . One girl took from a garbage can in her wooden shoe, which she used at night for urinating. . . . It was so barbaric, I don't believe the things that I survived, and I know that many survived longer and more than

I did. We didn't feel anything in Auschwitz. We weren't human. . . . I have a cousin in Israel who went in. She was a young married woman. She went in pregnant. She gave birth there.

INTERVIEWER: In Auschwitz?

SW: In Auschwitz. And they hid the baby for about three days and then the girls took the baby. They killed the baby. And I don't know what they did with the body. Because, otherwise, the mother would have carried the baby. I never knew it until she told it to me in Israel.

INTERVIEWER: She survived?

SW: She survived. Her husband survived.

When liberated by the Russians, SW became sick and was hospitalized. After recovering, she returned to Borod via Prague and Budapest. She received a letter from her aunt in New York and, in a complex series of maneuvers, was brought to the United States in 1947 by an American uncle who married her "on paper" in order to facilitate her entry. The uncle then decided he would like to marry SW in reality. They have two children, a son and a daughter. The son is in advertising; the daughter lives in New Jersey with her husband and three children. SW was a widow at the time of this interview.

Toward the end of her testimony, SW was asked when and with whom did she start talking about the Holocaust.

I always talked to my children. I have this bitterness in me. I have this bitterness because nobody survived. At least one person, that's close to me, that I grew up with, I was born with. Somebody. I have nobody.

Yugoslavia

ZVI STERN, 1929–

[Holocaust testimony (HRC-2020, videotape: 1 hour, 27 minutes), 13 December 1995; interviewed and indexed by Joseph J. Preil. D804.3/.S842 1995]

Zvi Stern [ZS] was born in Ilok on 4 September 1929. At the beginning of World War II, his immediate family consisted of six persons: his parents, three sisters, and himself. ZS's extended family consisted of approximately fifty-two people. In addition to the six in his immediate family, eight other people survived. Thus, some thirty-eight people in his extended family perished in the Holocaust.

ZS's father was a successful retail store owner and grain exporter. ZS remembers a pleasant life, a happy childhood wherein Jewish family life was a beautiful experience. The parents of ZS's mother had come to Bosnia from Poland.

The Germans invaded Yugoslavia in April 1941. They occupied Ilok the day before Passover. ZS's father's store was confiscated by the Germans; his father was among the ten prominent Jews in town who were imprisoned to frighten the Jewish population. When his father returned home after three weeks, ZS says, "I didn't recognize him." Several weeks later, ZS's father fled from Ilok to Ljubljana, a city that was originally part of Yugoslavia and was then occupied by Italy.

In two days, he took anything that he could take. I remember, he took tallis, tefillin, and maybe some money. And he left. I was about twelve years old. You know, I didn't understand all this tragedy what's going on. I was . . . in school. It was like, how do you say this in English? *Hefker* [Hebrew: "ownerless"]! Our house . . . it was no more the owner. . . . Chaos. This was what was happening with my father.

Three weeks later, he sent a non-Jewish person to my mother, to bring us over to the same place. . . . They left Ilok and went to Slovenia, what was occupied by Italians at this time, to the city by the name of Ljubljana. He was staying there, and seems to be waiting to bring over the rest of the family. So he sent over, after three, four weeks, the Italian or Slovenian non-Jewish person with the direction to come to our town, to my mother, and to bring us over, the rest of the family. So I remember, my mother, as he came, the person, he was talking to my mother, that he is here, to bring us over. My mother said, how can she leave everything and just go? She cannot do this. She needs more time. She has to try, maybe, to sell something. So she put together maybe some money, or whatever she had, and she gave it to the man and she said, "Give this to my husband and tell him I cannot leave now."

INTERVIEWER: As far as you know, your parents still had some of their money?

ZS: Yeah. They had some. We still had some chance to steal from our own money from the store. Maybe to steal some merchandise and sell it, you know, behind the curtains and not in the store, or to take some from the cashier. And the second time, when this person came back to my father and he gave the money to my father, my father told him, "I asked you to bring my family. I did not ask you for money." My mother did not want to leave. So he sent the same person, two, three months later. And in half an hour, my mother was ready with the children, to leave the house and everything. She locked the house, I remember. In my room, I had some pictures on the walls, from the family and from friends in the schools. And I took them down. I put them below my bed. And I said, "I will be back in three weeks. I will find them."

INTERVIEWER: You haven't been back since?

ZS: This is fifty-five years now. We did not go back to it, and this time my mother was ready and we left, and we came together with our father in Ljubljana.

The family remained about four months in Ljubljana. They were then deported to the Ferramonti camp in Italy where they remained approximately eighteen months, until September or October 1943, when they were liberated by the British. ZS reports that his education, synagogue, and Israel-related youth group were quite satisfactory in the Italian camp. In fact, ZS celebrated his bar mitzvah there and has photos of a public celebration of a bris and a Mishnah study group for adult men.

After liberation, the family lived in southern Italy, in Reggio Calabria. ZS's father learned a new trade, shoemaking. The family participated in a Hachshara (prepatory) program prior to their aliyah (immigration) to Palestine. They were the first family to arrive legally in Israel after the Holocaust, in April 1945.

ZS lived in Israel for thirty-five years, 1945–1980, and then emigrated to the United States with his wife and three of their children; his oldest son remained in Israel. His two oldest children are married, and he has three grandchildren. ZS is a builder and real estate developer. He and his family moved to central New Jersey for the Jewish community and education available to them.

Chapter Seven
Liberators

~~~~~~

T HE testimonies of the twenty liberators reveal the depth of their reactions to the Holocaust even though the total experience may have been only a short visit to a concentration camp followed by a speedy return to their unit for resumption of the military campaign. Following the camp visit, many of these young soldiers could not talk at all, yet their testimonies reveal the lifelong impact of witnessing the results of the Holocaust. It is obvious that practically every soldier was deeply affected by the experience. One is impressed that the Holocaust has changed many of these men into more sensitive and better human beings. In addition, it has elevated the sense of responsibility and the value systems of many of their families and communities.

These testimonies involve the following camps in Austria and Germany (the number in parentheses indicates the number of men who visited that camp): Austria—Wels/Straubing/Gunskirchen (1); Germany—Buchenwald (3), Dachau (9), Wöbbelin (1), Gardelegen (1), Lebenau (1), Nordhausen (3), and Ohrdruf (1).

Twenty Liberators[1]

Leon Bass	Reverend Elbridge Holland	Henry Ricklis
Henry Butensky	Sol Lasky	Chaplain Herschel Schacter
Herb Carlson	Leonard Linton	Richard J. Tisch
John B. Coulston	Albert Mazurkiewicz	Victor Wegard
John Farinella	Lee Merel	Alvin A. Weinstein
Irving Gerenstein	Chaplain Judah Nadich	Reuben Weitzman
Milton Goldberg	A. Kevin Quinn	

As we conclude the 172 testimonies in this book, let us evaluate what happened to each of the three types of individuals we have met: the survivors themselves, their children (the "second generation"), and the liberators.

The few victims who survived the Holocaust were, most often, young people and often the lone survivors in their families. As a group, they were remarkable in

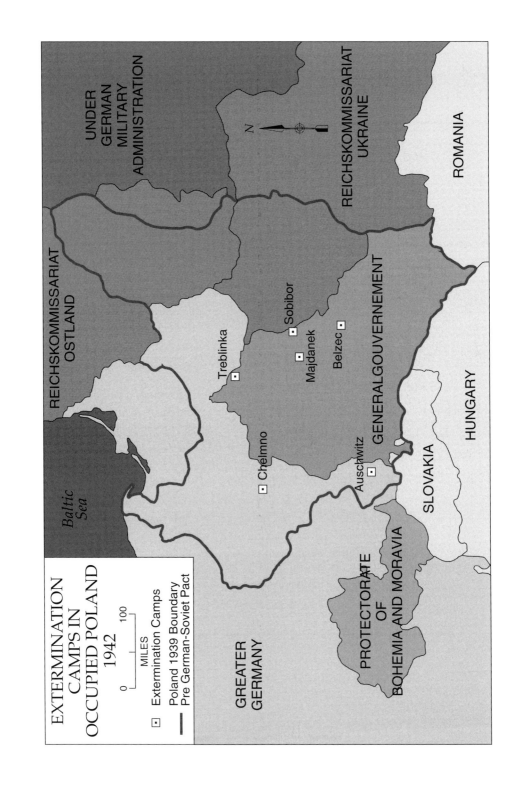

EXTERMINATION
CAMPS IN
OCCUPIED POLAND
1942

MILES
0   100

▫ Extermination Camps
━━ Poland 1939 Boundary
    Pre German-Soviet Pact

Baltic
Sea

REICHSKOMMISSARIAT
OSTLAND

UNDER
GERMAN
MILITARY
ADMINISTRATION

REICHSKOMMISSARIAT
UKRAINE

N

Treblinka ▫

Sobibor ▫

Majdanek ▫

Belzec ▫

Chełmno ▫

Auschwitz ▫

GENERALGOUVERNEMENT

GREATER
GERMANY

PROTECTORATE
OF
BOHEMIA AND MORAVIA

SLOVAKIA

HUNGARY

ROMANIA

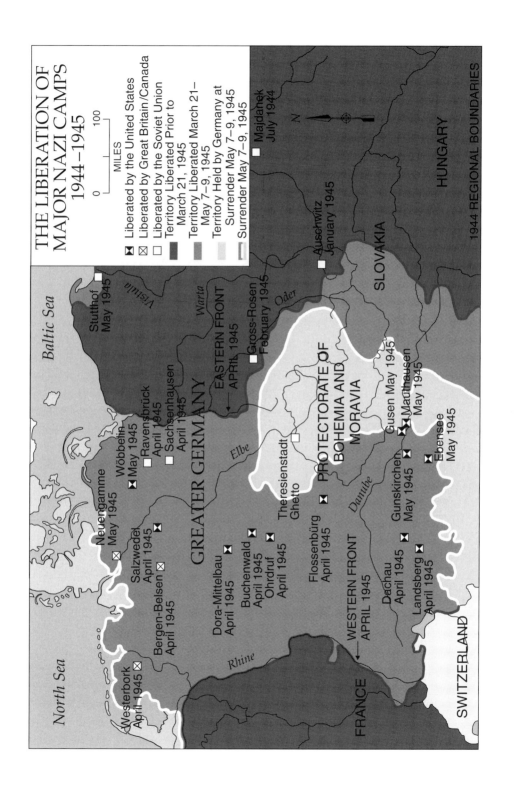

THE LIBERATION OF
MAJOR NAZI CAMPS
1944–1945

MILES
0   100

Liberated by the United States
Liberated by Great Britain/Canada
Liberated by the Soviet Union
Territory Liberated Prior to
March 21, 1945
Territory Liberated March 21–
May 7–9, 1945
Territory Held by Germany at
Surrender May 7–9, 1945
Surrender May 7–9, 1945

1944 REGIONAL BOUNDARIES

N

North Sea

Baltic Sea

Westerbork
April 1945

Neuengamme
May 1945

Wöbbelin
May 1945

Stutthof
May 1945

Vistula

Salzwedel
April 1945

Ravensbrück
April 1945

Bergen-Belsen
April 1945

Sachsenhausen
April 1945

Warta

GREATER GERMANY

EASTERN FRONT
APRIL 1945

Dora-Mittelbau
April 1945

Buchenwald
April 1945

Ohrdruf
April 1945

Elbe

Gross-Rosen
February 1945

Oder

Auschwitz
January 1945

Theresienstadt
Ghetto

PROTECTORATE OF
BOHEMIA AND
MORAVIA

Flossenburg
April 1945

Gusen May 1945

Mauthausen
May 1945

WESTERN FRONT
APRIL 1945

Danube

Dachau
April 1945

Gunskirchen
May 1945

Ebensee
May 1945

Landsberg
April 1945

SLOVAKIA

Majdanek
July 1944

HUNGARY

FRANCE

SWITZERLAND

organizing their lives under the most difficult circumstances. The need to build new families was a critical motivating force for most survivors. Their children, the "second generation," have generally received excellent educations and are pursuing responsible careers. And, finally, we consider the liberators. As they returned home, they resumed their education in college or their careers. They are obviously responsible leaders, both in their families and in their communities.

LEON BASS, 1925–

[Holocaust testimony (HRC-979, videotape: 1 hour, 14 minutes), 16 March 1988; interviewed by Bernard Weinstein and Mark Lender, indexed by Joseph J. Preil. D804.3/.B317 1988]

Leon Bass, retired Philadelphia high school principal and outstanding Holocaust lecturer.

The parents of Leon Bass [LB] were born in the 1890s in South Carolina where LB's father had been a sharecropper. Father was changed by his World War I experience in France, and as a result LB's parents migrated to Philadelphia in a quest for greater equality and opportunity. LB was born in Philadelphia in 1925. He describes the racism that he suffered in the years preceding and during World War II when he volunteered at the age of eighteen to serve in the United States Army as a member of the 183rd Engineer Combat Battalion, attached to General George Patton's Third Army.

In growing up, LB realized society was saying to him, "You're not good enough." His unit consisted of all black men with white officers. They had their basic training in Georgia, where LB recalls "denigrating experiences in the military and in town." Army training continued for another year in several southern states. As a result, LB reports he "became an angry, frustrated young black soldier."

LB describes his unit's participation in the campaign through Western Europe and his reaction on their arrival at the Buchenwald concentration camp as the war was ending. His description is highly effective and memorable.

We went right to Buchenwald and that was the day that I was to discover what had really been going on in Europe under the Nazis. Because I walked through the gates and I saw walking dead people—seriously—walking dead people.

I am not a doctor. I cannot assess things that accurately, but in just looking at these people who were skin and bones and dressed in those pajama-type uniforms, their heads clean shaved, and full of the sores through malnutrition, and here they were coming toward us, making all kinds of guttural statements, and using their own language. It was very difficult for me to comprehend what was going on. I just looked at this in amazement and I said to myself, My God, who are these people? What have they done? What was their crime?

It's hard for me to try to understand why anyone could be treated this way. I don't care what they had done. It just didn't grab me. . . . I had no frame of reference. I was only twenty. And so this young man, who spoke English, began to tell us about Buchenwald. . . . He spoke perfect English, and he was Polish. So he explained to us the composition of this place, that these people were Jews and Gypsies, they were trade unionists and Communists. . . . He went through a litany of groups, saying these people were incarcerated here because they, if I can use a term I used before, saying they were not good enough. Saying they had been put here for one purpose and that was to be worked until they died, starved until they died. . . .

INTERVIEWER: Terms like Auschwitz, Bergen-Belsen, Majdanek, and places like that were not known to you?

LB: Even when I went into Buchenwald, I had no idea that those places existed. Those names only came to me after I got out of the service. Later, much later, I began to hear of names and places and realize that there was more than just a Buchenwald. That there were many, many, many Buchenwalds of different names all over Europe and Russia.

That's what boggles the mind, to think that a group in society can organize and do it in a systematic way, such a program to remove from the world a whole group of people and any others that they didn't think were worthy. . . . But I saw what I saw in the camp. . . . I went into the crematorium where the bodies were piled up, the ashes to be used as human fertilizer.

After the war, LB attended West Chester State College in Pennsylvania, became a teacher and eventually a high school principal in the Philadelphia school system, and joined the civil rights movement. He describes additional racist experiences he suffered following the war.

LB never spoke about the Holocaust until 1970. As he was assuming his position as high school principal, a class had become so unruly that an Auschwitz survivor could not tell her story. LB lectured the students about the importance of the speaker and the significance of her testimony, and told them that he himself was a witness.

LB has become an articulate speaker on the Holocaust and civil rights.

I go around telling my story and, of course, I get people saying, Leon, why do you deal with this? This is not a black problem. I say, Hey, it's not a black problem. It's not a white problem. It's a human problem. And we've got to face it. And as Dr. King says, "Injustice anywhere is the loss of justice everywhere."

HENRY BUTENSKY, 1922–

[Holocaust testimony (HRC-1017, videotape: 57 minutes), 1 November 1988; interviewed by Bernard Weinstein and Selma Dubnick, indexed by Bernard Weinstein. D804.3/.B972 1988.]

Henry Butensky [HB] was born in 1922 in Manhattan and grew up in the Bronx. The son of a cantor, with his older siblings born in Jerusalem, HB was a committed Jew concerned about the fate of European Jewry even before he was drafted into the U.S Army in 1942. He served as a First Sergeant in the Second Battalion, Sixty-sixth Infantry, of General George Patton's Third Army. He was attached to a tank corps in the front line during the tail end of the Battle of the Bulge in December 1944.

HB's first exposure to a forced labor camp was in Wels, Austria. Several days later his unit came to Straubing, another Austrian camp, and "saw the bodies lying massacred and decimated by hunger and starvation. We had heard about the stupid uniforms they were made to wear. And we saw up front the way it was told."

HB's unit came to their third Austrian camp in Gunskirchen. They saw many hundreds of corpses, probably thousands, in the woods near the camp, and inside the camp.

> Yes, we saw some that were still alive. The ones that I came upon still alive were really incoherent. I spoke to one man in Yiddish, and he was in a daze. . . . I couldn't get from him where he came from. One man said he was from Lithuania. . . . Another . . . was from Poland. It was very difficult. . . . There were probably hundreds that were alive.

> *INTERVIEWER:* How did the men in your unit react when they came upon this?

> *HB:* With a lot of sympathy. I think, at that time, had the State of Israel been a fact, or at least had been in the works like it was in 1948, I think the American people at the time would have got up and fought for a Jewish homeland. It was very strong.

> The guys in my outfit came to me, knowing that I'm a Jew and I never hid the fact, and this other boy, Goodman, Michael, who was a radio operator in my outfit. We both talked together, one Jew to another. And many of the guys came over and said, "Gee, we never knew that your people had to go through so much." . . . And they were very sympathetic.

> These were all young men in their twenties. . . . These were guys who are hardened, tough infantry boys. Went through a lot of this war and saw a lot of death. We saw a lot of American boys, a lot of Germans. We saw a lot of death, going through. But I think this moved them. That people were just slaughtered, just for being Jewish. . . . I think it created at that time a very sympathetic feeling for the Jews and perhaps that's why the study of the Holocaust. . . .

HB reports that he was not able to discuss these experiences with his own children. At one time, a book describing the history of his division was damaged severely in a flood in the basement of their home. His son worked painstakingly to dry out each page and put the book together. Father and son were then able to sit together and discuss the history of the Holocaust as revealed in the pictures and descriptions of HB's wartime experiences.

HERB CARLSON, 1919–

[Holocaust testimony (HRC-961, videotape: 57 minutes), 22 October 1987; interviewed and indexed by Bernard Weinstein. D804.3/.C285 1987]

Herb Carlson, left, Stuttgart, July 1945.

Herb Carlson [HC], a corporation president at the time of this testimony, was twenty-six years old in 1945 as World War II was ending. He grew up in Bayonne, New Jersey, and graduated from the University of Alabama with a degree in journalism. He served in the Sixty-third Infantry Division. When the war ended in May 1945, he was transferred to Detachment 268 in Bavaria to serve in the military government. He was in the Counterintelligence Corps, assigned "to flush out Nazis."

HC witnessed the horror of the Holocaust when he went into Dachau at the end of the war.

[Dachau was] an experience beyond belief . . . going into the place, bodies. I'm not talking about those that were in the cribs that were still alive. I'm talking about the bodies that had been hastily thrown into the ditches, into pits that had been dug . . . and sprinkled with lime trying to decompose the bodies, I assume, before the American soldiers got there. We found cars, where they had hastily thrown bodies into boxcars . . . open cars. . . . I assume they were going to try to dispose of them in whatever way they could.

HC's perception of antisemitism in the army when he was trained in the United States was that there was very little among the "brass," much in the ranks. In Dachau, however, he was surprised to find different reactions. The less-educated types from states like Kentucky and Tennessee were outraged; the more-educated types "distanced themselves."

The men in the ranks were more visceral in their attitudes, in their reacting to it. [Unclear; probably: "They would take their rifle"—*ed.*] or automatic weapon and shoot every Kraut they could see, without being selective. I think they didn't go into tears. . . . They just reacted in that way. But I found very little, very little sympathy and understanding to what took place. We didn't realize . . . I think it was so horrible, we didn't realize what we were seeing, until long afterwards.

After the war, HC visited three other concentration camps—Theresienstadt, Oranienburg, and Buchenwald.

JOHN B. COULSTON, 1918–

[Holocaust testimony (HRC-983, videotape: 35 minutes), 3 November 1987; interviewed by Bernard Weinstein, indexed by Joseph J. Preil. D804.3/.C855 1987]

John B. Coulston [JC] was born in New York in 1918. His family lived in Brooklyn and moved to Montclair, New Jersey, in 1920. After volunteering for the National Guard in 1939, JC enlisted in the U.S. Army in September 1939. He was sent to Officer Candidate School after Pearl Harbor (December 1941) and graduated in April 1942. He was then assigned to the 602nd Tank Destroyer Battalion, Third Army. His group went to France in August 1944 and fought in the Battle of the Bulge.

General Bradley ordered his unit to move to the Ohrdruf concentration camp in Germany on 1 April 1945. There they found only a handful of living inmates; all the others had been marched away by German guards. JC described the horrors he had seen in a letter to his father. Toward the end of the interview, JC was asked about the effects of what he had witnessed in Ohrdruf and elsewhere. In a relatively lengthy but very significant response, JC articulates his view after forty years of thinking, as well as private and public speaking, about the Holocaust.

I suppose the dedication, from those early days my daughter talked about in 1950 and 1952, in 1953—I suppose it was starting to jell even before then. I've been trying to trace back, look backwards into my own past. Unfortunately I save things. I save letters and I see that I had written, or other people had written, that I had talked about this as early as 1946 and 1947 to various people who commented on it twenty years later, fifteen years later. I know that my friends thought of it. It was jelling. And as it jelled and we grew older and our children and the business of making money to support them and that sort of thing—that went on as usual within all of us. But also whatever was jelling inside of us seems to have sprouted out.

As far as I personally am concerned, it's resulted in what I call a brotherhood—a wish for, a fight for, and I'll do anything I can to do it—a feeling of a brotherhood through strength, a brotherhood where we can all shake hands and not the silliness of saying love or anything like that, but mutual understanding, of mutual respect, so that we can look each other in the eye, sit down, have coffee, talk, go into the most tragic or the happiest of subjects. And perhaps the more we can do that, the less likely it is that another Hitler or another tyrant who can change opinions on people and call them subhumans as they called the Russians or the Polish or nonhumans as they called the Jews—it could never, never have happened, or wouldn't happen again. It's a wish or dream but that's what happened at least to me.

JOHN FARINELLA, 1917–

[Holocaust testimony (HRC-969, videotape: 35 minutes), 1 October 1987; interviewed by Bernard Weinstein and Mark Lender, indexed by Bernard Weinstein. D804.3/.F225 1987]

John Farinella, retired, Clark (New Jersey) superintendent of schools and strong supporter of Holocaust education.

John Farinella [JF] was born and raised in Hartford, Connecticut. He was drafted in World War II and assigned to the Eighth Air Force in the European Theater of Operations and then to the Ninth Air Force. His group became the Tenth Air Force Disarmament Group.

On a beautiful day in April 1945, he and his group approached the Buchenwald concentration camp in Germany, which had just been liberated. The young Americans were unprepared for the shock. They saw, felt, and smelled the horror of the camp. A little red-haired Jewish boy in striped prison garb, no more than thirteen or fourteen years old, met JF's group and said, "I want nothing from you, only that you never forget what you hear or see here."

JF describes the so-called hospital in Buchenwald. He visited the crematoria and saw how bodies were hung on hooks prior to cremation. His immediate reaction was: "Disgust. You couldn't believe what you were hearing, and what you were smelling was not nice. It just was disgusting. It changed a beautiful day to one of horrors. . . . You couldn't conceive of human beings treating others in this manner." JF spent one day in Buchenwald, made a joint report with the other three men in his jeep, and they went on to their next job.

What happened to JF after the war? "It left an impression you will never forget. . . . Back at home, you began the task of rebuilding your own life." JF went on to an illustrious career in education, eventually becoming the superintendent of schools in Clark, New Jersey. JF recalls a meeting one evening in a Westfield home in the presence of the New Jersey commissioner of education. The discussion veered to atrocities in war. JF spoke up about the need to teach this subject. He has been speaking up ever since and has been in the forefront of educators advocating the teaching of the Holocaust in the schools of New Jersey.

IRVING GERENSTEIN, 1919–

[Holocaust testimony (HRC-1051, videotape: 56 minutes), 22 June 1989; interviewed by Bernard Weinstein and Joan Bang, indexed by Bernard Weinstein. D804.3/.G375 1989]

Irving Gerenstein [IG] was born in 1919 and grew up in Brooklyn during the Depression. He is currently a retired jeweler living in New Jersey. IG was drafted into the U.S Army in 1942 and was sent overseas in April 1944. He was at Omaha Beach, Normandy, shortly after D-Day, as part of the Fiftieth Signal Battalion of the First Army under the command of General Joseph Lawton Collins. He went through the Siegfried Line in September 1944.

IG's unit came to a concentration camp in the spring of 1945. Although he did not identify the camp, he said that while there he shared K rations with some prisoners. He was also in Nordhausen, where there were "corpses as far as one could see." These two events constituted the "deepest" experiences he had during the war. When asked how he felt, IG responded:

> Well, there was so much going on. . . . My feeling itself was anger, I suppose. . . . But I couldn't get over the fact how people could do such things to people. . . . I had never seen anything like that. I had never experienced anything like that. Of course, going through France and Belgium . . . seeing death in itself and dead bodies and planes shot down . . . you get hardened to certain things, like the concentration camp and Nordhausen. . . . My God, did this go on in Poland and Czechoslovakia? . . . It was unthinkable that one people would do this against another people . . . but when you witness it, you realize it was true. If you want to call it history, this was history.

IG reports this reaction was articulated by Protestants and Catholics in his outfit also, not only by Jews. And he concludes these were "the two deepest experiences I have ever gone through. . . . They weren't only Jews."

*Milton Goldberg and Reuben Weitzman,
Dora-Mittelbau concentration camp,
April 1945.*

MILTON GOLDBERG, 1918–1992
AND REUBEN WEITZMAN, 1923–

*[Joint Holocaust testimony (HRC-1016, videotape: 53 minutes), 28 September 1988;
interviewed and indexed by Bernard Weinstein. D804.3/.W435 1988]*

Milton Goldberg [MG], a New Jersey resident, was born on 5 October 1918. He was
a Pfc in the 104th Infantry. (MG died in 1992.) Reuben Weitzman [RW], also a resident of New Jersey, was born on 27 July 1923. He was attached to the Medical Battalion of the 104th Infantry during World War II. Both men were retired at the time
of this interview.

Before entering the army, MG was an accountant and RW a student at City College of New York. Both men were involved in the liberation of the Dora-Mittelbau
concentration camp in Germany on 11 April 1945. Both men knew little about the
camps until they stumbled on Dora-Mittelbau; neither was prepared for the shock.

MG estimates they saw about three thousand corpses. They each knew a little
Yiddish, and when MG started speaking to the victims, they hugged him. Both men
learned about the Final Solution after the war. The prisoners all cried the same
litany, about being treated like "animals."

The two men report that former New York Governor Hugh Carey and former
Mayor Ed Koch served in their unit; the memory of this experience has remained
with both public officials. MG and RW stress the importance of teaching the Holocaust in our schools, that we dare not be apathetic and indifferent when confronted
with evil in the future.

These former soldiers were asked about their initial reactions upon entering
Nordhausen.

MG: I didn't have a reaction. It was a shock, total shock. . . . I showed you a picture before of a baby. I don't think the baby was six months old. His stomach was ripped apart
with a bayonet. How would you feel if you saw a little infant with a stomach ripped
apart with a bayonet? What kind of a human being do you think would do a thing like
that? . . . Could a *person* do that?

RW: I think the gut reaction to it all was disbelief. We just couldn't believe that anything like this could happen. . . . The people were so emaciated that those who were alive really were not alive. They couldn't raise their hands, they couldn't raise their heads. . . . They had tears in their eyes, they were being liberated. . . . According to one of the doctors in our unit, they doubted very much that anyone would live a year or two beyond that. They were just sticks and bones. The living ones were living with the dead, and you couldn't tell them apart.

MG concludes with a memorable definition: "This was a labor camp. They worked until they died."

REVEREND ELBRIDGE HOLLAND, 1924–

[Holocaust testimony (HRC-1063, videotape: 40 minutes), 23 January 1990; interviewed and indexed by Bernard Weinstein. D804.3/.H761 1990]

Rev. Elbridge Holland, senior pastor, Bishop James Methodist Church, Basking Ridge, New Jersey, as photographed in 1943.

Currently senior pastor of the Bishop James Methodist Church in Basking Ridge, New Jersey, Reverend Elbridge Holland [EH] was a Pfc in the Twentieth Armored Headquarters Division, which was attached to General George Patton's Third Army and the Forty-second "Rainbow" Division. EH had begun to study for the ministry before he was inducted into the army. He was twenty-one years old when his unit arrived at Dachau to liberate the concentration camp, ten miles from the city of Munich.

EH reports that he heard a colonel say, "What the men would see, they would never forget, but they had to see it."

Just outside the camp, were these boxcars, with the doors open. You saw the bodies lying in there, all mangled. There were a number of prisoners from Dachau. This was my first experience to see them, just really skin and bones. . . . These were living. They were prisoners that were just beginning to wander out of the camp. . . . I was amazed that they could even walk, because when you looked at their arms, there was no place on their arm that was larger than my wrist . . . and their faces looked like skin was stretched over skeletons. So here they were in pajama-striped clothes . . . and they were just hobbling along.

The Dachau gas chamber had never been completed. The dead bodies were gassed somewhere else and brought back to Dachau, which served as a "coal bin."

He saw stacks of clothing twelve to fourteen feet high and forty feet long. The stench of Dachau was so great that EH held his breath longer than he ever had in his life. He saw the townspeople of Dachau; no Germans looked the Americans in the face, they exhibited only shame and fear.

EH describes the liberation of Dachau:

> It's very hard to describe because, on the one hand, believe it or not, it was something that was so deeply moving and exhilarating, because these people were experiencing freedom. They were marching. Here were the prisoners all marching up and down the central street in the camp and singing their national anthems. And so to see that, and to hear it, you wondered how they could sing because, you know, they were just at the point of starvation. You wondered how they had enough strength and energy to do that. And as I said, this was profoundly moving, just moved you to tears. . . . Yet, as you felt this exhilaration, it was so overwhelmingly overshadowed by the terrible nature of all this. Because here they were, skin and bones, with their health practically all gone, and to realize the suffering that they had been through and, as I realized later, these were the ones that survived. Here were the others, that were treated more horribly than they were, or else they did not have the stamina to survive. But any way you take it, to see this kind of inhumanity to people was just really beyond belief.

At first EH wanted to forget, but now he wants to remember. He took his family years later to see Dachau, but by then it had become so sanitized and mild, it made him feel that one could not really know the Nazi Dachau. EH concludes his testimony by reporting that teachers have been questioning him about his experiences and have been inviting him to speak to their students.

SOL LASKY, 1913–

[Holocaust testimony (HRC-1041, videotape: 53 minutes), 14 June 1989; interviewed by Bernard Weinstein and Joan Bang, indexed by Bernard Weinstein. D804.3/.L413 1989]

Sol Lasky [SL] was born in New York in 1913. He married and moved to New Jersey in 1937. He started to work for the federal government in 1942 and was drafted into the army in 1943. SL served as a Pfc in the Seventh Army, Forty-fifth Infantry, under General Alexander Patch; he was awarded two Bronze Stars in combat, three Battle Stars, and an Army of Occupation Medal. He served in Italy, France, and Germany. SL returned to government work after World War II until his retirement in 1974.

SL's unit was involved in liberating the Dachau concentration camp. SL reports that he never expected what he saw in Dachau, a fact revealed in the following exchange.

INTERVIEWER: What did you know about the Holocaust prior to being in the service?

SL: None whatsoever. The first time we saw it, when we hit Dachau, it's the first I realized anything like that existed. We had absolutely no knowledge. I don't know, because of low rank, I was a Pfc . . . but I don't think too many people knew about it. . . . The first indication we had was when we walked into Dachau and we were *shocked* by what we saw.

In Dachau, he saw bodies everywhere. The inmates who were still alive weighed as little as fifty pounds. He spoke to the survivors in his limited Yiddish. They informed him that prisoners capable of work had to work and at the same time they were being starved to death. He saw bodies of children also. Jews were being murdered up to the moment the Americans arrived.

The reaction of the American soldiers was universal: fierce anger. SL was particularly angry with Germans who claimed ignorance of events in the camp; the smell of death was in the air for miles around.

SL comments that, for a long time after the war, he spoke to no one but his wife about his Dachau experience. He thought he would not be believed. At the time of this interview, however, he had been talking to various groups in his community. SL lives in New Jersey. He has two sons, both lawyers, and five grandchildren.

LEONARD LINTON, 1922–

[Holocaust testimony (HRC-1020, videotape: 1 hour, 56 minutes), 16 December 1988; interviewed and indexed by Bernard Weinstein. D804.3/.L768 1988]

Leonard Linton [LL] was born in Germany on 1 January 1922. His family left Germany before the outbreak of World War II. LL attended school in Germany and France. He speaks German, French, Russian, and English.

During World War II, LL served as a paratrooper in the Eighty-second Airborne Division, which liberated the Wöbbelin concentration camp, near Ludwigslust, in northern Germany. His rank was sergeant T-3. He served in a G-5 unit (military government) and attended a military government school after the Battle of the Bulge.

LL learned about the existence of the Wöbbelin concentration camp on 2 May 1945. LL and the men in his unit knew nothing about the camp or the German Holocaust program. They thought the camp inmates were convicts. The Jewish prisoners in Wöbbelin represented a minority of the population incarcerated in the camp.

LL is highly articulate about his Wöbbelin experience. It has obviously affected his philosophy of life and his sense of values. The following excerpts from his testimony describe how one American soldier reacted to the shock of learning about the German extermination plan during the concluding days of World War II.

One thing we learned: There comes a point in their life when they don't want to live any more. We call them zombies. Because they are emaciated. Their eyes are bulging. Because all the skin, all the flesh, collapses. . . . They look right through you with those sad, huge eyes. They don't care about anything. They have lost the will to live. There is nothing worse than that, because you can't cope with it. And they will die, even though they are free. We could give them some food, but they will die.

A portion of LL's testimony refers to an aspect of the camps that was established deliberately by the Germans.

One other feature that is unforgettable about this camp, which to this day still shocks me and nauseates me, that is the odor. This was in May, northern Germany. The day was beautiful, clear, beautiful day, a little nippy. Not a warm day. But coming into the camp, and especially inside these barracks, was a stench the likes of which I have never smelled, before or after. It was not the stench of rotting corpses, which I have smelled . . . after we took some town which was heavily shelled or bombed. . . . And you can sort of smell, after you have been in the army for a while, and you can differentiate between the smell of human corpses from the smell of animals. Horses, or dead cows, or goats, or dead geese. . . . These kind of corpses have their own peculiar smell, which is nauseating and very unpleasant. I can't say I ever got used to it. But the concentration camp smell is so many degrees worse than the worst smell . . . elsewhere, that it fills you with disgust and horror. I tried to speak little, because I felt that I didn't want to keep open my mouth too much, because I could feel almost the particles of that smell getting on my lips. And when I talk, getting into my mouth. I wanted to avoid that. I didn't take a handkerchief or anything in front of my mouth. I guess I was too hard for that at the time. But I walked around, and that stench of those particular corpses rotting in the indescribable filth that surrounded them, their fecal matter and their urine right on the spot, and the rotting mattresses, but the straw that was rotting, their clothing were rotting. . . . It was a smell that sickens me when I think of it to this day.

And finally, LL's personal conclusion:

I must say, what amazes me is that so few of [the survivors] are vengeful. I am more outraged, personally, at what the Nazis have done, and I would like to see bloody revenge, if possible . . . than the survivors themselves.

ALBERT MAZURKIEWICZ, 1926–

[Holocaust testimony (HRC-1081, videotape: 38 minutes), 23 February 1993; interviewed and indexed by Joseph J. Preil. D804.3/.M394 1993]

Albert Mazurkiewicz, professor of education and department chair, Kean University, as photographed in 1945.

Albert Mazurkiewicz [AM] entered the U.S. Army in 1944 when he was eighteen years old. He served as a corporal in the 122nd Medical Unit of the Eighty-second "Rainbow" Division. His division fought in the Battle of the Bulge and then went on to liberate the concentration camp at Dachau two weeks after the death of President Roosevelt and two weeks before the end of the war.

AM had heard of German atrocities through articles in *Stars and Stripes,* the army newspaper. Many servicemen were interested in visiting the camp as sightseers, but General Collins forbade their entry. In retrospect, AM feels that, for historical and educational reasons, it would have been useful to bring all the servicemen into Dachau, but he understands General Collins's decision under the severe pressures of that time.

In his testimony, AM refers to a reaction typical of many soldiers who witnessed the last stages of the Holocaust.

> Over the years, of course, I've had very little opportunity to discuss these things. Most people don't want to talk about it unless there is some specific observation or activity, such as, for instance, we have here in the Holocaust Center, as such, and Holocaust education that goes on. Other than that, there is very little that seems to get into a discussion.
>
> How does it still affect me? Until you asked for me to participate in this, I was repressing much of this information or much of my . . . experience. It's not something that, essentially, in terms of a war activity that you revisit. It's conveniently forgotten. I know I go to certain movies that are war experiences, and they recall battles, and I have very uncomfortable feelings. Well, so too, these provide uncomfortable feelings and they're best, essentially, not brought to the fore.

AM brought a copy of a book published by the Rainbow Division to the interview, describing the experiences of the division in World War II. Sixteen pages are devoted to the concentration camps.

INTERVIEWER: Why does the Rainbow Division book not mention Jews [in those] sixteen pages?

AM: No, they don't for some reason. But even after the fact, when we're talking about displaced persons, they were not referring to them as Jewish. They refer to them as Gypsies or Romanians or Poles. But there wasn't a singling out of the fact that most of these people had been Jewish and of that faith and had been deliberately slaughtered.

INTERVIEWER: How do you understand that?

AM: It's incomprehensible. Just as today I find it incomprehensible that we have the atrocities being committed in Bosnia-Herzegovina, and so on. I don't understand the kind of thinking involved, and certainly I can't understand the thinking of individuals back in that particular period. . . . But there was a lot of antisemitism in that period. And that is something I don't understand. . . . It's just beyond me.

Upon his return to civilian life, AM returned to college and earned three degrees, including his doctorate, and is currently the chairperson of the Communication Sciences Department in the School of Education, Kean College of New Jersey.

LEE MEREL, 1924–

[Holocaust testimony (HRC-1075, videotape: 56 minutes), 20 November 1992; interviewed and indexed by Joseph J. Preil. D804.3/.M558 1992]

Lee Merel in 1944. Berlin native, United States military intelligence.

Lee Merel [LM] was born in Berlin on 7 April 1924. His immediate family consisted of his parents, an older sister, and LM. He attended an Orthodox Hebrew day school in Berlin. In 1935, his father decided suddenly to abandon his business and flee from the dangerous antisemitism in Germany. They went to Palestine, and in 1937 LM and his parents emigrated to the United States. His sister had married in Palestine and remained there.

LM reports that approximately twenty family members remained in Germany. Almost all of them perished in the Holocaust. Of the twelve to fifteen family members who left Germany, all survived.

LM's father decided to leave Palestine because of the Arab boycott, as many customers of his furniture business were wealthy Arabs. The family began their American life in New York City, in Washington Heights, and then moved to New Brunswick, New Jersey, to be near the father's furniture store. LM graduated from New Brunswick High School and then entered Rutgers University.

LM volunteered for military service in October or November 1941. He reports that he encountered much antisemitism in his early army days. He managed to transfer from combat engineers to military intelligence. LM relates two fascinating experiences. Because he was fluent in the language, he was assigned to interviewing many Germans.

> I was fortunate . . . to interrogate the head engineer of the Krupp works. . . . I made it a habit of putting a Nazi flag [on the floor] in front of my desk in order to antagonize those people I would have to interrogate. . . . They would have to walk across their own flag before they would come to me. . . . Then I would tell them, "Look, you better start talking, because I'm a Jew and I don't love you very much."
>
> This man had lost two of his sons on the Russian front, his wife was killed in a bombing, and he had lost a leg. . . . I questioned him, and I said, "Now that you know and you've had all the experience that you had, what would you do? Would you do something different?"
>
> He said, "Yes, now that we had all the experience, if I could do it all over again, I would do exactly the same thing, except that we would not make the same mistakes that we made."

In other words, he concluded, there was no regret for what had been done, but only for having lost the war. "They [Germans] couldn't care less. . . . I found the feeling was very widespread."

The second memorable experience was in Gardelegen, a concentration camp in the Ruhr valley. There were three thousand to four thousand dead prisoners and two thousand live prisoners. The stench from the corpses was felt miles away. LM was in charge of a company of approximately 125 men, including a medical unit, with the task of saving as many live prisoners as possible.

> There was one incident in that camp which was unbelievable. You could probably make a movie of this incident. After this camp had been cleaned up fairly well and everybody had been put into . . . hospital tents, I was walking down the camp street and there was a body lying there. And I thought the body was dead. And that body just had enough strength to grab my ankle to show me that this person was alive. It was a male person. I, of course, immediately called . . . somebody with stretchers. He was brought to the hospital tent.
>
> In the evening, I wanted to see how everything was going. . . . I went to the hospital tent and I walked over to this man who, by then, had recovered sufficiently, and he called me over. He turned out to be a deaf-mute person, who could not speak.
>
> As we started to talk, and I could sign a little bit because I had such a cousin when I was a very young boy. . . . He was able to read lips and I do speak German very fluently. We started to talk, and the more we talked, one thing brought to another and pretty soon I discovered he was my first cousin.

The cousin married a mute woman in London and was brought to Washington Heights by the Merel family, where LM's father set him up as a furrier.

INTERVIEWER: How did the 125 Americans react to the experience [of Gardelegen]?

LM: Very kind and very caring. They did everything they could possibly to make these people comfortable.

INTERVIEWER: It was a shining moment for them?

LM: Yes, I think so. It brought out their humanity, if you will. Yes . . . which many people lose very quickly. Morality and humanity is lost much too quickly in the daily struggle for living.

LM reports that his experiences at Gardelegen raised profound theological questions. He concludes his testimony by stating that his greatest struggle at this time is with his religious beliefs and how to transmit them to his three children and five grandchildren.

CHAPLAIN JUDAH NADICH, 1912–

[Holocaust testimony (HRC-1059, videotape: 1 hour, 12 minutes), 15 March 1990; interviewed and indexed by Bernard Weinstein. D804.3/.N335 1990]

Chaplain Judah Nadich [JN] was the senior Jewish chaplain in the European Theater of Allied Operations when he was appointed General Dwight D. Eisenhower's advisor on Jewish affairs and displaced persons camps in 1945, shortly after the European war ended. JN reported directly to Eisenhower or to his deputy, General Walter Bedell Smith.

JN visited Dachau several weeks after liberation and saw the furnaces, gas chambers, crematoria—the entire camp. The Germans had arranged to use the ashes as fertilizer for German soil. He does not recall meeting any surviving families or children, but mostly single adults. He also visited Feldafing, which was described as the best of the camps by the Harrison Commission, which was headed by Earl G. Harrison, dean of the Law Faculty of the University of Pennsylvania. He could not understand how this was "best"; he found terrible conditions in Feldafing.

JN found General George Patton to be unsympathetic to the plight of the survivors. This was reported to Eisenhower, and shortly thereafter Patton was relieved of his command. JN wonders whether this was part of the reason for Patton's demotion (in addition, of course, to Patton's slapping a soldier).

In the camp in Landsberg, JN found workshops that helped Jews learn new trades or revive knowledge of former trades. Because this was very constructive, Nadich recommended using the Landsberg model in other camps, and this was done.

JN describes David Ben Gurion's speech to the survivors in the camp at Zeilitzheim, the excitement of the survivors who recognized Ben Gurion, and the emotional singing of "Hatikvah." Ben Gurion spoke of their coming to Palestine, and the survivors sobbed throughout. "An unforgettable experience for Ben Gurion, for me, for the hundreds of thousands of Jews present." All this is described in JN's book, *Eisenhower and the Jews* (Twayne, 1953), where he expresses admiration for Eisenhower's positive attitude and sensitivity. He sees Eisenhower as a man without bigotry or prejudice.

JN concludes by reflecting on his personal religious problems after he saw the results of the murder camps. He did not return as a rabbi; instead, he accepted the post of Joint Distribution Committee director for Germany. He never assumed this position, however, because he was drafted to speak throughout the United States on behalf of the $100 million campaign for the United Jewish Appeal. He returned to the American rabbinate in 1947 and served for many years as rabbi of the Park Avenue Synagogue in New York City.

A. KEVIN QUINN, 1918–1995

[Holocaust testimony (HRC-1047, videotape: 1 hour, 37 minutes), 29 June 1989; interviewed and indexed by Bernard Weinstein. D804.3/.Q547 1989]

A. Kevin Quinn with his commanding officer, Dachau concentration camp.

Kevin Quinn [KQ] was born on 6 September 1918 in the Bronx, New York. He studied theology and law at Providence College and became a novitiate in the Dominican Order but chose to leave it in August 1941. The Dominican Order, however, had an impact on him throughout his life. His studies made him knowledgeable in Latin, philosophy, and church history.

KQ entered the U.S. Army in 1942 and received a Signal Corps commission in 1943. He served in the Forty-fifth Infantry of the Seventh Army under General Alexander Patch and also in the Third Army under General George Patton. KQ was promoted to the rank of captain and assigned to educational and religious affairs in Dachau after the camp had been liberated. KQ describes the impact on his men of their first entrance into Dachau.

I could not control my men. . . . It's important to get prisoners for information, even then. *Especially* then. But a lot of them died because they were shot down by American troops who would not listen to me. They would not have listened to George Patton.

KQ saw healthy-looking persons in prison garb. These were Germans, including doctors, trying to escape detection. When KQ questioned one German doctor regarding his deeds, the answer was, "It was for science." KQ wanted to kill that doctor. After his experiences in combat and in Dachau, he was appointed religious affairs officer in Munich. He understood his responsibility to be primarily humanitarian.

The survivors had a profound effect on KQ.

> The miracle of this century is that those people, mostly Jews but not only Jews, would undergo that, what they had to undergo, and still think, "My God, I believe in you. Why have you permitted this to happen?" They must have felt that way, or they did feel that way, and yet they keep their faith. They keep their love for humanity, which is the only real faith anyway. That's why there is a bond, I think, with most of the people that I meet. We're almost like brothers and sisters.

KQ remained in the army for many years. He returned to civilian life with the rank of colonel and became a secondary school teacher and church deacon. He did not wish to talk about his Dachau experiences, which caused nightmares that he was a prisoner himself. He feels he must speak out, however, to overcome the lies of Holocaust revisionists and deniers.

KQ sees himself as a witness. At the time of this interview, he lived in New Jersey. He concludes by quoting a newspaper reporter who referred to him as a "hero." He refers to himself as a "soldier." The heroes were those who protected others, people who risked everything.

HENRY RICKLIS, 1924–1989

[Holocaust testimony (HRC-971, videotape: 24 minutes), 29 October 1987; interviewed by Bernard Weinstein and Freda Remmers, indexed by Bernard Weinstein. D804.3/.R53 1987]

Born in New Jersey, Henry Ricklis [HR] was a student at the beginning of World War II. He entered the U.S. Army and became a Pfc in the Twentieth Armored Division of the Third Army. His unit fought its way through France, Holland, Belgium, and Germany. At last he arrived at Dachau, anxious to see the concentration camp.

> I had wanted to see for myself. I had a personal interest in this. I knew I had a lot of relatives that were from Lithuania. I knew that we hadn't heard from them. My father hadn't heard from brothers and sisters, nieces and nephews, and we had a lot of family there, a sizable family. I found out many years afterward on a trip to Israel that none of them had survived. They were all done away with.

HR describes what he saw upon entering Dachau.

There were still trains there, the dreaded death trains that carried people into the camps. They would carry in their live cargo and left empty to get more cargo. The first thing that was here were a couple of carloads of people. . . . Apparently whether they had suffocated or died or just been left to rot in these boxcars. . . .

That was the first thing. . . . And then as you got into the camp, you saw, it's hard to describe them as human beings. I mean, they were faceless and they would look at you. I don't think they realized what was happening. They were emaciated. They were bags of bones, really, in their striped uniforms. . . .

To a few of the people, they would come up toward you, stagger up to you. These people would talk in Polish or Yiddish so of course I understood some of what was said to me. Some of these people were not coherent really. I think they were not just abused. I think they were dazed. It's hard to describe these people really. I mean, they were hardly human beings at that stage.

HR tells how the discovery of Dachau affected the American soldiers.

Some of the soldiers that I had spoken to had gotten into the camp. Many of these servicemen were so-called veterans. They had never seen [such] sights and sounds, and been through a great deal. Many of these soldiers, when they saw this, got in there and retched. It was beyond belief. I spoke to a number of these people, these were people of various faiths. Whatever their background, they just couldn't comprehend the sights that they saw.

What was the reaction of Americans, and American Jews, back in the United States upon discovery of the concentration camps?

I think I was in a state of shock for a short period of time. Just having chanced on this, I don't think the mind could conceive of this type of thing. That's why it was understandable that people back in the States, even people who had relatives there, could not conceive of what was going on. I don't think the mind could imagine this.

HR had thought Germany was a cultured country, but he was awed that human beings could subjugate others in such a beastly manner. He believes that it is important to teach and commemorate the Holocaust. He was among the first to become active in this endeavor in his community.

HR developed a carpet retail business. Since his retirement, his son runs the business. In addition to his son, HR has a daughter and seven grandchildren.

CHAPLAIN HERSCHEL SCHACTER, 1917–

[Holocaust testimony (HRC-1093, videotape: 1 hour), 9 December 1993; interviewed and indexed by Joseph J. Preil. D804.3/.S329 1993]

Rabbi Herschel Schacter [HS] was ordained at Yeshiva University in 1941. His first pulpit was in Stamford, Connecticut. He volunteered as a chaplain in the U.S. Army in October or November 1942 and was shipped to Europe in 1944, where he served as Jewish chaplain for the Eighth Corps of the Third Army. He was at the Battle of the Bulge in Bastogne and then moved into Germany.

HS arrived at Weimar. He had known of German persecution of Jews but had not heard of Buchenwald. The day he entered, 11 April 1945, was "the most memorable day of my life."

We stopped . . . on the highway, learned that elements of American tanks had rolled through. Outside of Weimar I had my own jeep and my own driver and we left, with permission, our unit. We drove ahead on the Autobahn, got to Weimar; there were already American soldiers stationed and directing traffic.

We got to Buchenwald. And there we were in front of the huge gate at the entrance of Buchenwald. We drove through that gate and there was a big, open . . . *Appellplatz* where thousands and thousands of inmates gathered every single day, early morning, late at night, standing for hours in the freezing cold of the winter and the broiling heat of the summer. The *Appellplatz* at that time, of course, was empty. This is the afternoon of April 11.

INTERVIEWER: What they did at the *Appellplatz* was take attendance.

HS: Right, right, exactly. Take attendance, roll call. I stood and looked around. I looked up and I saw huge chimney stacks. And I wondered, What was that? And I ran over, and sure enough there were the crematoria. I looked about me, there were hundreds of human bodies, dead bodies, just strewn around, waiting to be shoveled into the ovens that were still hot. I stood riveted to that incredible scene. I stood there, I don't know how long, but I just couldn't tear myself away. My eyes were tearing—not only from the smoke that was through the chimney, going upward. . . . Every time I think of it, I choke up. The rage that was inside of me. I finally pulled myself away, and as I walked down from that one spot, I came upon a young second lieutenant . . . who had been there for a while now and seemed to know his way around. I approached him. He of course recognized that I was a Jewish chaplain from the insignia I wore.

I said to him, "Do you know, are there any Jews in this camp? Are there any Jews still alive?"

And he said, "Yeah, I think they're down in that area . . . called *das kleine Lager,*" the small camp within the larger Buchenwald. It was a tremendous camp, I learned later, over a quarter of a million people . . . over the course of some six years. Buchenwald was opened, I believe, in '37 or '38. Originally, it was purely a prison camp for political prisoners who were opposed to the fascist regime in Germany. . . .

I walked down into this area called *das kleine Lager*. There was a string of low barracks. I rushed into one of those barracks and again the scenes that met my eyes are just incredible. There they were—I'm sure many people have seen pictures of just raw planks of wood. There were hundreds, men, a few boys, there were no women in Buchenwald, looking down at me. There they were, strewn over stinking, scraggly straw bags. Just skin and bones. More dead than alive. Looking down at me out of haunting, crippling eyes, paralyzed with fear.

I looked around. I didn't know what to say. But I felt that the one language that most of these people would understand would be Yiddish. So in Yiddish I called out, "*Sholom Aleichem Yidden, ihr seit frei.*" You are free, the war is over! Utter silence. And again, those incredulous eyes. How these people survived defies again any understanding. Thank God, many did survive.

I went from barracks to barracks, repeated the same story, the same scenes, the same reactions. And slowly, those who were able to, began to follow me and try to talk to me and just touch my insignia, the little Star of David and the Hebrew letters. Blurted out: "Is it true? Is it really true? Is the war over? Does the world know what happened to us? Where do we go from here?"

For the next months, HS worked with the survivors to match them with relatives around the world or to help them to countries appropriate for them. He understood they could not return to their native countries. At the Yalta Conference, the victorious Allied nations agreed Weimar would be assigned to the Russian zone. HS had to complete his work with the remaining Buchenwald survivors.

HS's unit returned to New York to be reassigned to the Far East. The war with Japan ended suddenly, and HS returned to civilian life as rabbi of the Mosholu Jewish Center in the Bronx. He has served this congregation since 1946 and has also played a leading role in American Jewish affairs. Although he is recognized as a forceful and articulate orator, HS did not speak about the Holocaust during the first generation after the war.

Nobody talked about the Holocaust immediately. This is one of the remarkable phenomena. For years, when all these memories were so vivid in my mind, I had nobody to tell it to. Nobody asked. Nobody heard. Nobody spoke. The first ten years, the survivors never talked.

INTERVIEWER: Right. I always thought the survivors didn't talk because they were trying to rebuild their lives.

HS: Right. . . . I had no platform. Nobody asked me. Nobody wanted to hear.

INTERVIEWER: How do you explain that?

HS: There are no glib, easy explanations. Everybody was busy. It took time for this to sink in, to begin to realize what had happened. Very difficult. It wasn't until . . . the sixties when survivors began to organize and survivors began to invite me to talk with them. And slowly, slowly in the seventies and certainly by the eighties, Jewish communities all over America began to build memorials, began to organize meetings, when the one date began to take hold. That's . . . the twenty-seventh day in the Hebrew month of Nissan [late April or early May]. . . . And the story has yet to be fully told.

HS states that the focus of his life has changed because of his Buchenwald experience. He remains concerned. "What have we learned? This is the tragedy. We have not yet learned the lesson . . . and that's why we survived."

RICHARD J. TISCH, 1922–

[Holocaust testimony (HRC-2018, videotape: 41 minutes), 15 February 1995; interviewed and indexed by Joseph J. Preil. D804.3/.T541 1995]

A lifelong resident of New Jersey, Richard J. Tisch [RT] was born on 18 June 1922. He graduated from Hillside High School and Upsala College. He was in the Forty-second Infantry "Rainbow" Division, A Battery, 392nd F.A. Battalion of the Seventh Army during World War II.

After the war, RT enjoyed a successful career in business. He is married and has three children and five grandchildren. One daughter is a homemaker in Pennsylvania, his son is a lawyer in New York, and his younger daughter is a director of marketing in North Carolina.

RT knew nothing about the Holocaust before 29 April 1945, the day the Seventh Army liberated the Dachau concentration camp. The news spread quickly from the first men who entered Dachau. He describes the liberators' introduction to the camp.

> We also had some artillery positions so close to Dachau that they could walk to it. When some of the men walked over in that direction, they said the stench was so bad they couldn't believe it. They continued walking and saw it.

RT quotes from an article by Louis Lochner in the *New York Herald Tribune* of 1 May 1945. According to RT, Lochner composed an "accurate report" of the scene that greeted the Rainbow Division upon entering Dachau: thirty-two thousand inmates, fourteen hundred corpses, cattle cars, stench. He shows photographs of corpses in cattle cars, pictures taken by one of the Rainbow men immediately after liberation.

RT testifies that a large group of soldiers visited Dachau and remained briefly. They saw the crematorium. He was only twenty-two years old at the time. It was "a sight you would never forget. . . . [I] couldn't talk about it for a while. . . . This is in-humanity for no good reason."

RT returned to Dachau in 1992 for the dedication of the bronze plaque at the camp entrance. Five hundred Dachau survivors attended the ceremony. There was also a memorial for the five thousand prisoners of war murdered in Dachau as the war was ending. RT met a Russian POW, Yacob, at the ceremony, and they have been corresponding ever since. RT concluded his testimony by recalling a sign he saw at Dachau: "Now we know why we fight."

VICTOR WEGARD, 1917–

[Holocaust testimony (HRC-956, videotape: 1 hour, 20 minutes), 4 May 1987; interviewed by Bernard Weinstein and Mark Lender, indexed by Bernard Weinstein. D804.3/.W411 1987]

Victor Wegard, War Crimes Division.

Victor Wegard [VW] was born in New York City on 9 December 1917. He entered the army at the age of eighteen in 1936 and became a reporter for the Army War College. In 1943 he was an aide to General George Patton during the invasion of North Africa. Later, he served with the War Crimes Division and returned to the United States to be trained for entry into the concentration camps.

He returned to Paris in 1944 as part of the War Crimes Commission. His unit was No. 6832. There were four warrant officers and twelve enlisted men in his unit, attached to the Ninety-first Infantry Division. Although his unit entered Flossenbürg on the very first day of liberation, most of the prisoners had been marched out. In Namering, a nearby town, the people lied when they claimed to have seen "nothing," to have heard "nothing." His unit found bodies still bleeding, with heads blown off—mostly French and Czech clerics—and they forced the local citizens to line up and view the rotting corpses.

VW learned later that the Germans considered Flossenbürg their most "efficient" gas chamber. It was a death camp, and some one hundred thousand victims were murdered there, including Russians, Yugoslavs, Greeks, and German political prisoners. Not many Jews had been incarcerated in Flossenbürg.

VW was involved in war crimes trials conducted in Dachau. The defendants were generally honest, except for their own responsibility. Particularly frustrating to VW was the case of Andreas Müller, who played a leading role in the 1941 massacre of forty-four thousand Jews in Kovel in the Ukraine. A very strong case was mounted against Müller, who claimed he was not guilty because he was "following orders."

The case was ordered closed by U.S. Secretary of State Edward Stettinius. Müller was released to build airfields, and he died peacefully in 1961, a wealthy man.

At the time of this interview, VW was an investment banker, living in southern New Jersey. He remains dedicated to his mission of speaking to American audiences on justice done and justice aborted for German perpetrators of the Holocaust.

ALVIN A. WEINSTEIN, 1918–

[Holocaust testimony (HRC-2017, videotape: 59 minutes), 3 May 1995; interviewed and indexed by Joseph J. Preil. D804.3/.W427 1995]

Alvin A. Weinstein [AW] was born in Milwaukee on 4 October 1918. He graduated from Marquette University and earned his medical degree at Marquette's School of Medicine (now the Medical College of Wisconsin) in 1943. AW lives in New Jersey and has been practicing medicine there for forty-eight years.

AW volunteered for service in the U.S. Army on 1 August 1944. He was in the Medical Section, Second Battalion, 222nd Infantry, Forty-second "Rainbow" Division of the Seventh Army, responsible for 868 soldiers. AW was among the first Americans to enter Dachau on 29 April 1945. His first reaction was, "There but for the grace of God go I."

I never saw anything so pitiful, so horrible. Tortured human beings. It was hard to recognize them as being human beings. They looked like skeletons with a yellowish, parchmentlike skin pulled over them, with sunken eyes and sunken cheeks. . . . One man tore this Star of David off his would-be uniform and forced it in my hand. He said to me in Yiddish, "Never forget what you saw here today." I've carried this in my wallet until a week ago, when I took it and mounted it for another interview. In fifty years, that was the first time it was out of my wallet. I'll never forget what I saw or heard or smelled.

INTERVIEWER: Getting back to your entry into Dachau, you went with other service people. . . . How did the others react?

AW: Everyone couldn't believe it. I saw soldiers cry. They couldn't believe it. How could one human being do this to other human beings?

INTERVIEWER: How do you explain it?

AW: [quotes a line spoken by Errol Flynn in the film, *The Dawn Patrol*] "Man is a vicious beast who, once every generation, in order to relieve his nervous tension, tries to destroy himself with a war." . . . And I think it's so. There is enough beast within us, hate within us, that would let something happen.

A German doctor was anxious to show the results of his medical experiments at Dachau to AW. When he heard the inhuman details of this endeavor, AW was horrified and ashamed of his profession.

AW refers to a newspaper article from the *Munich Evening Press* of 19 April 1945, which he received recently from his colonel, now living in retirement in Texas. He asked AW to translate it for him. The article reported that the strongest of the Dachau prisoners were being transferred by train to build fortifications for a German last stand. The train could not go through to its destination because of heavy Allied bombing, including the railroad tracks. By the time the train of thirty-nine boxcars returned to Dachau, all the prisoners were dead. They had been on the train for twenty-eight days without food or water.

AW tells of a discussion he had with a German patient in his medical office in New Jersey. The patient lived in Germany during World War II. She told AW how shocked her father and brothers were when President Roosevelt died in April 1945 and the American army did not then join the Germans against Russia. Such was the power of German propaganda that FDR was leading the American effort in Germany against the will of the American people.

After Dachau, AW and his battalion moved on to Lebenau. They saw a prison for women where the conditions were good: there was sufficient food, adequate sanitation, and the women were healthy. Some of their "crimes" are described in AW's letter below. There was also a prison for Jewish men, which resembled Dachau, and held a group of 150 men, the survivors of a death march of 250 miles from Buchenwald, a march that started with more than 1,500 men.

AW was in Lebenau on 7 May 1945, as the war was ending in Europe. He wrote a letter that day to his wife describing his experiences and reactions.

May 7, 1945

My darling wife,

At one minute after midnight tomorrow night the war with Germany will be officially over. The 7th Army had the "Cease Fire" order at 12 noon yesterday so the war for us ended 3 days sooner.

I want you to know where I was when the "Cease Fire" order came. Believe it or not, I was the commandant of a concentration camp near the Alp mountains.

I saw 243 starved, tortured, diseased bodies that were once men. 170 of them were Polish Jews who were the only ones remaining alive of 1600 that left Buchenwald Concentration camp. They had walked 440 kilometers barefoot and in 28 days. They were given 5 potatoes a day and no water. All who fell or accepted food from civilians were shot by the SS troops. When they arrived at their new prison they were all huddled into a barracks with 73 Russians and Poles in as bad condition. The odor in that barrack made everyone who entered vomit or at least gag. When the American Army came in the SS fled and took with them Churchill's nephew, Field Marshal Alexander's son; Ambassador Winant's son; and several other prisoners of great renown from the nearby internment camp at Laufen.

Our Battalion was given the mission to take Laufen—release the celebrities kept in the Laufen castle internment camp and occupy Lebenau prison for women (where these 243 men and 306 women prisoners were kept). When we arrived the SS had fled with the celebrities and I was put in charge of the Lebenau Prison while the rest of the battalion occupied the Laufen internment camp.

This Lebenau prison was divided into 2 parts—the women's portion which was clean, healthful and a permanent prison with all facilities and the men's portion which were barracks without any plumbing, or ventilation. They had straw mattresses that were covered with lice and the men were barefoot and half-naked. They were all lousy and many were delirious with high fever. Many I am sure had typhus. When the American soldiers came in they cheered and cried that the Messiah had come at last and now they would be free. Everyone had been beaten and kicked and cut besides starved. The interim camp near by had sent them American Red Cross packages so they were eating the delicacies they had not known since the war. They had cigarettes and chocolates once again and meat—which they could not taste because of their swollen tongues. The things we take as every day habits were gifts of God to them.

I immediately set about preparation for bathing facilities, new clothes and new barracks. With the aid of 5 interns from South America and the States we got a program started. After a while one of the company commanders of our Battalion brought in two German soldiers that had taken off all their insignia. He placed them in the barracks with these tortured people and told them that they were SS troops. These men suddenly gained their strength and beat these Hitlerites until they were almost dead. We went in and stopped them and put the beaten Nazis on a jeep and took them out of the camp. They were so wild with fear that they jumped off of the jeep and tried to run but their guard killed both of them.

When the prisoners heard the shots they cheered and cheered and begged us to bring them more. They wanted no more food or baths or beds—just SS. In a few hours they were quiet again and I went to treat the very ill. It was hard to find any that were strong—none were healthy. I tried to arrange to have them transferred but the camp was in quarantine so they had to remain there. I had fear that the typhus might spread to the women (many of whom were French and Czech) but there was no way of taking them from the prison. There was nothing more that I could do for them. At 12 o'clock noon came the word that this war was over and these men wept with joy. I almost wept with them. Some of the women wandered over to the men's sector and upon seeing the misery wept bitterly. They all wanted to help make the men comfortable and clean but I had to keep them away for health purposes. One girl (who had worked for 36 hours straight through without sleep) cooked for the men and tried to clean the place up. She almost dropped of exhaustion (all of this was done before I came). She herself was the daughter of a German captain who was captured in Serbia and she was a German WAC working as a switchboard operator. She deserted because she hated the SS and was put in prison after being beaten and having had her teeth knocked out.

Another French girl who was now 22 years old had been in jail for 2½ years because she tore up Hitler's picture. Still another had called Hitler crazy and she was in prison for 4½ years. Many were there because they listened to the BBC or because they were Communists or Socialists. None had committed a crime worth punishing at home.

The women had a clean building, good food, and were well cared for. It was the two extremes of prisons in one institution and one could hardly believe they both were in the same country much less within the same gates.

Darling, no one will believe what I saw the last day of the war—I didn't believe it either—I also thought it was all propaganda but now I know it was all true. Every SS trooper should be tortured the way they tortured these poor refugees. These men whose greatest crime was to be born to a faith, deserve the right to try and sentence the sadistic torturers who killed four and one half million of their comrades.

I know you won't believe me either, darling, so I took movies of the whole thing and when I get home I'll show you in pictures what I saw in the flesh.

My heart is too full. I fought hard in this war but being a Jew I fought for my brother Jews as well as my country and on the last day of the war I was able to set free 100 of these poor people. My mission in this war is complete. My country defeated the armies of our enemy and I was able to free some men of my faith. I ask no more.

Darling I'll write more tomorrow. I cannot think of anything but the misery I've seen.

I adore you as always.

Your loving husband,
Obbie

When asked at the conclusion of his testimony what the message is for us from the Holocaust, AW referred to a sign he had seen in Notre Dame in Paris: "Forgive, but never forget."

Chapter Eight
The Survivors in Elizabeth

~~~~~~

A large number of survivor families settled in the greater Elizabeth area. This group immigrated in the same manner as struggling, non-English-speaking immigrants have come to the United States throughout American history. These survivors have played a very significant role in the development and growth of the Elizabeth Jewish community. Their activities remind us of the memorable statement of Harvard historian Oscar Handlin in the introduction to *The Uprooted:* "Once I thought to write a history of the immigrants in America. Then I discovered that the immigrants *were* American history." [1]

In projecting this book, I decided to interview members of the Holocaust Resource Foundation (HRF) regarding the survivors' involvement in important Elizabeth institutions. During the course of the interviews, it became obvious that we were seeking the answers to three key questions:

1. Why did you settle in Elizabeth?
2. What impact did Rabbi Pinchas M. Teitz and Rebbetzin Bessie Teitz have on your perception of life in Elizabeth?
3. How would you compare the role of the Jewish Educational Center (JEC) and the community involvement of Holocaust survivors in Elizabeth with the experiences of survivors elsewhere?

The original plan was to interview seven founding members of HRF's executive committee: Arie and Sam Halpern, Clara Kramer, Rae Kushner, Murray Pantirer, Joseph Wilf, and Abraham Zuckerman. In the course of these interviews, it became apparent that the perceptions of the community leaders who welcomed the survivors to Elizabeth should be researched: Rabbi Pinchas Teitz and his wife, Bessie Teitz, and Leonard Diener, three leaders who would have provided the perspectives of the rabbinical and lay leadership as the survivors became an integral part of the community from the 1950s on.

Unfortunately, and tragically, these three key people are no longer alive. Thus it was decided to interview the Elizabeth members of the Teitz and Diener families. One interview was conducted with Beatrice Diener and Marjorie Diener Blenden; the concluding interview involved Rabbi Elazar M. Teitz, Dr. Rivkah T. Blau, and Shulamith Teitz Ebner. As the brother of Bessie Teitz, I played two roles during the Teitz family testimony.

■ 293

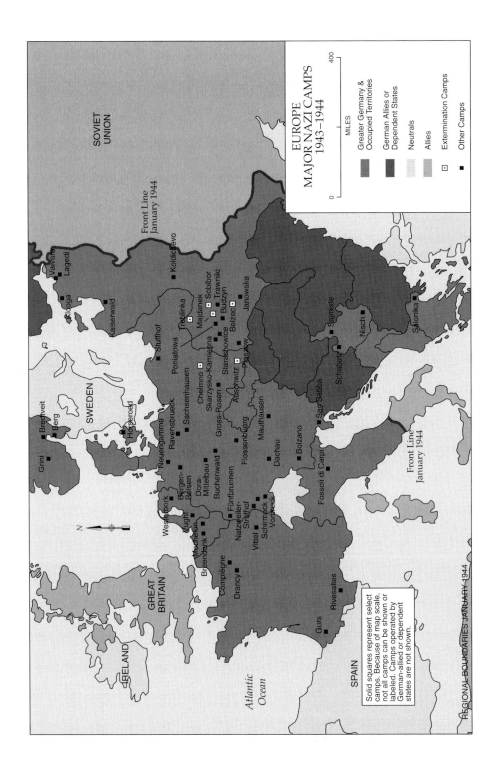

EUROPE
MAJOR NAZI CAMPS
1943–1944

MILES
0   400

Greater Germany &
Occupied Territories

German Allies or
Dependent States

Neutrals

Allies

☐ Extermination Camps

■ Other Camps

SOVIET
UNION

Front Line
January 1944

Valivara
Lagedi
Rioga
Kaiserwald
Klooga
Shuflhof
Poniatowa
Treblinka
Majdanek
Sobibor
Trawniki
Budzyn
Belzec
Janowska
Skarzysko-Kamienna
Chelmno
Starachowice
Plaszow
Auschwitz
Gross-Rosen
Sachsenhausen
Ravensbrueck
Semlin
Nisch
Schabatz
Sajmiste
Sar-Sahba
Salonika

Grini
Bredtveit
Berg
Hopserod
SWEDEN
Neuengamme
Bergen-
Belsen
Dora-
Mittelbau
Buchenwald
Flossenburg
Mauthausen
Dachau
Bolzano
Fossoli di Carpi
Front Line
January 1944

GREAT
BRITAIN
IRELAND
Westerbork
Vught
Mechelen
Breendonk
Compiègne
Drancy
Natzweiler-
Struthof
Vittel
Schirmeck
Vorbruck
Fünfbrunnen

N

Atlantic
Ocean

Gurs
Rivesaltes
SPAIN

Solid squares represent select
camps. Because of map scale,
not all camps can be shown or
labeled. Camps operated by
German-allied or dependent
states are not shown.

REGIONAL BOUNDARIES JANUARY 1944

Following are excerpts culled from the nine interviews. The reader will discern how the survivors arrived in Elizabeth following the Holocaust and, in their effort to build their lives and their families, how they also became pillars of the community under the dynamic leadership of Rabbi Teitz. (Unless otherwise indicated, brackets mean that the speaker used the Hebrew or Yiddish word or phrase.)

MURRAY PANTIRER [MP], 25 NOVEMBER 1996

At this time of the year, I have yahrzeit [date of murder of his family by the Germans], it's ten days in Kislev, in November. The days are getting shorter, and I was told that on Elmora Avenue, not far from Irvington Avenue, Hillside, there's a shul [synagogue] that they [pray] mincha-maariv every day. So I walked into the shul, there was a very distinguished young man, and his name was Rabbi Pinchas Teitz. . . . Between mincha and maariv, I walked over to Rabbi Teitz. I told him that I lost my entire family, and I have yahrzeit for the family. He asked me what's my father's name. It was Eliezer Pinchas. He said, "My name is Pinchas, and I have a son Eliezer." I told him, "Since I observe the yahrzeit, I always [lead the service]." Rabbi Teitz said, "By all means." As a matter of fact, he walked over to a person who was [leading the service] every day because . . . that year he had lost a father or mother.

Rabbi Teitz said, after maariv, "Don't run away. I want to talk with you." We talked about all the things that happened to us. And I said that I made a decision not to hand over to the Germans a victory. They tried to kill us all. If the war had been another six months, they probably would have succeeded. Thank God, in my case, it was Oskar Schindler who put me on the list, and I survived. And after the war, I looked around, and I had no one who survived from my family. I said to myself . . . I decided I'm going to get married. I got married in 1947, in January, in Austria, Linz. I decided, if I have children, I will give them a Jewish education, [especially] not to hand a victory to the Nazis. . . . It's my obligation as a sole survivor to give them a Jewish education.

I spoke with Rabbi Teitz and I said that I have an opportunity to . . . build a house in Hillside, but it's really too far to walk to shul. He said to me, "Go out and buy the lot. By the time you build the house, we will have a shul. I have plans to build a shul on North Avenue." And, sure enough, in 1954, we moved in . . . in May. For the first year . . . we had to walk to the Elmora shul. By 1955, with the leadership of the board, of Leonard Diener, Milton Levy, Sam Cohen, Joe Feldman, Natelson, Kalish, and a few more people. Of course, with the leadership of Rabbi Teitz, to build a Jewish community and build a Jewish school. . . .

Rabbi Teitz was a personality. It made an impression on me that he did not know me but, yet, he knew for whom I have yahrzeit, I have to say Kaddish. He let me [lead the service]. I got back the next morning. And since then, I respected and I liked Rabbi Teitz. As a matter of fact, when I moved in, my partners and I, when they built the North Avenue shul, we gave all the blocks and the paneling inside the shul. . . . The relationship with Rabbi Teitz grew more and more. I told everyone about the community. The Wilfs came in, the Halperns, the Kushners, and every one of them had the opportunity to give their children a Jewish education because of Rabbi Teitz.

INTERVIEWER: In that first conversation with Rabbi Teitz, when he said, "Don't go away yet, I want to talk with you," how long did he and you talk?

MP: Oh, we talked maybe an hour's time. He told me of his losses, and I started telling him about what things happened. Every time you walked into Rabbi Teitz's room-office, you walked away with a little bit more knowledge, and with a good feeling, because he would walk you to the door and say to you, "*Mazel* and *bracha*" ["Good luck" and "be blessed"]. He prayed for us, and I believe very strongly, I don't know how to say it in English, but in Jewish it's *bashert* [Yiddish, destined]. It's meant to be.

CLARA KRAMER [CK], 22 MAY 1997

After the war, Clara and Sol Kramer lived in Tel Aviv for eight years. They moved to Brooklyn to be near Sol's family because his only relatives had settled in the United States. After eight years in Brooklyn, they moved to Elizabeth in 1964 to be near the Sam Halperns. Gladys Halpern and Clara Kramer are second cousins. "The school [JEC], of course, was important for me also."

In Brooklyn, they sent their two sons to public school and an afternoon Hebrew school. They had applied to a major Brooklyn yeshiva, but they were refused admission because no scholarships were available at the time. Upon enrolling their younger son in the JEC in Elizabeth, Sol Kramer approached Rabbi Teitz regarding tuition. The rabbi responded, "No Jewish child will miss a Jewish education because of money."

CK talks about the Elizabeth community and Rabbi and Mrs. Teitz.

I love it here, I love it here. . . . I was privileged to know Rabbi Teitz. Wherever I go, in Israel, in Europe, when I mention Elizabeth, that goes together—Elizabeth and Rabbi Teitz. . . . And Mrs. Teitz, she was a mother. She wanted me to call her Bessie. I could never do that. To me, she was Rebbetzin. She was warm. She was wonderful.

On the importance of having a strong, organized Jewish community:

It's definitely unique . . . I feel a part of the community. When I meet with my friends who live in Long Island, the survivors are together, and then they have some American friends. I don't think they speak of their community [as] my community. . . . We don't have this Jewish center, that Jewish center. We have one center. And this same group [in Elizabeth] is active in the center, this same group was active in building the old age home, this same group supports the museum.

I think it's unique in Elizabeth. . . . I think the group of survivors is unique. I am sad to say, I know a lot of survivors . . . in other communities. They are not that involved in the community like we are here. . . . Rabbi Teitz gave us guidance, gave us motivation. He was a special person. He was a dynamic person.

CK concludes by recounting this incident to illustrate the relationship of Rabbi and Mrs. Teitz with all members of the community.

As you know, my mother was sick. She had Alzheimer's. It was hard to cope, and I had to put her in an old age home. And, to me, it was the biggest tragedy. Because I am European, and you don't put away parents. And, I thought, I am a nurse, and I could take care. But I couldn't.

Come High Holidays, I was in the synagogue. And I cried all the time.

When I walked out of the synagogue, and I was about the last one, because I'm sitting up front. The Rabbi, and the Rebbetzin, were waiting on the steps. There was almost nobody there anymore. They saw from the balcony that I am crying. And they were waiting for me to console me, to talk to me.

And that's it in a nutshell. It was like family. It was like a grandfather and grandmother, or a mother and father, consoling me. They saw me crying.

So you ask how I felt in that community. I am a part of the community because it's family. First of all, I don't have much family. It is extended family.

INTERVIEWER: How long had you been in the community at that time?

CK: Not too long. . . . We were not big givers at that time. . . . About six, seven years that we were in the community.

SAM HALPERN [SH], 28 MAY 1997

Sam and Gladys Halpern arrived in the United States in 1949 and settled in Manhattan. He changed his occupation from supermarket owner to real estate construction and moved to Elizabeth in 1959, because Sabbath observance was difficult in his retail business. The Halperns selected Elizabeth because of the school (JEC) and the leadership of Rabbi Teitz.

He was a great leader. If he would go in Zionism, he would be a great leader. Whatever he would do, he was able to do it. You will find a thousand people in the army, nine hundred ninety would be soldiers, nine would be officers, and one will become a general. He would become a general. He was a leader. . . .

We used to come to the board meeting. Everybody had something to say. And he used to listen to everybody. But when he came out with a proposition, somehow, everybody was satisfied. Because he had this leadership. . . .

I know, he told me, that Jabotinsky, who was a great leader . . . met with him, called him, and invited him that he should stay with him in the Zionist Party. He chose . . . and he went to learn Torah.

I came to Russia, I came to Moscow, I came to Leningrad. When I mentioned Rabbi Teitz, everybody knows him. He did this for us, he did this for us. Now, we have a time, if you want to send packages or money to Russia, there is no problem. I remember times . . . not too long ago, you couldn't send packages. He would work so hard to get approval, later on to raise money, and later on to send them. . . . I'm talking about tons of matzos that he used to send.

SH compares Elizabeth survivors with those in other communities.

I think our group of survivors worked as a team. In certain other towns, there are survivors, individuals, they will do. But we [thank God] worked as a team. If Rabbi Teitz called up, he has a problem, we came together with him. There is no such a thing to refuse him, God forbid, to give a little bit and let Rabbi Teitz worry. Yes, he worried, but we made sure that the problem should be solved.

We had a very fine team. I would give a lot of credit [to] the Wilf family. The Wilf family, under the leadership of Harry Wilf [of blessed memory], he also loved Rabbi Teitz. Joe, of course, later on was chairman of the board, after Leonard [Diener] passed away. When Leonard passed away, Harry became chairman. Now, we have Joe, he should be well.

INTERVIEWER: Is this community [Elizabeth] unique?

SH: In New Jersey, I couldn't stay in any other community but this. . . . In New Jersey, there are very fine communities, but they didn't give me what I wanted. I wanted my children should go to a good yeshiva.

INTERVIEWER: What made this group work as a team?

SH: Rabbi Teitz brought us together. Rabbi Teitz taught us how [unclear: probably "to support worthy institutions"]. Although in my house we knew how to give to charity. My father and mother taught us how to give to charity.

ABRAHAM ZUCKERMAN [AZ], 3 JUNE 1997

Abraham and Millie Zuckerman arrived in the United States in 1949 and settled in Newark. He joined forces with three Kraków friends—Murray Pantirer and the two Levenstein brothers. Two members of this group entered the construction industry and all four families were supported by the sixteen dollars in weekly wages of the two men who remained tailors. In 1953–1954, the Pantirer and Levenstein families moved into the Westminister section of Elizabeth. The Zuckerman family joined their partners when they moved into their new home in 1963.

In discussing Rabbi Pinchas Teitz, AZ said:

> He understood us. He understood the survivors. . . . He saw whatever we were do-
> ing was beautiful. Maybe we weren't as observant as we had to be, but I think he knew
> what we went through. So he was a great force behind us. . . . To have him, to be with
> him, to invite him, to talk to him. He was a great influence on us. . . .
>
> *INTERVIEWER:* The key to your feeling comfortable here was Rabbi Teitz?
>
> *AZ:* Absolutely, Rabbi Teitz. And also the survivors. . . .
>
> *INTERVIEWER:* So you enjoyed it here?
>
> *AZ:* Absolutely. Sure, I enjoyed it very much. Otherwise, I would leave this town if I
> didn't enjoy it. I could live in the nicest places, where I built. But I wanted this envi-
> ronment, which was beautiful.

AZ is asked to compare his survivor group in Elizabeth with survivors in other communities.

> What we have is, we have the group around us. . . . The others . . . are scattered. . . .
> I think the JEC was the reason. . . .
>
> *INTERVIEWER:* Do your friends elsewhere, do they realize that you feel there is some-
> thing different over here?
>
> *AZ:* That belongs to the bringing up, you know, before. My life was a Hasidic way of
> life. Other people did not, so maybe it didn't pull them so much. . . . But I was looking
> for Yiddishkeit [Jewish way of life].
>
> *INTERVIEWER:* And you found just what you wanted?
>
> *AZ:* Right. Thank God, yes.

ARIE HALPERN [AH], 19 AUGUST 1997

Arie Halpern arrived in the United States together with his wife and their eldest
daughter in November 1950 and resided in Manhattan for ten years. He and his
brother owned several supermarkets, but they left their thriving business because of
difficulty in observing the Sabbath properly. Their partners, the Rieder brothers, recommended that they move to Elizabeth and the JEC community. Their homes would
be near their new real estate construction activities.

> Rabbi Teitz [of blessed memory] gave me a warm welcome, which was very
> unique. I seldom meet people able to do the way he did. . . . It is unusual, that some-
> body who comes the first time to shul, the rabbi should come in, and give him a wel-

come, and ask questions . . . and become acquainted, which made on me a good impression. And Rabbi Pinchas Teitz, also in his looks, he was a man who left always an imprint. Once [I] met him, I fell in love with him. That was a relationship . . . until he passed away.

AH recognizes the importance of the JEC and Yeshiva University, which were established prior to the arrival of the survivors on the American scene. He and his friends support these institutions presently, but he recognizes the fact that they existed before the survivors arrived here.

INTERVIEWER: What stands out in Rabbi Teitz's approach to leadership that made him what he was?

AH: I think Rabbi Teitz was a good student of *Pirke Avot* ["Ethics of the Fathers"], and he realized what was good. In order to get [honor], you have to [honor] somebody else. . . . Rabbi Teitz did [honor] everybody, not a special class of Jews. Because of this, everybody [honored] him, did respect him very much. Number one.

Number two, he was [a man of action], he did. He was one of the first ones who made a [religiously forsaken city] like Elizabeth was, before he came to Elizabeth, made from it a Jewish community. And a yeshiva, that we have today [thank God] more than nine hundred students. . . . For this, he deserves the credit.

AH concludes this interview by mentioning *Daf Hashavua,* the weekly Talmud lecture broadcast on the radio for thirty-five years (1953–1988) by Rabbi Teitz, without commercial sponsorship. AH feels this program was very important for American Jewry and especially for Holocaust survivors.

JOSEPH WILF [JW], 10 SEPTEMBER 1997

Joe Wilf arrived in the United States in 1950. He lived in Forest Hills until 1955 when he moved to Elizabeth with his wife and joined his older brother, Harry, in the family's new construction business. Thus, the family settled in Elizabeth to be near their business and to join the developing JEC community, "a wonderful school and a synagogue, which was fully functioning with religious services daily." This was essential in 1954–1955, the year of mourning following their father's sudden death.

In discussing the spiritual leader of the JEC, JW says:

He [Rabbi Teitz] gave us the connection [to the community]. . . . He brought me out. I experienced . . . like newcomers are very uneasy. They don't fit in . . . and you felt that he alone did it.

INTERVIEWER: Were others involved?

JW: Basically, I would attribute it mostly to him . . . the entire community was cordial, but the openness.

INTERVIEWER: You have friends elsewhere, in other communities. When you talked to them, did you find there was something unique about him and this community as compared with their experiences in the other communities?

JW: Many communities, the survivors, they were very successful in business . . . but they were much, much less successful to be integrated into the community. . . . Elizabeth, actually, is an example. . . . Elizabeth was very unique. And I attribute it to Rabbi Teitz. . . . The people [survivors] became part of the community, they felt very comfortable. They contributed to the community, to the development. As a matter of fact, [they] brought in other people and, in some instances, nonsurvivors to be part of the Jewish community.

In order to discuss the essence of Rabbi Teitz's leadership, JW recalls the vibrant Jewish life in his small town in Poland during his boyhood years and the lack of outstanding leadership. He was fourteen years old at the beginning of World War II.

Rabbi Teitz, to me, on a personal level, was the first personality that I saw as a leadership in the Jewish community. During the war, and right after the war, I did not see anybody, I could not identify with anybody, as a leader of the Jewish community. . . . And even in the United States, it was the same thing. . . . [There was] not something I wanted to see in Jewish leadership. This was lacking. . . .

When I was invited the first time, there was a dinner. . . . When he walked into the room, it was leadership. . . . He was so eloquent. He made everybody feel good. . . . Wherever I went, when I traveled, I did not have to say where I lived. All I had to do [was to say] I lived in Rabbi Teitz's community. . . . I traveled a few times, because of him, to the Soviet Union. There was no question about it. Oh, Rabbi Teitz! Eyes opened up, I became something. Otherwise, who would care?

We did not know how much strength we actually gained from it [our association with Rabbi Teitz]. I'm talking strength in many areas. Our families—bringing up our families. All you have to do is look what happened in other communities, with other families, with our contemporaries who live in Long Island. . . .We have contact with friends, the survivor community, different gatherings. And I feel they miss a tremendous thing in life. It's been a long time, it's been forty-five years or whatever it is, and what happened to the group of survivors here [in Elizabeth]? . . . Almost without exception—actually there is no exception—everybody got involved, helped others, helped other Jews, helped Israel . . . naturally, helped the community build something. It gives a future to a generation of Jewish youngsters. . . .

We got a bonus. It's almost a gift from God.

RAE KUSHNER [RK], 3 DECEMBER 1997

Rae Kushner and her late husband, Joseph Kushner, moved to Elizabeth from Brooklyn in 1951. RK explains the move:

> We were looking for a place with a yeshiva, with a school, to give [our children] a Jewish education. We heard, here was Rabbi Teitz, with a yeshiva for the kids. Rabbi Teitz was our leader, our provider. We were orphans. . . . We didn't have any mothers, any fathers. . . . We didn't have too much money, but with what we had, we wanted to support the yeshiva and Rabbi Teitz. . . .
>
> The smartest thing that we did was that we gave [our children] a real Jewish education in the JEC. . . . In the beginning, we had a place where to come, with whom to talk. And Rebbetzin Teitz was a doll. She always protected us. She opened the door for us. And she loved us.

RK then describes her group of survivors in Elizabeth.

> *RK:* The whole group was not *Shomer Shabbos* [Sabbath observant]. . . . They were far away from religion. The first years . . . the Holocaust survivors, either they believed it or they didn't believe anything in religion. But Rabbi Teitz made us, the whole group, to become religious, to become more *frum* [observant]. . . .
>
> *INTERVIEWER:* So he brought the group back?
>
> *RK:* The whole group started to believe in him. Thank God for the JEC, I have all my kids are *Shomer Shabbos* [religiously observant], and they grew up *menschen* [fine human beings]. . . .
>
> *INTERVIEWER:* How do you compare the group of survivors . . . is there something different about this group? You know survivors all over, is there something special about this group?
>
> *RK:* The leader taught us, Rabbi Teitz, that we need to share, we need to give. . . .
>
> *INTERVIEWER:* The reason, you say, that this group is unique is because of Rabbi Teitz?
>
> *RK:* Rabbi Teitz, the closeness. Bessie Teitz, too. She kept us close.

BEATRICE DIENER [BD] AND MARJORIE DIENER BLENDEN [MB], 2 JULY 1997

Beginning with the construction of the JEC elementary school building in 1950 and 1951, until his death in 1987, Leonard Diener [LD] played a crucial role in the most dynamic years of growth of the Elizabeth Jewish community under the inspiring leadership of Rabbi Teitz. This interview sheds light on the period when the survivor-builders settled in Elizabeth and became a vital force in the community. This testimony defines the perspective of an active lay leader who arrived in Elizabeth one generation before the survivors.

Both Leonard and Beatrice Diener were born in small towns in Poland. BD came to Elizabeth as a young girl with her parents. She attended the synagogue wedding ceremony of Rabbi and Mrs. Teitz in Elizabethport in January 1935. LD arrived in the United States in 1932 and settled in Elizabeth. The Dieners have lived in Elizabeth during this entire period except for three years in upstate New York when MB was in the second, third, and fourth grades.

The Diener-Blenden testimony provides great insight on Elizabeth's Jewish history from a lay leadership perspective of the past four decades.

INTERVIEWER: What was it about Rabbi Teitz and/or Mrs. Teitz that was the secret of their successful leadership?

MB: They had charisma. They both had charisma.

BD: I was very much in awe of Rabbi Teitz. I wouldn't dare go close to him. I felt, I don't know, there was something about the Rabbi that inspired respect. And Mrs. Teitz was wonderful, too. She was a real asset to the community. And we became friendly. . . . I have never forgotten her and I never will. She was a wonderful person. And I'm not the only one. When you speak to people, they feel that they were the Royal Family of Elizabeth.

MB: The Rabbi was a presence. And yet . . . and this I can tell you from personal experience in later years, when I became an adult. Even though I was always in awe of him, like my mother. When I picked up the phone and I heard the Rabbi's voice, my hand kind of shook. . . . In times of need or in times of difficulty, he was a tremendous comfort. He was a very good friend.

I think one of the great things about him, outside of his intellect and his presence and his charisma, was that he treated everyone exactly the same. It didn't matter if you were president of Kean College, if you were someone who had just come to the community and you were just starting out. I always felt that about him.

And she was such a sweetheart, Mrs. Teitz. She was absolutely, probably had one of the loveliest hearts that I've ever come in contact with. . . .

INTERVIEWER: I'm sure that Mr. Diener spoke about the Rabbi's impact. I don't think there was a lay person in town who knew him better.

BD: They discussed many things over the phone. Once the Rabbi and Leonard got on the phone, you know, you couldn't get that phone for a while. They discussed many things. Everything concerning the school and the shul. For hours, it went on.

MB: My father always said that the Rabbi could have been anything in this world if he had not entered the rabbinate. Besides, obviously, being a great rabbi. He could have

been a great jurist. He always felt that way. He could have been a marvelous businessman. He said that whatever he would have chosen in life, he would have been successful, and eminently so. . . .

BD: Tell the story, if it's OK, about Richie not wanting to go home.

MB: Oh, what I said about different people. When we used to go to Florida, every year
in December, and Richie was about three years old, and it was time to go home, the
bags were packed, the taxi was waiting, and Richie didn't want to go. We were chasing him around the lobby of the Sterling Hotel. And no matter how hard Joel and I ran,
we couldn't catch him.

The Rabbi came into the lobby, he saw what was going on, and he called Richie
over and said, "Why are you running away from your parents?" And Richie said, "Because they want to go home, and I don't want to go home."

So the Rabbi put his hand into his pocket and pulled out a dime, a nickel, and three
pennies. He said "This is eighteen cents, eighteen is *chai* [life]." And he said, "You
take this." He put it into Richard's little, chubby hand. He said "You take that home,
and when you get home, the first thing you do, is put it in the *tzedakah* [charity] box."

So Richie said, "Of course." The Rabbi said, that's what you do.

So even at age three, he took the eighteen cents in his huddled hand, did not un-
clench his fist until we got into the house, which I was afraid he would never be able
to do it, and the first thing he did . . . was he put into the *tzedakah* box, because the
Rabbi said, "That's what you should do."

The discussion proceeded to the role of the survivors in the Elizabeth community.

INTERVIEWER: What would you say their impact has been on the community?

BD: A great impact. They're a great asset to the community. . . . They're interested in
education, so that helped the school. And they're interested in the shul as well as the
school. . . . They're very much active, and they are involved.

MB: The Jewish population, when I was growing up in Elizabeth, those people are no
longer here. . . . They died, or they moved away, and their children have not remained
in the community, so that the face of the community has changed tremendously in the
past twenty, twenty-five, thirty years. . . . I would imagine, if this group had not come
in, who knows what would have happened to our community?

INTERVIEWER: How do you explain the close relationship between Leonard and the
survivors? They say the Rabbi and Leonard taught them how to be lay leaders.

BD: Leonard's family was annihilated in Europe at the same time. . . . I think that's why
they became close and became friendly. He was interested in what they were doing, as
people and as survivors.

MB: I think Daddy understood them. He understood where they were coming from, in
a way that he was like one of them. . . . He intuitively, or maybe because of his background, understood them. . . . He came in 1932.

INTERVIEWER: They probably were close in age. The only difference being that he was fortunate enough to leave before the war, and they had to suffer what they suffered during the war.

MB: And, besides the Judaism, they also shared the bond of Zionism. . . . He liked them very much. . . .

I remember, as a young girl . . . in 1947 and 1948, a lot of people coming to the house, very nice people, and I always thought they were personal friends of my parents. What I didn't know, that my father was involved in helping the State of Israel. He was an asbestos manufacturer. They manufactured pipe covering. . . . He was able to help them ship supplies that they needed very urgently there during the fighting, when the Arabs declared the war on them, after the State was declared. He was able to give them the pipe covering and the cartons and send these supplies over there. . . . Camouflage . . .

That was something that no one knew. It wasn't until many years later, there was a book . . . *The Promise* by Leonard Slater, in which he described the activities of Americans who aided and abetted the Haganah in those days. A lot of the names that he mentioned were names of people who had been in our house.

I didn't know the story about my father doing this until I confronted him with this. And he said, "Oh, yes. And this is what happened."

INTERVIEWER: This also helped create a kinship. They saw a man who knew what to do. Thus, the survivors saw in Rabbi Teitz and Leonard Diener a dynamic duo. The Rabbi's personality attracted them to the community, and Leonard helped them, together with the Rabbi, in their development into community leaders.

BD: I really don't know what would have happened to Elizabeth, really, if the Rabbi wasn't here, and the survivors didn't come in. It would have been a ghost town, as far as Yiddishkeit is concerned.

RABBI ELAZAR M. TEITZ [EMT], DR. RIVKAH BLAU [RB], SHULAMITH EBNER [SE], INTERVIEWER JOSEPH J. PREIL [JP], 5 SEPTEMBER 1997

The late Rabbi Pinchas and Bessie Teitz were very interested in and impressed by the achievements of the Holocaust Resource Center at Kean University. They honored and encouraged us by attending all of our major functions. Had they been granted additional years, they would have agreed to be interviewed for this publication. This interview presents the role of a unique group of survivors in the Elizabeth Jewish community as viewed by three members of the Teitz family, from their younger years until the present time, when they have now assumed key leadership roles in the Jewish Educational Center.

JP: What attracted [the founding members of the Holocaust Resource Center] to Elizabeth?

SE: Initially, it may have been just gratuitous that they came here, and then there was the attraction that some are here. . . . I think there was also one other thing. Because of my father's presence, and the kind of *Rav* that he was, and the kind of community that it was, a community that had everything, that it was reminiscent for them of what they had in Europe. A relatively small town . . . with the yeshiva and the shul, the whole kehilla [community] was very close together and it had everything there.

And they had a *Rav* who they could look up to very much. He was a European. It was someone they could talk to, he spoke their [Yiddish language]. There was just very good chemistry . . . between these people and my father, my parents. The blend was very good for them.

RB: My mother was an American-born woman, really a Yankee in origin, who spoke a beautiful Yiddish, who could relate to them totally, who had been in Europe in 1935. So she knew where they came from. She had lived that life for close to two months. So she was very understanding to them . . . especially the women felt my mother's friendship. My mother cared about people. . . . I think that was a very important factor.

Incidentally, Elizabeth before that had been active in helping people, not only bringing people over on the affidavits through the yeshiva where the yeshiva, I think, had less students than staff at one point . . . but also people who were brought in to work in Elizabeth because my father wanted to see to it that they had a place where they were taken care of. . . . There was an attitude that you help survivors in any way you can, and that was very clear in the city. . . .

JP: My impression is, from talking to them [the survivors], that the school, the Jewish Educational Center, was very important to them, because they were having children, and the children were starting school. They came here, let's say some time in the fifties, and by the end of the fifties, certainly, their children were of schoolage.

EMT: They had the European attitude. You needed two things: you needed a shul to [pray] in, and a cheder [religious school] to send the children. That they found in Elizabeth under one roof.

SE: Many of them came on scholarships. Sol Kramer likes to tell the story of when he first came, he only enrolled one of the children in the school. My father called him in, and he said, "Tell me, Mr. Kramer, these two children that you have, are they both from the same wife? You're treating one better than the other." Sol said, "Listen, Rabbi, I really can't afford to send both." My father said, "Listen, you send the children. You pay for one, I'll pay for the other."

Both Rae and Clara served lunch because people who had children on scholarship did service in order to merit the reduction in tuition.

EMT: Mr. Kushner often remarked that he felt a debt of gratitude and that's why he remained a staunch supporter even afterwards, because of the fact that his children came in without tuition. . . .

RB: I understand that he got a [blessing] then, that Papa told him, "Now your children will come on scholarship but I hope [God] will bless you and that you will be able to help other people's children. . . ."

JP: They comment on the interest your father had in them and how he would sit down and talk with them. . . . One might say this was the pastoral side of [the rabbinate]. Did you see your father as being the one who could get that involved personally with people that he won them over that way?

RB: Well, first of all, he really enjoyed people. He enjoyed talking with people.

EMT: My father flew many times. There was never a flight in which he didn't get to know the people he was sitting next to. . . . I think there was more than that, too. In this particular instance, I think he felt that with survivors . . . I don't say it was done consciously, but he felt they had come from Yiddishkeit and, to some extent, some of them had not stayed with it to the extent that they did, and his method of getting people to be more observant was not by lecturing, but by getting them, as he used to say, *taamu ur'eu,* taste and you will see. . . . And I think he may have had an additional . . . that through *kiruv,* through bringing them close, they would reawaken what was in them.

JP: When he spoke in the synagogue or at a public forum, he spoke in global terms, and very sure of himself, with great strength. It wasn't the people person. It could be the people person too, but that was one time a year. That was at neilah [closing service of Yom Kippur].

RB: My father said that at neilah he was trying to recreate what it had been like in a European shul at neilah time. He said they used to have long candles, before they had electricity, burning. The longest candles were at the front of the shul, near the [cantor], and everybody would be coming closer and closer to the front as Yom Kippur was going on, as it was getting darker and darker in the rest of the shul. And he wanted to create that feeling of the light near the [Holy Ark] and the light at the front of the shul. And everybody coming together almost as one, just by the closeness of people, asking [God]. . . .

EMT: That's why, when he spoke before neilah was the only time he did not speak from behind the [lectern], he stood in front of the [lectern] to speak, to get closer to the people.

JP: True, the survivors whom I spoke to . . . remember him as the people person. This comes through. I suspect there are others in the community who would see him in shul as the *Rav* . . . who perhaps didn't see that. Is that possible?

RB: Yehudis Frankel asked me when we were kids, we were in the sixth grade, "Is a *Rav* allowed to smile?"

I said, "Why do you ask that, Yehudis?" She said, "I think your father always has to be serious. Isn't that part of being a rabbi?"

I said, "But he laughs at home." But I couldn't get over the question.

And Margie Blenden told me, it was only when she really got to know our family that she found out just how sweet and how soft my father is. And she said you could tell who knew him publicly and who knew him personally. People who knew him publicly saw a very strong leader, a very strong figure. They didn't know the sense of humor. They didn't know the kindness. Margie said he was the softest person. If he saw a child crying, he had to go over and do something about that child crying. . . .

JP: What you're saying then is that, with survivors, he immediately was the people person. . . .

SE: With the drama, that you saw when he was speaking from the pulpit, there was also tremendous passion because of his total commitment to what he was doing. And I think that same kind of warmth . . . came through in a private way, because he was also a very demonstrative person. . . . Even in my father's later years, if Jack Burstyn would walk into the office, he and my father would always embrace. . . . It was something that was mutually brought out from the survivors to my father and from my father to the survivors.

JP: The embraces were for survivors. What about others?

EMT: There was something else besides that, too. When the survivors started coming in, his role was already a different role. When he met the Milton Levys, and even the Leonard Dieners, it was early in his rabbinate. He had to overcome the extreme . . . the opposition or antipathy to what he was trying to do in the community. After all, the idea of opening a day school was just foreign to Elizabeth, it was foreign to the United States. . . .

His model of the *Rav* was the European model for himself. The European rabbanim, as I understand it, did keep at a distance from the [members]. It was only as he became recognized for the leader that he was, and had already established what he established here, that he could . . . loosen up. But the relationships that he formed from that point and on could be different.

JP: That's a very important point, because the opposition to what he was doing, he had to do battle in those years. Now, he was the person who was the leader of the community, they saw him as The Leader, and he was the one to make them comfortable. How do you make a person comfortable? By being friendly, by being warm, by embracing.

EMT: There was another transition, too. Until, roughly, the end of the fifties, the [rabbinate] consisted of the people who were here. And it involved convincing the ones who were here to go along with what he had in mind. . . . Starting from the end of the fifties and beginning with the sixties, the community was beginning to attract people because of what there was here. And, therefore, their relationship was going to be on a different level. These survivors are a case in point. They came, in part at least, because it was an established community.

RB: I have to say that shows something. The Fischmans came because of what was here. They came because of the school. He felt a very tremendous warmth to them, which he showed them immediately. And with Stanley, with Danny Fischman, he could be very open about how he cared for them. . . .

JP: Now let's consider something else. It's interesting that I, of all people, have latched onto the embracing.

[Laughter.]

RB: You're a Litvak [from Lithuania].

JP: Is it possible that part of it is the fact that the survivors themselves are very demonstrative in their feelings? . . . So, it wasn't that your father took the initiative, necessarily, but he was responding to them in the way that they understood?

SE: No, he was a very demonstrative person. . . . He was a very demonstrative parent. That's why I said, because his nature was this kind of dramatic, passionate. . . . It was strong, but there was also a lot of warmth that went with it. I think he sensed, he sensed that it was going to be well received. Not that he sensed it consciously. It was more just an instinctive knowing, that it would be the appropriate way. . . . Listen, they had lost so much, they had suffered so much. They needed that. . . . It was a combination of what he was always prone to be and what they were receptive to.

EMT: Just from the relationship among themselves, the way they all participate at each other's [joyous occasions], they are each other's family. Each one sees the group as a whole, as replacing the families that they lost.

RB: I always felt that sometimes he related to their kids as though they were the nieces and nephews he had lost, Fayga's children and Rivkah's children.

JP: Let's talk about the role of your mother in your father's career and in the development of the community.

SE: There was never a sense of my mother doing anything other than working to promote the [rabbinate] and the kehilla. She was so completely committed to it. . . . The biggest part of it was her love and commitment for my father and her belief in the verity of it, in her own spiritual commitment. But it was also because she had grown up, her father, Zaydie [of blessed memory], had been the *Rav.* So there was this ongoing feeling of continuity and commitment that she was very involved in.

RB: And I think she definitely was the one who made sure that my father stayed in Elizabeth when different things were being offered to him to leave Elizabeth. She had a tremendous commitment to the city because of her father's place in it and, I think, my father found other ways to express it, like working for Russian Jewry or *Daf Hashavua* [his weekly Talmud radio lecture]. . . . But Elizabeth was the home base.

I don't think that I fool myself. I seem to remember this conversation after Rabbi

Herzog [Chief Rabbi of Israel] had visited and had spoken to my father—something about, eventually, he should be a contender for the Chief Rabbinate, and my mother said, "What's the Chief Rabbinate? It's press releases, it's a lot of political stuff. . . . What do you need that for? And here, when you do something, you give a [Talmud lecture], it's a real accomplishment. You start a school, it's a real accomplishment. What will that be?" And she would not hear of any consideration of the Chief Rabbinate.

JP: Did you [EMT] ever hear that Herzog story?

EMT: It was not Herzog, because the trial balloon was floated after he passed away. Rabbi Herzog came here . . . for UJA . . . in 1950.

JP: Do you think there is something unique about the survivors-builders in this community as compared with elsewhere?

RB: Two special things. One is the relationship they created among themselves. They recreated themselves as a family. Since they had lost so much, they recreated themselves here as a family.

Then, I do think that their relationship to my parents was a unique relationship. That, somehow, my parents stood in for a lot of what they had lost, and they felt they could find it again through them. It was both a commitment to Halacha [Jewish law], being a very honest *Rav* and Rebbetzin, being very much the heads of the community. There was just a lot there that was answered for them by my parents' presence.

JP: What did it do for them?

RB: What did it do for them? It was restorative.

SE: It gave them a sense of the rightness of what they were doing.

RB: I've heard from a number of survivors that one of the main things they wanted to know was that life would be good again. . . . A woman told me that after the war, after getting out of the concentration camp, she was in Sweden, with her sister in a hospital. They weren't eating kosher food, they weren't keeping Shabbos. . . . All they were trying to do was rebuild from the skeletons that they were, to become people again.

And she and her sister went out for a walk. She wasn't even aware of the fact that it was Saturday. A button popped off her coat. Her sister said, "Fruma, don't pick it up. It's Shabbos, we can't pick the button up. We'll come back after Shabbos and get it."

And she said, suddenly, she felt life would be normal again. Because if it was Shabbos again, and you didn't pick up a button again, things were going to come back. That was the moment when she started getting over the concentration camp experience.

I think that for all these families, coming to Elizabeth and seeing a full, functioning, *frum* [pious] community, with a *Rav* and Rebbetzin who were very understanding to them, and knew what they had lost, was a very significant part of the restoration of normalcy.

SE: It inspired hope in them. I think they looked upon my parents, there was a warmth. . . . I know, I heard this phrase so many times, that they were the Royal Couple. There was a certain regal quality that they appreciated in my parents. And so it was a combination of them being both very regal and very approachable. Also, it gave them hope.

EMT: The fact that everything in the community is combined and that to go to the shul, you have to come to the school, I think it made an impact on them to see the continuity in the children growing up as Jews as well as Americans. [It] had an impact on them which, in other cities, where they didn't have contact with the schools necessarily . . . when they came to [pray], they didn't go to a school building and see the children.

Here, they came to say Kaddish [prayer said for the dead], to keep a yahrzeit [anniversary of a death] . . . they were in the school building. And this made an impression on them, too. Because of the fact . . . that everything is under one roof here, it may have made a difference in how they reacted earlier than they did in other communities where they didn't have this.

JP: There are survivors in many communities in New Jersey and elsewhere. Do you have any impression as to what's going on there? Did it take off the way it did here, or is it different?

RB: I know of individuals in other communities, but I don't know of a group that formed a cohesive society the way that this group did.

SE: It's a combination of what my sister said, you know, the numbers. They were a fairly large cluster. I think it is that they really took to Elizabeth, to what it had to offer, to my father.

EMT: In other communities, you have survivors. Here, you have a survivors' group. . . . They are a distinct entity within the town. . . . They are mishpachah [family]. When one gets an aliyah [Torah honor], he makes a [blessing] for all the others. This stems from a feeling of kinship. I have a sense this . . . does not exist in other communities.

JP: I suspect this has to be studied. You mentioned the Breuer group. The Breuer group was all survivors [and refugees]. . . . There are tremendous groups out there. Probably, we have to know more about them before we make a definitive statement about the uniqueness of this group. In other words, something has happened that is beautiful over here. How unique it is, I suspect it is, but I'm not sure. . . . What we did, we sharpened up how beautiful the Elizabeth part is, but we're not sure about the uniqueness over here. . . . Who knows what's going on in Monsey or Los Angeles?

RB: In a . . . movie about Hasidim, it's mentioned that the Bobover Rebbe created the same kind of community around himself . . . by finding people jobs, finding people someone to marry, to take care of all kinds of things. So, he created a community of survivors.

JP: You know, the Rebbe, then, becomes very important, because it's the Bobover, it's the Satmarer . . . it's Rav Breuer. What happened over here is, you had the *Rav* already.

SE: Many of them come from Hasidic stock, of the builders. . . . They can relate to having this kind of tremendous loyalty to a *Rav* as though he were their Rebbe.

JP: But, in order to have this kind of story, you need a rabbinical figure who is regarded by the group and respected. . . .

EMT: Who can be looked up to as the Rebbe.

JP: And the others have their Rebbe from Europe over here. They [builders] came and found a *Rav*. This is what they wanted. They wanted someone who had been somewhat Americanized. . . .

EMT: Something else, too, in terms of why his [rabbinate] was different. A Rebbe wasn't just somebody you went to for matters of the spirit. When you had a business matter to discuss, you knew you could talk to him, and get advice. And I think they saw the same thing in my father. I don't know if they came actually for business advice, but they realized they could talk to him about . . . worldly things, too, not just about matters of the spirit, which maybe some other communities did not feel in their leaders.

Epilogue: Faith after the Holocaust

The Holocaust nearly ended a thousand years of magnificent Jewish spiritual development on the European continent. Although the Jewish population was generally very poor, certainly by our standards at the beginning of the twenty-first century, most communities of European Jews experienced rich standards of religious activities in their daily rounds and in their pursuit of learning. This is apparent in many of the testimonies of our survivors.

The interviews also reveal that it was well-nigh impossible to observe the tenets of Judaism during the Holocaust. We marvel when we hear that some survivors came through these horrible years avoiding nonkosher food. Any effort to maintain spiritual practices, such as conducting religious services, were judged to be crimes punishable by death in Hitler's "thousand-year Reich." Nearly all Talmudic centers of learning and practically all the great Talmudic scholars perished. This is the background for our appreciation of the interviews with Rabbis Alter Pekier, Jack Ring, and Abraham Shlomowitz. They describe how two of the greatest Torah centers were transplanted to American and Israeli soil. This also explains the reverence of the survivors in Elizabeth for a dynamic leader such as Rabbi Pinchas Teitz, who was able to create a model Jewish community in the United States for survivors as well as for native-born Americans.

The return to religious life was not always a simple matter. This is apparent in many of our interviews. Quite a few of the survivors discuss their decision to return as their determination not to provide Hitler with a posthumous victory.

It is appropriate to conclude this study by listening to two of the survivors in the Kean University Library of recordings, Elie Wiesel and Adela Ulka Sommer.

ELIE WIESEL

Wiesel was Kean University's distinguished Scholar in Residence during the week before he received the Nobel Peace Prize in December 1986. His struggle with his faith at Auschwitz, as described in *Night,* is revealed in the following exchange.

> *INTERVIEWER:* You have been quoted as saying, "I don't want an easy answer. I have problems. I have questions. Mine is a tragic faith." And another time, you quoted Rav Nachman of Bratslav: "No heart is as whole as a broken heart." And then you stated, "I would like to rephrase his words to say, No faith is as pure as a broken faith."

■ 313

However, probably the most famous words you have ever written were used by François Mauriac in his foreword . . . to your book, *Night,* back in 1955. You, yourself, quoted the passage in its entirety when you spoke in 1979 at the Yom Hashoah program, the Day of Holocaust Remembrance program, in the Capitol Rotunda before our government leaders. This is the statement that our students read, and I can tell you that these students, who are teachers, as well as *their* students, are deeply moved by that statement.

The question is how do we teach this most famous passage of yours?

"Never shall I forget that smoke. Never shall I forget the little faces of the children, whose bodies I saw turned into wreaths of smoke beneath a silent blue sky. Never shall I forget those flames which consumed my faith forever. Never shall I forget that nocturnal silence which deprived me, for all eternity, of the desire to live. Never shall I forget those moments which murdered my God and my soul and turned my dreams to dust. Never shall I forget these things, even if I am condemned to live as long as God himself. Never."[1]

How do we teach that passage?

WIESEL: Two words are key in my entire work, in all my work. These two words are: *And yet.* What do they mean?

At that moment, that's what I felt, and that's why I had to write it. Ten pages later, I describe a service I attended on Rosh Hashanah evening. And the next book is already about something else. And the tenth book is already about Hasidic fervor. And the twentieth book is about my total commitment to study the Bible and the Talmud.

In 1944, when I saw what I had seen, that is what I had to say because that is what I felt. But not to stop there. The main thing is not to stop there, but continue. And I said it. OK, I said it. And now you say, "And yet. Continue." And if you continue, you learn very much.

ADELA ULKA SOMMER

Adela Ulka Sommer joined us during the interview of her husband, Julius, on 1 July 1997, when he described the effect of the Holocaust on his religious observance. She related the following story.

I will never forget it. It was a Friday afternoon in the winter . . . of '45. I came there because I was afraid to be in the village . . . and his cousin sent me in to a neighbor. I don't remember what it was, the proverbial cup of sugar, or whatever. It was a Friday afternoon, it was dark, in wintertime. And I opened the door.

I will be emotional. I cannot tell the story without crying. Candles lit, challahs on the table, the young wife is standing, and a little girl. He is making kiddush.

When I saw this, I don't know, something in me turned, and I said, "My God, there is a world. People still believe." I remembered my home, my parents. And at that time, I picked my head up, and I made a deal with God. God willing, if he comes back, wherever he is, and we get married, I promise you, every Friday night, I will light candles, and I will make him make kiddush [blessing over wine]. And I will live like I was raised. Hitler won't kill my background. He killed my family. I am one, a survivor of eighty-three in my family. I am the only survivor but for a cousin who survived in Russia.

From that day on, when we got married, I lit my candles, I made him make kiddush. . . . The day I came to the United States, I didn't have much money, but I came with two sets of dishes, two sets of pots and pans, and the Passover dishes I bought already in the United States. And I kept a kosher home. I had a little bit of resistance. My husband was angry with God. And I said, "In my home, you'll put away the fleishige [meat dishes] here, and the milchige [dairy dishes] there," and little by little you found when you met him, you met a good Jew. But it wasn't easy.

A CONCLUDING THOUGHT

In conducting interviews, I tried to discuss with survivors the careers of their children. In the Sommer interview, Julius said they have two daughters, "one works for me, and one is a professor at Harvard University. . . . She teaches South American literature." This led to a fascinating discussion of the outstanding achievements of many of the survivors' children. Ulka Sommer referred to this intriguing development as her "revenge against Hitler."

We learn a great deal about the loss to humanity when we listen to these 172 survivors. We must ever bear in mind what each survivor represents. After all, for each and every survivor represented in this volume, more than 33,000 Jews perished in the Holocaust.

The message of twentieth-century history should be obvious. Revenge does not mean our total involvement in seeking and destroying the criminals. Rather, we must endeavor to develop ourselves and to inspire future generations to live as fine human beings. Our life on earth should not be merely a never-ending pursuit of destroying evil. Rather, let us devote our short lives to build families and to create communities to serve as constructive contributions to our traditions and to humanity.

Appendix A: Holocaust Resource Center of Kean University

The establishment of the Holocaust Resource Center at what was then Kean College of New Jersey was achieved after eighteen months of negotiations during the early 1980s between a group of community leaders, mostly Holocaust survivors, and the administration of Kean College.

The first plan was suggested to me by Arie Halpern, a Holocaust survivor and an outstanding leader of the Elizabeth Jewish community. Halpern was distressed about the campaign of Holocaust deniers in the United States. His idea was to collect every single Holocaust book in a central location in town to be made available to all citizens. This led to consideration of the need for Holocaust education and the logical involvement of Kean College.

The local community group, all neighbors of Kean College, began to meet with me during the summer of 1981. They requested that I introduce the concept being developed to Kean College President Nathan Weiss. This was the first stage of establishing a Holocaust Resource Center (HRC) in Kean College to be sponsored jointly by the college and the community group.

In September 1981, I met with President Weiss, then with Vice President Vera King Farris, and finally with Deans Frank Esposito, T. Felder Dorn, and Richard Nichols. President Weiss asked me to prepare a memorandum describing the proposed program. This was delivered to Vice President King Farris on 1 October 1981.

In reading this memorandum today, nearly sixteen years after it was presented to the Kean College leadership, what is apparent is the clarity of the thinking of the local community group. The essence of the three-page document is captured in the following:

Holocaust Resource Center (HRC) Activities

(*a*) To teach and encourage public school teachers, especially on the secondary level, to incorporate Holocaust units into social studies and literature curricula.

(*b*) To house print and nonprint media in the Kean College Library and the Instructional Resource Center. Books and media will be available to students, teachers in neighboring school districts, and residents of our vicinity.

(*c*) To sponsor . . . lectures each year that will be open to the Kean College family as well as residents of our community.

(*d*) To produce and preserve a series of oral history videotapes based on the personal experiences of Holocaust survivors who reside in our community.

In addition to these four activities, one additional program was added during the year of review and negotiation, and two others were developed during the first fifteen years of the HRC's history:

(*e*) The Kean College HRC cosponsors the annual Yom Hashoah (Holocaust Memorial Day) program with the Jewish Federation of Central New Jersey.
(*f*) Teaching Prejudice Reduction is offered as a follow-up course to Teaching the Holocaust.
(*g*) The Diversity 2000 Council of Kean College has been organized by Kean's School of Education and the HRC for school districts wishing to join together to network for the purpose of teaching students to live together peacefully and constructively in America's increasingly diverse society.

The year of negotiations culminated on 10 September 1982 with agreement to establish a Holocaust Resource Center at Kean College. The center is located in the Kean College Library and is cosponsored by the college and the Holocaust Resource Foundation, a privately endowed entity organized to support the HRC.

Murray Pantirer served as foundation president from October 1982 until June 1994. Clara Kramer has been president since then. I have been privileged to serve as director of both the foundation and the center. Dr. Henry Ross was the Kean College administration liaison to the center from 1982 until his appointment as Kean College interim president for the 1995–1996 academic year. Dr. Michael Lampert, executive assistant to President Ronald Applbaum, has been administration liaison since September 1995. Rose Pinchas served as the coordinator of activities during the center's first two years. Helen Walzer succeeded Ms. Pinchas in February 1985 and continues to serve in that position.

The following persons have served on the foundation's executive committee: Marjorie Blenden, Jack Burstyn, Beatrice Diener, the late Leonard Diener, Rella Feldman, Erwin Fisch, Meyer Gold, Arie Halpern, David Halpern, Sam Halpern, Clara Kramer, the late Joseph Kushner, Rae Kushner, the late Isak Levenstein, Larry Pantirer, Murray Pantirer, Esther Schulder, Betty Schwartz, Julius Sommer, the late Harry Wilf, Joseph Wilf, Judith Wilf, Zygmunt Wilf, Abraham Zuckerman, and Wayne Zuckerman.

HRC Accomplishments

TEACHER EDUCATION

The founders of the Holocaust Resource Center agreed that education should be the foundation for all our endeavors. The HRC's first activity was the preparation of a graduate course for teachers, Teaching the Holocaust, which was offered for the first time in the spring 1983 semester. The course has always been offered tuition-free, being sponsored by the Holocaust Resource Foundation. The course has been exceptionally well received by the students and has been consistently fully enrolled since the HRC's founding.

During the early years, Teaching the Holocaust was offered on campus at Kean College. Teachers often traveled great distances from many communities. This led to a request that we move the course location to school districts, for maximum impact, with twenty-five to thirty teachers in a district involved in each group. This was done for the first time in the spring 1985 semester in the Tenafly school district. The off-campus courses have proven to be so effective that all courses have been offered in school districts since the 1990–1991 academic year, beginning with the Westfield and Scotch Plains–Fanwood school districts.

The enrollment statistics reveal the success of the program most effectively: more than eight hundred educators have taken the course in thirty-three sections, an average of twenty-six per class, over a sixteen-year period. The HRC's leadership adopted this approach after concluding that it is essential for teachers to be involved in a three-credit graduate course in order to become sufficiently inspired and knowledgeable Holocaust educators.

During the early semesters of the Holocaust course, the students would often say, "This course was great, but what is the follow-up?" Teaching Prejudice Reduction was considered to be the logical study after completing the Holocaust program. This new course was introduced during the spring 1989 semester, and has been offered regularly ever since. More than four hundred educators have enrolled in the Prejudice Reduction course in nineteen sections, an average of twenty-one students per class.

Twenty-one school districts have served as course sites during the past twelve years: Elizabeth, Chatham, Fort Lee, Highland Park, Jersey City, Monmouth Regional High School, Montville, North Brunswick, Old Bridge, Paramus, Parsippany–Troy Hills, Passaic, Plainfield, Rahway, Scotch Plains–Fanwood, South Orange–Maplewood, Summit, Tenafly, Wayne, Westfield, and West Milford.

HRC's education program includes the following two approaches: First, we serve as a resource for many undergraduate students at the college. An increasing number of faculty bring their classes to the center every year. Second, as many as six hundred Kean College students and teachers visit the United States Holocaust Memorial Museum in Washington every year. This unique experience is required of every student in the HRC's graduate courses as well as in several General Education courses on the undergraduate level. Dr. Daniel O'Day is director of the General Education program.

ORAL HISTORY

The oral history program is an especially important component of the HRC activities. At the very outset, we were confronted with a philosophical issue: Should we emphasize a psychological or a historical approach in interviewing survivors? We consulted with Holocaust and oral history scholars in the United States and in Israel and, after the first years, we resolved that our program would emphasize the importance of testimony regarding Holocaust experiences. Our oral history committee agreed the testimonies should provide information on the fate of all members of the survivor's family and other pertinent and available details of survivor family and community history.

In developing an oral history program, the greatest challenge occurs immediately after the interview. How can scholars make use of the large number of tapes? In our case, the question was; How can Holocaust centers avoid the risk of producing a plentiful supply of tapes which become useless and merely collect dust on shelves as a result of lack of sophistication and commitment in the postinterview phase of the program?

We were fortunate in the composition of the Kean College Oral History Committee and in the scholars who consulted with us and who enabled us to reach this stage, the publication of *Holocaust Testimonies,* wherein we report the results of our endeavors. In this regard, we note especially the assistance of three persons: Dr. Yaffa Eliach, Holocaust Professor at Brooklyn College and creator of the Tower of Faces at the United States Holocaust Memorial Museum; Dr. Dov Levin, Director of the Oral History Program at Hebrew University, Jerusalem; and Howard Green, oral history specialist of the New Jersey Historical Society.

During an early period in our history, we sent copies of our videotaped interviews to the Yale University Oral History Program. After the opening of the United States Holocaust Memorial Museum in Washington, the HRC determined that all our testimonies would be sent to the museum. We have also been sending selected videotapes to the impressive oral history collection at the Hebrew University in Jerusalem.

The two faculty members who preceded me as directors of the Kean College Oral History Program are Sidney Langer, who was the early pioneer in launching this program, and Bernard Weinstein, who was most productive in his years at the helm in conducting more than half the interviews in our collection. Throughout his administration of the program, he was ably assisted by Phyllis Ziman Tobin.

The following persons have served on the Oral History Committee: Selma Dubnick, Howard Green, Bonnie Kind, Michael Lampert, Mark Lender, Vincent Merlo, Joseph Preil, Henry Ross, Helen Walzer, and Bernard Weinstein.

LECTURE SERIES

Which aspect of HRC activities reaches the greatest number of people? One may suppose that the in-service graduate courses, which have inspired 849 teachers to teach the Holocaust to more than 20,000 students, are the best approach to influence the thinking of future generations. Many of us in the HRC agree with this theory.

On the other hand, our lectures have attracted many thousands of people. The audiences have consisted of high school, undergraduate, and graduate students as well as college faculty and community members. In December 1996, for example, Daniel Jonah Goldhagen of Harvard addressed a total of twenty-six hundred people in three lectures during the course of his two-day visit. Similar audiences were in attendance in December 1986, when Elie Wiesel was our guest several days before receiving the Nobel Peace Prize in Sweden.

Our lecturers during the past sixteen years comprise a *Who's Who* of international leaders in Holocaust scholarship. Each guest lecturer made a profound impact on the Kean College community. The videotapes of their lectures and question-and-answer sessions are treasures of Holocaust education and oral history. The roster of distinguished guest lecturers includes Leon Bass, Yehuda Bauer, Michael Berenbaum, Christopher Browning, Robert Clary, Yaffa Eliach, Daniel Jonah Goldhagen, Raul Hilberg, Jan Karski, Gerda Weissman Klein, Lawrence Langer, Israel's Chief Rabbi Israel M. Lau, Deborah Lipstadt, Franklin Littell, Rose Thering, Elie Wiesel, and David Wyman.

During his appearance at Kean College, Elie Wiesel encouraged educators to invite survivors to their schools and classes. "They are the best teachers," he said, and he was right. During these years, the following sixteen survivors (including three of the Schindlerjuden in our midst) and one liberator have enthralled audiences at the college and in many of the schools in this area: David and Julia Altholz, Ernest and Helene Bokor, Gladys and Sam Halpern, Gladys Helfgott (who has spoken practically every semester in one of our classes), Clara Kramer, the late Isak Levenstein, Anne and Paul Monka, Murray Pantirer, Rabbi Alter Pekier, Chaplain Herschel Schacter, Rabbi Jack Ring, Siggi Wilzig, and Abraham Zuckerman.

The testimonies of all thirty-four lecturers have been videotaped and may be studied through the facilities of the HRC.

COMMUNITY-WIDE YOM HASHOAH PROGRAM

The involvement of the HRC in cosponsoring the annual Yom Hashoah (Holocaust Memorial Day) program with the Jewish Federation of Central New Jersey has resolved the sensitive question every year of which institution should host the program. Locating this important community event in the college's Wilkins Theatre has provided a convenient and spacious auditorium for the entire audience, and the theater's dedicated staff ensures an essential professional touch to the highly significant evening.

PRINT AND NONPRINT MEDIA

As of June 1997, the several collections in the HRC are categorized as follows: 2,700 books, 269 videotapes, 32 distinguished lecture series, and 217 oral history testimonies.

Our resources are used mainly by Kean faculty and students and also by educators whose districts have joined the Diversity 2000 Council. We have received greatly appreciated praise for the effectiveness of our collections from visiting scholars connected with premier academic institutions. In the spirit of "imitation is the sincerest form of flattery," the scholars often express the wish that a similar facility would be established in their own institutions.

THE NEW HOLOCAUST RESOURCE CENTER

For the first twelve years of our history, the HRC was located in an adequate room on the second floor of the library. The original center was designed and furnished most attractively under the direction of Abraham Zuckerman.

An impressive expansion and complete renovation of the Kean University Library was implemented during the 1990s, a fortuitous development for the HRC, which had outgrown its original quarters. In its beautiful location in the new wing of the second floor, the HRC has approximately triple the space of its original room. We moved into the new quarters during the summer of 1995.

DIVERSITY 2000 COUNCIL OF KEAN COLLEGE

One of the most significant achievements of the HRC has been its role in organizing the Diversity 2000 Council of Kean College. As stated in the council's bylaws,

> The Diversity 2000 Council of Kean College exists for the purpose of providing education and training to its members in multiculturalism and diversity; to transmit through its members, to other teachers and their students, the skills a multicultural education can give students to understand others, and to thrive in a rapidly changing and diverse world.

How did the Council evolve into today's highly effective and productive organization? I had the privilege of introducing Teaching Prejudice Reduction during the spring 1989 semester. During the second semester of Prejudice Reduction (fall 1989), the teachers in the course and I discussed the advisability of conducting a two-day seminar with scholars in the field. I consulted with School of Education Dean Ana Maria Schuhmann regarding this possibility. The dean responded enthusiastically, just as she has always responded on all issues and programs involving the HRC and the Diversity Council. Associate Vice President Catherine Dorsey-Gaines accepted the responsibility to chair the faculty planning committee. We were fortunate to involve three outstanding personalities in the two-day program: James Banks, Samuel Betances, and Frances Sonnenschein.

Thus the originally projected seminar for fifty educators became a wonderful two-day conference for two hundred fifty teachers and administrators from many school districts on 22 and 23 March 1990.

Obviously, the time had come for Kean College to work with New Jersey school districts on multicultural education and prejudice reduction. The group met informally and organized two successful conference days during the 1991–1992 school year. The conferences and workshops in 1992, on 7 February and 1 May, featured New Jersey district superintendents and educational leaders. Dr. Mary Lee Fitzgerald, then superintendent of the Montclair school district and subsequently New Jersey Commissioner of Education, played a leading role in the February conference. Many of the fourteen participating districts in those two conferences have continued to serve among the council's leaders.

The council is blessed with the participation of many gifted educators. The high caliber of leadership is reflected in the council's three presidents: David Rock, Brenda Patterson, and Gerry Melnick—all were very active in planning the conferences described above. The fourteen school districts, which met informally back in 1991–1992, have developed into a vibrant and powerful organization of forty-three dues-paying school districts as of June 1997.

The council developed into an effective, lively organization during the first six years of its existence. It is housed in Kean College's School of Education. It would be appropriate, then, to have Dean Ana Maria Schuhmann's (AMS) responses to two questions:

How would you describe the council's progress during the past six years?

AMS: The council's progress has surpassed our expectations. It has been steady progress. There has been progress every year.

What are the underlying causes for this progress?

AMS: Excellent leadership, both from the college and from the districts. People see a need for the council's work, for prejudice reduction and multicultural education competencies in the schools. Also, support from the college has been significant. It's a very inclusive organization, attracting urban, suburban, rural, large and small districts, including primarily public and also some private schools.

The importance of council members' networking was made clear at one meeting when it became obvious that many are involved in seemingly similar organizations on the state and national levels. The reader should appreciate that average attendance at our four meetings a year is between thirty-five and forty. I asked the membership at that meeting:

Inasmuch as many of you belong to similar organizations, what attracts you to our Diversity Council?

COUNCIL: This is the one organization that is really diverse, both in the districts as well as the individuals involved.

HRC EVALUATIONS BY KEAN COLLEGE LEADERSHIP

Two individuals offered their views on the HRC's role in Kean College and its achievements. Henry Ross, interim president during the 1995–1996 academic year, was the administration's liaison to the Holocaust Resource Center during the first thirteen years of the center's existence. Ronald Applbaum had just completed his first year (July 1997). The author met with Dr. Ross on 25 June 1997, when Dr. Ross was asked several questions:

How do you view the progress and achievements of the Holocaust Resource Center during its fifteen-year history?

H. Ross: The original concept was accepted by the administration for its clearly defined tasks. Vice President Vera Farris was enthusiastic about the proposal and appointed me to chair a feasibility committee. The committee studied your memorandum of October 1, 1981, and concluded that Kean College *could* and *should* undertake the project.

We *could* because the project was well defined and thought out. A crucial aspect of the committee's conclusion was the involvement of the surrounding community in the concept development and in providing some support.

We *should* because the project spelled out the significance of the Holocaust for all humans, a lesson to be understood and taught, a matter basic to the mission of Kean College and all educational institutions.

Is the HRC achieving these goals?

H. Ross: The Holocaust Resource Center has exerted influence far beyond the college. The courses have had an impact directly on many teachers throughout the state. With the ripple effect, the lessons of the Holocaust were then transmitted to the students as well as to numerous colleagues of these teachers.

Within Kean College, the HRC plays a visible role on behalf of intergroup relations, mutual understanding, and respect for diversity. It has become a powerful symbol in this endeavor.

President Ronald Applbaum was interviewed on 2 July 1997. At the outset, he recalled his very first meeting at the college with Murray Pantirer and Abraham Zuckerman. The two survivors impressed him as fine, gentle individuals who were concerned with the college's responsibility for providing excellent education for all its students.

In referring to his first visit to the Holocaust Resource Center, for a September 1996 meeting of the Diversity 2000 Council, Dr. Applbaum said:

My first impression of the facility was the symbols, the artifacts, conveying the impression of suffering and sadness. To counter that was the attitude of the people in the Diversity Council, working with commitment to reduce prejudice based on a real understanding of the consequences of the Holocaust, not only on the Jewish people, but on all people who suffer as a result of prejudice based on race, religion, or ethnic background.

After observing the Holocaust Center throughout the year, what do you think the HRC's role should be in the educational community?

R. APPLBAUM: I think what HRC does is to provide a focus based on a singular event, a very special event in the history of humankind, a time of great inhumanity.

The Holocaust Resource Center should provide:

1. An understanding of the Holocaust in historical context;
2. A better understanding of how prejudice and, in this case, antisemitism have such a pervasive effect on a person's attitudes, values, and behavior.

In essence, the HRC is an educational forum where people can come together for discussion and to learn techniques and pedagogy working to reduce prejudice. It is a vehicle for bringing disparate groups together to focus on the Holocaust, and it brings the internal and external communities together for the purpose of building America's diverse society of the future.

Appendix B

It is appropriate to record how Kean University's oral history program developed into this book. At the very beginning of our activities in 1983, Holocaust Resource Foundation (HRF) president Murray Pantirer foresaw the advisability of producing such a publication. This was discussed at an early foundation meeting. I believe the book is faithful to the guidelines formulated at that meeting, namely, an introductory brief description of each survivor's background followed by the survivor's Holocaust experiences, and concluding with a short statement of each individual's status at the time of testimony.

As indicated in the appendix, the Kean University oral history program was guided by the highly regarded program at Yale University. We had also been fortunate in appointing an outstanding committee of oral history scholars to advise and monitor our work This helped us to organize:

  a. the pre-interview preparations,
  b. the interview itself,
  c. the post-interview recording procedure, a most, important and demanding aspect of the entire program, and
  d. the criteria for determining which interviews would be published.

During the course of our fifteen year history (1983–1998), a questionnaire was developed to prepare the survivor and the interviewer for the experience. A copy of the questionnaire appears below.

KEAN COLLEGE OF NEW JERSEY
Holocaust Resource Center

Name of Interviewer: _____

Date of Interview: _____

HOLOCAUST ORAL HISTORY QUESTIONNAIRE

I. Please provide the following information about yourself:

Name _____

Address _____

Telephone Number (Home): _____ *(Work):* _____

Date of Birth _____

Place of Birth _____

Principal Occupation _____

Education _____

Marital Status _____ *# Children* _____ *# Grandchildren* _____

II. Where possible, please provide the following information about your family:

Father's Name _____ Birth Year _____

Occupation _____

Location in 1945 _____

Mother's Maiden Name _____ Birth Year _____

Occupation _____

Location in 1945 _____

Significant Others (e.g., siblings) _____

Name	Birth Year	Relationship	Location in 1945

III. Please provide the following information about your experiences during the war and after:

Where were you at the outbreak of the war? _____

_____

If you were segregated in a ghetto, please provide the following information:

Where _____

Dates _____

If you were ever in a concentration camp(s), please provide the following information:

Name of Camp(s)   Dates

_____

_____

_____

If you were involved with a partisan group, please identify the group and explain:

_____

_____

If you were hiding, where and with whom?

_____

_____

Where were you at the time of liberation? _____

Identity of your liberators? _____

Where did you go immediately following liberation? _____

_____

Place of first residence in USA _____

Date of arrival in USA _____

Occupation after arrival in USA _____

Date of arrival in New Jersey _____

Reason for settling in N.J. _____

IV. For each of your children, please provide the following:

Year of Birth	Sex M/F	Location	Occupation	Married?	Number of Children

Please provide the name and phone number of one or two of your children (or other close relative) that we may contact for information should you be unavailable.

_____

_____

_____

V. Please think about the next five questions for discussion before and during the interview. These are questions about the meaning and impact of your experiences, and we are interested in your reactions. Of course, there are no right answers.

1. When did you start talking about the Holocaust? With whom?
2. How has the Holocaust affected your outlook on life and your understanding of human nature?
3. What should be taught to your children and to American students about the Holocaust?
4. Has the Holocaust affected your faith and religious observance?
5. Do you have any recollections of particular significance you would like to comment on?

Call #   HRC #

1/93

KEAN COLLEGE OF NEW JERSEY
Holocaust Research Center

Notes

ACKNOWLEDGMENTS

1. On 26 September 1997, Kean College of New Jersey was designated by the New Jersey Commission on Higher Education and its name changed to Kean University. References to either Kean College of New Jersey or Kean University are based on the date of an event.

1. GERMANY AND AUSTRIA

1. *Encyclopedia of the Holocaust,* s.v. "Germany."
2. Ibid.
3. Ibid.
4. Ibid.
5. Ibid., s.v. "Austria."

2. WESTERN POLAND

1. *Encyclopedia of the Holocaust,* s.v. "Poland: General Survey."
2. Ibid., s.v. "Poland: The Jews in Poland."
3. Christopher R. Browning, *The Path of Genocide* (New York: Cambridge, 1992), 169.
4. Anne Frank, *The Diary of a Young Girl* (New York: Pocket Books, 1953).
5. Judith Miller, *One, by One, by One: Facing the Holocaust* (New York: Simon and Schuster, 1990).

3. EASTERN POLAND

1. *Encyclopedia of the Holocaust,* s.v. "Poland: General Survey"

6. CENTRAL EUROPE

1. Reuben Weitzman's testimony is included with that of Milton Goldberg.

8. THE SURVIVORS IN ELIZABETH

1. Oscar Handlin, *The Uprooted,* 2d ed. (Boston: Little Brown, 1973).

EPILOGUE: FAITH AFTER THE HOLOCAUST

1. Elie Wiesel, *Night* (New York: Bantam, 1982), 32.

Index

About the Editor

JOSEPH J. PREIL holds a Ph. D. from New York University in teaching effectiveness. During his first two decades as professor of education at Kean University, Preil served as graduate coordinator in the department of instruction, curriculum, and administration. By that time, his scholarly interest centered on teaching the Holocaust and prejudice reduction. In addition to creating and teaching the graduate courses in this program, he also played the leading role in organizing the Holocaust Resource Center, the Diversity 2000 Council, and the Holocaust Resource Foundation—all for Kean University in New Jersey.